Technology, Work and Globalization

The Technology, Work and Globalization series was developed to provide policy makers, workers, managers, academics and students with a deeper understanding of the complex interlinks and influences between technological developments, including information and communication technologies, work organizations and patterns of globalization. The mission of the series is to disseminate rich knowledge based on deep research about relevant issues surrounding the globalization of work that is spawned by technology.

Päivi Aaltonen · Emil Kurvinen
Editors

Contemporary Issues in Industry 5.0

Towards an AI Integrated Society

palgrave
macmillan

Editors
Päivi Aaltonen
Lappeenranta University of Technology
Lappeenranta, Finland

Emil Kurvinen
University of Oulu
Oulu, Finland

ISSN 2730-6623 ISSN 2730-6631 (electronic)
Technology, Work and Globalization
ISBN 978-3-031-74778-6 ISBN 978-3-031-74779-3 (eBook)
https://doi.org/10.1007/978-3-031-74779-3

This work was supported by LUT University and University of Oulu.

This Palgrave Macmillan imprint is published by the registered company Springer Nature Switzerland AG
The registered company address is: Gewerbestrasse 11, 6330 Cham, Switzerland

Preface

This book aims to create an interdisciplinary theoretical overview of Artificial Intelligence (AI) in our current society. In addition to understanding managerial and global business perspectives, the book highlights state-of-the-art industrial applications, as well as scenarios of potential societal impacts and the evolving reality of human and machine collaboration—Industry 5.0 and beyond.

This book is inspired by the constantly evolving and increasing usage of computational terminology, emergent discussions and theories on Artificial Intelligence (AI), and the seemingly overwhelming increase of new skill acquisition. AI technologies and functional applications have been around for decades in some form or another, yet, we still occasionally lack a common grounding framework and a horizontal view of the multiple fields of research and their perspectives on AI. This includes for example the simple differentiation between algorithms and functional applications—the former referring to mathematical models and the latter to a user-ready combination of ones, such as ChatGDP. Advanced disciplines in the area have published extensive work on AI and AI applications—such as cloud computing, Cyber-Physical-Systems

(CPS), Digital Twins (DT), and Machine Learning (ML), yet, reading further on any discipline alone leads to a rabbit hole. To understand the practical implications, ethical dilemmas, and prospects of AI, it is unreasonable to suggest full societies become data scientists overnight. On the other hand, research can only arrive at straw-man arguments on strategic AI integration without understanding the core concepts of phenomena—data hierarchies construction, user interface significance, and mandatory inter-organizational collaboration. In the age of Industry 5.0, even the simplest questions could remain unanswered without a truly interdisciplinary effort.

To first touch base with the black box that is AI, we have created a book that does not shy away from technical details, yet aims to understand the core of AI's significance for businesses, and where the future opportunities and challenges lie. The purpose of this book is to provide a guiding introduction to scholars and practitioners who navigate ambiguous and heterogeneous research of AI and provide a systematic source for the basics from a holistic viewpoint.

Compiling this book has taken a village and some very dedicated individuals. The editors would like to acknowledge and thank the highly esteemed expert panel for their help in the early stages of designing the content and for their excellent advice in both practical and contextual directions. We would also like to express our gratitude to the long list of anonymous reviewers for their extensive and high-quality feedback, as well as to all the authors for their patience and rapid responses, for their excellent contributions, and for their enthusiasm towards the book from the early stages on. Finally, we would like to thank our supporting facilities and funders, especially the Business Finland projects SANTTU (project 8859/31/2021), VIIMA (project 7290/31/2023), and the ITEA Eureka Cluster project AIToC (project 19027), that have made possible the publication of this book and given an insightful view to what is Industry 5.0.

Helsinki, Finland
August 2024

Päivi Aaltonen
Emil Kurvinen

Contents

Notes on Contributors

Päivi Aaltonen LUT University, Lappeenranta, Finland

Ryan Armstrong Department of Business, Universitat de Barcelona, Barcelona, Spain

Erkko Autio Imperial College London, London, UK

Isa Banagar Machine and Vehicle Design (MVD), Materials and Mechanical Engineering, Faculty of Technology, University of Oulu, Oulu, Finland

Ilkka Donoghue Department of Industrial Engineering and Management, School of Engineering Sciences, LUT University, Lappeenranta, Finland

Kalle Elfvengren Department of Industrial Engineering and Management, School of Engineering Sciences, LUT University, Lappeenranta, Finland

Nampuraja Enose Kamalabai Industrial Engineering and Management, LUT University, Lappeenranta, Finland

Tero Frondelius Machine and Vehicle Design (MVD), Materials and Mechanical Engineering, Faculty of Technology, University of Oulu, Oulu, Finland;
R&D Engineering, Wärtsilä, Vaasa, Finland

Jukka Hallikas LUT Business School, LUT University, Lappeenranta, Finland

Ari-Pekka Hameri Université de Lausanne, Lausanne, Switzerland

Lea Hannola Department of Industrial Engineering and Management, School of Engineering Sciences, LUT University, Lappeenranta, Finland

Aapo Hölsä Machine and Vehicle Design (MVD), Materials and Mechanical Engineering, Faculty of Technology, University of Oulu, Oulu, Finland

Heidi Huuskonen The Rescue Department of South Karelia, Lappeenranta, Finland

Mika Immonen LUT Business School, LUT University, Lappeenranta, Finland

Johan Kask CREDS—Center for Research on Digitalization and Sustainability, University of Inland Norway, Kongsvinger, Norway

Timo Kärri LUT Industrial Engineering and Management, LUT University, Lappeenranta, Finland

Qasim Khadim Machine and Vehicle Design (MVD), Materials and Mechanical Engineering, Faculty of Technology, University of Oulu, Oulu, Finland

Sini-Kaisu Kinnunen LUT Industrial Engineering and Management, LUT University, Lappeenranta, Finland

Mikkel Stein Knudsen Finland Futures Research Centre, University of Turku, Turku, Finland

Jouni Koivuniemi School of Engineering Sciences, LUT University, Lappeenranta, Finland

Kirsi Kokkonen Department of Industrial Engineering and Management, School of Engineering Sciences, LUT University, Lappeenranta, Finland

Juho Konnö Machine and Vehicle Design (MVD), Materials and Mechanical Engineering, Faculty of Technology, University of Oulu, Oulu, Finland

Emil Kurvinen Oulu University, Oulu, Finland

Antero Kutvonen School of Engineering Sciences, Industrial Engineering and Management, LUT University, Lappeenranta, Finland

Hervé Legenvre EIPM 59 Rue Antoine Rédier, Archamps, France

Gabriel Linton CREDS—Center for Research on Digitalization and Sustainability, University of Inland Norway, Kongsvinger, Norway

Amin Mahmoudzadeh Andwari Machine and Vehicle Design (MVD), Materials and Mechanical Engineering, Faculty of Technology, University of Oulu, Oulu, Finland

Amin Majd Faculty of Engineering and Business, Turku University of Applied Sciences, Turku, Finland

Lasse Metso LUT Industrial Engineering and Management, LUT University, Lappeenranta, Finland

Anna-Greta Nyström Faculty of Social Sciences, Business and Economics, and Law, Åbo Akademi University, Turku, Finland

Katayoon Pourmahdi Faculty of Social Sciences, Business and Economics, and Law, Åbo Akademi University, Turku, Finland

Paavo Ritala Business School, LUT University, Lappeenranta, Finland

Ellen Saltevo School of Engineering Sciences, Industrial Engineering and Management, LUT University, Lappeenranta, Finland

Jyrki Savolainen LUT Business School, LUT University, Lappeenranta, Finland;
CSC-IT Center for Science, Kajaani, Finland

Mira Timperi Department of Industrial Engineering and Management, School of Engineering Sciences, LUT University, Lappeenranta, Finland

Marko Torkkeli School of Engineering Sciences, Industrial Engineering and Management, LUT University, Lappeenranta, Finland

Luke Treves Business School, LUT University, Lappeenranta, Finland

Maija Worek FHWien der WKW University of Applied Sciences for Management and Communication, Vienna, Austria

List of Figures

List of Tables

Part I

The Operational Core of AI

1

Introduction to the Concepts: The Past, Present, and Future of AI

Päivi Aaltonen and Emil Kurvinen

1.1 Introduction to the Book

Artificial intelligence (AI) refers to an umbrella of technologies, from unsupervised machine learning to regression analysis and data management (Lichtenthaler 2020; Lee 2020). There is a long tradition of AI research in operations management and information systems, however, other management fields have only recently been interested in AI's organizational impacts (Michael et al. 2019; Iansiti and Lakhani 2020). For example, in databases such as EBSCO and Scopus using the terms 'AI' and 'Artificial Intelligence', over 250,000 manuscripts starting from 1975; most of which were in the field of computer science and engineering, while 3135 were in management field, of which 2149 were

P. Aaltonen (✉)
LUT University, P.O. Box 20, 53851 Lappeenranta, Finland
e-mail: paivi.aaltonen@lut.fi

E. Kurvinen
Oulu University, Oulu, Finland
e-mail: emil.kurvinen@oulu.fi

P. Aaltonen and E. Kurvinen (eds.), *Contemporary Issues in Industry 5.0*, Technology, Work and Globalization, https://doi.org/10.1007/978-3-031-74779-3_1

journal articles. Nonetheless, this 'fifth industrial revolution', stands apart significantly from its predecessors, marked by an exponential surge in opportunities and a simultaneous upheaval in the global landscape (Andreas and Michael 2019; Xun et al. 2021; Dąbrowska et al. 2022).

In the modern day, the available technology is no longer an issue. In prior decades, the competitive race between firms to develop technology played a much larger role. In contrast, in the current day the operational environment, skilled personnel, and internal coordination can determine success (Glikson and Woolley 2020; Frankiewicz and Chamorro-Premuzic 2020). However, while staying completely ignorant of AI technology is no longer possible, not all of us need to become data scientists overnight. In this introductory chapter, we first take a look and the recent history and terminology related to AI. While there are multiple definitions for AI, none are particularly clear nor universally agreed upon. For example, the dictionary defines AI as

> a software designed to imitate aspects of intelligent human behavior; a branch of computer science dealing with the simulation of intelligent behavior in computers; software designed to imitate aspects of intelligent human behavior; an individual program or set of programs designed in this way; something (such as a robot) that operates using AI software

In the first part, we open the details and background of these definitions to position the various definitions in their context. In the second, we apply an interdisciplinary lens to AI applications—how it is evident in everyday firm operations, how it can be a crucial part of firm strategy, and how to benefit from it as a tool for solving future challenges. The rest of the chapters in this book dwell on each of these points in more detail with empirical evidence.

1.2 Fundamental Concepts and Background

In the story of the blind men and the elephant, each of the men touches a different part of the elephant—declaring what it likens to. It is both a story about collaboration and communication in understanding complexity and about appreciation of a different viewpoint. Similarly, defining AI in a single sentence is challenging:

> AI represents a highly capable and complex technology that aims to simulate human intelligence (Glikson and Woolley 2020).

> (AI) encompasses logic, probability, and continuous mathematics; perception, reasoning, learning, and action; and everything from microelectronic devices to robotic planetary explorer (Russell 2010).

> ML lacks sentience and relies on formal rationality, or impersonal quantitative calculations, to select a small set of statistical models that best describe the specific context of historical data. (Balasubramanian et al. 2022).

> Artificial intelligence (AI) technologies are edging closer to human capabilities and are often positioned as a revolutionary resource promising continuous improvements in problem-solving, perception, and reasoning. (Lebovitz 2022).

> AI tends to refer to either macro-economic development, e.g., labor market,'world-fist' innovations, i.e. Uber and Netflix, or deep conceptualizations regarding distant future (Aaltonen et al. 2024).

The definition of *Artificial Intelligence* is simultaneously complex and clear. On the other hand, *Artificial* refers to something man-made, and *Intelligence* refers to some processing capability. A simple calculator. One might want to clarify what type of calculator, does it deal with Large Language Models (LLM), or generative AI in particular? Or, where does it get its input? Sensors? Simulation? Us pushing the buttons? On the other hand, however, the mere concept of AI is filled with symbol-laden discussion on, for example, theft of opportunities (Fleming 2019), mistrust (Glikson and Woolley 2020), and accountability (Perc and Hojnik 2019). Both are very valid and important lenses to study AI, yet can lead easily to a mixed view of the phenomena for anyone unfamiliar with the ontological assumptions paradigms carry. Our perception of AI is not as simple and value-free as algorithm construction. Unlike a keyboard or a mouse, we have a complex relationship with AI, yet is equally as much of an integrated part of many of our daily lives. And continues to increasingly be so. This creates a particularly evident dualism to AI, that applications of simpler technologies might not have—although, humans have a habit of naming and growing attached to everything.

1.2.1 Elements of AI

We have selected three questions to illustrate how AI has multiple built-in, dualistic, contradictions following the equally contradictory concept of being both man-made, human-like, yet of superior intelligence (Lindebaum et al. 2020; Ramaul et al. 2025). These relate to *interaction, scope assumptions, and inscrutable rationality*.

This dualism in interaction refers to the question—is it us or them who should change? Do humans need to follow the rules and recommendations created by AI, even if we do not always want to—or should we build AI and revise algorithms based on our comfort? After all, seems funny to force traditionally hard-headed human individuals conditioned to certain behaviors since birth to follow fully rational actors. In other words, should we alter systems to complement our capabilities, where then the pure rational efficiency of AI does not suffice as a 'positive outcome', but the net positive of human experience included does? Or, are we the recipients of benefits and need to act accordingly, as we are inherently biased and lacking in certain cognitive capabilities? Secondly, the dualism based on scope assumptions essentially highlights our relationship and expectations toward AI. Do we discuss AI's potential to become religion-like [see e.g., EM Forster's short story 'The Machine Stops' from 1909 (Lindebaum et al. 2020)], or do we want to develop economic implications for transfer learning? The latter sees AI from a pragmatic micro-level perspective, a calculator and statistical mathematical algorithm that uses data provided to it, and acknowledges that understanding full details requires often deep domain-specific knowledge. The former conceptualizes AI as an abstract contextualization, an intelligent agent that can perform humanlike functions—such as beating world champions in games (see Fig. 1.1). Thus, we tend to create unrealistic expectations of its capabilities as exemplified by science fiction such as The Terminator. Our final question is the perspective of dualism in inscrutable rationality. Is AI rational or does it lack the capability to fully comprehend reality as we are unable to describe it properly? Is AI a *black box* of inscrutable, powerful, and opaque technologies, or is it a *bias box* that is a contextual result of data work that is inherently biased? These perspectives are summarized in Table 1.1.

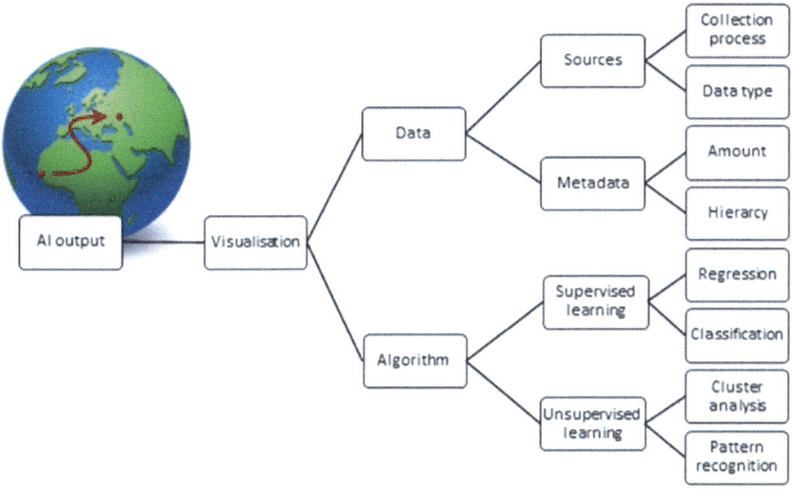

Fig. 1.1 Defining AI [based on Lee (2020)]

Table 1.1 Perspectives on AI

Viewpoint		
Interaction	Humans adapt to AI	AI is created around humans
Scope assumptions	AI transforms everything	Incremental improvements with AI
Inscrutable rationality	We cannot understand AI	AI cannot understand physical reality

For the purpose of this book, we use the following example to capture the various elements forming a general output that could be considered AI in Fig. 1.1.

While this is a simplification, it encapsulates many of the elements often overlooked in the general discussion around AI. For example, we humans tend to need a visualization of the outputs created by an algorithm to comprehend it, the calculator does not. Yet, this definition also leaves out many elements, such as context awareness. This can be exemplified with the help of Digital Twins. Digital Twins—digital copies of real-world objects, such as factories and machines—can exist as a separate entity (Digital Twin Prototype), or as an entity constantly connected to its physical counterpart (Digital Twin Instance). Both may or may not exist additionally in a digital environment, that can be used to either predict future behavior (Digital Twin Prototype) or investigate past behavior (Digital Twin Instance) (Aaltonen et al. 2024; Kurvinen et al. 2022; Grieves and Vickers 2017). Furthermore, the description in Fig. 1.2 leaves out details of algorithms themselves, for example linear, polynomial and support vector regression; decision tree and neural network classification; K-means Clustering and DBSCAN; Gaussian Mixture Model and Hidden Markov Model in pattern recognition (Lee, 2020). On the other hand, the larger picture of the combination of technologies, applications, and mutual hierarchies is best described as *AI maturity* (Lichtenthaler 2020; Aaltonen et al. 2024). Maturity here refers to the organizational capabilities and not the reliability of the algorithm itself. Level 1 maturity indicates a company that has taken initial steps toward experimentation with selected technologies and applications, but implementation is limited. Level 2 indicates ongoing initiatives and in level 3, multiple solutions are exploited, and there is clear coordination between organizational units. Level 4 describes how AI is used for purposes beyond simple efficiency, and level 5 indicates that truly novel solutions are created (Lichtenthaler 2020; Aaltonen et al. 2024). However, this evaluation does not take into account different AI *technologies* (mathematical models) or different *applications* (or functional applications—such as speech recognition or computer vision), nor the field of application (e.g., medical industry, agriculture, or transportation). AI technologies can relate to data technology, analytic technology,

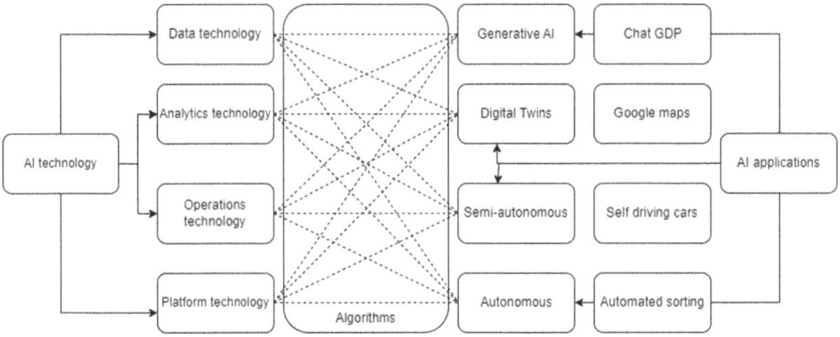

Fig. 1.2 Levels of AI

platform technology, or operations technology (Lee 2020) (see also CH 6 in this book), whereas AI applications in this book refer to particular, often named, uses—such as Google maps—that can utilize any type of AI technology and algorithms or a combination. Figure 1.2 represents these differences and in Table 1.2 we have collected a short list of various terms used in this book and literature.

Following Table 1.2, this book uses a multitude of the above terms to highlight the rich variety of studies and paradigms related to AI and Industry 5.0. In the first part of this book, where the focus is on current-day operations management in established industrial firms, Chapter 3 authors focus on the usage of AI especially autonomous and semi-autonomous systems, describing in detail current functional applications used and the planned future advances. For example, companies tend not to see the 'mistrust' toward AI as an issue, unlike some literature has suggested (Fleming 2019; Glikson and Woolley 2020), as the change in technological advances at the company grassroots level is incremental and slow. In Chapter 4, the authors discuss in detail how firms could formally organize their functions to support AI applications, using Digital Twins as an example. As each stage in the manufacturing system process is affected by human, equipment, material, process, and environmental problems, the perspective minimizes invisible problems and leverages the creation of a holistic perspective when aiming toward higher AI maturity levels (Kurvinen et al. 2024; Lichtenthaler 2020). Chapter 5

Table 1.2 Some AI terminology

General terminology	
ICT	
Data	Data that includes the relevant information that the AI algorithm can use as input
Input	Information and data inputs for the AI
Output	Results from the AI algorithm applied in an application
Visualization	Input or output information presented in a visual format for human interpretation
Maturity (algorithm)	The algorithm sufficiency and confidence level of a given application
Maturity (AI)	The amount of interconnections, future plans, and coordination between AI applications in a given organization
Industrial AI	AI applied to industrial context and cases
Internet of Things (IoT)	Platform for data visualization and gathering
Intelligent industry (II)	Industry that uses advanced data processing for the benefit of innovation in business
Cyber-physical-systems (CPS)	Hardware and software are closely connected
Data technology (DT)*	(Any) CPS technology used for handling, collecting, and organizing data
Analytic technology (AT)	(Any) CPS technology used for analyzing data collected
Operations technology (OT)	(Any) CPS technology used for monitoring and controlling processes in DT, AT, or HMT and their interconnections
Human–machine technology (HMT)	(Any) CPS technology used for communication and inter-action between humans and machines
Platform technology (PT)	Combination of all CPS technologies used in DT, AT, HMT and OT
General AI	Refers to the general umbrella of AI or functional applications

(continued)

Table 1.2 (continued)

General terminology	
Narrow AI	Refers to a single or well-defined model, functional application, or use
Functional applications	
Virtual simulation	A category of simulation
Cloud computing	
Centralized external storage of data and hardware to be used online open-source	
Software or a part of it that is free to Can create different kinds of information such as text, visual use or modify Generative AI (G-AI) representations	
Digital twins (DT)	An accurate representation of a real asset or a piece of asset in a virtual world
Digital twin prototype (DTP)	A representation of a real asset or a piece of asset used to predict behavior
Digital twin instance (DTI*	A representation of a real asset or a piece of asset used to asses previous behavior
Digital twin environment (DTE)	A virtual world created for a Digital Twin that can be based on real life as well
Autonomous	Capable of making independent decisions without human intervention
Semi-autonomous	Capable of deciding with human intervention
Algorithms and models	
Deep learning (DL)	Multilayered neural networks used
Machine learning (ML)	Statistical algorithm that can learn from data
Transfer learning (TL)	Pre-trained model can be used in a related but different task
Neural networks (NN)	Artificial mathematical models estimating nonlinear models
Large language models (LLMs)	General purpose language generation
Supervised learning (SL)	Uses labeled data sets

(continued)

Table 1.2 (continued)

Algorithms and models	
Unsupervised learning (UL)	Uses non labeled data sets
Reinforcement learning (RL)	Trains software to make the most optimal results
Regression	Statistical method for estimating variable relationships
Classification	Classifies data into different sets
Cluster analysis	Grouping of similar information datasets to clusters
Pattern recognition	ML-based methodology that identifies different patterns and regularities in data

examines the risk and potential of investments toward Industry 5.0 technologies and AI functional applications, as the future of technology benefits is uncertain. In the second part of this book, which discusses AI from a firm ecosystem level, Chapter 6 serves as an introduction to the levels of AI technologies similar to Fig. 1.2 and the core competitive capabilities they enable. However, Chapters 7, 8, and 9 each illustrate how it is far from simple to integrate AI into operations. Chapter 7 focuses here on established industries, Chapter 8 on entrepreneurial start-ups and Chapter 9 takes a special approach to value-laden leadership roles that are idiosyncratic—family firms, local businesses, and diaspora entrepreneurship (Elo and Volovelsky, 2017) are examples of this.

1.2.2 The Multilayer History of AI

The question

> Is AI "just" an influential digital technology among others, or should we more fundamentally alter how we theorize organizations, their employees, and their relationship to AI?

is the main theme of the first chapter of this book [also see (Ramaul et al. 2025)], along with an extensive look at the history of revolutions dating back to the agricultural revolutions of the Stone Ages. However, before anything comes to a world-changing technology, it tends to go through incremental changes, evolving from niche technology to dominant applications (Geels 2005).

Multiple events are connected to the history of AI, such as the invention of the Turing test, 'AI winter', and remarkable technological feats—such as IBM's Deep Blue defeating world leader Kasparov in chess. Here, we conceptualize roughly three parallel but thematically different development paths in AI (1) technologies and functional applications, (2) management practices adopted and theoretical frameworks developed, and the general, (3) societal interest. The latter, in addition to news and media, also impacts funding and government support initiatives. This section is not an extensive and all-inclusive timeline of AI nor does it represent the entire history of mathematics, but it focuses on common events and theories developed. Borrowing from Chapter 2:

> Beginning in Britain in the mid-eighteenth century and spreading to Europe and North America, the First Industrial Revolution introduced steam power and mechanization, transforming textile manufacturing and other industries. The societal changes brought by this "revolution" were enormous, and yet, it took nearly a century for the impacts to fully manifest (Ashton 1948). Thereafter, the "Second Industrial Revolution," often dated from 1870 to 1914, introduced further significant changes. These included the widespread electrification of factories, the development of rail and telegraph networks, and the introduction of internal combustion engines. The diffusion of these technologies was faster than that of the First Industrial Revolution, reflecting a quickening pace of technological change (Mokyr 1998)

Around the turn of the century theories on organization and management began to appear [e.g., the works of Schumpeter (Schumpeter 1906) and the Hawthorne studies (Muldoon 2017)]. After World War II, the developing industrial nations adopted wartime managerial systems in statistical analysis and automation—for example, Standard Process Theory (SPT), Computer Numerical Control (CNC), and soon after Computer-Aided Design (CAD) (Lee 2020). However, during the famous Dartmouth conference and the scholarly work of Alan Turing in the 1950s, the term 'Artificial Intelligence' was officially coined, closer to the origins of the Third Industrial Revolution, despite often being connected to the 2020s and the Fifth Industrial Revolution. Notable in these revolutions, nonetheless, is the decrease in the lengths of the waves, i.e., time difference, between revolutions—when the first wave of innovation to the second took 60 years, the fifth only 30 (Ziemnowicz, 2020)—current evidence between Industry 4.0 and Industry 5.0 development suggests even shorter lengths of merely a decade (Xun et al. 2021). Simultaneously to Turing, in 1956, an American inventor named George Devol and a physicist named Joseph Engelberger invented the world's first industrial robot, Unimate (Lee 2020). As its research field, AI was initiated in 1955 (Andreas and Michael 2019), and the first dedicated academic journal was established in the mid-1970s, titled 'Artificial Intelligence' (Waterman 1970). In the World of Science (WOS) database there are in 2024 over half a million publications on AI, and additional and earlier publications exist in for example in European Patent Office (EPO) databases, having closer to two million publications in total.

The terms *AI winter*—often the first and second are acknowledged—refer to brief periods of decreased interest in general AI. The first takes place around the mid-1970s to the beginning of the 1980s and the second between the late 1980s and 1990s. It has been suggested that the first was due to the limited capabilities of the technologies and the second to the collapse of the specialized hardware industry in the late 1980s. Before this, microprocessor development in the 1970s had reduced the cost of computing machine tools. However, actual technology development never ceased to exist. Furthermore, firms in the field during those times successfully developed strategies by product diversification [e.g., Intel and semiconductors (Burgelman 1983, 1994, 2002) Corning and fiber optics (Cattani 2006)] or joined the field through alternative technologies—the CD-ROM technology was originally invented to improve the durability and sound quality of vinyl records, yet had a unique characteristic of being capable to store enormous amounts of data (Aaltonen et al. 2020; Aaltonen 2020). Thus, AI winters refer, in general, largely to the popular interest decrease and shifts in development focus, rather than complete pauses in technology development. Since the mid-1990s, the increased computational power has steered toward data-driven systems, such as cloud computing, Amazon recommendations, and finally Siri (Zhang et al. 2011; Aaltonen et al. 2020; Andreas and Michael 2019), then evolving into driverless cars and Chat-GDP (Manzl et al. 2024). However, looking into purely the economic literature under the term 'AI', less than 10 000 have been published, with only 2017 more than 200 annually (note that the term ICT has been in much wider use in past decades with equally 10,000 results, hitting past 200 a decade earlier). Interestingly, most cited publications on AI focus on larger societal issues, such as expressing a growing concern about job security (Fleming 2019) and the role of AI in service (Wirtz et al. 2018; Huang and Rust 2018)—highlighting the increasing impact of AI and Industry 5.0 in the wider society. Surprisingly, based on an industrial survey, Chapter 3 concludes that such concerns do not reflect the opinion of all firms, especially as many focus on field-specific functional applications and narrow AI. Yet, as Chapters 7, 8, and 9 highlight, organizational structures and environmental impact remain barriers to overcome.

As literature under one paradigm ponders whether robots will replace humans, *robotics*—as a relatively simple assistance tool to begin with—has been the most common functional application of AI since the 1980s. Robots followed the advances in computer vision in the 1970s, and by the 1990s natural language processing, distributed AI and predictive analytics began to be of more frequent use. As noted before, the terms Industry 4.0 and 5.0 refer to European manufacturing industries and the European Union launched terms describing the commonly used technologies in particular fields of applications. However, the line between operations management practices, functional applications of AI technologies, and scholarly theories—such as the Technology-Organization-Environment (TOE) and TAM (Technology Acceptance Model) models (Tornatzky 1990; Davis 1989)—is vague. For example, the management practice titled the PDCA cycle (Plan, Do, Check, Action), or 'Kaizen' originates from Japanese organizational culture in the mid-1900s focused on continuous improvement, that has largely impacted the Lean management practices of the 1990s (Lean Womack et al. 1991). However, it essentially originates from the efficiency generated by the Computer Numerical Control (CNC), whereas AI also originates from (Lee 2020). Similarly, Toyota's and General Motors's manufacturing development in the 1980s and 1990s led to the project management quality insurance management practice 'Six Sigma', still popular decades later (Fig. 1.3).

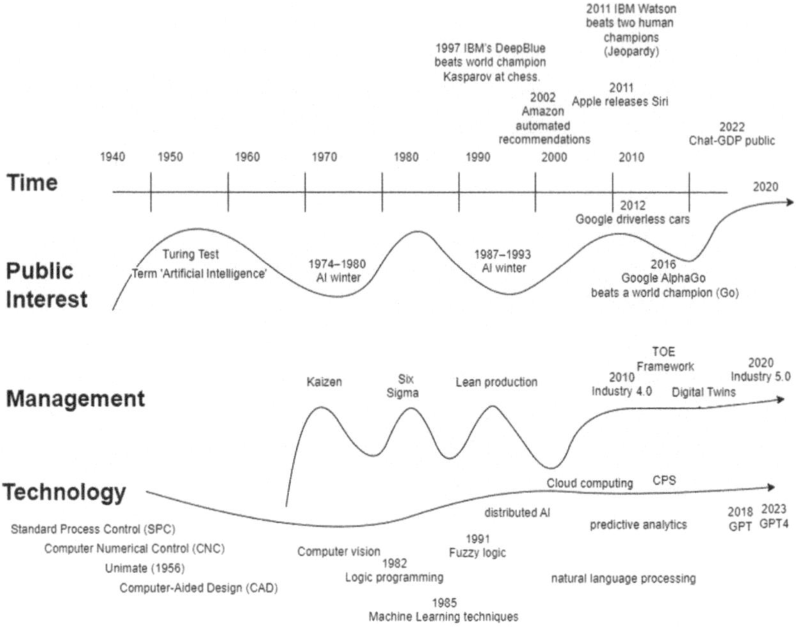

Fig. 1.3 Multilayer timeline

Popular and public advances in AI bring much of the underlying technology and applications development narrowly to public knowledge, steering interest toward them. Only in the past few years has AI become an increasingly popular search term, following the Chat-GDP launch. A similar increase in interest is notable during the launch and spreading of Google driverless cars, Siri, and IBM beating the top Jeopardy contestants. These events have caused a need to revise educational guidelines on cheating, and futuristic scenarios in movies, TV, and literature (Lindebaum et al. 2020) have geared the general perception of AI toward something far beyond possible with current technologies. A sentient AI is in practice very far from reality taking into consideration that humanity does not even comprehend all the *human* cognitive functions yet. As mentioned before, we have divided our parallel streams of the AI timeline into three levels, roughly following the widespread uses of technologies, the development of ones, and the major milestones.

Firstly we have the development of the underlying technology (Manzl et al. 2024). Second, the academic theories and managerial practices developed as a consequence. Finally, we have the notable milestones and trailblazer functional applications reaching the public eye—Deep Blue, IBM Watson, and Chat-GDP for example—and the fluctuating general interest of the society.

1.3 Industry 5.0 and Beyond

This book has been divided into three parts, each consisting of chapters addressing a particular area of AI, starting from the very practical insights on the current use of AI in day-to-day operations. In the first part, the chapters discuss the contemporary status of AI functional applications in twelve industrial sectors (according to the NACE Rev. 2 classification system of economic activities in the European Union) in Chapter 3, and how model-based systems engineering (MBSE) can eliminate technical barriers between personnel and data in Chapter 4. Chapter 5 highlights how economic theories can adeptly address numerical uncertainties in mathematical models and enable the usage of decision frameworks in making investment decisions on AI technologies and applications. These chapters form what we understand as the narrow core of modern-day AI in companies. Figure 1.4 summarizes the focal point of each part.

In the next part, we widen our perspective and focus on the development strategies and capabilities potential of AI applications. Chapter 6 opens this part by examining the strategic use of these technologies and the technological infrastructure of Google and similar players in building new services and products. Chapter 7 discusses the infrastructural and managerial competencies needed to leverage firm AI maturity, and 8 compares the differences in innovation processes of technological startups and the impact of these processes on their early-stage success. Chapter 9 points out the challenges created by existing strong ecosystem relations, risk aversion, and non-financial goals by using family firms as an example. In the final part of the book, we highlight the promise of AI as a society changing. The grand challenges, complex, uncertain, and evaluative (Ferraro et al. 2015; George et al. 2016), may be

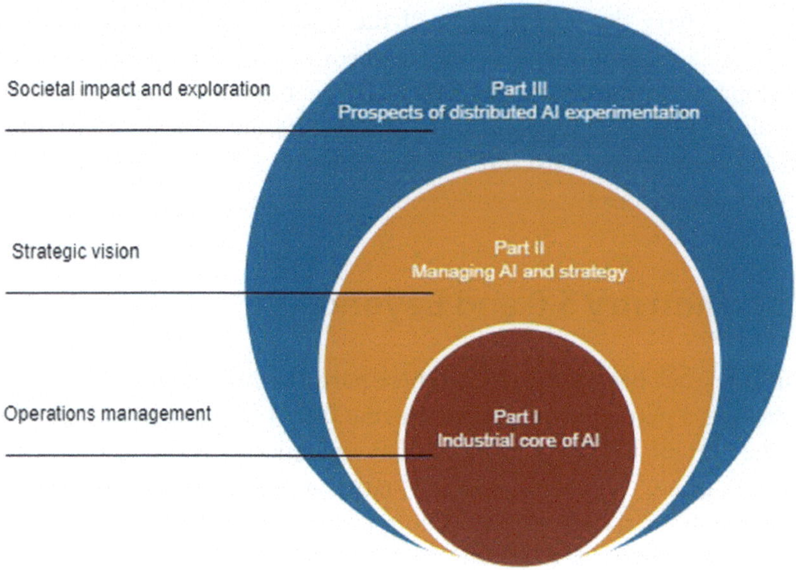

Fig. 1.4 Scope of book

addressed with AI applications—by for example gathering data on how pricing can impact sustainable consumer decisions as in Chapter 11, or how rescue departments can utilize ML techniques simulating potential emergency scenarios in Chapter 13. Chapter 10 opens this part with an integrative literature review addressing socio-technical transition toward sustainability, and the joint role of humans and AI within. Chapter 12 summarizes how the principles of Industry 5.0 enable the inclusion of social and sustainable goals in the techno-centric worldview of the previous decade. Finally, this part and the book ends with Chapter 14, a pedagogical discussion on how we can teach current and future generations to utilize AI applications to their fullest.

1.3.1 The Operational Core of AI

Is AI as significant in current organizational reality as we are led to believe? If so, what is the level of AI utilization in firms across industries, how do they select in what technologies to invest and how do they handle data collection and internal co-alignment between functional applications across business sectors?

Chapter 2 questions indeed whether a transition is currently taking place toward a new Industrial Revolution, or if AI is just a modern buzzword. The authors question the increasingly popular narrative of technological advancement as a series of abrupt Industrial Revolutions—instead of an incremental trajectory of technological and industrial evolution (also Geels 2005). The essay advocates for a nuanced understanding of the development of AI and encourages practitioners to adopt a long-term perspective and balance in transforming organizational structures [similarly, (Aaltonen et al. 2024)].

Chapter 3 focuses on the current plans for AI utilization in organizations, the common benefits and drawbacks of AI application integration, and the challenges in scaling. The chapter provides a comprehensive overview of the current state of the art of AI's business use and future implications for academics and practitioners, highlighting the increasing need to identify effective integration strategies and study how AI affects organizational performance, strategic management, and capabilities development. Industry 5.0 emphasizes the integration of digital technologies and automation while placing a strong emphasis on enhancing the well-being of workers, customization, and sustainability (Xun et al. 2021). As an integral part of the Industry 5.0 vision, Chapter 4 identifies a method for effective integration and illustrates how AI can facilitate the challenges of operations systems engineering, and simulation can patch up uneven data repositories and create new data rapidly—a requirement of efficient algorithm development. The systems engineering approach highlights how all the information can be centrally captured, and instead of many, the system can act as a singular source of truth that can act as a justification for development decisions, and in comparing alternative solutions to specific problems. To build systematic infrastructures enabling efficient AI utilization, the significance of these supporting hierarchical structures is crucial.

The central question of Chapter 5 is to evaluate the potential and investment risk in AI and Industry 5.0 technologies. Essentially, how one can grasp the emerging opportunities of technological change while avoiding sunk cost investments in, possibly, soon-to-be-obsolete technology applications, when should companies engage in transitional investments and how could they approach the investment decision and technology integration systematically? The authors introduce how strategic foresight tools can help organizations choose an optimal path forward by understanding the potential consequences of their decisions.

1.3.2 Managing AI and Strategy

> Novel technologies are a double-edged sword for companies. Technological advances enable scalable global operations and support growth, equality, and inclusivity—yet, traditional industries can be slow to adopt new technologies and some challenges cannot be avoided.

Despite the growing interest in AI, organizations can struggle to realize and transform the value of AI and solutions in practice (Fountaine et al. 2019; Raisch and Krakowski, 2021). Organizations encounter major hurdles in realizing the full AI benefits; financial constraints, cultural resistance, skill gaps, and ethical concerns, among other challenges. Furthermore, while AI shows promise in improving organizational efficiency, decision-making, and adaptability, its implementation often remains confined to specific operational segments. While AI indeed provides a remarkable opportunity for firms' growth (Lannon et al. 2023), it is not yet widely applied: less than 5% of German family firms apply AI in their daily business and only successful experimentation tends to be reported (Raisch and Krakowski 2021; Rammer et al. 2022; Soluk and Kammerlander, 2023).

In Chapter 6 of this book, the authors elaborate on the potential of AI as a core competitive capability through the examples of multinational giants such as Google, Meta, Amazon, and IBM [see also (Zhang et al. 2011)]. Especially, they highlight the pivotal role of cloud platforms within the broader cloud technology ecosystem, as these occupy a central position and serve as access points that interconnect various sub-ecosystems of open technologies and explain how constraints across heterogenous technology ecosystems emerge and how to deal with such bottlenecks.

Chapter 7 then provides in-depth empirical evidence on how firms can develop such capabilities in operational practice, yet also what can be hindering factors for advancing holistic AI maturity and leveraging one's competitive advantage. The authors introduce a framework for addressing Industry 5.0 competencies by adding *soft competencies* to the previous TAM and TOE models (Davis 1989; Tornatzky 1990), emphasizing the need for talent, conflict management, and emotional intelligence [similarly (Frankiewicz and Chamorro-Premuzic 2020; Glikson and Woolley 2020)].

Chapter 8 examines the challenges faced by deep technology start-ups as they navigate across the critical *Valley of Death*—the phase of financing their long and capital-intensive development processes. The author focuses on the systemic nature and interdependencies involved in innovation processes. The chapter concludes how concluding how deep-tech start-ups require an effective innovation system to be successful, diverging from conventional methods, as financing and human capital are critical components of an effective innovation system.

Chapter 9 highlights and opposite end of the spectrum in terms of AI maturity and willingness for technology adoption and focuses on the social values, talent, and human resource management areas in times of change in legacy firms. Due to the concentrated ownership structures, family firms pursue efficient decision-making processes that can be a source of competitive advantage but also a barrier. The cases serve as an example of challenges in AI technology integration in the presence of non-financial goals that strongly impact the company's strategic preferences.

1.3.3 Prospects of Distributed AI Experimentation

> Grand challenges are formulations of global problems that can be plausibly addressed through coordinated and collaborative effort (George et al. 2016).

Industry 5.0 is expected to do what Industry 4.0 did not achieve—a more just and sustainable society (Coelho et al. 2023). A Sustainable society is a combination of inclusive health, equal opportunities in economics and educational pursuits alike, and protecting the environment that requires participatory architecture and distributed experimentation (George et al. 2016; George et al. 2016). However, the discussion on AI often addresses how technologies revolutionize their sectors, underscoring their importance for and in societal development. Industry 4.0, characterized by its heavy reliance on automation and data-driven technologies, poses risks of social inequalities and reduces human oversight, potentially leading to ethical dilemmas and decreased job satisfaction among workers. For example, Chapter 4 discusses how the production of defective metal products consumes substantial quantities of natural, financial, and energy resources, contributing to environmental degradation. Learning how to benefit from AI is the core of a sustainable future society, yet we are still to understand the possibilities of augmenting human capabilities with AI.

Chapter 10 presents an integrative literature review that elucidates the underlying factors that influence the process and role of individual learning in sustainability transition and develops a conceptual framework to discuss the alignment of AI with these elements. The analysis identifies key points where AI can synergistically enhance the learning process, particularly in the restructuring of learning spaces and the facilitation of learning approaches that improve competency development, and illustrates the optimized alignment of roles and responsibilities between humans and AI in the creation of an improved learning function necessary to steer sustainability transitions.

Chapter 11 seeks to understand the key components of marketing strategies with a focus on pricing strategies in an era of increased orientation toward sustainable consumption and AI. The study uses agent-based simulations as a tool to analyze the impacts of pricing changes on customer behavior related to green products. Further, it identifies and discusses how this method can help reduce the risk of systems' failure and improve service precision as well as managers' awareness of suitable pricing strategies for green products. The results of this chapter reveal the optimal product pricing strategies that companies should pursue to convince and nudge their customers' buying behavior toward choosing sustainable products over other, substituting products. We specifically address how managers may benefit from pricing simulations facilitated by technology.

According to Chapter 12, Industry 5.0 enables embracing the original principles of sustainability, as the recent paradigm shifts have only brought to light the limits of the techno-centric approach of Industry 4.0. To create a balance between societal and economic goals, an adaptation of the traditional linear model to a circular operational model, mutual cognitive coordination between humans and AI, and a human-centric approach is required. While a standard approach to embedding these complexities is still developing, the authors provide a preliminary framework for creating circular economy operations by using AI technologies systematically.

Chapter 13 highlights the potential of AI in times of disruption, risk, and uncertainty as creasing the capabilities of rapid, societal resilience complex networks. Managerial literature outlines societal challenges related to an aging population, healthcare politics, and safety risks involved in decentralized home care plans. In industrialized Western nations, up to 80% of people are living in or near urban regions, and the fastest-growing areas are those surrounding the urban regions of major cities.

According to forecasts by the Ministry of the Interior (2016), approximately 25% of the population will be aged over 65 in 2030. For example, the authors demonstrate how trained artificial neural networks (ANNs) can be utilized in rescue service assessment in residential areas, where societal changes and healthcare reforms drive fire station networks, addressing challenges emerging from decentralized home care plans.

Chapter 14 highlights how companies need new types of professionals, and how the shortage of skilled workforce hinders the exploitation of advanced technologies (Brynjolfsson and McElheran 2016; Gürdür Broo et al. 2022; Pomp et al. 2022). However, while the increased amount of data is collected with sensors and IoT-related advanced technologies, not all data and technologies available are utilized as the support of decision-making by managers. The authors focus on creating a systematic process to use AI in operations provide a guiding framework to improve tactic knowledge and skills in everyday decision-making, and offer a systematic process to use as an educational element in company operations.

References

P. Aaltonen, L. Ramaul, E. Kurvinen, A. Kutvonen, and A. Nemeh. *Organizational Barriers and Enablers in Reaching Maturity in Digital Twin Technology*, chapter 19, pages 386–400. CRC Press, 2024.

Päivi Aaltonen, Lasse Torkkeli, and Maija Worek. The effect of emerging economies operations on knowledge utilization: The behavior of international companies as exaptation and adaptation. In *International business and emerging economy firms*, pages 49–87. Springer, 2020.

Päivi Hanna Maria Aaltonen. Piecing together a puzzle—a review and research agenda on internationalization and the promise of exaptation. *International Business Review*, 29(4):101664, 2020.

Kaplan Andreas and Haenlein Michael. Siri, siri, in my hand: Who's the fairest in the land? on the interpretations, illustrations, and implications of artificial intelligence. *Business horizons*, 62(1):15–25, 2019.

T. S. Ashton. *The Industrial Revolution, 1760–1830*. Oxford University Press, 1948.

Natarajan Balasubramanian, Yang Ye, and Mingtao Xu. Substituting human decision-making with machine learning: Implications for organizational learning. *Academy of Management Review*, 47(3):448–465, 2022.

Erik Brynjolfsson and Kristina McElheran. The rapid adoption of data-driven decision-making. *American Economic Review*, 106(5):133–39, 2016.

Robert Burgelman. Corporate entrepreneurship and strategic management: Insights from a process study. *Management Science*, 29:1349–1364, 1983.

Robert A. Burgelman. Fading memories: A process theory of strategic business exit in dynamic environments. *Administrative Science Quarterly*, 39(1):24–56, 1994. https://doi.org/10.2307/2393493.

Robert A. Burgelman. Strategy as vector and the inertia of coevolutionary lock-in. *Administrative Science Quarterly*, 47(2):325–357, 2002. https://doi.org/10.2307/3094808.

G. Cattani. Technological pre-adaptation, speciation, and emergence of new technologies: How corning invented and developed fiber optics. *Industrial and Corporate Change*, 15(2):285–318, 2006. https://doi.org/10.1093/icc/dtj016.

R. Coelho, S. Jayantilal, and J. J. Ferreira. The impact of social responsibility on corporate financial performance: A systematic literature review. *Corporate Social Responsibility and Environmental Management*, 30(4):1535–1560, 2023.

Fred D. Davis. Technology acceptance model: Tam. In *Information Seeking Behavior and Technology Adoption*, pages 205–219, 1989.

Justyna Dąbrowska, Argyro Almpanopoulou, Alexander Brem, Henry Chesbrough, Valentina Cucino, Alberto Di Minin, Ferran Giones, Henri Hakala, Cristina Marullo, Anne-Laure Mention, Letizia Mortara, Sladjana Nørskov, Petra Nylund, Calogero Oddo, Agnieszka Radziwon, and Paavo Ritala. Digital transformation, for better or worse: A critical multi-level research agenda. *R&D Management*, 53 (5):930–954, 2022.

Maria Elo and Erez Katz Volovelsky. Jewish diaspora entrepreneurs-the impact of religion on opportunity exploration and exploitation. *International Journal of Entrepreneurship and Small Business*, 31(2):244–269, 2017.

Fabrizio Ferraro, Dror Etzion, and Joel Gehman. Tackling grand challenges pragmatically: Robust action revisited. *Organization Studies*, 36(3):363–390, 2015.

P. Fleming. Robots and organization studies: Why robots might not want to steal your job. *Organization Studies*, 40(1):23–38, 2019.

Tim Fountaine, Brian McCarthy, and Tamim Saleh. Building the ai-powered organization. *Harvard Business Review*, 97(4):62–73, 2019.

B. Frankiewicz and T. Chamorro-Premuzic. The post-pandemic rules of talent management. *Harvard Business Review*, 13, 2020.

Frank W Geels. *Technological transitions and system innovations: a co-evolutionary and socio-technical analysis*. Edward Elgar Publishing, 2005.

Gerard George, Jennifer Howard-Grenville, Anjali Joshi, and Laszlo Tihanyi. Understanding and tackling societal grand challenges through management research. *Academy of Management Journal*, 59(6):1880–1895, 2016.

Manzl P. Gerstmayr J. and Pieber M. Multibody models generated from natural language. *Multibody System Dynamics*, 29(5):1–23, 2024.

Elan Glikson and Anne W. Woolley. Human trust in artificial intelligence: Review of empirical research. *Academy of Management Annals*, 14(2):627–660, 2020.

Michael Grieves and John Vickers. Digital twin: Mitigating unpredictable, undesirable emergent behavior in complex systems. In *Transdisciplinary perspectives on complex systems*, pages 85–113. Springer, 2017.

D. Gürdür Broo, O. Kaynak, and S. M. Sait. Rethinking engineering education at the age of industry 5.0. *Journal of Industrial Information Integration*, 25:100311, January 2022.

Ming-Hui Huang and Roland T. Rust. Artificial intelligence in service. *Journal of Service Research*, 21(2):155–172, 2018.

Marco Iansiti and Karim R Lakhani. *Competing in the age of AI: strategy and leadership when algorithms and networks run the world*. Harvard Business Press, 2020.

D. Kurvinen, A. Kutvonen, P. Aaltonen, J. Salakka, and B. Ghalamchi. Physics-based digital twins leveraging competitive edge in novel markets. In *Handbook of Digital Twins*, pages 185–199. CRC Press, 2024.

Emil Kurvinen, Antero Kutvonen, Juhani Ukko, Qasim Khadim, Yashar Shabbouei Hagh, Suraj Jaiswal, Neda Neisi, Victor Zhidchenko, Juha Kortelainen, Mira Timperi, Kirsi Kokkonen, Juha Virtanen, Akhtar Zeb, Ville Lämsä, Vesa Nieminen, Jukka Junttila, Mikko Savolainen, Tuija Rantala, Tiina Valjakka, Ilkka Donoghue, Kalle Elfvengren, Mina Nasiri, Tero Rantala, Ilya Kurinov, Eerik Sikanen, Lauri Pyrhönen, Lea Hannola, Heikki Handroos, Hannu Rantanen, Minna Saunila, Jussi Sopanen, and Aki Mikkola. Physics-based digital twins merging with machines: Cases of mobile log crane and rotating machine. *IEEE Access*, 10:45962–45978, 2022. https://doi.org/10.1109/ACCESS.2022.3170430.

Lannon, R. Lyons, and C. O'Connor. Generation ai and family business: a perspective article. *Journal of Family Business Management*, 2023.

James P. Lean Womack, Daniel T. Jones, and Daniel Roos. *The Machine That Changed the World: The Story of Lean Production*. Harper Paperbacks, 1991.

Lifshitz-Assaf H. Lebovitz S. and Levina N. To engage or not to engage with ai for critical judgments: How professionals deal with opacity when using ai for medical diagnosis. *Organization science*, 33(1):126–148, 2022.

Jay Lee. *Industrial AI: Applications with Sustainable Performance*. Springer, 2020

Ulrich Lichtenthaler. Five maturity levels of managing ai: From isolated ignorance to integrated intelligence. *Journal of Innovation Management*, 8(1):39–50, 2020.

Dirk Lindebaum, Mikko Vesa, and Frank Den Hond. Insights from "the machine stops" to better understand rational assumptions in algorithmic decision making and its implications for organizations. *Academy of Management Review*, 45(1): 247–263, 2020.

Zhang J. Marston S., Bandyopadhyay S. and Anand G. Cloud computing—the business perspective. *Decision Support Systems*, 51:176–189, 2011.

Haenlein Michael, Kaplan Andreas, Tan Chee-Wee, and Zhang Pengzhu. Artificial intelligence (ai) and management analytics. *Journal of Management Analytics*, 6 (4):341–343, 2019.

J. Mokyr. *The Second Industrial Revolution, 1870–1914*. Northwestern University, 1998.

J. Muldoon. The hawthorne studies: An analysis of critical perspectives, 1936-1958. *Journal of Management History*, 23(1):74 – 94, 2017.

Ozer M., Perc M. and J. Hojnik. Social and juristic challenges of artificial intelligence. *Palgrave Communications*, 5(1), 2019.

A. Pomp, A. Burgdorf, A. Paulus, and T. Meisen. Towards unlocking the potential of the internet of things for the skilled crafts. In *Proceedings of the 24th International Conference on Enterprise Information Systems (ICEIS 2022)*, volume 1, pages 203–210, 2022.

Sebastian Raisch and Sebastian Krakowski. Artificial intelligence and management: The automation–augmentation paradox. *Academy of Management Review*, 46(1): 192–210, 2021.

L Ramaul, Paavo Ritala, Alexandros Kostis, and Piia Aaltonen. Rethinking how we theorize ai in organization and management: A problematizing review of rationality and anthropomorphism. *Journal of Management Studies*, 5(1), 2025.

Christian Rammer, Gastón P Fernández, and Dirk Czarnitzki. Artificial intelligence and industrial innovation: Evidence from german firm-level data. *Research Policy*, 51(7):104555, 2022.

Stuart J Russell. *Artificial intelligence a modern approach*. Pearson Education, Inc., 2010.

Joseph Alois Schumpeter. *Über die mathematische Methode der theoretischen Ökonomie*. Wien Braumüller, 1906.

J. Soluk and N. Kammerlander. Digitale transformation und künstliche intelligenz in familienunternehmen. In *Handbuch Digitale Wirtschaft*, pages 1–17. Springer Fachmedien Wiesbaden, 2023.

Louis G. Tornatzky. *The Processes of Technological Innovation*. Lexington/DC Heath & Company, 1990.

Donald Arthur Waterman. Generalization learning techniques for automating the learning of heuristics. *Artificial Intelligence*, 1(1-2):121–170, 1970.

Jochen Wirtz, Paul G Patterson, Werner H Kunz, Thorsten Gruber, Vinh Nhat Lu, Stefanie Paluch, and Antje Martins. Brave new world: service robots in the frontline. *Journal of Service Management*, 29(5):907–931, 2018.

Xun Xu, Yuqian Lu, Birgit Vogel-Heuser, and Lihui Wang. Industry 4.0 and industry 5.0—inception, conception and perception. *Journal of Manufacturing Systems*, 61:530–535, 2021. ISSN 0278–6125. https://doi.org/10.1016/j.jmsy.2021.10.006. URL https://www.sciencedirect.com/science/article/pii/S0278612521002119.

C. Ziemnowicz. Joseph a. schumpeter and innovation. In E.G. Carayannis, editor, *Encyclopedia of Creativity, Invention, Innovation and Entrepreneurship*. Springer, Cham, 2020.

2

Another Industrial Revolution? It's All Evolution!

Johan Kask and Ryan Armstrong

2.1 Introduction

References to industrial eras (e.g., "Industry 4.0", "Industry 5.0", "Fourth Industrial Revolution") have recently exploded in academic and popular literature, reflecting increased interest in socio-technological change. While such interest is most welcomed, both the scientific soundness and purpose of the "Fourth Industrial Revolution" and related terms have been questioned (Cetrulo and Nuvolari 2019; Drath and Horch 2014). The more recent discussion of a "Fifth Industrial Revolution" or "Industry 5.0"—the terms are not equivalent but are used interchangeably—further calls into question the appropriateness of such

J. Kask (✉)
CREDS—Center for Research on Digitalization and Sustainability, University of Inland Norway, Kongsvinger, Norway
e-mail: Johan.kask@inn.no

R. Armstrong
Department of Business, Universitat de Barcelona, Barcelona, Spain
e-mail: ryan.armstrong@ub.edu

P. Aaltonen and E. Kurvinen (eds.), *Contemporary Issues in Industry 5.0*, Technology, Work and Globalization, https://doi.org/10.1007/978-3-031-74779-3_2

terms within scholarly discussion. The question emerges: Do these terms refer to actual events, or are they just buzzwords, marketing devices devoid of any real substance? In this chapter, we seek to address this question. Our paper is conceptual, though we employ bibliometrics and our research data to support the arguments and illustrate our points. The first aim of this chapter is to consider the value of such terms so that scholars can distinguish between their use as a buzzword—a pathologically vague description of events, linked to a strong belief in what they are meant to bring about (Rist 2007), versus scholarly discussion. Drawing on a bibliometric analysis of recent publishing trends, we suggest its use is mainly promotional rather than scientific. With some exceptions, this use creates confusion and redundancy with existing concepts. Perhaps worse, such use obscures plausible explanatory mechanisms of technological change. Rather than viewing the industrial period as a series of distinct "revolutions" or stages, we suggest it is more accurate to perceive industrial progress as a continuous process of cumulative, path-dependent interaction between technology and society at a varying pace, with each iteration of evolution adding new elements to the existing system (Murmann and Frenken 2006). Technical innovation, driven by competition and the pursuit of efficiency and effectiveness, interacts with other factors such as government regulations, consumer preferences, and social attitudes, to (re)shape the industrial landscape.

The second aim of the chapter is to propose that technological shifts are better understood as "Industrial Evolution," which holds greater descriptive and explanatory value. To illustrate this perspective, we use the case of technological development in the music recording industry, in which the recent development is driven by an evolutionary change in human values, countering the progressivist rhetoric of the Industrial Revolution. Data from interviews, industry reports, news archives, and patent databases, highlight that disruptive changes in the marketplace, occurring within a limited time frame, such as the shift from physical CDs to streaming-on-demand as a dominant way of distributing recorded music, are not a sudden revolution. Instead, they are preceded by a decades-long build-up of technologies and patents, as well as social habits, across several interacting sectors.

The chapter concludes by proposing the term Industrial Evolution as a more accurate descriptor of this multi-dependent, dynamic process where technological advancements are both the causes and results of ongoing sociotechnical and economic transformations. This term offers a more in-depth and nuanced understanding of the dynamics of industrial development.

2.2 A Brief History of Technological Evolution: From Hand Axes to AI

The evolution of technology across human history has been a slow but enduring process, marked by periods of gradual development and accelerating change. Examining this historical progression provides essential insights into the dynamics of sociotechnical transformation and helps put the idea of "Industrial Revolutions" into perspective. The earliest human technologies were strikingly durable. The Acheulean hand axe, for example, is an artifact of the Early Stone Age (Lower Paleolithic), dating back nearly 1.7 million years (See Fig. 2.1). These tools, created by our early human ancestors, Homo erectus, remained virtually unchanged for over a million years (Handwerk 2021). They represent an essential technological adaptation that helped our ancestors survive in diverse environments across Africa and Eurasia.

Following this, the "Neolithic Revolution"—sometimes referred to as the "First Agricultural Revolution"—saw the widespread transition of human societies from hunting and gathering to settled farming. This transition occurred over thousands of years, beginning around 10,000 BCE (Diamond 1997). This era introduced domesticated crops and animals, as well as technological innovations like the plow and pottery, dramatically altering human societies and the environment. However, the pace of technological change remained very slow compared to the pace of change in our modern era, with innovations often taking centuries to spread across different regions.

What is referred to as the "First Industrial Revolution" marked a significant turning point in this slow trajectory of technological evolution. Beginning in Britain in the mid-eighteenth century and spreading

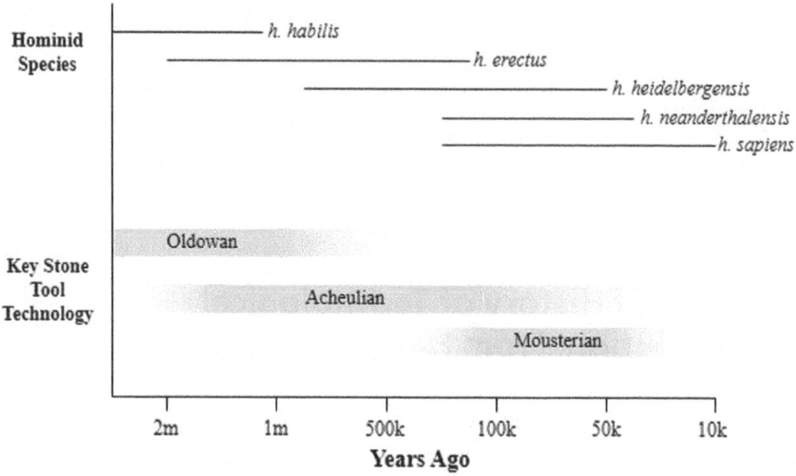

Fig. 2.1 Stone age technologies and human evolution [*Source* The authors, drawn from data from Wood (2012) and Mcbrearty and Brooks (2000). Note that the timeline is not at scale]

to Europe and North America, the First Industrial Revolution introduced steam power and mechanization, transforming textile manufacturing and other industries. The societal changes brought by this "revolution" were enormous, and yet, it took nearly a century for the impacts to fully manifest (Ashton 1948). Thereafter, the "Second Industrial Revolution," often dated from 1870 to 1914, introduced further significant changes. These included the widespread electrification of factories, the development of rail and telegraph networks, and the introduction of internal combustion engines. The diffusion of these technologies was faster than that of the First Industrial Revolution, reflecting a quickening pace of technological change (Mokyr 1998).

More recent discussions of industrial eras—the "Third Industrial Revolution" (associated with digital technologies and often dated from the late twentieth century), the "Fourth Industrial Revolution" or "Industry 4.0" (related to cyber-physical systems and Internet of Things, and spanning the early twenty-first century), and even a proposed "Fifth Industrial Revolution" and "Industry 5.0" (focusing on artificial intelligence and machine learning)—implies even shorter time frames for each "revolution." These periods are increasingly compressed, with each new "revolution" predicted to unfold over mere decades, reflecting an unprecedented acceleration in technological change (Makridakis 2017; Schwab 2015).

2.3 The Problem with Revolution

The word *revolution* to describe technological developments is problematic. For one, it introduces ambiguity at the expense of specificity. Ambiguous definitions hinder scientific progress and the accumulation of evidence (Rousseau et al. 2008). Drawing valid conclusions is impossible when people use the same term to refer to different things and, it appears, this is what is happening when the term "Fourth Industrial Revolution" and its derivatives are employed.

Unlike the first three industrial revolutions, which emerged in scholarly literature, the fourth emerged from practice, beginning with the term "Industrie 4.0" in 2011 (Drath and Horch 2014), to refer to a subset of technologies including automation, Big Data, digitization, Internet of Things (IoT), networking and smart manufacturing (Lasi et al. 2014). The notion of "revolution" appeared shortly after. To be clear, it is not its non-scholarly origins that make the term problematic—plenty of now widely accepted concepts in scholarly literature began in this way (Macey and Schneider 2008). It is precisely its use in research where one expects conceptual clarity that appears most problematic.

Indeed, most scholarly discussion that includes a Fourth Industrial Revolution are not talking about a revolution at all but rather some aspect of it, i.e., the effects of the implementation of some particular aspect of a technology rather than a composite suite of technologies. Just which technologies are included, and the degree of concern for revolutionary aspects is unclear. To be sure debates around delineating exactly when and what things are is a hallmark of scientific debate and are not germane to the Fourth Industrial Revolution—they exist for the First Industrial Revolution, as well as technological developments in the Stone Age. For example, De Vries (1994) notes that while much discussion on the First Industrial Revolution places it in the late eighteenth century, the foundations and key developments had already taken place in the seventeenth century, and possibly earlier. Mcbrearty and Brooks (2000) level a comparable critique against oversimplifications of the "human revolution," a relative acceleration in technology that occurred around 50,000 years ago and marked the beginning of the later Stone Age.

The demarcations between Industrial and non-Industrial, and Middle and Late Stone Age, despite being separated by tens of thousands of years of human development, suffer similar deficiencies that any attempt to define a clearly defined era or "revolution" is likely to share. These are a general dismissal of heterogeneity and richness in design in favor of a wider scope, a tendency for Euro or Anglo-centricity, and a progressivist framing in which technological development is taken for granted to be good (Lycett and Norton 2010; Mcbrearty and Brooks 2000). But unlike these terms, the Fourth and possibly Fifth "Industrial Revolution" are ongoing, and therefore present a further deficiency. Revolution is a term that refers to an event, rather than a tendency. The term is almost always applied retrospectively and implies a subversive element—a significant change in the way of life and social order (Nickles 2006). Kuhn's (1970) discussion of scientific revolutions speaks to the depth of this change: a revolution alters deep-seated assumptions that underlie fundamental and wide-ranging ways of thinking and behaving. There is a before and after, such that after, the "world of his research will seem, here and there, incommensurable with the one he had inhabited before" (p. 112). None of these criteria necessarily applies to the current context. While technologists have claimed the mantel for subversion in certain fields (e.g., that it will revolutionize education by providing expanded access), so far, the benefits of Industry 4.0 technology have not displaced wealth (Center 2020). There is little evidence of any widespread shift in the thinking of the type Kuhn referred to within industry that would suggest revolution—the rules governing systems of production remain largely unchanged, beyond some espoused recognition of its harm to the environment. On the contrary, we would expect the ecological impacts of an industrial revolution, clearly visible in the "Neolithic Revolution" as well as the "First Industrial Revolution." Despite these limitations, academia appears to buy into the concept wholly and enthusiastically: since 2011, "Industry 4.0" and related terms have generated over 30,000 citations (Fig. 2.2). Compare this number to the combined total for the first three revolutions: Just over 1,000, with the majority also appearing in the past decade (Fig. 2.3). Such growth has not, to our knowledge, been accompanied by a related growth in academic departments whose remit is sociotechnical transitions, but rather, as Xu et al. (2021) warn against, more indicative of a marketing device to generate interest and justify grant applications.

Finally, the labeling of these periods as distinct revolutions may also obscure the true nature of technological development as an enduring process of cumulative, path-dependent technological development that has characterized human history from the Acheulean hand axe to today's AI. Technological change is an iterative process, with each innovation building upon previous ones in complex, interactive ways. Understanding this can provide a deeper perspective on our current era of rapid technological change and help us anticipate the trajectory of future developments.

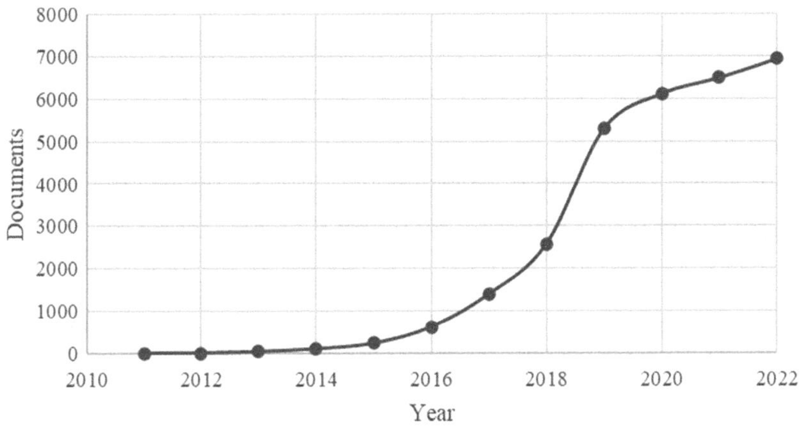

Fig. 2.2 Publications on the 4th industrial revolution, 2011–2022

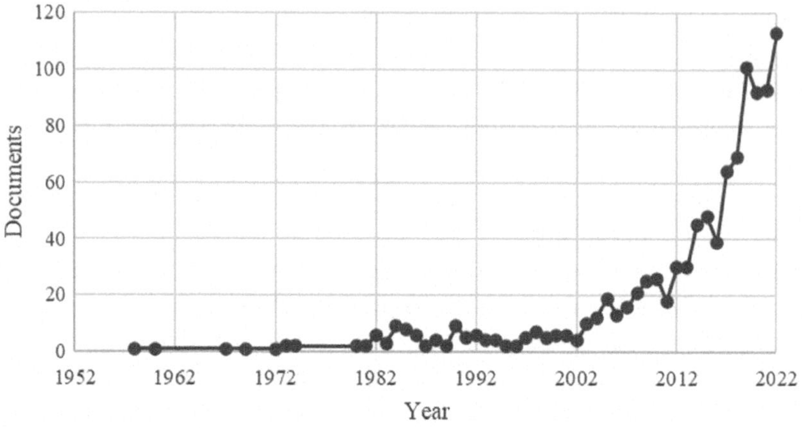

Fig. 2.3 Publications on 1st, 2nd and 3rd industrial revolutions to 2022

2.4 The Continuity of Technological Evolution

The concept of technological *revolutions* may be deceptive, obscuring the complex, continuous processes of technological evolution that underpin apparent "breakthroughs." The narrative of sudden, disruptive change often overshadows the reality that these transformations are built on a cumulative foundation of previous innovations, patents, and technological advancements that have developed over the years, even decades. The model of *evolution* rather than *revolution* is more accurate, as evolution suggests continuity: technological variation comes about through innovation, some are selected if they outperform the competition, and some are retained through generations. Often, co-evolution occurs where the evolution of one entity—a species, technology, or practice—exerts a causal influence on another and is itself responsive to that evolution (Breslin et al. 2021).

The evolution of humans and human tools in the Stone Age is an example of this co-evolutionary development. Consider solar photovoltaic technology. Although the wider adoption of solar energy and its recognition as a viable alternative to fossil fuels is a relatively recent development, the foundational research goes back much further. The photovoltaic effect was discovered, and the first patents for solar cells were filed, already in the 1800s by Becquerel Sr and others Lincot (2017). This early invention, although groundbreaking, had limited efficiency and high production costs. However, since then, the field has seen a cascade of patents, each building on, refining, and evolving from the accomplishments of their predecessors. For example, a later invention that substantially improved the efficiency of solar cells by, employing layered nanostructures would not have been possible without a firm grounding in earlier developments. Thus, what might seem like a recent "revolution" in energy production is the culmination of over a century of incremental improvements and persistent research.

The narrative of continuity and evolution is also evident in other technological systems, such as the development of electric vehicles (EVs) and the corresponding advances in battery technology. While the commercial success of companies like Tesla may seem to signify a sudden shift, the history of EVs extends back to the nineteenth century. Advances in battery technology, a key component for the operation of EVs, have been the result of long-term, incremental research and development (Mom 2004). Also, this progress has been characterized by a series of patented inventions that build on, revise, and develop previous inventions. For example, a rechargeable lithium battery with a particular arrangement of the anode and cathode (Mizushima et al. 1980), laid the groundwork for subsequent improvements, including those that have resulted in the high-performance lithium-ion batteries in today's EVs.

Similarly, the internet—a technological innovation that has radically transformed societies worldwide—did not emerge suddenly. Its roots can be traced back to the 1960s with the development of *ARPANET*, a project funded by the *U.S. Department of Defense*. The protocols that form the foundation of the internet, such as *TCP/IP*, were developed in the 1970s, and the *World Wide Web*, which made the internet accessible and useful to the public, did not come into being until 1989 (Leiner et al. 2009). This multi-decade evolution underscores that even the most transformative innovations are products of extended, cumulative processes.

Artificial intelligence (AI)—so labeled by Turing, and defined as the science and engineering of creating intelligent machines (Turing 1950)—and virtual reality (VR) are other examples where the origins of the technologies predate their widespread use and societal impact by several decades. AI research began in earnest in the 1950s and 1960s (McCorduck 2004), but its potential is only being realized recently due to advances in computational power and data availability (Hassabis et al. 2017; Silver et al. 2016). Similarly, the conceptual groundwork for VR was laid in the mid-twentieth century, with key developments like the *Sensorama* (1962) and the *Head-Mounted Display* (1968) (Biocca and Levy 1995). Nevertheless, VR technology only started to gain mainstream attention and commercial success in the 2010s with products like the Oculus *Rift*.

These examples above demonstrate that while we may perceive technological change as occurring in leaps and bounds or "revolutions," it is a cumulative and ongoing evolutionary process. The apparent breakthroughs we see are often just the most visible aspects of long, complex journeys of technological innovation happening on multiple fronts in parallel, often barely or loosely connected. Recognizing this can provide us with a more nuanced understanding of technological change and its implications for society.

2.5 Lessons from the Recording Industry: The Evolutionary Path to On-Demand Streaming

The evolution of the music recording industry provides a clear illustration of the complex interplay, or co-evolution, of technological advancements that culminated in apparent sudden disruptions. Spotify and other on-demand streaming services didn't suddenly emerge and transform the music industry; they are the visible outcomes of a long-standing evolutionary process encompassing several technological breakthroughs.

The internet is a fundamental prerequisite for streaming services. Developed over decades, the internet has profoundly impacted the music industry by providing a platform for global music distribution. Additionally, the creation of the *World Wide Web* in 1989 and the subsequent development of web browsers during the 1990s made the internet more accessible and user-friendly, enabling the rise of digital music platforms (Leiner et al. 2009).

Advancements in digital storage technology played a crucial role as well. The introduction of CDs in the 1980s signaled the transition from analog to digital music formats, revolutionizing the recording industry by offering superior sound quality and durability. The proliferation of CD-ROM writers in the late 1990s allowed consumers to copy CDs and create their compilations, a step toward the personalization of music consumption (Kask 2011; Wikström 2009).

The development and popularization of the *MP3* format in the mid-1990s further accelerated the digitization of music. MP3s compress audio files without significantly compromising sound quality, enabling users to store more songs on their devices and share music online. This led to the rise of peer-to-peer file-sharing services like *Napster*, which marked the beginning of digital music distribution and sharing, even though it ran afoul of copyright laws (Wikström 2009). Fast broadband connections have been another essential factor, enabling quick and seamless music streaming. In the early days of the internet, slow dial-up connections made online music streaming impractical. With the advent of broadband, music could be streamed smoothly, paving the way for the growth of online music platforms (Kask 2011).

It is in this context that *Spotify* and other music streaming services emerged, integrating these various technological advancements into a single user-friendly platform. Through a longitudinal study, Kask (2011) underscored how the evolution of technologies and innovative market channels, underpinned by technological advancements, paved the way for Spotify. The study highlighted how Spotify leveraged the existing technological infrastructure— digital music formats (first CDs and then MP3s), internet, digital storage, broadband connections, Peer to Peer sharing—to offer a new way of consuming music. Further, Kask and Öberg (2019) posited that Spotify's success is not only due to technological innovation but also to its alignment with the music consumer's will to use such a service. By providing unlimited access to a vast music library through a subscription model, these platforms have fundamentally changed the way we purchase, own, and listen to music.

Yet, despite the disruptive impact of these platforms, they are simply the latest manifestation of a nested, path-dependent process of technological evolution that has been reshaping the music industry for decades. Understanding this historical context can help us appreciate the nuances and dynamics of this transformation and anticipate the future direction of various industries.

2.6 Discussion

Our exploration of the evolutionary processes underlying technological development challenges the prevailing notion of industry "revolutions." Through a historical review of technological progression and the lessons learned from the music recording industry's transformation, we argue that the concept of Industrial Evolution holds greater descriptive and explanatory value. Technological shifts, from the creation of the first hand axe to the rise of music streaming services, have unfolded through a cumulative evolutionary process, often misunderstood as a series of abrupt revolutions. The notion of industrial revolutions, often perpetuated by the media and corporations, creates a perception of radical discontinuity and emphasizes the newness of technologies over their historical underpinnings. This perspective can distort our understanding of technological change by presenting it as a series of leaps and breakthroughs rather than as a long-term, path-dependent process (Frenken and Leydesdorff 2000; Kask 2013). We acknowledge that the narrative of distinct "Industrial Revolutions" may appear attractive for its simplicity and the way it neatly categorizes periods of drastic change.

However, this narrative overlooks the fact that the time interval between these so-called revolutions is diminishing, and the rate of technological innovation is accelerating. The increase in the number of patents issued, the growing population of educated individuals involved in research and development, and the exponential pace of advancements in fields like computing power (Moore's law), bandwidth, energy storage, and solar power (Kask et al. 2022; Kittner et al. 2017). All demonstrate this acceleration. This tendency for technological growth to follow an exponential, rather than a linear trajectory, is a significant factor. This can be attributed to the cumulative and interconnected nature of technological development. Each innovation serves as a building block for future inventions, creating a positive feedback loop that fuels faster and more sophisticated advancements (Arthur 2009). While disruptive technologies certainly emerge, it is misguided to think of these as "revolutions." The accelerating pace of technological advancements implies that there will be no final "Industrial Revolution." Instead, we are likely to witness a continual, rapid evolution of technologies and industries. The concept of an "Industrial Revolution" may, thus, increasingly become a buzzword or a sales pitch for the most recent "big thing," rather than a meaningful description of a distinct period of more drastic change. This perspective aligns with the view that we are now in an era of constant, high-speed innovation, where the acceleration of technological progress has become the norm (Schwab 2015). Therefore, rather than focusing on labeling and differentiating "revolutions," we might do better to understand the broader, continuous, and accelerating process of Industrial Evolution. Recognizing the cumulative, interconnected, and exponential nature of technological progress can provide a more nuanced and accurate understanding of the socio-technological landscape, its trajectory, its pace, and its implications for society.

Moreover, in this chapter we address that technologies do not emerge from a vacuum; they build upon previous achievements, knowledge, and structures. The sum of numerous improvements and developments in the details at the niche level in technologies and sociocultural norms can yield and accumulate significant macro-level transformations over time. The story of Spotify's rise, for example, is not simply about a single breakthrough, but about a long-term accumulation of technologies and patents, as well as changes in consumer habits and societal norms. In this context, Spotify's success was more the outcome of a gradual technological evolution in the condition of this kind of service than a sudden revolution (Kask and Öberg 2019). Acknowledging, instead, the evolutionary and co-evolutionary nature of industrial development—focusing on the interdependency between actors or between technology and sociocultural norms (Abatecola et al. 2020)—has profound implications. It can help decision-makers and policymakers craft more informed strategies and policies, educators provide a more realistic portrayal of technological progress, and the public cultivate a deeper understanding of how technology and industry evolve. It also encourages us to pay attention to the less glamorous, incremental advancements that, while often overlooked, form the basis for the "breakthroughs" that, often much later, capture our imagination.

The concept of Industrial Evolution also compels us to recognize the multidimensionality of technological change. It is not only about the evolution of hardware and software but also about the evolution of regulatory frameworks, market structures, social norms, and cultural values. All these elements interact to shape the path of technological development, with each "revolution" simply reflecting a particular and temporal stage in this ongoing process. Hence, we claim that technological change is better conceptualized as a co-evolutionary process—a series of small, history-dependent steps rather than giant leaps. We believe that adopting this perspective can deepen our understanding of the past and present technological landscape and, importantly, guide us as we navigate the uncharted territories of the future.

2.7 Conclusions and Implications

This chapter has endeavored to reframe our understanding of technological change as a process of Industrial Evolution a concept that emphasizes path-dependent change rooted in cumulative knowledge. We posited that so-called "industrial revolutions" often overlook the historical context and cumulative advancements, resulting in a distorted understanding of the nature of technological change. By analyzing the music recording industry, we demonstrated how perceived revolutionary shifts are better understood as the long-term, cumulative evolutionary processes, inherently driven by previous innovations and societal shifts. Hence, challenging the existing discourse of a series of so-called "Industrial Revolutions" has implications for research and practice. Firstly, it serves as a rallying call for a shift in our conceptual understanding of industrial change. The concept of Industrial Evolution necessitates a reconsideration of existing ideas, theories, and frameworks that too often label technological progress into isolated, discrete "revolutions." We contend that a reframing of this nature has the potential to enhance the discourse in fields like innovation, technological change, and industrial organization. For one, it suggests that scholars interested in technological development would be better served by focusing on specific technologies or technology groupings and their context-dependent effects, rather than trying to divine or evaluate a set of "Industry 4.0" technologies. Otherwise, they may miss out on adaptive heterogeneity as the technologies develop in different contexts and for different purposes. Second, our proposed concept of "Industrial Evolution" demands a change in research methodologies. The focus should shift toward longitudinal studies that meticulously trace the intricate and gradual processes leading to major technological changes. Additionally, given the diverse range of factors at play in these transitions, an interdisciplinary approach becomes paramount. This is an audacious demand, but one we believe is crucial for capturing the genuine essence of technological progression.

For practitioners, acknowledging "Industrial Evolution" could reshape the way one thinks about strategic decision-making. Instead of being captivated by the lure of the next "big thing," firms would need to cultivate a deep, historical understanding of long-term technological-evolutionary trajectories. Policymakers, too, would need to transition from short-term, reactive policymaking to a more visionary, long-term perspective that fosters sustained and inclusive innovation. To this end, direction and pace in the change processes are as important as the current state-of-the-art.

Despite the arguments presented here, there remains terrain to be explored. We encourage future research to undertake detailed longitudinal case studies across various sectors to further enrich the concept of "Industrial Evolution." Additionally, investigating the pace of socio-technological evolution across different contexts and its interaction with broader societal trends remains a largely uncharted but potentially rewarding area of study.

To conclude, this chapter is a call for a rethinking of our understanding of technological change, bringing in more of the longer lines and the parallel societal change. By advancing the concept of "Industrial Evolution," we aim to provoke thought, incite debate, and inspire a more rigorous, comprehensive, and realistic appreciation of the dynamic interplay between society and technology. This is a daring stance, but it is in these audacious challenges to the status quo that we believe lies the key to understanding our ever-evolving social, technical, and economic world. Because, after all, it is worth noting that the term *evolution* stems from the Latin word *evolvere*, which means "to roll forward." In contrast, *revolution* implies a "rolling back." It is an inherent trait of history and time that they never roll back, but rather, continuously move forward.

References

Gianpaolo Abatecola, Dermot Breslin, and Johan Kask. Do organizations re- ally co-evolve? problematizing co-evolutionary change in management and or- ganization studies. *Technological Forecasting and Social Change*, 155:119964, 2020. https://doi.org/10.1016/j.techfore.2020.119964.

W. Brian Arthur. *The Nature of Technology: What it is and how it evolves*. Penguin Books, 2009.

Thomas Southcliffe Ashton. *The Industrial Revolution, 1760–1830*. Oxford Univer- sity Press, 1948.

Frank Biocca and Mark R. Levy, editors. *Communication in the Age of Virtual Reality*. Routledge, 1995.

Dermot Breslin, Johan Kask, Michael Schlaile, and Gianpaolo Abatecola. Devel- oping a coevolutionary account of innovation ecosystems. *Industrial Marketing Management*, 98:59–68, 2021.

Pew Research Center. Most americans say there is too much economic inequality in the us but fewer than half call it a top priority (issue january), 2020. URL https://www.pewresearch.org/social-trends/2020/01/ 09/trends-in-income-and-wealth-inequality/.

A. Cetrulo and A. Nuvolari. Industry 4.0: revolution or hype? reassessing recent technological trends and their impact on labour. *Journal of Industrial and Business Economics*, 46(3):391–402, 2019. https://doi.org/10.1007/s40812-019-00132-y. URL https://doi.org/10.1007/s40812-019-00132-y.

Jan De Vries. The industrial revolution and the industrious revolution. *The Journal of Economic History*, 54(2):249–270, 1994.

Jared Diamond. *Guns, Germs, and Steel: The Fates of Human Societies*. W. W. Norton & Norton Company, 1997.

Rainer Drath and Alexander Horch. Industrie 4.0: Hit or hype? *IEEE Industrial Electronics Magazine*, 8(2):56–58, 2014. https://doi.org/10.1109/MIE.2014.2312079. URL https://doi.org/10.1109/MIE.2014.2312079.

Koen Frenken and Loet Leydesdorff. Scaling trajectories in civil aircraft (1913- 1997). *Research Policy*, 29(3):331–348, 2000. https://doi.org/10.1016/S0048-7333(99)00037-2. URL https://doi.org/10.1016/S0048-7333(99)00037-2.

Brian Handwerk. An evolutionary timeline of homo sapiens, 2021. URL https://www.smithsonianmag.com/science-nature/ essential-timeline-understanding-evolution-homo-sapiens-180976807/.

Demis Hassabis, Dharshan Kumaran, Christopher Summerfield, and Matthew Botvinick. Neuroscience-inspired artificial intelligence. *Neuron*, 95(2):245–258, 2017. https://doi.org/10.1016/j.neuron.2017.06.011

Johan Kask. Evolving market channels in the swedish music industry: A domi- nant design approach. In *Studies in Industrial Renewal: Coping with Changing Contexts*, pages 95–116. Örebro University, January 2011.

Johan Kask. *On Business Relationships as Darwinian Systems*. PhD thesis, Örebro University, 2013.

Johan Kask and Christina Öberg. Why "majors" surge in the post-disruptive record- ing industry. *European Journal of Marketing*, 53(3):442–462, 2019. 10.1108/ EJM-11-2017-0841. URL https://doi.org/10.1108/EJM-11-2017-0841.

Johan Kask, Per Carlborg, Nina Hasche, Vladislav Klézl, and Gabriel Linton. Futures beyond myopia: Pathways for the swedish electric power market 2030, 2022. Unpublished work.

Noah Kittner, Felix Lill, and Daniel M. Kammen. Energy storage deployment and innovation for the clean energy transition. *Nature Energy*, 2(9):1–6, 2017. https://doi.org/10.1038/nenergy.2017.125. URL https://doi.org/10.1038/nenergy. 2017.125.

T. Kuhn. The structure of scientific revolutions. Chicago, IL: University of Chicago Press, 1970.

Heiner Lasi, Peter Fettke, Hans-Georg Kemper, Thomas Feld, and Michael Hoff- mann. Industry 4.0. *Business and Information Systems Engineering*, 6(4):239– 242, 2014. https://doi.org/10.1007/s12599-014-0334-4. URL https://doi.org/10.1007/s12599-014-0334-4.

Barry M. Leiner, Robert E. Kahn, Jon Postel, Vinton G. Cerf, Leonard Kleinrock, Lawrence G. Roberts, David D. Clark, Daniel C. Lynch, and

Stephen Wolff. A brief story of the internet. *ACM SIGCOMM Computer Communication Review*, 39(5):22–31, 2009. URL http://www.acm.org.

Daniel Lincot. The new paradigm of photovoltaics: From powering satellites to powering humanity. *Comptes Rendus Physique*, 18(7-8):381–390, 2017.

S. J. Lycett and C. J. Norton. A demographic model for palaeolithic technological evolution: The case of east asia and the movius line. *Quaternary International*, 211(1–2):55–65, 2010. https://doi.org/10.1016/j.quaint.2008.12.001.

W. H. Macey and B. Schneider. The meaning of employee engagement. *Industrial and Organizational Psychology*, 1(1):3–30, 2008. https://doi.org/10.1111/j.1754-9434.2007. 0002.x.

S. Makridakis. The forthcoming artificial intelligence (ai) revolution: Its impact on society and firms. *Futures*, 90:46–60, 2017. https://doi.org/10.1016/j.futures.2017.03.006.

S. Mcbrearty and A. S. Brooks. The revolution that wasn't: A new interpretation of the origin of modern human behavior. *Journal of Human Evolution*, 39(5): 453–563, 2000. https://doi.org/10.1006/jhev.2000.0435.

P. McCorduck. *Machines Who Think: A Personal Inquiry into the History and Prospects of Artificial Intelligence*. A K Peters/CRC Press, 2004.

K. Mizushima, P. C. Jones, P. J. Wiseman, and J. B. Goodenough. Li_x coo_2 (0<x<-1): A new cathode material for batteries of high energy density. *Materials Research Bulletin*, 15(6):783–789, 1980. https://doi.org/10.1143/jjap.42.6131.

J. Mokyr. *The Second Industrial Revolution, 1870-1914*. Northwestern University, 1998. https://doi.org/10.1016/j.wavemoti.2014.01.006.

G. Mom. *The electric vehicle: Technology and expectations in the automobile age*. Johns Hopkins University Press, 2004.

J. P. Murmann and K. Frenken. Toward a systematic framework for research on dominant designs, technological innovations, and industrial change. *Research Policy*, 35(7):925–952, 2006. https://doi.org/10.1016/j.respol.2006.04.011.

T. Nickles. Scientific revolutions. In Sarkar S. and Pfeifer J. editors. *The Philosophy of Science: An Encyclopedia*, pages 754–764. New York: Routledge, 2006.

G. Rist. Development as a buzzword. *Development in Practice*, 17(4-5):485–491, 2007. https://doi.org/10.1080/09614520701469328.

D. M. Rousseau, J. Manning, and D. Denyer. Evidence in management and organiza- tional science: Assembling the field's full weight of scientific knowledge through synthesis. *Annals of the Academy of Management*, 2:475–515, 2008.

K. Schwab. The fourth industrial revolution: What it means and how to respond, December 2015. URL https://www.foreignaffairs.com/articles/2015–12–12/fourth-industrial-revolution. Foreign Affairs.

D. Silver, A. Huang, C. J. Maddison, A. Guez, L. Sifre, G. Van Den Driessche, J. Schrittwieser, I. Antonoglou, V. Panneershelvam, M. Lanctot, S. Diele- man, D. Grewe, J. Nham, N. Kalchbrenner, I. Sutskever, T. Lillicrap, M. Leach, K. Kavukcuoglu, T. Graepel, and D. Hassabis. Mastering the game of go with deep neural networks and tree search. *Nature*, 529(7587):484–489, 2016. https://doi.org/10.1038/nature16961.

A. M. Turing. Computing machinery and intelligence. *Mind*, 59(236):433–460, 1950. URL http://mind.oxfordjournals.org/.

P. Wikström. *The music industry: Music in the cloud*. John Wiley & Sons, 2009.

B. Wood. Palaeoanthropology: Facing up to complexity. *Nature*, 488(7410):162– 163, 2012. https://doi.org/10.1038/488162a.

X. Xu, Y. Lu, B. Vogel-Heuser, and L. Wang. Industry 4.0 and industry 5.0—in- ception, conception and perception. *Journal of Manufacturing Systems*, 61 (October):530–535, 2021. https://doi.org/10.1016/j.jmsy.2021.10.006. URL https://doi.org/10.1016/j.jmsy.2021.10.006.

3

Industrial Transformation via AI and Autonomous Systems: Evidence from a State-of-the-Art Survey

Luke Treves, Paavo Ritala, and Päivi Aaltonen

3.1 Introduction

The development of Artificial Intelligence (AI) and autonomous systems is transforming operations across industries (Fountaine et al. 2019; Thomson et al. 2021). While AI and its applications are not new [e.g. (Xu et al. 2021)], they have received increasing attention in recent years due to the rapid advancement of AI technologies and the increasing availability of data (Ransbotham et al. 2018). AI now performs tasks once imagined impossible for machines, such as driving cars (Banerjee 2020), diagnosing diseases (Lebovitz et al. 2022), and with the advent of Generative AI, conducting creative and knowledge-intensive tasks such as writing and editing creative content (Ritala et al. 2023). This capability has led to a surge of interest in AI applications, such as autonomous systems and digital twins, from businesses, governments, and the public

L. Treves (✉) · P. Ritala · P. Aaltonen
Business School, LUT University, Yliopistonkatu, 53850 Lappeenranta, Finland
e-mail: luke.treves@lut.fi

P. Aaltonen and E. Kurvinen (eds.), *Contemporary Issues in Industry 5.0*, Technology, Work and Globalization, https://doi.org/10.1007/978-3-031-74779-3_3

(Enholm et al. 2022). Another important factor driving the growth of AI is the increasing availability of data. Organizations use this data to train AI and autonomous systems, and the adage goes that the more data they train with, the better they perform. The development of technologies like the Internet and the Internet of things (IoT) in the last decade (Xu et al. 2021) has led to an explosion in the amount of data available, enabling AI to be trained on massive datasets, resulting in significant performance improvements (Acciarini et al. 2023), increasing the need to rethink business strategies (Ruokonen and Ritala 2023) and organizational practices (Berente et al. 2021; Brock and von Wangenheim 2019). Given the ubiquity of digital technologies and the breadth of data available in different industries (Dabrowska et al. 2022), organizations are increasingly exploring ways to deploy and scale AI and other predictive and autonomous systems to achieve business benefits such as increased revenue, cost savings, and improved efficiency (Enholm et al. 2022; Davenport and Mittal 2023; Bouschery et al. 2023). However, despite the growing interest in AI, organizations are struggling to realize and transform the value of AI and solutions in practice (Fountaine et al. 2019; Raisch and Krakowski 2021). Even if organizations invest time, effort, and resources in AI adoption, the expected benefits may not be realized (Makarius et al. 2020). Common challenges include a lack of time and money, cultural challenges, resistance to change, a lack of necessary knowledge and skills, and ethical, security, and privacy concerns (Enholm et al. 2022; Acciarini et al. 2023; Glikson and Wooley 2020). Against this backdrop, this chapter addresses the research question:

> What is the current state of the art of AI and semi-autonomous/autonomous systems used by industry, and what has been its impact?

To address our research question, we present findings from a Summer 2023 survey of 207 Finnish and international companies headquartered in Finland across various industries. The chapter comprises eight main sections. After the introduction, Sect. 3.2 defines AI and autonomous systems in the context of our study. Sections 3.3–3.7 form the main body of the chapter. We describe the results of our survey, which focus on (1) how organizations are currently and plan to use AI and semi-autonomous/autonomous systems, (2) strategy and management, particularly the future objectives and management commitment to applying these technologies within organizations, (3) the impact of AI and semi-autonomous/autonomous capabilities on organizations. (4) the benefits and drawbacks of access to data, and (5) the challenges organizations encounter when implementing and scaling AI and semi-autonomous/autonomous systems in their organizations. The final section (8) provides concluding remarks and an outlook.

3.2 Theoretical Background: AI and Scaling Within Organizations

3.2.1 Conceptual Foundations of AI

AI has transformed the business world in recent years, with its applications streamlining productivity and efficiency across all industries. Initial research on AI in business began in the late 1950s with the early development of artificial neural networks. However, it was not until the early twenty-first century that AI truly took off in the business world, with the introduction of more sophisticated algorithms such as deep learning, reinforcement learning (Haenlein and Kaplan 2019), and generative AI, involving generative pre-trained transformers and related large language models (Dwivedi et al.2023; Ritala et al. 2023). Building on existing definitions (Mikalef and Gupta 2021; Enholm et al. 2022), AI is a field of technology that combines computer science and large datasets to solve problems and make predictions. It also includes the subfields of machine learning and deep learning, that may be used in a variety of industrial applications, such as semi-autonomous/autonomous systems or digital twins [further see e.g. (Holopainen et al. 2022)], and more recently, in a variety of Generative AI applications. In the context of this chapter, AI describes the ability of a system to identify, interpret, make inferences, and learn from data to achieve predetermined organizational and societal goals (Haenlein and Kaplan 2019). In line with this definition, an AI application is any system that can generate insights from data and act based on these to reach a set of objectives. This capability is also referred to as 'cognitive ability' whereby AI resembles the human brain's ability to think and act intelligently (Bytniewski et al. 2020) while using different technological means to do so.

Further, we focus on the most recent technologies under the AI umbrella, excluding technologies present in Industry 4.0 applications, such as IoT and cloud computing, and aim to follow more closely the definition of Industry 4.0 and 5.0 (Xu et al. 2021). Industry 4.0 and 5.0 are concepts not that far from classical Schumpeterian waves—also sometimes called the 4th or 5th Industrial Revolution—which embody transformative stages in economic development marked by innovation and technological progress that pave the way for more agile, efficient, and personalized production systems. Specifically, Industry 4.0 refers to a German-led strategic initiative in 2010, describing the highly advanced technologies in use—IoT is one of them. Industry 5.0, a term coined by the European Commission in 2020, is a movement beyond Industry 4.0 that focuses on human-centered design, sustainability, and augmentation of human intelligence with digitalization and AI-driven technologies to increase production efficiency and flexibility (Xu et al. 2021).

3.2.2 Artificial Intelligence and Industrial Change

Today, AI applications are ubiquitous in the workplace and are rapidly transforming how organizations operate. Fueled by access to large amounts of data and advances in computational power (Enholm et al. 2022), AI is allowing organizations to automate, augment, optimize, and streamline, their business and operational processes across the entire value chain, including HR, manufacturing, marketing, sales, quality control, IT, and finances. As such, AI promises to deliver significant advantages in terms of decision-making and creating and capturing added value (Chui et al. 2018; Mikalef and Gupta 2021). Organizations are integrating AI into their business activities in a variety of ways (Haenlein and Kaplan 2019; Iansiti and Lakhani 2020). For example, AI can automate repetitive and time-consuming tasks, enabling employees to focus on more strategic and creative work (Raisch and Krakowski

2021), *improve decision making* by analyzing large amounts of data and by identifying patterns and trends that would be difficult or impossible for humans to see (Waardenburg and Huysman 2022), and finally, AI potentially *enables the creation of previously unthinkable products and services*—such as self-driving cars, personalized healthcare plans, and intelligent virtual assistants and 'copilots,' among other things (Enholm et al. 2022; Ritala et al. 2023).

Additionally, AI is creating new opportunities for organizations to create value for their customers and stakeholders (Haenlein and Kaplan 2019; Przegalińska et al. 2019). *Semi-autonomous* and *autonomous systems* (Thomson et al. 2021) are at the forefront of this transformation by embedding AI's predictions and affordances into broader solutions and technological frameworks. AI-powered semi-autonomous and autonomous systems can automate complex tasks and enable better decision-making. They have become an essential part of organizations of all sizes and industries helping them achieve their goals more effectively by improving efficiency and automating tasks that were once time-consuming and prone to errors (Chui et al. 2018; Mikalef and Gupta 2021). For instance, in the finance industry, AI-powered systems can automate risk assessment and fraud detection, and in the manufacturing industry, they are enabling organizations to optimize production lines, reduce waste, and improve quality control.

3.3 Methods

The findings presented in this chapter were gathered through a cross-industrial survey. When gathering primary data, this technique has several advantages, including the ability to obtain a high response rate, improve data quality, and reduce non-responses, as well as the ability to collect data on complex issues because interviewers can explain issues if interviewees have uncertainties (Newsted et al. 1998; Dillman et al. 2014). The telephone survey used a Likert questionnaire to gather data on five key themes: (1) AI usage, (2) strategy and management, (3) capabilities and technology, (4) data usage, and (5) challenges in AI integration. All constructs were measured by using a 7-point Likert scale, ranging from 1 (not at all) to 7 (to a great extent) and ranging from 1 (strongly disagree) to 7 (strongly agree). A 7-scale Likert questionnaire was chosen as it allowed us to gather nuanced responses on a range of phenomena, reduces central tendency bias, increases reliability and validity, and enhances data analysis (Dawes 2008). The questions were developed using peer-reviewed academic articles relevant to the research phenomenon and the five key topics.

The organizations surveyed represent twelve industrial sectors defined by the official NACE Rev. 2 classification system of economic activities in the European Union (Table 3.1), which presents a framework for collecting and presenting a large range of statistical data according to economic activity in the fields of economic statistics (e.g., production, employment, national accounts) and other statistical domains. Providing uniformity and comparability for assessing data across EU member states (Eurostat 2008). This framework is suitable for our research as it comprehensively covers a broad range of industrial sectors, facilitates comparative and trend analysis, and enables us to develop insights into the state-of-the-art impact of AI and semi-autonomous and autonomous systems on organizations.

3.3.1 Sampling and Data Collection

Our research encompassed a sample of approximately 2738 organizations within the industrial sectors outlined in Table 3.1. Per the European Union's definition, these enterprises have a workforce exceeding 50 employees (EUR-Lex 2023). The selection of medium and large organizations was strategic, given their substantial resources, varied applications, and significant market impact compared to smaller entities. Facilitating a deeper insight into the effects and evolving patterns of AI alongside semi-autonomous and autonomous systems.

Out of this sample, we surveyed 207 Finnish-owned and international organizations with headquarters in Finland during the summer of 2023. The survey was conducted via telephone and recorded electronically into a database. The response rate we received was 7.6%, which represents the diversity of our chosen industrial sectors and provides a comprehensive

Table 3.1 Descriptive details of survey

	n
Area of operations	
Administrative and support service activities	18
Professional, scientific and technical activities	28
Real estate	1
Information and communication services	15
Accommodation and food services	3
Transportation and storage services	8
Distributive trade sector	36
Construction	25
Water supply, waste and remediation activities	3
Electricity, gas, steam andair conditioning supply	5
Manufacturing	64
Mining and quarrying	1
Turnover	
EUR 20 million or more	121
EUR 10–19.999 million	46
EUR 1–9.999 million	37
EUR under 1 million	3
Employees	
10,000+	4
500–999	8
250–499	28
249–50	167

insight into the dynamic landscape of AI adoption. Our cross-sectional approach also ensured that the study's findings provide a comprehensive and generalizable overview of the current state of knowledge in this rapidly evolving field.

3.4 Findings

In the following sections, we provide a descriptive analysis to summarize and provide a clear description of the state-of-the-art situation in AI integration and use by industries from five perspectives:

- *AI usage* relates to the number of ongoing AI projects organizations have, the types of AI technologies they currently use and intend to use in the future, and in which operational areas.
- *Strategy and management* relate to current and future organizational and management commitment to use AI technologies in their organization. Specifically, this perspective looks at the extent of AI use in an organization's business and operational processes and the importance of investment and resource commitment when it comes to AI.
- *Capabilities and technology* relate to how AI technologies affect job roles, skills, and responsibilities within organizations and subsequent employee attitudes toward AI.
- *Data use* relates to an organization's collection, analysis, and use of vast and complex datasets to gain insights, enhance decision-making, and drive business strategies. It also relates to data sharing among internal and external partners and its drawbacks when used to train AI technologies.
- *Challenges* in AI integration relate to challenges organizations face when implementing and scaling AI technologies, including lack of time or money, cultural challenges, resistance to change, and security and privacy concerns.

Additionally, we categorize our findings in two distinct ways:

- For a Likert scale ranging from 1 (not at all) to 7 (to a great extent), we report and analyze responses from 2 (to a limited extent) to 7 (to a great extent). This indicates the level of engagement an organization has in a specific AI-related activity. One means that there is no engagement.
- For the Likert scale, ranging from 1 (strongly disagree) to 7 (strongly agree), responses falling between 5 and 7 indicate agreement (ranging from agree to strongly agree). A response of 4 denotes a neutral stance, while responses between 1 and 3 reflect various degrees of disagreement (from disagree to strongly disagree).
- We do not report non-responses.

In this study, we opted for a descriptive-analytical methodology to present our results as it allows us to provide a clear and more widely accessible account of the survey findings. This approach also allows us to simplify the initial understanding of the large dataset gathered through the survey and ensure the reliability of subsequent detailed statistical analyses by providing a clear overview of patterns, trends, and potential anomalies within the data.

3.4.1 AI Usage: How Industries Are Using These Technologies to Transform Their Businesses

The rapid evolution of AI is fundamentally altering business landscapes, compelling organizations across diverse industrial sectors to harness these technologies to achieve a multitude of objectives, ranging from automating repetitive tasks to effectively forecasting and satisfying customer demands. Our survey investigates the state of AI adoption in organizations and how it will evolve over the next three years by examining the number of AI projects organizations are working on and the types of AI technologies they use.

Despite emerging as a top technological priority of organizations in recent years (Mikalef and Gupta 2021), the survey found that 79 organizations have no ongoing AI projects, 122 have between one and ten ongoing projects, and only 5 organizations have more than ten (Fig. 3.1). The findings suggest that, while organizations recognize the strategic importance of AI they are still in the early stages of implementation. This situation may be due to factors, including a lack of expertise, resources, or data. However, it is also possible that organizations are taking a cautious approach to AI, launching a limited number of projects to assess their impact before scaling up. The findings are also consistent with those of a global survey of Chief Information Officers (CIOs) from leading companies and industry experts conducted by MIT Technology Review Insights (2023), which reports that while AI is viewed as strategically important, current ambitions are limited.

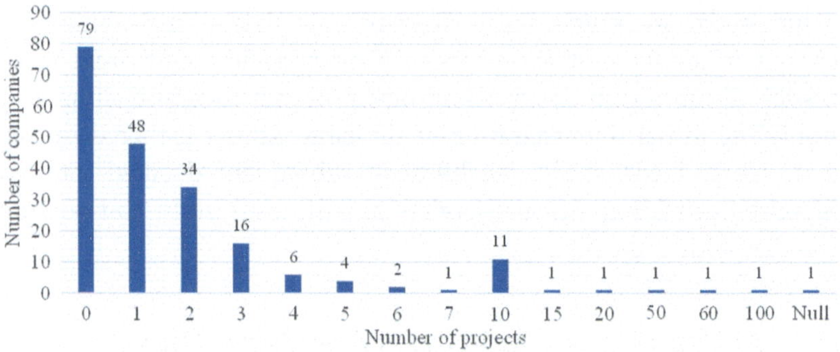

Fig. 3.1 Number of ongoing AI projects

3.4.2 Current and Future Applications of AI

When it comes to AI technologies, literature (Haenlein and Kaplan 2019; Enholm et al. 2022; Bouschery et al. 2023; Chowdhury et al. 2023) provides various classifications based on the types of intelligence and their corresponding applications. In this chapter, we examine AI technologies at three levels of abstraction:

- *Automated intelligence* (including machine learning, computer vision, sensor systems, speech synthesis systems, robotic process automation, and rules-based expert systems) which can perform automated and repetitive rule-based routines, freeing human workers to focus on more strategic and creative tasks.
- *Assisted intelligence* (including Natural language processing (NLP); Generative AI tools for natural language processing (such as ChatGPT); Generative AI tools for visual material (such as Dall-E or Midjourney) which can aid data-driven decision-making by analyzing and extracting meaningful insights from large datasets, and by creating new data, insights, and outputs based on users' prompts.
- *Autonomous intelligence* (semi-autonomous and fully autonomous systems, including self-driving vehicles and robots in warehouses) which can adapt to a working environment and function independently under certain conditions but requires human intervention in functions like design, development, governance, and management

of such systems. Moving to complete autonomy where systems can operate and adapt to dynamic environments and scenarios independently.

3.4.2.1 Automated Intelligence Technologies

The survey results indicate that the most used Automated Intelligence technologies (Fig. 3.2) are 'Robotic Process Automation (RPA) (68%)' and 'Sensor systems (62%).' These technologies are relatively mature and are being used in various industrial sectors to perform tasks that would be dangerous, repetitive, or difficult for humans. For example, in manufacturing, RPA robots are used to automate machine loading and unloading and to detect defects. The use of other AI technologies is relatively low. For example, 71% of respondents are not using 'speech synthesis systems.' These findings may be due to factors including the newness of technology, lack of skills and knowledge, and industry fit.

Looking to the future, the survey results show a different picture with most respondents indicating that their organizations intend to use automated technologies to an extent. Notable the intention to use 'machine

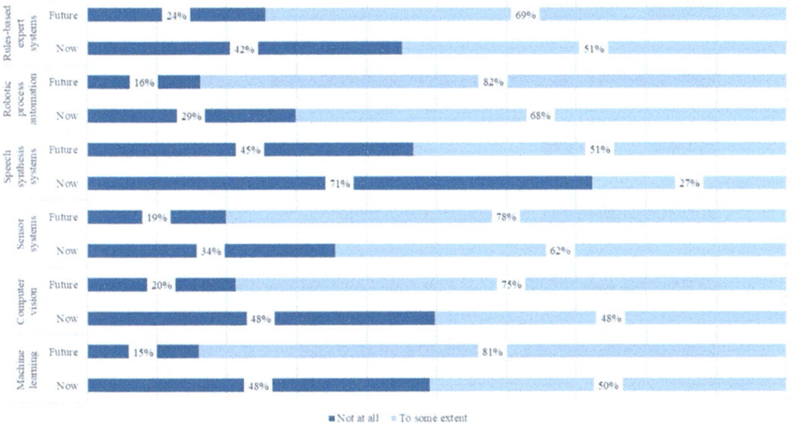

Fig. 3.2 Current and future intention to use automated intelligence technologies (%)

learning' (from 50% organizations currently using this technology to 81%) and 'computer vision' (from 48% of organizations currently using this technology to 75%).

3.4.2.2 Assisted Intelligence Technologies

The survey results show that current use of Assisted Intelligence technologies is low (Fig. 3.3), with over half of respondents reporting that they are not using any form of these technologies: Natural Language Processing (NLP) 56%, Generative AI tools for NLP 52%, and Generative AI tools for visual material 61%. The low use of these technologies may be due to factors, including awareness of the technologies or their potential applications. Accessibility barriers due to the current high costs associated with them. Complexity of their use, or their trustworthiness and reliability to produce consistent and accurate results. However, respondents are forecasted to rapidly increase the use of these technologies in the coming years, with 64% indicating their intention to utilize NLP to some extent and 72% expressing their intention to use Generative AI tools for both NLP and visual material.

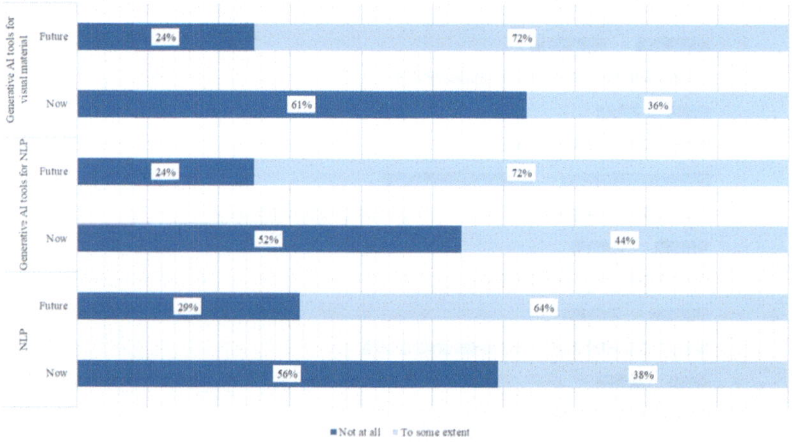

Fig. 3.3 Current and future intention to use automated intelligence technologies (%)

3.4.2.3 Autonomous Intelligence Technologies

The survey results show that when it comes to Automated Intelligence technologies (Fig. 3.4), 60% of respondents currently use a form of semi-autonomous system in their business compared to 28% using autonomous systems. These findings may be due to factors, including semi-autonomous systems being more available than fully autonomous systems, allowing users to become more familiar and comfortable with applying semi-autonomous systems in their operations. Organizations may also be more willing to use semi-autonomous systems now as they want to maintain an element of human oversight or intervention in their operational control and do not see fully autonomous systems as being mature, dependable, or safe enough in their current stage of development to contribute effectively to their business or operational processes.

However, the results suggest that organizations are becoming increasingly interested in using a form of autonomous intelligence technology in the future. The intention to use fully autonomous systems more than doubles from its current use, with 59% of respondents indicating their intention to use these systems to an extent in the next three years. At the

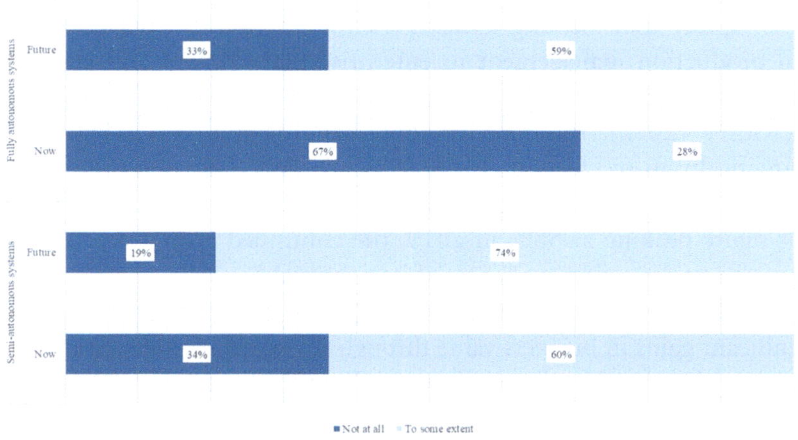

Fig. 3.4 Current and future intention to use autonomous intelligence technologies (%)

same time, 74% of respondents intend to use semi-autonomous systems in the next three years.

3.4.2.4 Outlook for the Future

While the current use of AI technologies is relatively low within most organizations, our survey results suggest that this picture is about to change. Several factors are driving this rapid increase. First, AI technologies are becoming more accessible and affordable. For example, cloud computing allows organizations of all sizes to access powerful AI tools, and the cost of training and deploying AI models has fallen significantly in recent years. Second, the benefits of AI technologies are becoming more apparent. AI allows organizations to solve real-world problems in industries ranging from manufacturing to finance, such as optimizing production lines and making more accurate financial predictions. These results suggest that as AI technologies mature and costs decrease, their use will become more common in the workplace.

3.4.3 Business Areas AI Is Being Used in

AI is rapidly transforming industries across the globe, from marketing and production management to enterprise management and customer service (Alsheibani et al. 2018; Jelonek et al. 2019). According to McKinsey (2022), business AI adoption and application have risen dramatically in recent years, with 20% of respondents reporting adoption in at least one business area in 2017, rising to 50% today. Despite this figure peaking at 58% in 2019, the continued growth in AI adoption reflects a growing awareness of its potential benefits. AI applications can be deployed across the entire value chain of an organization to realize significant gains in business value through increased revenue, cost reduction, and increased business efficiency (Wamba-Taguimdje et al. 2020). Reflecting these possibilities, organizations are adopting and applying AI throughout their operations, including business planning and decision-making, customer relationship management, finance and budgeting, human resources, logistics and supply management, manufacturing and production, and product and service design (Enholm et al. 2022; Acciarini et al. 2023). Our survey asked respondents to what extent their organizations use AI in these business areas and their plan to do so in the next three years (Fig. 3.5).

The results show that currently AI is being used to an extent across all the business areas we examined. The most prominent application area is customer relationship management (CRM), where 82% of respondents indicate they are using AI technologies to some extent. Organizations are also using AI technologies to a high extent in finance and budgeting, where 57% of respondents indicate they are using AI technologies. Additionally, the survey found that in other business areas, approximately half of the respondents report using AI to some extent as follows: manufacturing and production 50%, product service and design 49%, business planning and decision-making 48%, in logistics and supply chain 45%, and human resources (HR) 41%.

However, looking to the future respondents indicate that they believe that AI will be in use increasingly across all business sectors. Looking at logistics and SCM, business planning and decision-making, product service and design, and HR, we can see the intention to use increases to 71%, 74%, 76%, and 64%, respectively.

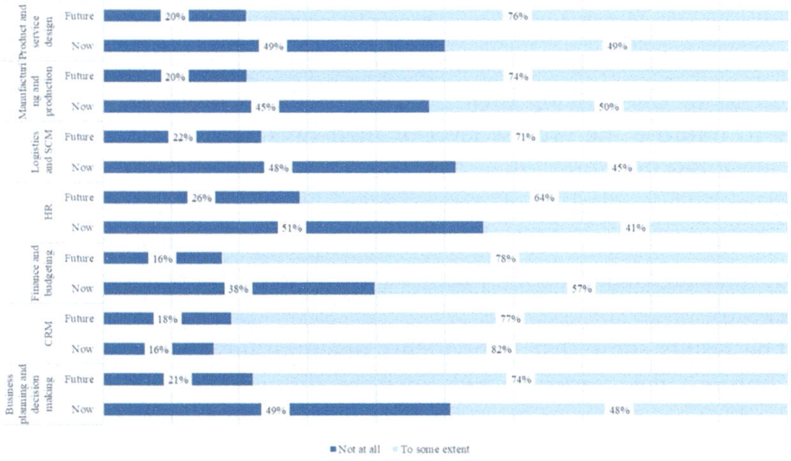

Fig. 3.5 Business area AI is being used in and plans to use in the next 3 years

3.5 Strategy and Management: Revolutionized by AI in Business

Organizations are interested in how AI can lead to improved operational and competitive performance and seek to find unique approaches to make themselves distinctive from their competitors with data, algorithms, and execution based on that (Ruokonen and Ritala 2023). To understand how AI is affecting organizational approaches to strategy and management, we study the effects of AI at both the process (first-order) and organizational (second-order) levels proposed by Enholm et al. (2022). The first-order effects of AI use are related to changes it causes at the 'process level,' including process efficiency, insight generation, organizational agility, and business process transformation. Second-order effects are related to AI use effects at the 'organizational level,' including operational performance, financial or accounting performance, market-based performance, and sustainability performance (Enholm et al. 2022). These process and organizational level effects are described in more detail in the following section of this chapter.

3.5.1 Process (First-Order) Effects

While the survey results suggest that AI is still in the early stages of use within organizations, we found that it is already impacting how they think about and develop their business strategies and associated activities to improve the process level of their organization. AI is enabling organizations to improve their efficiency by automating tasks, improving decision-making, and developing new products and services. To understand the extent to which AI is impacting organizational strategy we performed an extensive survey across a diverse range of business processes (Fig. 3.6).

The results show that respondents organizations are using AI most 'to improve data security' and 'increase throughput (the amount of a product or service that a company can produce and deliver to a client within a specified period (Hayes 2023), with 72% and 80% of respondents respectively indicating their organizations are using AI in

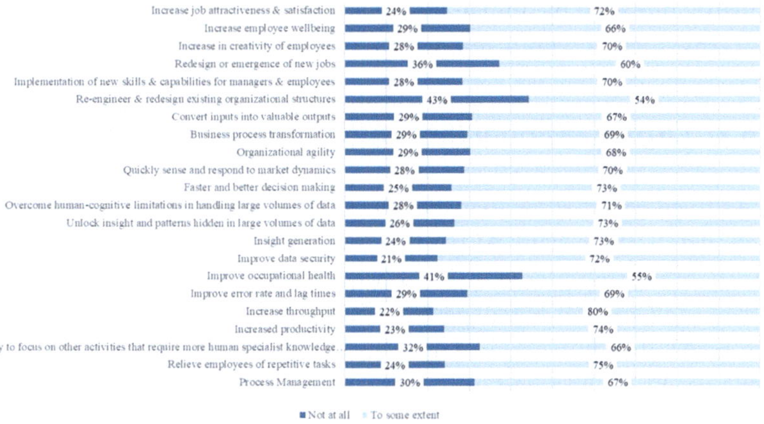

Fig. 3.6 AI's current effect on organizations' business processes

these areas to some extent. The reasons that organizations are using AI in these areas may be due to its benefits being more immediate and tangible than in other areas. For example, organizations are using AI to create more sophisticated security systems capable of detecting and responding to threats more quickly and effectively. AI is also being used to automate time-consuming or error-prone tasks, increasing productivity, responding to market and operational changes more quickly and accurately (Eriksson et al. 2020), and freeing human operators to perform more rewarding activities (Enholm et al. 2022).

At the other end of the spectrum, AI is least used in re-engineering and redesigning existing organizational structures (54%) and improving occupational health (55%). One explanation is that these are more difficult and complex areas to apply AI. For example, re-engineering organizational structures necessitates a thorough and often human understanding of how the organization operates and how different organization sections interact to instigate and implement changes, which AI is currently unable to do. Similarly, improving occupational health and safety is a complex issue involving factors including employee physical and mental health, workplace design, and work organization, which require nuanced understanding and human judgments. Although AI is powerful, it may lack the contextual understanding and empathy provided by human interactions. There are also legal and ethical concerns, such as who is responsible if AI makes a mistake.

3.5.2 Organizational (Second-Order) Effects

The survey results show that the impact of AI varies at the organizational level (Fig. 3.7). To date, AI has had the greatest impact in enhancing the quality of existing products and services (61%), operational performance (60%), and market-based performance (59%). These results are likely due to AI already being widely used in these fields. For example, AI is being used to collect and utilize data on the use of products and services new offerings, improve the quality of existing products and services, more effectively target customers, and cut costs.

Although AI has demonstrated a positive effect on organizational processes, the findings from the survey indicate areas where enhancements are needed. For instance, only 41% of respondents indicated a favorable impact of AI on their capacity for precise customer segmentation. Similarly, only 48% of participants reported a positive influence of AI on their efforts to enhance targeted and personalized marketing and the introduction of new products and services. An explanation for why AI has had less impact on these areas is that they are more complex and nuanced than others, making AI automation more difficult. For example, customer segmentation and marketing necessitate a thorough

Fig. 3.7 AI's current effect on organizations' business processes

understanding of customer's wants and needs, and the ability to create and deliver personalized messages and experiences. These are still tasks AI is unable to perform well.

3.6 Capabilities and Technologies: Rethinking Industry Approaches Through AI

AI capabilities are critical for organizations across all industrial sectors seeking to thrive and remain competitive in the twenty-first century (Schmidt et al. 2020). Organizational capabilities are an organization's collective skills, abilities, and expertise it employs to adapt to changes in its business environment and identify, create, and capture value for itself, its stakeholders, and its customers. Furthermore, they are the result of investments in human resource staffing, training, compensation, communication, and other areas (Smallwood and Ulrich 2004). In the context of AI, the core capabilities (referred to 'AI capabilities' from this point) are an organization's ability to select and leverage hard-to-imitate AI-specific resources, such as data, methods, processes, and people, to unlock new possibilities for automation, decision-making, collaboration, develop new products and service, and improve existing ones, and more (Davenport and Ronanki 2018; Mikalef and Gupta 2021; Karttunen et al. 2023; Chowdhury et al. 2023). This definition underscores the importance of looking at AI through the lens of organizational capabilities rather than technologies on their own (Davenport and Ronanki 2018). In other words, the capability lens focuses on what the technology allows the organization to do, rather than what the technology is as such.

Our study seeks to understand to what extent AI capabilities are impacting organizations, particularly their employees. We adopt this perspective as AI is predicted to have a significant impact on employees from eliminating jobs to creating new and different ones based on new ways of working (Davenport and Ronanki 2018; Mikalef and Gupta 2021; Chowdhury et al. 2023). Specifically, the survey aimed to understand the extent to which:

(i) AI capabilities are changing job roles and responsibilities.
(ii) AI capabilities are freeing workers up from repetitive, physical, manual, and dull tasks to creative ones.
(iii) Employees' perceptions and attitudes are relevant factors in AI acceptance and use.
(iv) AI capabilities have/are changing job roles and necessary skills.
(v) AI capabilities require ongoing reskilling and upskilling of employees.
(vi) Trust in AI capabilities is higher among high-skilled employees than low-skilled employees.
(vii) Overpromising AI capabilities have led to mistrust and dissatisfaction among employees.
(viii) Employees and AI can coexist, resulting in a more technologically evolving workforce.

Figure 3.8 shows the percentage of survey respondents who agree or strongly agree (on a scale of 5–7) that AI capabilities affect their organizations in different areas.

The results show that only 27% of respondents agree that AI capabilities are significantly changing job roles and responsibilities. There is a similar picture when it comes to the impact of AI capabilities

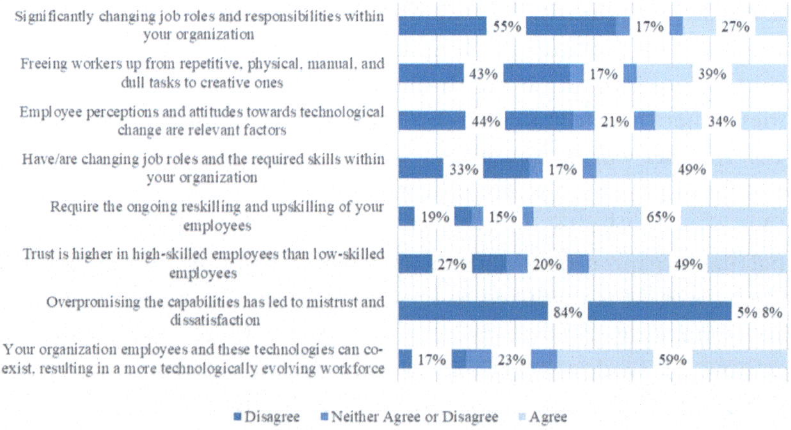

Fig. 3.8 Are AI capabilities impacting organizations employees?

on freeing workers from repetitive, physical, manual, and dull tasks to perform more creative ones and the relevance of employee perceptions and attitudes toward technological change and the use of AI. Respectively, only 39% and 34% of respondents agree that these factors impact their assessment of these technologies' integration and scaling in their organizations.

One explanation for these findings is that the current iteration of AI is introducing relatively new technologies into the workplace, and their impact is not yet fully felt. Another possibility is that employees are skeptical that these technologies will affect their jobs. Skepticism may be due to a lack of evidence that AI capabilities will change their jobs or because they believe their tasks are too complex or unsuitable for automation. The results also show that respondents feel that the perceptions and attitudes of employees toward AI capabilities are not relevant factors that influence the successful integration and scaling of these technologies within their organizations. This lack of awareness of the importance of the employee's role may be due to a focus on the technological aspects of change at the expense of including human elements.

Despite these findings, the situation is different when examining the impact of AI capabilities on job roles and employees' skill requirements. The survey results show that 49% of respondents agree that AI capabilities have or are changing job roles and the required skills within their organization. While 65% agree that AI capabilities require ongoing reskilling and upskilling of employees. These results can be attributed to AIs to automate tasks previously performed by humans. At the same time, these technologies will create new opportunities for workers to focus on more complex and strategic tasks. The findings also suggest that organizations should invest in reskilling and upskilling their employees to adapt to a changing workplace.

Employee trust and dissatisfaction with AI capabilities also affect the successful integration of these technologies within organizations. Previous research suggests that highly skilled workers are more likely to trust AI because they understand how these technologies work and how to use them safely and effectively (Enholm et al. 2022). Additionally, high-skilled employees may be more likely to work in roles that complement these technologies rather than ones that are likely to be replaced by them. The results show no clear consensus on whether high-skilled employees trust technology more than low-skilled employees. Suggesting that there is still uncertainty and a need to understand the relationship between employee skill level and trust in AI capabilities.

Finally, the results show respondents do not think that overpromising the AI capabilities has led to mistrust or dissatisfaction within their organizations with only 8% of respondents agreeing that this is an issue. This finding is complemented by 59% of respondents agreeing that employees and AI can coexist to create a technologically evolving workforce. In other words, most respondents are aware of the limitations of AI capabilities but are also optimistic about the potential for these technologies to coexist with human workers in a way that benefits both. Together, the responses suggest a growing understanding of the need for a balanced approach to integrating and scaling AI in organizations as they strive to achieve their goals.

3.6.1 Data Use: The Fuel Behind AI

Data is the fuel that powers AI and enables it to learn and make accurate predictions. The higher the quality and variety of data an AI model is trained on, the better it will be at learning the patterns and relationships in the data and making quick and accurate predictions (Mikalef and Gupta 2021; Acciarini et al. 2023). The amount of data available has reached unprecedented proportions, and businesses and governments are increasingly turning to it to gain new insights and make better decisions (Acciarini et al. 2023). Underling the significance of data, the Economist stated in 2017 that 'The world's most valuable resource is no longer oil, but data' (Economist 2017), with the data market being forecast to grow to $103 billion by 2027 (Statista 2011).

To better understand how the availability and use of data affect the development and integration of AI in organizations, we sought to understand the extent to which they currently collect and use data to train their AI technologies, and the extent to which they share and collaborate with their external partners in this process (Fig. 3.9).

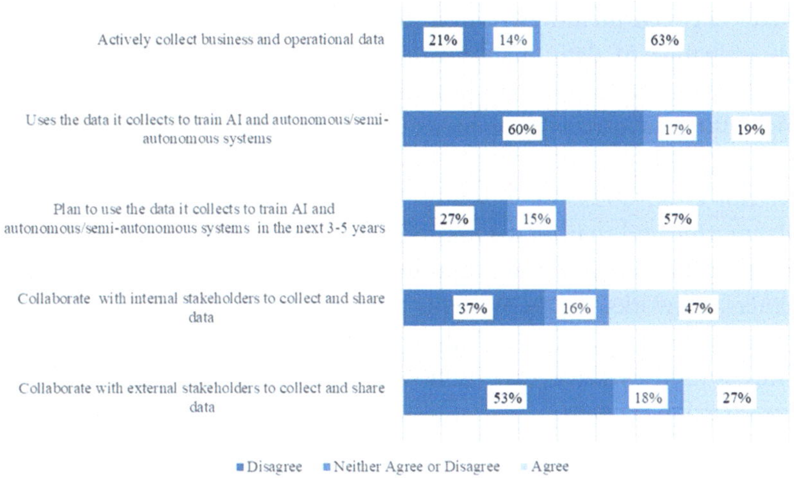

Fig. 3.9 Is the availability and use of data affects the development and integration of AI in organizations

The results showed that 63% of respondents strongly agreed or agreed that their organizations collect business and operational data. However, only 19% of respondents strongly agreed or agreed that their organizations currently use business and operational data to train their AI.

Nonetheless, the use of business and operational data to train AI is expected to grow over the next 3–5 years, with 57% of respondents strongly agreeing or agreeing that their organizations plan to use data they collect to train AI systems. These findings are consistent with other research on the adoption of AI by organizations. For example, McKinsey & Company the State of AI in 2020 report (McKinsey 2020), only 16% of organizations use the data they collect to scale AI beyond pilot projects. Even though organizations that successfully implement AI reap significant benefits such as increased productivity, improved customer service, and new product and service innovation.

Collaboration and data sharing are essential for organizations to succeed in the AI economy, as they enable the development of better AI capabilities and lead to competitive advantage by establishing internal and external digital (supply chain) platforms that facilitate the exchange of data between members related to operational and business activities. This exchange of data enables organizations to gain insights that are more accurate and actionable than those derived from isolated data sets, which allow them to make better decisions, improve their utilization of resources, and enhance product and service offerings (Li et al. 2020; Acciarini et al. 2023). The survey results show that when it comes to collaborating and sharing data only 27% of respondents strongly agree or agree that their organizations currently collaborate with external business partners, networks, and ecosystems to collect mutually beneficial data to be used to train AI. As for collaborating and sharing data internally, the picture is more positive, with 47% strongly agreeing or agreeing with the same question.

Our survey also sought to understand the main drawbacks organizations encounter when it comes to data in terms of data quality and relevance issues, unauthorized access and misuse, lack of standardized practices, and information overload. These drawbacks can be significant as they can compromise the accuracy and effectiveness of these technologies. Additionally, the lack of universally accepted industry norms hinders seamless integration and interoperability, creating inefficiencies and complexity. The sheer volume of data also poses a problem of information overload, reducing the ability to extract meaningful insights. Respondents' perceptions of these drawbacks are crucial in understanding the challenges of the use of data in AI systems (Mikalef and Gupta 2021; Enholm et al. 2022; Acciarini et al. 2023).

The survey explored to what extent these are drawbacks when using data to train AI (see Fig. 3.10).

According to the results, there are certain limitations to using data for training AI. However, the degree to which these limitations are perceived as drawbacks varies among respondents. Most respondents consider the unavailability of quality (93%) and relevant (88%) data as the biggest drawbacks to using data for training AI. It is important to note that AI depends heavily on precise and relevant data to produce accurate predictions and recommendations and automate processes. Low-quality and irrelevant data can lead to inadequate performance, biased decisions, or harmful actions.

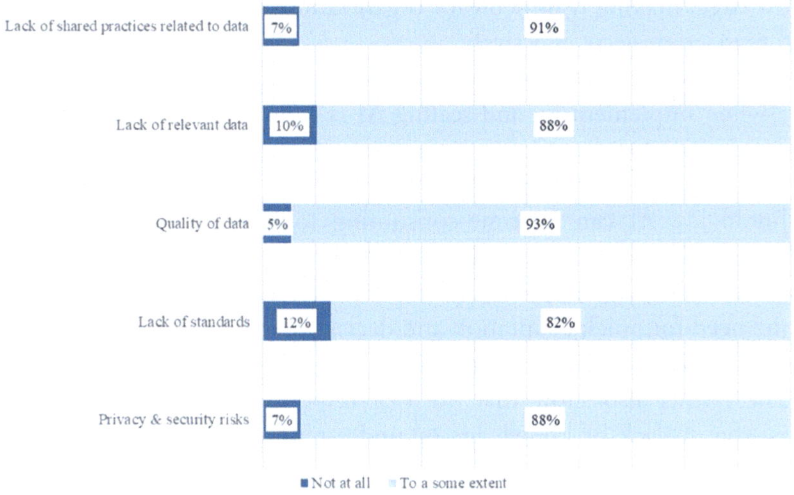

Fig. 3.10 Drawbacks to using data to train AI

91% of respondents also think that a lack of shared practices related to the collection, storage, and use of data is a disadvantage. The absence of standards can make it difficult for organizations to share data or concerns about privacy and security. The survey also revealed that 88% and 82% of the respondents believe privacy and security risks, and a lack of standards are drawbacks when it comes to data.

3.6.2 Challenges in AI Integration

Despite the growing interest in AI and the value it can provide, organizations face challenges that make integrating it with their existing systems and processes and realizing value identification, creation, and capture gains difficult (Enholm et al. 2022; Mikalef and Gupta 2021) producing a modern productivity paradox (Brynjolfsson et al. 2018). The main challenges in AI include time, money, expertise, and resistance to change due to disruption, unfamiliarity, and legal and ethical concerns. These complex technologies also require large amounts of data, training, and knowledge, making it difficult for organizations to find suitable partners and manage projects effectively.

The survey results show the most significant challenge organizations face when implementing and scaling AI is a 'lack of time' with 58% of respondents strongly agreeing or agreeing that this is a challenge when implementing and scaling AI (Fig. 3.11). As relatively new and complex technologies, AI can be time-consuming to develop and implement. Additionally, in increasingly disruptive business environments, allocating time for technology implementation and scaling can be challenging due to the need for quick adaptation and decisive decision-making while also developing complex new technologies.

The results also show that 56% of respondents strongly agree and agree that a 'lack of knowledge or understanding' is a challenge when implementing and scaling AI. These findings support previous research, that organizations face challenges in effectively implementing AI due to a lack of knowledge and expertise, shortage of skilled workers, and high competition for talent retention, leading to delays and errors when implementing and scaling AI (Enholm et al. 2022; Acciarini et al. 2023). However, the results show that respondents are more optimistic about other potential challenges. Respondents were positive, for example, when it came to addressing'lack of clear usage cases' and'external cultural factors.' with only 19% and 13% of respondents 'strongly agree or agree'

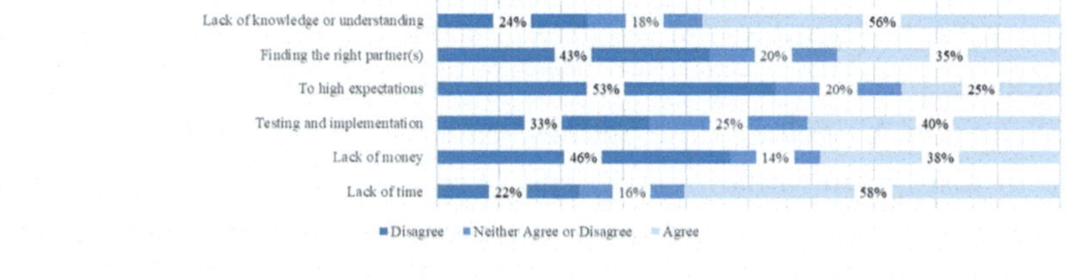

Fig. 3.11 Challenges organizations face implementing and scaling AI (%)

that these are challenges when it comes to implementing and scaling AI, respectively.

3.7 Conclusion and Outlook

In this chapter, our research examines the current state-of-the-art of AI and semi-autonomous/autonomous systems used by industry, examining their consequential effects. To provide clarity in our investigation, we undertake a descriptive analysis centered on five pivotal themes: (1) AI usage, (2) strategy and management, (3) capabilities and technology, (4) data usage, and (5) challenges in AI integration. The results suggest that AI is a rapidly growing field with the potential to transform industries. The results show that 61% of the organizations we surveyed are exploring the use of AI in their business. The most forward-thinking in developing AI plans is the 'information and communication services,' with all companies surveyed reporting at least one ongoing AI project. Furthermore, the findings indicate outliers in specific industries, with some organizations reporting significant investment in AI projects. For example, one respondent operating in the 'Professional, scientific, and technical activities sector' reported that their organization has 100 ongoing AI projects. As AI technologies continue to mature and become more accessible, we can expect to see a significant increase in their use by organizations of all sizes. Most organizations report increased plans to utilize AI and autonomous systems in the future (when inquired about their intentions 3 years to the future). We believe that AI as a general-purpose technology will be eventually adopted by nearly all digital and later, physical systems, transforming both unprecedented as well as difficult to forecast. For this reason, it is partially surprising that there are still companies (with over 50 employees) that do not report using AI or semi-autonomous/autonomous systems now, nor plan to in the future. It might of course be that they are not implementing such systems themselves but benefit from the AI-driven services provided by other companies, which could partially explain the result. Nevertheless, given the prominence and breadth of the 'AI revolution' with both classic machine learning but also the newer Generative AI models, our advice to the companies regardless of the industry is to make a strategic assessment of the potential of AI and semi-autonomous/autonomous systems, and then deliberate choices of whether and how to implement this technology.

3.7.1 Academic and Practical Contribution

The findings and reflections in this chapter provide a comprehensive overview of the current state-of-the-art of AI's business use and future implications for various industries. It highlights the increasing importance of AI and associated semi-autonomous/autonomous systems across different industrial sectors and the need for long-term studies to understand its impact and to identify effective integration strategies. Academically, it calls for further investigation into how AI affects organizational performance, strategic management, capabilities development, and data governance. The study highlights the importance of strategy agility, the correlation between AI capabilities and performance, and the complexities of data management in AI applications. From a practitioner perspective, our findings highlight the importance for organizations to constantly monitor and assess AI and semi-autonomous/autonomous system advancements in the context of their business and industrial sectors they operate in and plan to operate in the future and develop their business strategies applying appropriate forms of these technologies accordingly. It also underscores the importance of aligning AI initiatives with broader business strategies and addressing integration challenges proactively to ensure coherent growth and maintain a competitive edge.

Finally, the findings and interpretations provide actionable insights for both the academic community and practitioners, highlighting the critical necessity of grasping and systematically incorporating AI and semi-autonomous/autonomous systems to harness their transformative power in the digital era.

3.7.2 Limitations and Future Research

While providing valuable insights our study has several limitations. Firstly, it is important to recognize that the survey results are just a snapshot of the current state of AI adoption by organizations in Finland, and they may not be representative of all organizations and the situation in different countries. Secondly, while the diverse industry representation in our sample aids in providing a comprehensive overview, the survey may not have captured every way organizations use AI and semi-autonomous/autonomous systems. For example, organizations may use these technologies to develop new products or services, while others may use them to improve their internal operations. Our sample consists mostly of SMEs. Replicating this study in larger organizations could yield additional insights.

Finally, as a descriptive analysis of statistical results, our research serves as a foundational step for further statistical analysis. Future research should also explore the use of AI in organizations in more detail, including how different types of organizations use AI, organizations located in other countries, the impact of AI on organizational performance, and the challenges and opportunities associated with AI adoption. Additionally, more in-depth research methodologies, including organization case studies and interviews, would provide more nuanced and rich descriptive findings.

References

C. Acciarini, F. Cappa, P. Boccardelli, and R. Oriani. How can organizations leverage big data to innovate their business models? a systematic literature review. *Technovation*, 123:102713, 2023. https://doi.org/10.1016/j.technovation.2023.102713.

S. Alsheibani, Y. Cheung, and C. Messom. Artificial intelligence adoption: AI-readiness at firm-level. In M. Tanabu and D. Senoo, editors, *Proceedings of PACIS2018 : Pacific Asia Conference in Information Systems (PACIS) Article 37*. Association for Information Systems, 2018. URL https://aisel.aisnet.org/pacis2018/37/.

S. Banerjee. Autonomous vehicles: A review of the ethical, social, and economic implications of the ai revolution. *International Journal of Intelligent Unmanned Systems*, 9(4):302–312, 2020. https://doi.org/10.1108/IJIUS-07-2020-0027.

N. Berente, B. Gu, J. Recker, and R. Santhanam. Special issue editor's comments: Managing artificial intelligence. *MIS Quarterly*, 45(3):1433–1450, 2021.

S. G. Bouschery, V. Blazevic, and F. T. Piller. Augmenting human innovation teams with artificial intelligence: Exploring transformer-based language models. *Journal of Product Innovation Management*, 40(2):139–153, 2023. 10.1111/ jpim.12656.

J. K.-U. Brock and F. von Wangenheim. Demystifying ai: What digital transformation leaders can teach you about realistic artificial intelligence. *California Management Review*, 61(4):110–134, 2019. https://doi.org/10.1177/1536504219865226.

E. Brynjolfsson, D. Rock, and C. Syverson. *Artificial intelligence and the modern productivity paradox: A clash of expectations and statistics*. University of Chicago Press, 2018.

A. Bytniewski, K. Matouk, A. Chojnacka-Komorowska, M. Hernes, A. Zawadzki, and A. Kozina. The functionalities of cognitive technology in management control system. In *Proceedings of the Asian Conference on Intelligent Information and Database Systems*, page 230–240, Hanoi, Vietnam, 2020. Springer.

S. Chowdhury, P. Dey, S. Joel-Edgar, S. Bhattacharya, O. Rodriguez-Espindola, A. Abadie, and L. Truong. Unlocking the value of artificial intelligence in human resource management through ai capability framework. *Human Resource Management Review*, 33(1):100899, 2023. https://doi.org/10.1016/j.hrmr.2022.100899.

M. Chui, J. Manyika, M. Miremadi, N. Henke, R. Chung, P. Nel, and S. Malhotra. Sizing the potential value of ai and advanced analytics, 2018. Retrieved October 20, 2023, from https://www.mckinsey.com/featured-insights/artificial-intelligence/notes-from-the-ai-frontier-applications-and-valueof-deep-learning.

Dabrowska J., Almpanopoulou A., Brem A., Chesbrough H., Cucino V., Minin A. D., Giones F., Hakala H., Marullo C., Mention L., Mortara L., Nørskov S., Nylund P. A., Oddo C. M., Radziwon A., and Ritala P. Digital transformation, for better or worse: A critical multi-level research agenda. *R&D Management*, 52(5):930–954, 2022. https://doi.org/10.1111/radm.12531.

T. H. Davenport and N. Mittal. How companies can prepare for the coming 'ai-first' world. *Strategy and Leadership*, 51(1):26–30, 2023. 10.1108/ SL-11-2022-0107.

T. H. Davenport and R. Ronanki. Artificial intelligence for the real world. *Harvard Business Review*, pages 108–116, January-February 2018.

J. Dawes. Do data characteristics change according to the number of scale points used? an experiment using 5 point, 7 point, and 10 point scales. *International Journal of Market Research*, 51(1), 2008. URL https://ssrn.com/abstract=2013613.

D. A. Dillman, J. D. Smyth, and L. M. Christian. *Internet, phone, mail, and mixed-mode surveys: The tailored design method*. John Wiley & Sons, 2014.

Y. K. Dwivedi, N. Kshetri, L. Hughes, E. L. Slade, A. Jeyaraj, A. K. Kar, and R. Wright. So what if chatgpt wrote it? multidisciplinary perspectives on opportunities, challenges and implications of generative conversational ai for research, practice and policy. *International Journal of Information Management*, 71:102642, 2023.

I. M. Enholm, E. Papagiannidis, P. Mikalef, and Krogstie. Artificial intelligence and business value: A literature review. *Information Systems Frontiers*, 24:1709–1734, 2022. https://doi.org/10.1007/s10796-021-10186-w.

T. Eriksson, A. Bigi, and M. Bonera. Think with me, or think for me? on the future role of artificial intelligence in marketing strategy formulation. *The TQM Journal*, 32(4):795–814, 2020. https://doi.org/10.1108/TQM-12-2019-0303.

EUR-Lex. Small and medium-sized enterprises, 2023. Retrieved December 13, 2023, from https://eur-lex.europa.eu/EN/legal-content/glossary/small-and-medium-sized-enterprises.html.

Eurostat. Nace rev.2 statistical classification of economic activities in the european community, 2008. Retrieved October 20, 2023, from https://ec.europa.eu/eurostat/documents/3859598/5902521/KS-RA-07-015-EN.PDF.

T. Fountaine, B. McCarthy, B. and T. Saleh. Building the AI-powered organization. *Harvard Business Review*, 97(4):62–73, 2019.

E. Glikson and A. Wooley. Human trust in artificial intelligence: Review of empirical research. *Academy of Management Annals*, 14(2):627–660, 2020. 10.5465/ annals.2018.0057.

Haenlein M. and Kaplan A. A brief history of artificial intelligence: On the past, present, and future of artificial intelligence. *California Management Review*, 61 (4):5–14, 2019. https://doi.org/10.1177/0008125619864925.

A. Hayes. What is throughput? definition, formula, benefits, and calculation, 2023. Retrieved October 20, 2023, from https://www.investopedia.com/terms/t/throughput.asp.

M. Holopainen, M. Saunila, T. Rantala, and J. Ukko. Digital twins' implications for innovation. *Technology Analysis & Strategic Management*, 34(5):575–589, 2022. https://doi.org/10.1080/09537325.2022.2115881.

M. Iansiti and K. R. Lakhani. Competing in the age of AI: Strategy and leadership when algorithms and networks run the world. Harvard Business Press, 2020.

D. Jelonek, A. Mesjasz-Lech, C. Stępniak, T. Turek, and L. Ziora. The artificial intelligence application in the management of contemporary organization: Theoretical assumptions, current practices, and research review. In *Future of Information and Communication Conference*, 2019.

E. Karttunen, M. Pynnönen, L. Treves, and J. Hallikas. Capabilities for the internet of things enabled product-service system business models. *Technology Analysis & Strategic Management*, 35(12):1618–1634, 2023. https://doi.org/10.1080/09537325.2021.2012143.

S. Lebovitz, H. Lifshitz-Assaf, and N. Levina. To engage or not to engage with ai for critical judgments: How professionals deal with opacity when using ai for medical diagnosis. *Organization Science*, 33(1):126–148, 2022. https://doi.org/10.1287/orsc.2021. 1549.

Y. Li, J. Dai, and L. Cui. The impact of digital technologies on economic and environmental performance in the context of industry 4.0: A moderated mediation model. *International Journal of Production Economics*, 229:107777, 2020. https://doi.org/10.1016/j.ijpe.2020.107777.

E. E. Makarius, D. Mukherjee, J. D. Fox, and A. K. Fox. Rising with the machines: A sociotechnical framework for bringing artificial intelligence into the organization. *Journal of Business Research*, 120:262–273, 2020. https://doi.org/10.1016/j.jbusres.2020. 07.045.

McKinsey. The state of ai in 2020, 2020. Retrieved October 20, 2023, from https://www.mckinsey.com/capabilities/quantumblack/our-insights/global-survey-the-state-of-ai-in-2020.

McKinsey. The state of AI in 2022–and a half decade in review, 2022. Retrieved October 20, 2023, from https://www.mckinsey.com/~/media/mckinsey/business%20functions/quantumblack/our%20insights/the%20state%20of%20ai%20in%202022%20and%20a%20half%20decade%20in%20review/the-state-of-ai-in-2022-and-a-half-decade-in-review.pdf.

P. Mikalef and M. Gupta. Artificial intelligence capability: Conceptualization, measurement calibration, and empirical study on its impact on organizational creativity and firm performance. *Information and Management*, 58(3):103434, 2021. https://doi.org/10.1016/j.im.2021.103434.

MIT Technology Review Insights. Laying the foundation for data- and ai-led growth, 2023. Retrieved October 20, 2023, from $https://www.databricks.com/sites/default/files/2023-11/mittr-x-databricks_survey-report_final_06nov2023.pdf$.

P. R. Newsted, S. L. Huff, and M. C. Munro. Survey instruments in information systems. *MIS Quarterly*, 22(4):553–554, 1998.

A. Przegalińska, L. Ciechanowski, A. Stróż, P. Gloor, and G. Mazurek. In bot we trust: A new methodology of chatbot performance measures. *Business Horizons*, 62(6):785–797, 2019. https://doi.org/10.1016/j.bushor.2019.08.005.

S. Raisch and S. Krakowski. Artificial intelligence and management: The automation–augmentation Paradox. A*cademy of Management Review*, 46(1):192–210, 2021. https://doi.org/10.5465/amr.2018.0072.

S. Ransbotham, P. Gerbert, M. Reeves, D. Kiron, and M. Spira. Artificial intelligence in business gets real, 2018.

P. Ritala, M. Ruokonen, and L. Ramaul. Transforming boundaries: how does chatgpt change knowledge work? *Journal of Business Strategy*, 2023. 10.1108/ JBS-05-2023-0094.

M. Ruokonen and P. Ritala. How to succeed with an ai-first strategy? *Journal of Business Strategy*, 2023. https://doi.org/10.1108/JBS-08-2023-0178.

R. Schmidt, A. Zimmermann, M. Moehring, and B. Keller. Value creation in connectionist artificial intelligence–a research agenda. In *AMCIS 2020 Proceedings*, volume 14, 2020. URL https://aisel.aisnet.org/amcis2020/ai_semantic_for_intelligent_info_systems/ai_semantic_for_intelligent_info_systems/14. Retrieved October 20, 2023.

N. Smallwood and D. Ulrich. Capitalizing on capabilities, 2004. Retrieved December 13, 2023, from https://hbr.org/2004/06/capitalizing-on-capabilities.

Statista. Big data market size revenue forecast worldwide from 2011 to 2027, 2022. Retrieved October 20, 2023, from https://www.statista.com/statistics/254266/global-big-data-market-forecast/.

The Economist. The world's most valuable resource is no longer oil, but data, 2017. Retrieved from https://www.economist.com/leaders/2017/05/06/the-worlds-most-valuable-resource-is-no-longer-oil-but-data.

L. Thomson, A. Kamalaldin, D. Sjödin, and V. Parida. A maturity framework for autonomous solutions in manufacturing firms: The interplay of technology, ecosystem, and business model. *International Entrepreneurship Management Journal*, 18:125–152, 2021. https://doi.org/10.1007/s11365-020-00717-3.

L. Waardenburg and M. Huysman. From coexistence to co-creation: Blurring boundaries in the age of ai. *Information and Organization*, 32(4):100432, 2022. https://doi.org/10.1016/j.infoandorg.2022.100432.

Serge L. Wamba-Taguimdje, Samuel Fosso Wamba, Jean R. K. Kamdjoug, and Christian E. T. Wanko. Influence of artificial intelligence (ai) on firm performance: The business value of ai-based transformation projects. *Business Process Management Journal*, 26(7):1893–1924, 2020. https://doi.org/10.1108/BPMJ-10-2019-0411.

Xun Xu, Yang Lu, Birgit Vogel-Heuser, and Lihui Wang. Industry 4.0 and industry 5.0—inception, conception and perception. *Journal of Manufacturing Systems*, 61:530–535, 2021. https://doi.org/10.1016/j.jmsy.2021.10.006.

4

Industry 5.0 Vision Through Model-Based Systems Engineering and Artificial Intelligence

Aapo Hölsä, Isa Banagar, Qasim Khadim, Tero Frondelius, Juho Konnö, Amin Mahmoudzadeh Andwari, and Emil Kurvinen

4.1 Introduction

Industry 5.0 emphasizes the integration of digital technologies and automation while placing a strong emphasis on enhancing the well-being of workers, customization, and sustainability (European Commission and Directorate-General for Research and Innovation 2022). As an integral part of the Industry 5.0 vision, physics-based real-time simulations can provide data for the artificial intelligence (AI) algorithms (Han et al. 2021) to automate and optimize different phases of the product life-cycle by monitoring and adjusting processes in real time to maximize efficiency, reduce waste, improve quality and optimize the entire supply

A. Hölsä (✉) · I. Banagar · Q. Khadim · T. Frondelius · J. Konnö ·
A. Mahmoudzadeh Andwari · E. Kurvinen
Machine and Vehicle Design (MVD), Materials and Mechanical Engineering,
Faculty of Technology, University of Oulu, 90014 Oulu, Finland
e-mail: aapo.holsa@oulu.fi

T. Frondelius
R&D Engineering, Wärtsilä, P.O. Box 244, 65101 Vaasa, Finland

P. Aaltonen and E. Kurvinen (eds.), *Contemporary Issues in Industry 5.0*, Technology, Work and Globalization, https://doi.org/10.1007/978-3-031-74779-3_4

chain (Javaid et al. 2022). Further, the safety and ergonomics of work environments and human–machine interactions can be improved significantly when optimized AI models are utilized together with system architecture to create a virtual representation of the system in operation (Leng et al. 2021). Enhanced with Kalman filters and AI algorithms, real-time simulations also enable online condition monitoring, predictive maintenance, and product retirement decisions at the fingertips (Khadim et al. 2023a). However, the subject of combining model-based systems engineering (MBSE) and physics-based real-time simulations in the context of Industry 5.0 is a relatively less investigated area.

Manufacturing of metal products poses a concrete application where the benefits of Industry 5.0 can be materialized. The production of defective metal products consumes substantial quantities of natural, financial, and energy resources, contributing to environmental degradation. To foster the creation of sustainable products, seamless management of production data across the design, development, materials, manufacturing, and deployment phases is imperative. This integrated approach facilitates the realization of products that align with the principles of 'first-time-right' and 'zero-defect.' However, concurrently, it is crucial to ensure that products adhere closely to design specifications, mitigating the allocation of resources toward excessive quality (over-quality). Currently, the establishment of robust data management protocols and data formats across the various phases of a product's life cycle remains inadequate, leading to substandard products and services. Systems engineering, as a management methodology, has evolved to streamline the efficient development of well-defined systems designed to address customer objectives translated into system requirements (Weilkiens 2008). A fundamental aspect of the systems engineering process lies in the exchange of diverse documentation, serving to encapsulate information spanning the developmental phases from problem definition to testing. As the scope of a system expands, introducing heightened complexity, the task of maintaining and sharing up-to-date documentation grows increasingly intricate. Consequently, this challenge has precipitated the emergence of Model-Based Systems Engineering (MBSE), where the system model becomes the singular source of truth, accurately portraying the present state of the system under development (Madni and Sievers 2018).

The MBSE approach enables the representation and analysis of diverse information across different phases of the product lifecycle through the use of models (Ramos et al. 2012). These models help in the visualization, simulation, and documentation of system requirements, design, and behavior, enabling multiple team members to collaborate on the shared model simultaneously. Integrating MBSE with physics-based real-time simulations can contribute to providing real-time feedback on system parameter changes (Han et al. 2021), facilitating improved communication and detailed analysis for all stakeholders. Further, with real-time simulation models, the end-users and customers can be engaged in the various phases of the product lifecycle (Khadim et al. 2021). The integration of MBSE with real-time physics-based simulations aligns with the vision of Industry 5.0, also known as the human-centric industry, which represents the future of manufacturing and industry (European Commission and Directorate-General for Research and Innovation 2022). This chapter delves into the combination of MBSE and AI as a means to propel the industry toward the aspirations of Industry 5.0. Offering an overview of the MBSE concept and a holistic perspective of its alignment with Industry 5.0 goals, this chapter proceeds to illustrate its vision through a case study centered on the development and optimization of steel product manufacturing.

4.2 Model-Based Systems Engineering

In document-based systems engineering, information on the system is captured in textual specifications and design documents (Friedenthal et al. 2014). These data should be transferred and iterated between different departments for decision-making, (Fig. 4.1a), which is an error-prone and time-consuming procedure. The development of new engineering methods, tools, and means of communication has greatly improved the accuracy and efficiency of the design process. However, this progress requires novel methods to manage the massive volumes of digital data produced by modern engineering procedures. MBSE has developed

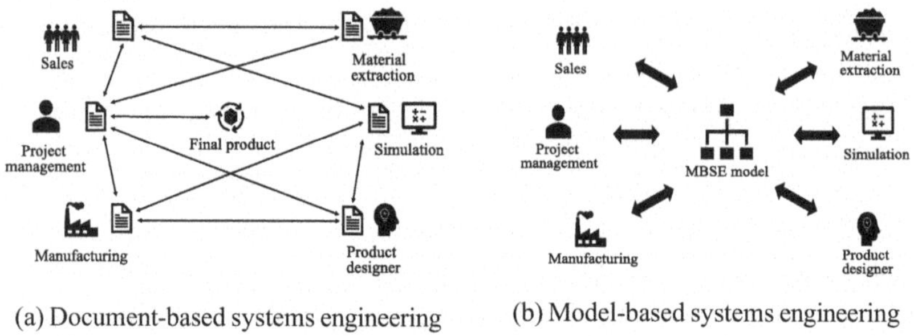

Fig. 4.1 Comparison between document-based and model-based systems engineering

based on document-based systems engineering to be capable of handling the development process through a central model, (Fig. 4.1b). The adoption of an MBSE model to capture all critical system data not only improves traceability but also provides a unified comprehension of the system's status (Ramos et al. 2012).

The key perspectives highlighted in a system presentation through an MBSE model are the system's requirements, structure, behavior, and parametric representation. The use of the system model as the sole source of truth leads to a decreased risk of mismatched or disregarded information during the system's life cycle phases.

The MBSE approach is emerging as a standard for exercising systems engineering for the development of systems in a vast variety of fields in technology.

Benefits to the approach have been claimed in numerous publications, although measured benefits have not yet been demonstrated sufficiently in publicly available research (Henderson and Salado 2021). Quantitative evidence of realized MBSE value propositions could alleviate resistance to the transformation from a document-centric to a model-centric systems engineering approach. The model-centric approach enables visualization of the system and makes it easy to comprehend for non-technical stakeholders, making it a successful platform for broader development, e.g., for evaluating business models or considering the sustainability aspects more comprehensively.

4.2.1 Adoption of MBSE

The collection of essentials that enable the adoption of the MBSE for varying development challenges is referred to as methodology (Fig. 4.2). A comprehensively defined methodology gives the user answers to questions about what is to be done and how it should be done (Estefan and Weilkiens 2020). A defined process gives steps that are needed to accomplish a complete model. A method is needed to provide information on how to approach and complete the tasks defined by the process. Finally, a tool is necessary to enable the compilation of a system model. In the commercial use of MBSE, it is commonplace that a tool is tailored for adoption with a certain process and method to ease the adoption. This leads to multiple similar options being available from different vendors for new adopters of the new systems engineering approach. Often overlooked additional factors that either support or obstruct the adoption and maintenance of the practice but that are not physically tied to the methodology are the environmental factors (Estefan et al. 2007).

Organizational factors such as reluctance to change and unwillingness to dedicate the workforce are key obstructions to wider adoption—especially when radical changes are desired. This is because the radical changes might impose risk on the main business by influencing the design and manufacturing of products. Demonstrated quantified benefits of the approach and openly available, well-defined methodologies could alleviate the effects of organizational resistance to this transformation. To have a real impact the change should be driven by the willingness

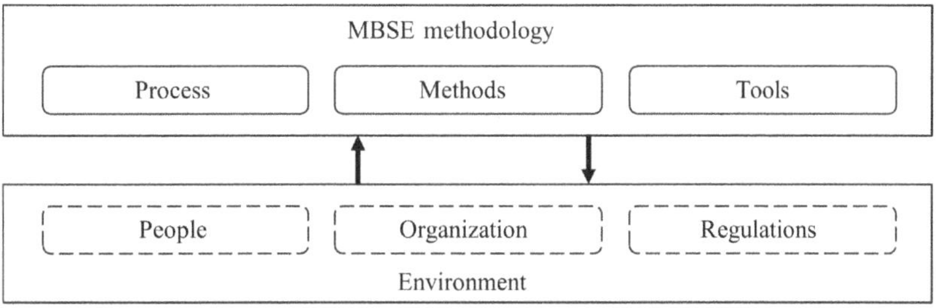

Fig. 4.2 Contents of a methodology and other factors that affect the adoption of MBSE

to improve and not by the necessity to change. An incentive for the transformation might also come from other suppliers that exploit MBSE successfully and thereby gain a competitive edge.

The methodologies for MBSE have been developed to facilitate a sufficient capturing of system information during the modeling process. A scan through the methodology surveys (Estefan et al. 2007) reveals that most MBSE methodologies employ a top-down approach of functional decomposition for system modeling and development, similarly as the business analysis is conducted. Common activities in the order of application include stakeholder need analysis, system requirement definition, logical architecture definition, and verification and validation. Functional analysis is often utilized as a step to assist the compilation of system logical architecture. These common MBSE activities roughly follow the traditional systems engineering lifecycle models such as the V-model. The V-model is a widely adopted product development framework that was originally developed for software development but has since been adapted for wider use in the development of different systems (Graessler et al. 2018). For MBSE, these frameworks have been optimized to produce modeling from viewpoints that enable a step-by-step development of the system. Contents of these viewpoints connect and produce a satisfactory model that provides a complete representation of the system for all life cycle development needs. While the completeness of the model is highly desirable, a well-formed methodology that is suitable for the particular application enables the creation of a good enough system model with the least amount of resources. This challenge has been an incentive for the development of many methodologies. This has led to some different approaches to the modeling process. Common to most of the MBSE methodologies is the iterative nature of the development process following a top-down approach. Modeling for each discovered system branch could be stopped at any level when the original problem is deemed as sufficiently, fulfilling predefined conditions, solved.

4.2.2 Benefits and Challenges of MBSE

MBSE is claimed to provide various benefits when compared to traditional product development approaches. Benefits commonly associated with the approach in the literature include improved communication, complexity management, increased reusability, and cost reduction (Henderson and Salado 2021). In another study, some examples of frequently used positive attributes of Model-Based Systems Engineering (MBSE) were listed to be verifiability, reasoning, consistency, and communication capability (Campo et al. 2023). These attributes demonstrate the original vision of MBSE that promotes a model as a singular source of truth. To provide comprehensive reasoning for decision-making the model should be complete and thus verifiable and consistent. These requirements demand a suitable methodology, a compatible toolset, and a proficient dedicated workforce.

The MBSE can still be regarded as an emerging approach to product development. It can be common that the benefits of the approach are presented with no consideration of possible drawbacks (Campo et al. 2023). The changing and tool-specific field of methodologies and the difference to the traditional systems engineering approach can raise questions about the feasibility and profitability of adopting a new approach. These doubts can be seen in the list of most frequently negatively perceived attributes toward Model-Based Systems Engineering (MBSE) gathered in a study (Campo et al. 2023; Huldt and Stenius 2019). The list of these attributes includes acceptability, familiarity, affordability, and feasibility. To combat these doubts, the development of the approach and methodologies should aim for universal semantics and guidelines for adoption while supporting the development of individual discipline-specific methodologies. One of the leading advocates for systems engineering and MBSE practices, the International Council on Systems Engineering (INCOSE), has noted technical challenges as one of the limitations for wider adoption of MBSE in their Systems Engineering 2020 Vision (INCOSE 2020). The listed challenges concern the difficulty of integrating models across boundaries of e.g. organizations or system lifecycle phases and the limitations of model and data exchange between modeling tools. Sharing models and data along supply chains should be facilitated to eliminate the need for overlapping activities. Models have been supporting part of system development for a long time in the phases of system analysis and design. Integration of the existing models and discipline-specific modeling tools with the system level to capture the system as a whole is one of the challenges that MBSE needs to solve shortly.

Despite its unavoidable limitations, MBSE has become a go-to approach for the development of new and existing systems. Already in its current state, the modeling practices of MBSE enable the creation of machine-readable representations of increasingly complex systems in commonly adopted languages such as SysML. This characteristic of MBSE permits the employment of machine intelligence as a tool in the essential quest toward sustainable and efficient systems. Hence the authors see MBSE as an important enabler of widespread adoption of Industry 5.0 including multidisciplinary viewpoints. In the following sections, a vision of employment of MBSE for Industry 5.0 is presented.

4.3 MBSE Vision in Industry 4.0 and 5.0

Industry 4.0, which emerged in the twenty-first century, integrates intelligent systems across industries. This revolution fully automates processes by utilizing flexible AI and machine learning in ambiguous situations (Akundi et al. 2022). Moreover, the implementation of machine learning and optimization methods aims to enhance operational efficiency (Vinitha et al. 2020).

In contrast, Industry 5.0 provides cooperative robots that communicate with human operators and reduce risk while comprehending objectives and duties. It represents the fusion of AI into daily life while boosting human capabilities using cutting-edge IT, IoT, robotics, AI, and augmented reality (Akundi and Lopez 2021). Industries have been pursuing Industry 4.0 visions such as digitalization (Verdugo-Cedeño et al. 2023), AI, and cyber-physical systems (CPSs) as integrated physical and software systems. Despite all the advantages Industry 4.0 has brought, it has been detected that it is not the right framework to achieve

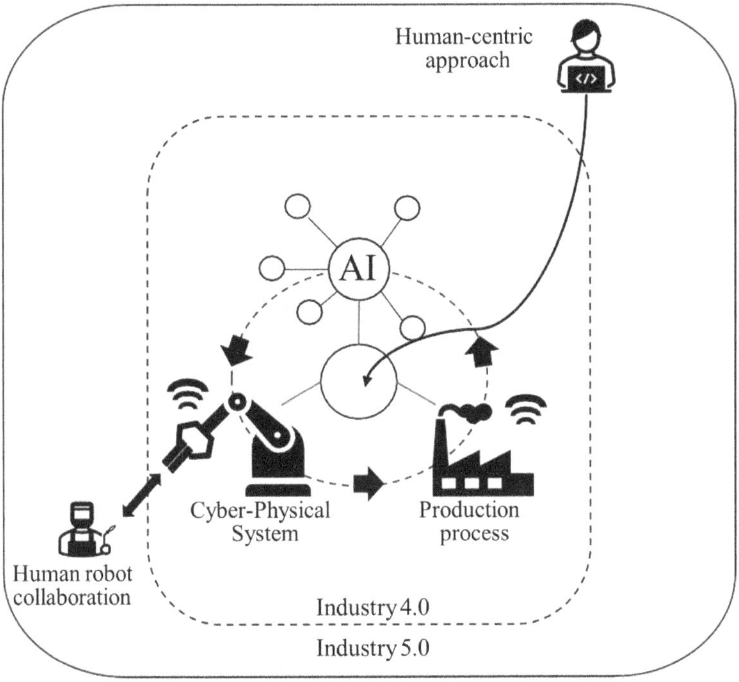

Fig. 4.3 Industry 5.0's integration of human-centric values and societal goals with industry 4.0's vision

European 2030 goals, which leads to promoting Industry 5.0 (European Commission and Directorate-General for Research and Innovation 2022). Industry 5.0 nested the Industry 4.0 vision and added other pillars as the main targets, such as a human-centric approach, personalized production, and decentralized decision-making, to direct industry toward societal challenges (Fig. 4.3).

4.3.1 Key Technologies in Industry 4.0

Utilizing key enabling technologies such as AI, the Internet of Things (IoT), and digital twins (DT) as the key technology to represent the behavior of the manufacturing process has become a critical practice in pursuing Industry 4.0 goals. These technologies increased the complexity of the design and manufacturing processes of a CPS. The uncertainties rooted in human behavior and safety considerations will also increase the complexity, even to a higher level, by placing humans at the center of the manufacturing process in Industry 5.0. To ensure the robustness and flexibility of cyber-physical production systems (CPPS) to real-time changes in the environment, reconfigurability is identified as a major need of Industry 5.0.

It is crucial to have models that cover business, processes, and control views to combine a wide variety of information and obtain the optimum reconfiguration approach. However, Industry 4.0 relies heavily on automation and data-driven technologies such as generative AI (Cámara et al. 2023). This shift could increase social inequalities and reduce human oversight, potentially leading to ethical dilemmas and decreased job satisfaction among workers. Further, the extensive integration of CPS and CPPS will increase vulnerability to cyber security threats, posing risks to both individual privacy and industrial security. The regulatory push for ethical AI practices in Industry 4.0, as highlighted in Mittelstadt (2019), has paved the way for Industry 5.0 to further balance technological advances with human-centric values. Next, the role of MBSE in Industry 5.0 is explained in more detail.

4.3.2 Role of MBSE in Industry 5.0

By encouraging cross-disciplinary cooperation, utilizing model-based design, and managing complex system structures, MBSE enhances automated production systems. MBSE offers benefits including increased efficiency, productivity, and consistency in managing complex systems, despite facing implementation difficulties. An assessment of MBSE deployment in the manufacturing and industrial sectors has been carried out by Akundi and Lopez (2021). MBSE provides an extensive foundation to tie different system models and methodologies together since there has not been any dedicated methodology in the Industry 5.0 context. It provides a suitable foundation for managing the complexity of various standards, languages, and methodologies used in software and systems engineering to increase productivity, flexibility, and the level of automation in general as nested targets of the Industry 4.0 paradigm within Industry 5.0. Moreover, it provides extensive possibilities for personalizing the product and decentralized decision-making through an emphasis on a human-centric framework design which is in line with the Industry 5.0 paradigm.

4.3.3 Integrating AI in MBSE

DTs (Khadim et al. 2021; Verdugo-Cedeño et al. 2023), AI, and key enabling technologies of Industry 5.0 can improve the performance of the MBSE models in a variety of ways. Using systems engineering tools enhanced with AI algorithms allows system engineers to focus more on creative tasks and less on data input or report generation. The production cycle becomes more difficult when people are involved since modeling non-deterministic behavior is involved. For control strategies based on observations, cognitive approaches, and AI techniques are stated as essential, and models can help with the learning processes of AI algorithms by supplying the required information for evaluating the system's present condition. AI for MBSE (AI4MBSE) has been introduced to facilitate the challenges of MBSE practice by contributing to task automation, improving analysis, and optimizing system designs (Chami et al. 2022).

Utilizing various AI techniques such as natural language processing (NLP) (Gerstmayr et al. 2024) and pattern recognition (Dunne 2007) by the Industry 5.0 vision not only improves the performance of MBSE model generation but also allows humans to return to the correct place in the production cycle. Moreover, the utilization of DT models and having them linked to the MBSE model as the executable part of a holistic model and virtual representative of a system of interest (SoI) will lead to agile decision-making and increase traceability in the early stages of the design. Nevertheless, the implementation of AI techniques and large language models (LLMs) will require huge computational resources in Industry 5.0. However, this challenge can be overcome by using low-fidelity models such as in Khadim et al. (2023b, 2024).

In the latest release of Systems Engineering Vision by INCOSE (2020), the concerns of Industry 5.0 have been covered by considering the Industry 4.0 and Society 5.0 approaches. This vision covers the idea of human-centered production while pursuing Industry 4.0 (Miller 2022). Implementing the MBSE approach, human intelligence can map and orchestrate design and manufacturing by considering different points of view and drawing linkages between related activities to improve the efficacy of design and manufacturing procedures.

4.4 Applications of MBSE for Industry 5.0 in a Case Study

The Industry 5.0 vision through MBSE and AI can be demonstrated in a case study. This case study examines the application of MBSE in the manufacturing of a marine engine connecting rod (Fig. 4.4) in the Industry 5.0 context. A modular product portfolio of the supplier facilitates that the component can also be used in a separate application as an engine power plant component. As a result, the operational requirements for the component can include a lot of variation in static and dynamic loading. The specified design loads are determined by simulations of differing fidelities which are typically validated by physical testing of limited coverage and accuracy. As such, the design loads contain multiple sources of uncertainty and have to be defined conservatively to provide a product that fulfills its function with an acceptable rate of failure.

The physical realization of the connecting rod is a cumulative result of a multi-stage, multisubcontractor manufacturing chain. Each stage of the process has to be specified to a level that ensures the realization of satisfactory product quality. The output of manufacturing stages is inherently affected by both epistemic and aleatoric uncertainty. Epistemic uncertainty in the output characteristics can be reduced by existing means (Lemaire 2014) but this process is often resource-intensive after a certain point. A compromise has to be made about good enough knowledge. The resulting leftover epistemic uncertainty has to be taken into account with an additional margin on product specification (Pelz 2021), similar to aleatoric uncertainty born from the inevitable randomness of phenomena (Lemaire 2014). This leads to over-quality in the majority of the components.

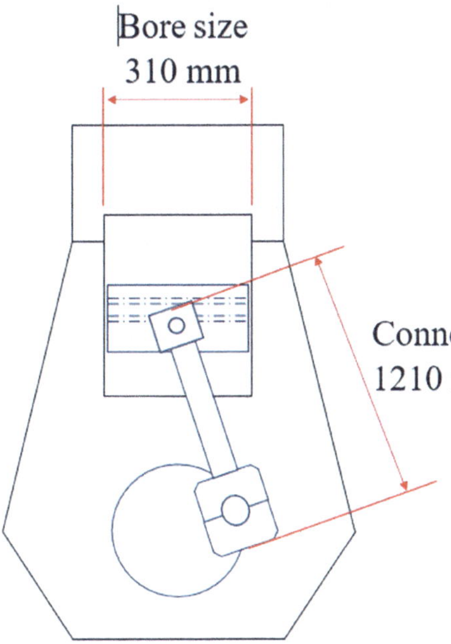

Fig. 4.4 Principle diagram of a marine engine crank train with dimensions

Simultaneously, a small number of manufactured parts will experience failure due to unforeseen circumstances and the unaccounted-for variation that was deemed not significant. The connecting rod, as a part of the engine in its use context, interacts directly with other engine components and indirectly with the operational environment. In this context, the engine can be seen as a system whose function is to generate mechanical power from chemical energy and an infinite air reservoir called an atmosphere. This main system, the engine, can be decomposed into different subsystems which each correspond to specific requirements and sub-functions. One of the primary sub-functions of a reciprocating engine is typically the conversion of gas forces into rotational torque. This function can be assigned to a subsystem called cranktrain. A decomposition of subsystems reveals another level of subsystems and components. Component level has been reached when at least part of subsystem functions can be directly realized by individual elements or parts. In this example connecting rod is a component that fulfills the function of transmitting reciprocal forces from the piston to the crankshaft.

An engine can be considered the SoI if the concern is primarily to develop an engine to a given specification. This definition for the SoI boundary is highly rational since it narrows the complexity and scope to a level that is comprehensible and maintainable by human actors with reasonable resources and only considers intellectual property up to the level of a whole engine. The exchange of information from one service and software to another within the system boundary is an existing problem with today's technology, and that challenge becomes more prominent with additional system complexity. However, a more comprehensive approach to systems and system lifecycle is inevitably needed to permit the development and production of systems with increased efficiency and sustainability. To enable that, the scope of SoI should be switched from system level to system of systems (SoS) level. An SoS is an SoI with individual systems as system elements (SFS-ISO/IEC/IEEE 2015). Systems that constitute an SoS work together to fulfill a task that is not realizable by the individual systems.

4.4.1 Natural Language Processing for Improved Accessibility of Captured Knowledge

Transition to SoS-viewpoint leads to exponential growth in information within the model. A level where a system is transformed into SoS can be reached when extending the scope of the SoI boundary vertically or horizontally. Here vertical extension would mean going up the structure from the component level to the application-specific level, for instance, a level of the complete vessel or a power grid. For optimization of manufacturing, we can extend horizontally on the component level to examine the connecting rod alongside its manufacturing chain as an SoS that provides both the design and the physical means for reliably transmitting forces to the engine crankshaft (Fig. 4.5). Regardless of the extension direction, the added complexity of managing systems on the SoS level generates challenges for model maintenance and information integration. A common, machine-readable system modeling language is necessary to facilitate the integration of models of different systems. The Systems Modelling Language (SysML) has been widely associated with MBSE as a semi-formal language for systems modeling (Saqui-Sannes et al. 2022). SysML was developed as a general tool-independent language and as such, leaves a lot of modeling decisions up to the modeler. This feature poses a challenge for model exchange between multiple disciplines and stakeholders for example in manufacturing SoS modeling cases. In addition, the specification of SysML doesn't facilitate direct verification and validation of the model by executable simulations. This limitation has led to the development of extended versions of SysML. One tool-dependent extension of SysML is the Arcadia method used with the software tool Capella (Saqui-Sannes et al. 2022). The current limitations of SysML have been noted by the developers and are alleviated in the upcoming SysML specification v2 by increasing interoperability and introducing analysis as an integral part of the system model (Bajaj et al. 2022).

With a developed model exchange capability, the manufacturing partner's system models could be integrated as a part of the SoS-level manufacturing chain model. The SoS-level model acts as a centralized representation of the current state of the manufacturing process and could be queried for desired information about subsequent manufacturing states. If the used modeling language is stable and machine-readable, this interpretation of model information could be automatically performed by AI via a prompt through a typical chat-type interface that utilizes an LLM. Similar document and report generation via NLP

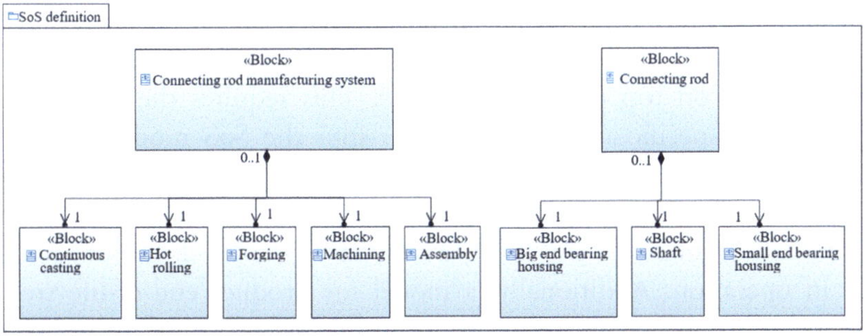

Fig. 4.5 Block definition diagram for case study system of systems definition

techniques has been demonstrated in Delp et al. (2013). This approach would make the knowledge captured within the system model accessible to stakeholders regardless of their ability to use specific tools or interpret a specific language. The practicality of such an approach suffers from some of the challenges regarding the compatibility of models from different tools and also from unavoidable cautiousness about data-sharing. This potential need has already been accounted for in the specification of the forthcoming SysML version 2 by defining the API to support requirements change impact assessment and querying the traceability of model elements (Bajaj et al. 2022). Automatic report generation for each stakeholder viewpoint is a promising concept that would relieve personnel from repetitive auxiliary duties that don't directly serve the goal of system development. In a practical example, a report could include a mapping of all processes whose output requirements are affected if the lifetime of a connecting rod in a certain application is to be altered. The result would be a trace from application-specific lifetime requirements to fatigue analysis to inclusion formation during manufacturing. A decision about the change feasibility could then be made based on the report. The use of LLMs for expanding the usability of system models is not limited to information queries. An extension of this technique is the automated AI-assisted building of SysML models and diagrams, which has already been demonstrated (Apvrille and Sultan 2024; Zhong et al. 2023).

4.4.2 System Model as a Structure for DTs

A deeper and more advantageous integration of MBSE into the Industry 5.0 concept is achieved by creating and maintaining an executable simulation model on top of the SoS model. This requires the integration of discipline-specific simulation models into the SoS model structure (Madni et al. 2019). For the connecting rod, this would include simulation models for the continuous casting of steel bars, forging simulation, machining simulations, and finally a simulation model of the connecting rod in operation. Additionally, a model for product end-of-life treatment is also necessary when the product's environmental impact over its full life cycle is to be considered. Such a simulation toolchain would inevitably be computationally inefficient to use frequently with high-fidelity models. A more realistic approach is to utilize data-driven models of different processes in a fidelity that is deemed sufficient. Data-driven models provide an additional benefit by protecting the underlying intellectual property of the owner of a manufacturing stage.

A comprehensive, full life cycle simulation toolchain constitutes a DT of the metal product. The DT can be used for assessing and quantifying impacts of proposed changes, and optimization of the manufacturing process. If we use the component lifetime requirement change as an example, the increase would result in a reduced allowed size of inclusions within the material. This sub-requirement change then propagates into a concrete set of requirements for the manufacturing stages: for steel composition, casting process parameters, etc. The optimization of the manufacturing SoS can be performed against a variety of goals, including improvement of business and sustainability metrics. The complete manufacturing chain contains a significant number of variables and various combinations of parameter values can lead to the same outcome. Simultaneously, the targets of optimization can be conflicting. Hence the task of finding the Pareto-optimal set of solutions requires multi-objective optimization algorithms. Machine-learning-based optimization algorithms have proved to provide a good compromise between accuracy and efficiency (Liu et al. 2015; Schweidtmann et al. 2018).

4.4.3 Employing Patterns and Optimization to Accelerate Product Development

The given examples of MBSE utilization use the existing SoS model of the manufacturing process to guide the development of the SoS toward specified targets. The SoS model itself needs to be built to materialize these applications, and the model development itself is certainly a task for an informed systems engineer. At present, the systems that form the SoS can be described internally in a multitude of ways that do not obey the conventions of MBSE. The fragmented field of MBSE and the various languages used for system modeling lead to there being incompatibilities between those already utilizing the approach for their processes. A skilled human operator is needed to interpret and tie together information on manufacturing processes to form a coherent and consistent picture of the complete SoS. This integration phase will become more straightforward if more concrete evidence of the benefits is published and the MBSE approach is adopted more widely. Additionally, the maturation of the MBSE approach will inevitably lead to better interoperability of tools and methodologies.

The unnecessary, recurring manual integration work that would be done for similar systems and systems of systems could be greatly reduced by employing previously created models as patterns. Each sufficiently described and complete system and SoS model defined according to the conventions of MBSE presents a solution to a defined problem. This entity of problem and its solution can be referred to as a Solution Pattern (Anacker et al. 2020, 2022). A Solution pattern captures solution knowledge in a reusable and well-documented way. This is contrary to the traditional practice of having that information stored as experience of individual employees (Anacker et al. 2022). Reuse of this captured solution knowledge would enable a higher level of efficiency during the development of future products (Anacker et al. 2020). A relevant solution pattern for the connecting rod manufacturing development would represent for instance each stage of the manufacturing process. One example problem could be the manufacturing of high-quality steel bar for connecting rod stock. This domain-specific knowledge is not necessarily essential for the connecting rod manufacturer and could easily be unofficially a responsibility of one senior employee. Future development of similar steel components would benefit from documenting this model of a system that constitutes one part of the manufacturing SoS as a solution pattern. A solution pattern can equally be the model of the connecting rod manufacturing chain. This pattern can then be used to configure the manufacturing process of connecting rods for different applications and operating conditions. The solution pattern provides a re-configurable template for a family of similar products. While the initial development of patterns is highly manual labor, the pattern can later be used for configuring new products for alternative sets of requirements. This configuration could employ AI for selecting optimal parameters for a specific set of requirements based on models of manufacturing stages.

4.4.4 Benefits and Challenges for Integrating MBSE in Industry 5.0

The given three approaches for applying MBSE to facilitate the efficient transition toward Industry 5.0 demonstrate merely a limited set of possible advantages that arise when the approach is adopted. The main value proposition of MBSE is to provide an organic and commonly agreed upon database that captures the whole architecture of SoI together with its functions and interactions. Making this centralized database accessible to all technical and non-technical stakeholders leads to the decentralization of knowledge, which ultimately facilitates more stakeholders to take part in development and innovation. DTs can be built on top of the captured knowledge to efficiently test system performance against numerous scenarios and to find the optimal configuration and parameters for each use case. Finally, the development of new systems inherently needs the creativity that is currently provided solely by us, the human actors within the development cycle. One key benefit of well-built and standardized models is their reusability as patterns. Employing AI and optimization techniques as assisting tools to provide the best possible starting points from previous configurations enables the human actor in the loop to concentrate on the more creative parts of development instead of repetitive configuration of similar types of products.

Key barriers that inhibit the realization of these benefits stem from the current limitations regarding the interconnectivity of created system-level models and models that capture subsystem and component behavior. This issue has been recognized as an important research area and a lot of advances have been made recently on this front. Nevertheless, existing methods and tools fail to provide a generally applicable solution to achieve truly integrated DTs that benefit fully from the system models that are created in a growing level of detail as product development proceeds. Another more fundamental barrier was already partly discussed in section two of this chapter. This barrier is created by the scattered compilation of methods, tools, and processes that are currently offered as separate and non-interconnected solutions. The threshold for adoption of the approach is high since no established processes exist for varying sizes of product development teams. Lowering this threshold requires quantified benefits and demonstrated success stories. This would eventually lead to a cumulative effect that leads to the natural prosperity of the best available solutions.

4.5 Conclusion

Systems engineering is an approach that has been developed for the efficient development of systems to specific and well-defined needs. Model-based systems engineering (MBSE) extends this approach by capturing all the information about the system of interest (SoI) in a centralized representation of the system called a system model. The system model acts as a singular source of truth that is used by stakeholders to communicate, act as a justification for development decisions, and compare alternative solutions to specific development problems. The field of MBSE is still developing and no common understanding about the best modeling languages or methodologies exists. The lack of consensus and abundance of options for methodologies creates challenges for integrating information from different sources. Despite its inherent challenges, MBSE can be seen both as a contributor and a beneficiary for the transition toward Industry 5.0. The use of system models can contribute to a platform for managing the development of complex cyber-physical systems (CPSs) and the various models that are an essential part of today's product development. System models can additionally provide a structure for integrating simulation models to form digital twins (DTs) of complex systems. The DTs can be used as a tool to quantify the effects of design decisions.

Several benefits of utilizing MBSE to advance Industry 5.0 concepts can be recognized in the context of manufacturing development, such as for a marine engine connecting rod. The centralized documentation provided by the fully integrated manufacturing chain system of systems (SoS) model can be used to trace the impacts of development decisions. This impact tracing could utilize AI for report generation to relieve personnel from repetitive tasks. The structure and behavior modeling from the SoS model provide a structure that facilitates the integration of simulation models for each of the manufacturing stages. When applied to the complete chain, this DT can be used for further optimization of the manufacturing process. A comprehensive DT with advanced machine-learning-based optimization algorithms can provide an optimized solution for multi-objective optimization tasks. Another benefit provided by MBSE is the use of patterns to promote reusability, reconfigurability, and personalization. The SoS and system models developed during the development of the manufacturing stages and the whole chain provide documentation on development problems and solutions, which can be used to provide Solution Patterns for solving future problems. Similarly, the whole manufacturing process model can be reused as a general Solution Pattern for any connecting rod, reducing repeated and overlapping human work and freeing human resources for creative tasks.

This chapter offers a vision of how MBSE can be used to promote the goals of Industry 5.0 and encourages integrating MBSE as an integral part of Industry 5.0. Additionally, the chapter highlights challenges that hinder the wider adoption of MBSE in the industry and its role in Industry 5.0.

Acknowledgements This research was co-funded by the European Union (Grant Agreement No. 101058179; ENGINE). Views and opinions expressed are, however, those of the authors only and do not necessarily reflect those of the European Union or the European Health and Digital Executive Agency. Neither the European Union nor the granting authority can be held responsible for them.

References

A. Akundi and V. Lopez. A review on application of model based systems engineering to manufacturing and production engineering systems. In *Procedia Computer Science*, volume 185, pages 101–108. Elsevier, 2021.

A. Akundi, D. Euresti, S. Luna, W. Ankobiah, A. Lopes, and I. Edinbarough. State of industry 5.0—analysis and identification of current research trends. *Applied System Innovation*, 5(1):27, 2022.

H. Anacker, R. Dumitrescu, A. Kharatyan, and A. Lipsmeier. Pattern based systems engineering–application of solution patterns in the design of intelligent technical systems. In *Proceedings of the design society: DESIGN conference*, volume 1, pages 1195–1204. Cambridge University Press, 2020.

H. Anacker, M. Günther, F. Wyrwich, and R. Dumitrescu. Pattern based engineering of system of systems-a systematic literature review. In *2022 17th annual system of systems engineering conference (SOSE)*, pages 178–183. IEEE, 2022.

L. Apvrille and B. Sultan. System architects are not alone anymore: Automatic system modeling with ai. In *International Conference on Model-Driven Engineering and Software Development*, volume 1, pages 27–38, 2024.

M. Bajaj, S. Friedenthal, and E. Seidewitz. Systems modeling language (sysml v2) support for digital engineering. *INSIGHT*, 25:19–24, 2022.

K. X. Campo, T. Teper, C. E. Eaton, A. M. Shipman, G. Bhatia, and B. Mesmer. Model-based systems engineering: Evaluating perceived value, metrics, and evidence through literature. *Systems Engineering*, 26(1):104–129, 2023.

M. Chami, N. Abdoun, and J-M. Bruel. Artificial intelligence capabilities for effective model-based systems engineering: A vision paper. In *INCOSE International Symposium*, volume 32, pages 1160–1174. Wiley Online Library, 2022.

J. Cámara, J. Troya, L. Burgueño, and A. Vallecillo. On the assessment of generative AI in modeling tasks: an experience report with ChatGPT and UML. *Software and Systems Modeling*, 22(3):781–793, 2023.

C. Delp, D. Lam, E. Fosse, and C.-Y. Lee. Model based document and report generation for systems engineering. In *2013 IEEE Aerospace Conference*, pages 1–11. IEEE, 2013.

R. A Dunne. *A statistical approach to neural networks for pattern recognition*. John Wiley & Sons, 2007.

J. A. Estefan. Survey of model-based systems engineering (MBSE) methodologies. *INCOSE MBSE Focus Group*, 25(8):1–12, 2007.

J. A. Estefan and T. Weilkiens. MBSE methodologies. In *Handbook of Model-Based Systems Engineering*, pages 1–40. Springer International Publishing, 2020.

European Commission and Directorate-General for Research and Innovation. *Industry 5.0, a transformative vision for Europe: governing systemic transformations towards a sustainable industry*. Publications Office of the European Union, 2022.

S. Friedenthal, A. Moore, and R. Steiner. *A Practical Guide to SysML: The Systems Modeling Language, Third Edition*. Elsevier, 2014.

J. Gerstmayr, P. Manzl, and M. Pieber. Multibody models generated from natural language. *Multibody System Dynamics*, pages 1–23, 2024.

I. Graessler, J. Hentze, and T. Bruckmann. V-models for interdisciplinary systems engineering. In *DS 92: Proceedings of the DESIGN 2018 15th International Design Conference*, volume 2, pages 747–756. Faculty of Mechanical Engineering and Naval Architecture, 2018.

S. Han, H.-S. Choi, J. Choi, J. H. Choi, and J.-G. Kim. A dnn-based data-driven modeling employing coarse sample data for real-time flexible multibody dynamics simulations. *Computer Methods in Applied Mechanics and Engineering*, 373: 113480, 2021.

K. Henderson and A. Salado. Value and benefits of model-based systems engineering (mbse): Evidence from the literature. *Systems Engineering*, 24(1):51–66, 2021.

T. Huldt and I. Stenius. State-of-practice survey of model-based systems engineering. *Systems Engineering*, 22:134–145, 2019.

INCOSE. *Systems engineering vision 2020*. Incose, 2007. INCOSE. *Systems engineering vision 2035*. Incose, 2021.

ISO/IEC/IEEE. *Systems and software engineering—System life cycle processes (ISO/IEC/IEEE 15288:2015)*. International Organization for Standardization, 2015.

M. Javaid, A. Haleem, R. P. Singh, and R. Suman. Artificial intelligence applications for industry 4.0: A literature-based study. *Journal of Industrial Integration and Management*, 7(01):83–111, 2022.

Q. Khadim, Y. S. Hagh, D. Jiang, L. Pyrhönen, S. Jaiswal, V. Zhidchenko, X. Yu, E. Kurvinen, H. Handroos, and A. Mikkola. Experimental investigation into the state estimation of a forestry crane using the unscented kalman filter and a multiphysics model. *Mechanism and Machine Theory*, 189:105405, 2023a.

Q. Khadim, L. Hannola, I. Donoghue, A. Mikkola, E.-P. Kaikko, and T. Hukkataival. Integrating the user experience throughout the product lifecycle with real-time simulation-based digital twins. In *Real-Time Simulation for Sustainable Production: Enhancing User Experience and Creating Business Value*. Palvgrave, 2021.

Q. Khadim, E. Kurvinen, A. Mikkola, and G. Orzechowski. Efficient and accurate real-time simulations of coupled mechanical systems using the universal hydraulic surrogate. In *International Design Engineering Technical Conferences and Computers and Information in Engineering Conference*, volume 87387, page V010T10A030. American Society of Mechanical Engineers, 2023b.

Q. Khadim, E. Kurvinen, A. Mikkola, and G. Orzechowski. Simulation-driven universal surrogates of coupled mechanical systems: Real-time simulation of a forestry crane. *Journal of Computational and Nonlinear Dynamics*, pages 1–14, 2024.

M. Lemaire. *Mechanics and Uncertainty*. John Wiley & Sons, Ltd, 2014.

J. Leng, D. Wang, W. Shen, X. Li, Q. Liu, and X. Chen. Digital twins-based smart manufacturing system design in industry 4.0: A review. *Journal of Manufacturing Systems*, 60:119–137, 2021.

R. Liu, A. Kumar, Z. Chen, A. Agrawal, V. Sundararaghavan, and A. Choudhary. A predictive machine learning approach for microstructure optimization and materials design. *Scientific Reports*, 5, 2015.

A. M. Madni and M. Sievers. Model-based systems engineering: Motivation, current status, and research opportunities. *Systems Engineering*, 21:172–190, 2018.

A. M. Madni, C. C. Madni, and S. D. Lucero. Leveraging digital twin technology in model-based systems engineering. *Systems*, 7(1), 2019.

W. D. Miller. The future of systems engineering: Realizing the systems engineering vision 2035. In *Transdisciplinarity and the Future of Engineering*. Incose, 2022.

B. Mittelstadt. Principles alone cannot guarantee ethical ai. *Nature Machine Intelligence*, 1(11):501–507, 2019.

P. F. Pelz. Introduction. In *Mastering Uncertainty in Mechanical Engineering*, pages 1–24. Springer Science and Business Media Deutschland GmbH, 2021.

A. L. Ramos, J. V. Ferreira, and J. Barceló. Model-based systems engineering: An emerging approach for modern systems. *IEEE Transactions on Systems, Man and Cybernetics Part C: Applications and Reviews*, 42:101–111, 2012.

P. D. Saqui-Sannes, R. A. Vingerhoeds, C. Garion, and X. Thirioux. A taxonomy of mbse approaches by languages, tools and methods. *IEEE Access*, 10:120936–120950, 2022.
A. M. Schweidtmann, A. D. Clayton, N. Holmes, E. Bradford, R. A. Bourne, and A. A. Lapkin. Machine learning meets continuous flow chemistry: Automated optimization towards the pareto front of multiple objectives. *Chemical Engineering Journal*, 352:277–282, 2018.
M. Verdugo-Cedeño, S. Jaiswal, V. Ojanen, L. Hannola, and A. Mikkola. Simulation-based digital twins enabling smart services for machine operations: An industry 5.0 approach. *International Journal of Human–Computer Interaction*, pages 1–17, 2023.
K. Vinitha, R. A. Prabhu, R. Bhaskar, and R. Hariharan. Review on industrial mathematics and materials at industry 1.0 to industry 4.0. *Materials Today: Proceedings*, 33:3956–3960, 2020.
T. Weilkiens. *Systems Engineering with SysML/UML: Modeling, Analysis, Design*. Elsevier, 2008.
S. Zhong, A. Scarinci, and A. Cicirello. Natural language processing for systems engineering: Automatic generation of systems modelling language diagrams. *Knowledge-Based Systems*, 259, 2023.

5

Managing Strategic Flexibility in Industry 5.0 Transition: An Integrated Real Options and Strategic Foresight Approach

Jyrki Savolainen and Mikkel Stein Knudsen

5.1 Introduction

After a decade-long interest in the concepts of Industry 4.0 among both academics and policy stakeholders, contours now emerge of an Industry 5.0 (I5.0) society shaped by digitalization and novel applications of artificial intelligence (AI). In this chapter, we look at corporate investment strategies through the lenses of Strategic Foresight (SF) and Real Options (RO) theory with a specific focus on Industry 5.0 and system-level Digital Twinning. The chapter is written out on the authors' beliefs that an important part of theorizing about AI and Industry 5.0 relates to theorizing about investments on them: when should companies engage

J. Savolainen (✉)
LUT Business School, LUT University, Lappeenranta, Finland
e-mail: jyrki.savolainen@lut.fi

CSC-IT Center for Science, Kajaani, Finland

M. S. Knudsen
Finland Futures Research Centre, University of Turku, Turku, Finland

P. Aaltonen and E. Kurvinen (eds.), *Contemporary Issues in Industry 5.0*, Technology, Work and Globalization, https://doi.org/10.1007/978-3-031-74779-3_5

in transitional investments and how could they approach them systematically. Integrating Strategic Foresight and Real Options Analysis could be one such way to attain strategic flexibility under such rapidly evolving conditions.

Strategic foresight as a tool involves a set of practices that help organizations choose an optimal path forward by understanding the potential consequences of their decisions and, subsequently, attain a superior position in future markets (Metz and Hartley 2020; Rohrbeck and Kum 2018). The Real Options theory introduced by Myers (1977, 1984) suggests that companies should assign value to their potential investment opportunities like investing in publicly traded options of financial assets. Following this logic, the value of an investment can be calculated using the analytical option valuation formula developed by (Black and Scholes 1973), which takes into consideration asset volatility, time until expiration, and the possibility of alternative risk-free investment.

This chapter considers the requirements of Industry 5.0 in the capital budgeting decisions of companies. The central question is how one can grasp the emerging opportunities of technological change while avoiding sunk-cost investments in, possibly, soon-to-be-obsolete technology applications. Misinformed or ill-timed strategic bets on losing technologies might result in significant company write-offs and, in the worst-case scenario, even jeopardize the company's existence. On the other hand, a simple wait-and-see strategy that postpones major investments "until the future becomes clear" (Courtney et al. 1997) can create windows of opportunity for new competitors. This managerial myopia may lead to situations that neither defend the company against new threats nor take sufficient advantage of new opportunities. It is not an optimal way to approach fast technological transitions.

As for the definition of Industry 5.0, we acknowledge it to be a contested concept in the sense that there is no clear and accepted definition, and the common conceptualization has drawn "mixed reactions" (cf. Lu et al. 2022). There is already an extensive stream of research aimed at investigating challenges and enabling technologies (Huang et al. 2022), but summarily, we see the extant vision of I5.0 as human-centric and recognizes the role of industry in achieving societal goals beyond jobs and growth. It remains unknown what the new technological and societal landscape will look like, how the pace of the technological transformation will unfold, and how companies should prepare themselves. In this vein, the key question that this chapter strives to answer is how market incumbents, with technologically mature product/service portfolios, should attain strategic flexibility considering the I5.0 transition.

The novelty of the contribution rests on the attempt to produce a meaningful combination of two theoretical schools of real options and strategic foresight, which both can help strategy-making under uncertainty, but which have hitherto been siloed from each other. That is, this chapter discovers, surprisingly, that very few previous academic works have sought to integrate the two fields of ROs and SF. It is suggested here that ROs could be utilized for exploiting opportunities when the uncertainty is mainly of parametric (numerical) type whereas SF could serve as a more qualitative vehicle of opportunity exploration under structural and/or radical uncertainty. This is followed by an introduction of a sketch of a high-level decision-making framework applied to an emerging technology of system-level digital twinning referring to virtual models of the whole (industrial) systems, identified as one of the Industry 5.0 technologies.

This chapter continues with a literature survey which is followed by a more general introduction to the two schools of thought. Thereafter, we present an integrated framework of SF and ROs derived from the exploration versus exploitation dilemma. The primary contribution of this text follows as the applicability of the integrated framework is evaluated for I5.0. Since the integration of strategic foresight and real options is at such an early stage, this is presented as an explorative and conceptual model. Finally, the chapter closes with conclusions and discussion.

5.2 Earlier Works

The original idea of this paper was to draw insights from the previous literature that had already considered the integration of the two theoretical streams of Strategic Foresight and Real Options. To do this, the Scopus citation database was queried using the keywords “Real Option”,

"Real Options", and "foresight". A total of fifteen works were identified of which only three studies were selected after reading the abstracts. One of the main reasons for heavy filtering was that even though several RO papers did use term the "perfect foresight", they did it in a narrow sense to depict a situation where the pre-set numerical uncertainties would be known before something happens. Such studies did not fit into the scope of our inquiry, as we are specifically interested in circumstances without access to such information.

The first research effort found in this area was made by Collan and Liu (2003), who propose a partially automated decision support system that would collect and analyze information related to ongoing projects and employ a real options framework as a means of facilitating ongoing dialogue with decision-makers about alternative future courses of action. By assigning a value to each alternative, the proposed system helps decision-makers make informed choices.

Eriksson and Weber (2008) examined the role of real options in adaptive foresight and aimed to establish a tangible connection between foresight that generally promotes open participation of all interested parties in society, and decision-making that focuses on implementing targeted strategy development on an organizational level. The authors suggest that adaptive planning highlights the importance of keeping options open and postponing decisions to adapt to changing circumstances. As uncertainties become resolved, gradual increases in bets for different technologies should be made (ibid.). While the paper of Eriksson and Weber (2008) purportedly limits itself to public policymaking, the insights are applicable also on a corporate-organization level.

The last paper is a recent literature review on radical innovation by Tiberius et al. (2021). They imply that incorporating strategic foresight can boost creativity, while the use of real options can provide valuable insights for financial evaluations. However, Tiberius et al. (2021) note that the financial aspects of radical innovations remain a relatively unexplored area of research and suggest that further investigation, perhaps within the framework of a real options strategy, is needed to shed light on this topic.

As a conclusion of the few results of the literature survey, the intersection of real options and foresight has been acknowledged by a few authors so far. The possibilities of integrating the fields remain mostly unexplored. Probably, multiple reasons can help explain this conundrum. A simple explanation could be that, traditionally, the discipline of capital budgeting, and more importantly real options framework, has looked at investment with a limited timeframe and constrained uncertainty whereas strategic foresight takes a long-term perspective. Even though investments in capital budgeting are planned for 20–30 years, the practice of heavily discounting distant returns tends to result in decisions with short-term value maximization. On the other hand, the lack of interest in the topic in the literature may indicate that the idea has been considered too far-fetched to address previously.

As a conclusion, it is highlighted that this work is not a review of the literature but rather a literature-based attempt to synthesize accumulated knowledge of Strategic Foresight and Real Options. Hence next, we cover the foundations of SF and RO individually and then discuss the points of connection between these two schools that both deal with decision-making under uncertainty.

5.3 Theory

5.3.1 Foresight

The term foresight has been applied since the 1980s to describe an inherently human activity aimed at increasing organizational future preparedness (Schwarz et al. 2020). Foresight is *"the discipline of exploring, anticipating and shaping the future to help building and using collective intelligence in a structured, and systemic way to anticipate developments"* (Commission 2020). Strategic foresight practices in profit-oriented organizations seek to enable flexibility and responsiveness to counter potential disruptions (Marinković et al. 2022). Corporate strategic foresight is applied to build and support competitive advantages by interpreting changes in the business environment (ibid.). In contrast, corporate strategy refers to the process of making choices about resource deployment within an organization (see Bowman and Hurry 1993).

The well-known dynamic capabilities theory (see, e.g., Teece et al. 1997) revolves around the reconfiguration of firms' resources to remain competitive in the current market environment. Strategic foresight in companies links to these ideas as it is considered as a series of micro activities aimed at negotiating an organizational path toward the future (Fergnani 2022; Marinković et al. 2022). Here we use the terms *strategic foresight, organizational foresight, and corporate foresight* interchangeably, as is often the case in foresight literature (Schwarz et al. 2020). Interest in these activities is fueled by the expectations that these practices will help companies with high future preparedness attain a superior position in future markets (Rohrbeck and Kum 2018). Longitudinal analysis (ibid.) does suggest the hypothesis is true: firms with higher levels of corporate foresight practices seem to overperform the average on growth and profitability.

Strategic foresight in business literature is often manifested through scenario planning, although it is an umbrella term for a range of methodological approaches. SF encompasses agile focus groups, such as panels and workshops, narrative techniques such as storytelling or world-building, and more complex techniques such as road mapping, horizon scanning, or, indeed, scenario planning (Sakellariou and Vecchiato 2022). A unifying component is that the primary value of the mostly qualitative approaches stems from high uncertainty situations that render traditional (quantitative) forecasts less applicable (Metz and Hartley 2020; Wack 1985). If companies are looking at a "clear-enough future" (Courtney et al. 1997), there is little need for introducing alternative methods for exploring the future.

A risk of being too preoccupied with foresight has also been identified: when firms' peripheral vision capabilities exceed their needs, they are said to be "neurotic" (Rohrbeck and Kum 2018). Too much emphasis on managing distant futures, while failing to provide sufficient attention to short-term matters has been coined "managerial hyperopia" (ibid.). Therefore, good corporate foresight practices should trigger *appropriate* organizational responses instead of lethargy (Rohrbeck et al. 2015).

5.3.2 Real Options

The Real Options theory builds on the neoclassical assumption of a rational decision-maker who is interested in maximizing her current wealth by making informed decisions under uncertainty by balancing between the risk and return. It has been implied (e.g., Adner 2007; Trigeorgis and Reuer 2017) that ROs could serve as a framework for guiding investment allocation decisions under uncertainty. Anand et al. (2007) distinct two foundational strategic option types as *growth* to add commitment and *switch* to embrace flexibility. In the context of forecasting, Eriksson and Weber (2008) distinct between *robustness* to describe fixed/passive uncertainty mit igation measures and *flexibility* that require active monitoring and decision-making. The "success indicator" of Real Option Analysis (ROA) is the perceived economic value of the decision and the extant literature has found numerous use cases for ROA including Research and Development (R&D) (Rogers et al. 2002), closing industrial operations temporarily during market downturns (Brennan and Schwartz 1985), or managing construction projects (Guma and de Neufville 2008), among others. For an in-depth review of the most common uses of ROs, we recommend referring to Trigeorgis and Tsekrekos (2018) and Bengtsson (2001) which gives a more comprehensive account of how to apply real options analysis at the manufacturing system level. In the big picture, most corporate strategy-related decisions are optional and can be theorized in terms of ROA of alternative actions. Lee et al. (2018) write that essentially *"real option theory helps isolate optimal choices"*. Research has shown that real-world managers tend to follow *real options reasoning*, i.e., they implicitly or explicitly respond to the value of preserving future investment decision rights (Gunther McGrath and Nerkar 2004).

In this chapter, we are interested in the strategic-level problem setting with more than one real option at the management's disposal. Within this RO-portfolio context, qualitative considerations include, for instance, the fact identified by Barnett (2008) that ROs noticed and selected by the company are shaped by the contextual and concrete channels of information filters where the managerial attention for sales pitches is dependent on the decision environment. Ghemawat and Ricart i Costa

(1993) define two types of organizational entities: first, *control-driven* steered by a top-down decision-making institution to pursue static efficiency and, second, a *knowledge-driven*, bottom-up one with an emphasis to resort to new opportunities that foster dynamic efficiency. The extant RO literature seems to be focusing on the former, which can be considered as exploitative-type, whereas more scholarly efforts to operationalize ROs for explorative capability building would be required. And, to do this, strategic foresight is considered here.

5.4 Toward an Integrated Framework of Strategic Foresight and Real Options

5.4.1 Dilemma of Control

By definition, the term exploitation, following March (1991), is characterized by refining, being efficient, and implementing existing knowledge to produce positive short-term returns whereas exploration, as its opposite, involves the acquisition of information through innovation, discovery, and experimentation with uncertain and distant returns. Already Bowman and Hurry (1993) proposed that, in general, organizations are more toward exploitation activity until a major change in the environment forces them to initiate exploration activities. The contradiction between exploration versus exploitation in the face of Industry 5.0 is at the core of our interest.

The problem of optimal balance between exploration and exploitation investments in dynamic markets can be viewed from several perspectives. First, the risk of obsolete exploration investments is evident that can constrain the exploitation of future opportunities [see, discussion, e.g., in (Uotila et al. 2009)]. On the other hand, the Collingridge Dilemma highlights the role of control—*"When change is easy, the need for it cannot be foreseen; when the need for change is apparent, change has become expensive, diflcult and time-consuming"* (Collingridge 1980). A similar view on the assessment of new technologies being adopted is summed up by the maxim of Buxton's law, which states that rigorous assessment is always too early, until, unfortunately, it's suddenly too late (Barkun et al. 2009).

The dilemmas show the inherent challenges of acting optimally today to prepare for the future which is the shared foundational concern of both Strategic Foresight and Real Options. Over time, these two schools seem to have arrived at different conclusions on how. As the key difference, SF mostly builds on qualitative expert knowledge, while ROs build on the existence of traceable numerical uncertainties that are utilized to evaluate asset values. As observed by (Marinković et al. 2022), it is notable that (corporate) foresight methods lack profitability indicators as analysis outputs which is a gap in research that this chapter touches upon.

The requirement of traceable numerical uncertainties (or uncertainty proxies) practically limits the scope of ROs as documented, e.g., in Adner and Levinthal (2004) who write that ROs should be utilized in projects with specific technical implementations and whose value depends on quantifiable uncertainties. This observation is supported by Eriksson and Weber (2008) who note that the real options literature has primarily focused on simple exploitation problems in corporate finance, overlooking the existence of structural uncertainties. Barnett (2008) deducts that externally oriented organizational attention structures support exploratory, large innovative portfolios whereas the opposite favors small portfolios of incremental, "close-to-marker" options. It is not surprising that the bulk of existing literature on ROs to date has primarily focused on discrete, one-off investment projects treated as numerical exercises aimed at selecting optimal actions while at the same time, it is acknowledged (see, e.g., Bowman and Hurry 1993; Myers and Read 2022) that the long-term success of companies depends on the ability to strategically manage their portfolio of real options. We argue that the portfolio effects of having multiple ongoing projects in parallel are seldom addressed quantitatively as they bring several additional complexities and qualitative factors into the mathematical formulations taking the edge off the available RO methods. With regard to complexity, referring to Anand et al. (2007), the value of an option portfolio is dependent not only on the volatility and the number of individual opportunities but also on the correlation between the returns of underlying assets and the number of how many options can be exercised (resource constraints)—since new real options decrease the probability of exercising the existing options in the portfolio. Furthermore, having an organizational resources aspect in the RO context brings it close to dynamic capabilities theory (Teece et al. 1997).

5.4.2 From Sensemaking to Strategy

To bridge the gap between Strategic Foresight and Real Options, the role of strategy should be considered. Bowman and Hurry (1993) write that opportunities for strategies emerge only once they are recognized and require "making sense" of organizational resources that serve as access to them. Strategic foresight offers one possible primer for such sensemaking activities (Sakellariou and Vecchiato 2022). Foresight activities do not seek to predict the future but rather support organizations in *sensing* (Teece 2007) or *perceiving* (Højland and Rohrbeck 2018) different possible futures, opportunities, and challenges. Hence, we suggest that the nature of SF, as an act, locates itself closer to exploration than exploitation.

Others have pointed out that incumbent companies may have challenges in digital transformation, as managers often rely on prior experience and prefer familiar strategic choices (see, e.g., (Warner and Wäger 2019) for a discussion on the digital transformation of incumbent firms). Creating systematic sensing and foresight capabilities in an organization can help overcome this potential legacy bias.

Literature on SF highlights its participatory nature (Dufva and Ahlqvist 2015). Stakeholder involvement can help produce better SF results by reducing potential biases and blind spots, and, simultaneously, SF processes can be a vehicle for aligning organizational visions and strategies across involved participants. Consensus may not be a target, however, as dissent among stakeholders in itself can be built into scenario development as an important component (Metz and Hartley 2020). One possible benefit of strategic foresight capabilities for companies is to limit exploration costs by ensuring a truly future-oriented strategic basis of investment activities by narrowing down the initial scope of opportunities for *value creation*. Therefore, at best SF could function as an open discussion tool to focus information-gathering efforts before the capital budgeting processes are initiated (with ROs) that are confidential and aimed at *value capture*. In this two-stage process, feasible investments would most likely emerge once the high-value-creation capability implied by SF can be topped with a doable blueprint of value capture devised by the RO framework. For a detailed discussion about the value creation and value capture, we advise the reader to refer to Baden-Fuller and Haefliger (2013).

While strategic foresight might be useful as an input for one-off projects and investments, the conceptualization of foresight as a set of future-oriented capability-creating activities underscores the necessity of *continuous* foresight. Foreseeing and hitting a home run on one set of market trends—like Blockbuster anticipating the market for home video rentals or Nokia the explosion of mobile telecommunications—does not guarantee long-term success, if companies fail to foresee and adapt to market disruptions.

Eastman Kodak Company, one of the market leaders in analog photographing products, is often regarded as a "classic example" of strategic failure as it filed for bankruptcy protection in 2012. A less-known fact is that already in 1997 a seminal paper by Courtney et al. (1997) commended Kodak's strategic bet on digital photography products. The aspect that remains missing is that for decades the value capture element existed only in analog photography while digital photography was at an exploratory stage with value promise that was not realized until technological leaps were made in other sections of computing. From the management perspective driven by maximal monetary returns, it probably did make sense for Kodak to exploit its leading position to the maximum while keeping the, yet uncertain, digitalization as an R&D-based real option until the expiration date. When looked at this way, the case of Kodak's failure could be seen as a failure of strategic foresight on a large scale and, subsequently, the inability to exercise its existing call option(s) for digital photography timely enough to keep up with the competitors.

Summarily, strategic foresight *in itself* is hardly valuable in a company; the value rests almost entirely in the interpretation and uptake of its contributions, and, first and foremost, in the actions to which a company's SF might lead. Successful implementation relies on obtaining organizational buy-in across multiple levels, while also emphasizing the importance of consistent updates to ensure its ongoing value. It is essential to recognize that this tool serves as a decision support system rather than providing explicit paths to the future.

5.4.3 Narrowing Down the Strategy to Actionable Options

In contrast to SF, Real Options theory starts from an assumption that explicit, alternative futures are described, and the decision-maker is in a position to bet on them based on probabilities of resolving uncertainties. As such, RO theory provides two key insights for companies struggling to make choices of emerging technology. The first is the importance of keeping options open in uncertain markets to see how uncertainties unfold, while the second is the advantage of reducing the uncertainty with one's actions. To implement these guidelines effectively, it is often necessary to establish "toehold" positions in projects and monitor their value, allowing these real options to be exercised promptly when the time is right to capture the value held by the RO.

The above guidance is much easier said than done: in reality, first, many of the investments are large, lump-sum projects that do not allow for gradual betting, and second, it is hard or even impossible to devise exact rules for the right timing that would trigger the pre-structured organizational actions. To complicate the situation further, a concept of "shadow options" has also been identified (Barnett 2008), referring to opportunities that exist but are not currently being systematically managed or pursued. At the same time, these shadow options might be the most valuable, for instance, in cases where structural or radical uncertainty unfolds in unpredictable directions that result in futures not included in the initially drafted RO analysis.

The discussion of Strategic Foresight and Real Options theory is summarized in Table 5.1 for comparison. It can be stated that the SF in the general business context is a qualitative tool aimed at identifying scenarios and their future value-creation opportunities that one should explore to maintain long-term competitiveness. The difference in the RO

Table 5.1 Comparison of problem formulation of corporate foresight and real options

Problem characteristic	Strategic foresight	Real options theory
Business orientation	Exploration	Exploration and exploitation
Business value focus	Value creation	Value capture
Main type of analysis	Qualitative	Quantitative
Wealth maximization	Long-term	Current
Organization	Open and participatory, broad stakeholder involvement	Closed and confidential; specialist committee/manager
Renew unsuccessful projects	Not stated	No
Uncertainty type in projects	Qualitative (narrative)	Mathematical (parametric)
Development of uncertainties	Yes/continuous	No/static probabilities
Portfolio effects of technology	Sometimes/context dependent	No/restricted to single investment

theory should not be overstated, but Real Options are more restricted to the current state of affairs highlighting the exploitation of opportunities with given uncertainties to produce numerically proven wealth as of today. Due to market competition, the nature of the Real Options Analysis process is expert-driven and confidential. It strives to excel others by implementing specific projects while SF is kept open and produces holistic insights that as such may not contain a tangible business value.

5.4.4 Budgeting Toward Industry 5.0

It is posed here that the frameworks of SF and RO could complement each other. We expand on this proposition with two main objectives: firstly, to explore the potential of a combined strategic foresight and real options approach for identifying promising exploratory opportunities on a theoretical level; secondly, to evaluate the suitability of this framework for analyzing Industry 5.0 opportunities. According to Eriksson and Weber (2008), the role of strategic foresight is to first look across the identified scenarios and then select the technology options and policies with the maximum robustness and adaptivity. The primary task for the decision-maker is to assess the problem complexity for the task/organization and use strategic foresight to scope the landscape, relevant challenges, opportunities, changes, and options for value creation.

Strategic foresight is best suitable for situations that involve system-level changes and non-quantifiable uncertainties. It should be utilized to narrow down the feasible scenarios of interest. Then, *Strategic Flexibility*, discussed in recent research (see e.g. Brozovic 2018; Chanphati and Thosuwanchot 2023), can be drafted in broad terms starting with the aim of value creation. This can mean a long-term plan involving such elements as capability development through education to acquire a new skill base. In a landscape of rapidly evolving technologies, this type of broad flexibility fostering "shadow options" has value (Mankins and Gottfredson 2022) as it is still unclear what the right bet on the "winning" assemblage of technologies will be. Only after finite and discrete scenarios are possible to formalize explicitly, real options can serve as a vehicle for taking strategic actions aimed at value capture.

Capital-intensive industries typically make investments with a long-term horizon of 10–20 years or longer, which can limit their flexibility to change course in the rapidly evolving technological landscape, even when new, more efficient ways of doing business become available. While real options theory recognizes the option to abandon unprofitable ventures, often induced by technology changes, it's not a decision to be taken lightly due to the possibility of positive developments that could make the business profitable again. In other words, despite the "theory-level" valueadding flexibility of ROs, a company with limited resources is tied down with the investment decisions taken previously.

Therefore, the importance of being able to write down a discrete presentation of the problem in a manner that is compatible with the limits of RO methodology is underscored. This requires the uncertainties to be mainly of *parametric* type [see discussion (Langlois 1984)] and be able to represent them numerically. If the problem does not meet the requirements of quantitative RO formulas, also the benefit is likely to be negligible.

5.4.5 Managing Portfolios

The importance of investment decision formalization calls for more elaboration as it omits some of the flexibility aspects identified in the current real options literature on strategy. We suggest that from the point of view of a decision-maker, the ability to invest resources into multiple uncertain projects can be viewed as a "problem of multi-armed bandits" to a player at an imaginary casino who can choose between several slot machines and each time a machine is played it produces information on its return distribution. An extension to this problem is called "restless bandits" where the probability distributions change dynamically. As it is not known which of the slot machines bet at a certain point in time, one should conduct exploration by dividing bets before the exploitation phase—in this case, the investment decision.

As a well-known solution to this general problem, Gittins (1979) suggests that a rational decision-maker should utilize the best opportunity to the maximum before moving on to the next one which we see is the common case with capital budgeting aimed at producing maximum returns. That is, in terms of risk, rational businesses, like in the Kodak example, should prioritize the lowest risk—highest return activities when choosing between alternatives with different expected rates of return, and often there are no natural incentives for exploratory activities (= changing slot machine to another) over the exploitation. Therefore, system-level changes in the industrial landscape, driven by high-level legislation and top-down initiatives like Industry 5.0, are crucial in providing companies with guidelines for navigating their future economic risks when the actual business value remains distant.

Real Options Analysis falls short of identifying these faraway, yet possible, system-level changes in the business environment. Here, strategic foresight could help firms "build specialized sensors that reduce blind spots in their peripheral vision" (Højland and Rohrbeck 2018). This, for example, enables firms to identify relevant technological developments that are not yet directly affecting their operational environment today, being excluded from the capital budgeting analyses, but which *could* profoundly alter their industry in the mid or long term. The potential emergence of novel Industry 5.0 and AI solutions are one such example that are widely known but as abstract concepts, rarely convert directly into value capture propositions formalized as actionable real options.

With the help of strategic foresight, mature companies are, ideally, better primed to anticipate relevant change drivers in their given market space, which would make them gain lead-time advantages against competitors (Højland and Rohrbeck 2018) and limit their risk of legacy bias associated with relying on past experiences (Warner and Wäger 2019). However, since SF analyses are subject to inherent structural uncertainties, it is borderline impossible to assign precise economic values to the various opportunities identified.

5.4.6 Evaluation Framework Proposition

Based on the discussion provided so far, a sketch of an integrated framework is visualized in Fig. 5.1.

Reiterating some of the previous points, the integrative framework suggests the following stepwise actions: (i) *Assess the level and type of uncertainty* The first step for companies seeking to take strategic actions with technology investments is to assess the level of uncertainty surrounding their concerns. Different levels of uncertainty call for different approaches to devising a path to the future (Courtney et al. 1997). This step effectively precedes the visualized model, and given the assessment of the level of uncertainty may render the rest of the steps

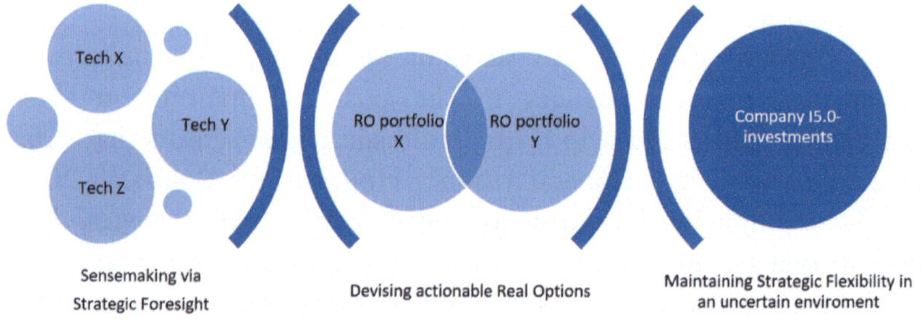

Fig. 5.1 Toward an integrative framework of strategic foresight and real options

unnecessary. After all, there is little need to maintain strategic flexibility if there is sufficient certainty about the right course of action.

(ii) *Sensemaking via Strategic Foresight* In investment cases surrounded by structural uncertainty, as the case is for mature companies pondering the transition to Industry 5.0, strategic foresight can help in sensemaking. When several simultaneous developments, some mature and some early stage, are happening in the technological and operational landscape, strategic foresight enables a better understanding of technological trajectories and potential consequences thus helping to provide insights into possible futures relevant to the given company. This narrows down the range of relevant courses of action.

(iii) *Devising Actionable Real Options* Once explicit, alternative futures are described, and the decision-maker is in a position to bet on them based on, at least subjective, probabilities of resolving uncertainties, real options theory can help isolate and highlight optimal choices. Real options thereby provide decision support for companies looking to put their money where their mouth is by investing in small "toehold" positions in emerging technologies.

(iv) *Maintaining Strategic Flexibility in an Uncertain Environment* The targeted outcome of the process is for the company to obtain strategic flexibility in uncertain and fast-changing conditions. It is important to note that to maintain strategic flexibility in this environment, the process has to be continuous and iterated.

5.4.7 Illustrative Application

To give an idea of how this framework could be used for budgeting in the Industry 5.0 context, we focus on real-time digital twinning (DT) of entire systems (system-level Digital Twins) which has been identified as one of the five critical technology areas of I5.0 by the European Commission et al. (2020). Instead of an off-the-shelf product, digital twinning is essentially a technology bundle consisting of several system components making the investment decision setting inherently complex for capital budgeting. While the system-level DT remains at rather a conceptual level at the time of writing [see discussion, e.g., in Savolainen and Knudsen (2021)], an evident potential exists to generate significant, positive impacts in many foreseeable future scenarios, which makes the technology relevant for detailed analysis.

In the scale of exploratory versus exploitative investments, the real-time, system-level DT falls in the former category: for mature manufacturing companies, it represents a potential disruptive shift in the organizational set-up and its manufacturing processes as well as in the ways how the end-products are being used. Therefore, the uncertainty is structural at the uncertainty assessment phase (i). However, at the same time, partial investments in individual parts of the manufacturing systems to enable digital twinning in the future might be considered more of an incremental technological adaptation linked with the current business model exploitation. In this regard, value capture potential exists, but sensemaking of the future (ii) could be further exercised to focus constrained resources toward the most potential directions of development.

Suppose a company arrives at a realistic plan during the initial phases of analysis to build a customized, real-time, system-level DT for its key product that is, say, some type of moving equipment. In that case, it would be necessary to position itself in the market to understand the most likely scenarios and, subsequently, identify relevant, traceable indicators that can trigger RO positions [phase (iii)] from the current set of options aimed for DT-product launch. Since the technology remains in the development stage standards are in constant flux, one has to resort to strategic foresight to formulate these underlying scenarios and then build capabilities that align with most of them.

The prospect of having to switch the entire Real Option (RO) portfolio has to be kept in mind in case of scenario breakdown which calls for constant revision of the selected course of action as suggested by the framework phase (iv). In the case of digital twinning, one could imagine some type of standard DT model that works irrespective of the underlying application and its embedded ICT technology which at this moment seems impossible. However, keeping the scenario breakdown in mind would enable the company to respond proactively and effectively to changes in the market and capitalize on new opportunities as they arise. This is in line with strategic RO literature, where Anand et al. (2007) states that a large portfolio of independent growth options should be preferred in high-volatility environments.

Due to the impossibility of predicting the future, it would be desirable for real option portfolios to have overlapping investments that are relevant irrespective of the scenario. We can think of these as "no-regret investments"; investments that would serve their purpose in any of the most plausible futures. It is worthwhile to consider whether some of the portfolio investments are "platform" projects that serve multiple purposes. For example, cloud computing capabilities can be used for both digital twinning projects (exploration) and advanced data analytics for refining existing business processes (exploitation). From the corporate perspective, developing such platforms may be more easily justified regardless of the scenario, as they are ambidextrous with regard to exploration and exploitation (see also, e.g., Sinha 2015) providing several opportunities for return on investment.

Summarily, putting the above example in context, companies can employ foresight to assess and contextualize potential disruptions (to their operations, organizational set-up, supply-chain relations, markets, etc.) entailed by leaps in digital twin capabilities. Foresight may also help illuminate possible implications caused by developments in peripheral fields, e.g., advancements in artificial intelligence. A viable guess is that foresight would also underline the possible future benefits of having access to greater amounts of data with higher levels of granularity, suggesting an incentive for initiating increased generation and collection today (Savolainen and Knudsen 2021). *Exaptation* (the utilization of existing knowledge or technologies, hitherto unutilized, for novel purposes) is a well-recognized source of innovation and expected future AI and digital twin capabilities make incumbents' large amounts of data make a promising exaptive pool (Garud et al. 2016) for potential future exploitation. Even if derived investments would not be economically feasible at present, this effectively represents a shadow option (Andriani and Cattani 2016) for future exaptation. Once the potential and plausible scenarios are laid out, companies can use real options tools to align their investment strategy for digital twins, taking into consideration also the value of shadow options. An investment portfolio that supports both exploration and exploitation activities is possible but calls for rigorous allocation of limited resources. If successful, the company can flourish across a wide range of possible technological trajectories of system-level digital twinning.

5.5 Conclusions and Discussion

This chapter focused on the strategic allocation of corporate resources in the transition process to Industry 5.0 (I5.0). It explored on a conceptual level how organizations could combine the theories of Strategic (or corporate) Foresight and Real Options as a practical tool to make better-informed decisions about resource allocation and position themselves viably in the rapidly evolving I5.0 landscape. The interest in the integration of SF and ROs lies in the authors' shared aspiration of finding more valuable, yet workable, means to navigate in uncertain technological transitions that would circumvent the method-specific problems of SF and ROs once utilized individually in the investment decision-making process. The key takeaway of this chapter is that SF could serve as a tool of organizational sensemaking and value creation that can be utilized to formulate more rigorous real options problems, while RO-framework should be seen as a tool that improves the value capture.

Technological advancements, not least in the realm of artificial intelligence, leave mature, incumbent organizations faced with radical uncertainty about the near-future operating environment. Investment choices about whether and how to commit to Industry 5.0 technology investments—exemplified in this chapter with system-level digital twins—are inherently difficult under these conditions. We believe that the suggested integrative framework could provide valuable decision support for organizations seeking to navigate through uncertain waters. Each of the two theories seeks to increase the number of areas that organizations can explore while decreasing the cost of each exploratory foray (Gunther McGrath and Nerkar 2004)—when applied together, we believe this is even more true.

As shown in the literature study, the idea of using strategic foresight and real option methodologies in concert has remained largely unstudied until now. Therefore, several future research directions exist out of which some of the most fruitful areas could include example case studies where the proposed integrated framework has been adopted and documenting its applicability. Secondly, a more rigorous, theoretical development of the integrated framework would be valuable as well that could meaningfully bring together the qualitative insights of strategic foresight with the numerical analysis of real options in the context of several uncertainties.

Acknowledgements This work was supported by The Strategic Research Council (SRC) at the Academy of Finland under Grants 313396, 335980, and 335989 (Manufacturing 4.0).

References

R. Adner. Real options and resource reallocation processes. In *Real Options Theory*, volume 24, pages 363–372. Emerald Group Publishing Limited, 2007.

R. Adner and D. A. Levinthal. What is not a real option: Identifying boundaries for the application of real options to business strategy. *Academy of Management Review*, 29:74–85, 2004.

J. Anand, R. Oriani, and R. S. Vassolo. Managing a portfolio of real options. In *Real Options Theory*, volume 24, pages 275–303. Emerald Group Publishing Limited, 2007.

P. Andriani and G. Cattani. Exaptation as source of creativity, innovation, and diversity: Introduction to the special section. *Industrial and Corporate Change*, 25(1):115–131, 2016. https://doi.org/10.1093/icc/dtv053.

C. Baden-Fuller and S. Haefliger. Business models and technological innovation. *Long Range Planning*, 46(6):419–426, 2013. https://doi.org/10.1016/j.lrp.2013.08.023.

J. S. Barkun, J. K. Aronson, L. S. Feldman, G. J. Maddern, and S. M. Strasberg. Evaluation and stages of surgical innovations. *The Lancet*, 374(9695):1089–1096, 2009. https://doi.org/10.1016/S0140-6736(09)61083-7.

M. Barnett. An attention-based view of real options reasoning. *Academy of Management Review*, 33(3):606–628, 2008.

J. Bengtsson. Manufacturing flexibility and real options: A review. *International Journal of Production Economics*, 74(1-3):213–224, 2001. https://doi.org/10.1016/S0925-5273(01)00128-1.

F. Black and M. Scholes. The pricing of options and corporate liabilities. *The Journal of Political Economy*, 81(3):637–654, 1973.

E. H. Bowman and D. Hurry. Strategy through the option lens: An integrated view of resource investments and incremental choice process. *Academy of Management Review*, 18(4):760–782, 1993.

Michael Brennan and Eduardo Schwartz. A new approach to evaluating natural resource investments. *Midland Corporate Finance Journal*, 3(1):42–47, 1985.

D. Brozovic. Strategic flexibility: A review of the literature: Strategic flexibility. *International Journal of Management Reviews*, 20(1):3–31, 2018. https://doi.org/10.1111/ijmr.12111.

J. Chanphati and N. Thosuwanchot. Strategic flexibility: A systematic review and future research directions. *Journal of Strategy and Management*, 2023. https://doi.org/10.1108/JSMA-08-2022-0134.

Mika Collan and Shouhong Liu. Fuzzy logic and intelligent agents: Towards the next step of capital budgeting decision support. *Industrial Management and Data Systems*, 103(6):410–422, 2003.

D. Collingridge. *The social control of technology*. Pinter, 1980.

European Commission. Strategic foresight—charting the course towards a more resilient europe. 2020 strategic foresight report, 2020. URL https://eur-lex.europa.eu/legal-content/EN/TXT/PDF/?uri=CELEX:52020DC0493. European Commission.

H. Courtney, J. Kirkland, and P. Viguerie. Strategy under uncertainty. *Harvard Business Review*, 75(6):66–79, 1997.

Mikko Dufva and Toni Ahlqvist. Knowledge creation dynamics in foresight: A knowledge typology and exploratory method to analyse foresight workshops. *Technological Forecasting and Social Change*, 94:251–268, 2015. 10.1016/j. techfore.2014.10.007. URL https://doi.org/10.1016/j.techfore.2014. 10.007.

Erik A. Eriksson and K. Matthias Weber. Adaptive foresight: Navigating the complex landscape of policy strategies. *Future-Oriented Technology Analysis (FTA): Impact on Policy and Decision Making*, 75(4):462–482, 2008. https://doi.org/10.1016/j.techfore.2008.02.006.

Directorate-General for Research European Commission, Innovation, and Jan Müller. Enabling technologies for industry 5.0: Results of a workshop with europe's technology leaders, 2020.

Alessandro Fergnani. Corporate foresight: A new frontier for strategy and management. *Academy of Management Perspectives*, 36(2):820–844, 2022. https://doi.org/10.5465/amp.2018.0178.

Raghu Garud, Joel Gehman, and Alessandro P Giuliani. Technological exaptation: A narrative approach. *Industrial and Corporate Change*, 25(1):149–166, 2016. https://doi.org/10.1093/icc/dtv050.

Pankaj Ghemawat and Joan E Ricart i Costa. The organizational tension between static and dynamic efficiency. *Strategic Management Journal*, 14:59–73, 1993

John C Gittins. Bandit processes and dynamic allocation indices. *Journal of the Royal Statistical Society: Series B (Methodological)*, 41(2):148–164, 1979.

Ali Guma and Richard de Neufville. *A Real Options Analysis of a Vertically Expandable Real Estate Development*, volume Master of *Department of Urban Studies and Planning*. MIT, 2008.

Rita Gunther McGrath and Atul Nerkar. Real options reasoning and a new look at the r&d investment strategies of pharmaceutical firms. *Strategic Management Journal*, 25(1):1–21, 2004. https://doi.org/10.1002/smj.358.

Jonas Højland and René Rohrbeck. The role of corporate foresight in exploring new markets—evidence from 3 case studies in the bop markets. *Technology Analysis & Strategic Management*, 30(6):734–746, 2018. https://doi.org/10.1080/09537325.2017. 1337887.

Shaowei Huang, Bin Wang, Xiaomeng Li, Peng Zheng, Dimitris Mourtzis, and Lihui Wang. Industry 5.0 and society 5.0—comparison, complementation and co-evolution. *Journal of Manufacturing Systems*, 64:424–428, 2022. doi: 10. 1016/j.jmsy.2022.07.010.

Richard N Langlois. Internal organization in a dynamic context: Some theoretical considerations. In M Jussawalla and H Ebenfield, editors, *Communication and Information Economics: New Perspectives*, volume 49, pages 23–49. North-Holland, 1984.

Joon Mahn Lee, Jae Chul Park, and Timothy B Folta. Ceo career horizon, corporate governance, and real options: The role of economic short-termism. *Strategic Management Journal*, 39(10):2703–2725, 2018. https://doi.org/10.1002/smj.2929.

Yushun Lu, Hongwei Zheng, Salil Chand, Wenjun Xia, Zhong Liu, Xun Xu, Lihui Wang, Zhiqiang Qin, and Jiale Bao. Outlook on human-centric

manufacturing towards industry 5.0. *Journal of Manufacturing Systems*, 62:612–627, 2022. https://doi.org/10.1016/j.jmsy.2022.02.001.
Michael Mankins and Mark Gottfredson. Strategy-making in turbulent times. a dynamic new model. *Harvard Business Review*, 100(9–10):60–69, 2022.
James G. March. Exploration and exploitation in organizational learning. *Organization Science*, 2(1):71–87, 1991.
Marko Marinković, Omar Al-Tabbaa, Zubair Khan, and Jin Wu. Corporate foresight: A systematic literature review and future research trajectories. *Journal of Business Research*, 144:289–311, 2022. https://doi.org/10.1016/j.jbusres.2022.01.097.
Anna Metz and Paul Hartley. Scenario development as valuation: Opportunities for reflexivity. *Technological Forecasting and Social Change*, 155:120027, 2020. https://doi.org/10.1016/j.techfore.2014.10.007.
Stewart C. Myers. Determinants of corporate borrowing. *Journal of Financial Economics*, 5:147–175, 1977. https://doi.org/10.1016/0304-405X(77)90015-0.
Stewart C. Myers. Finance theory and financial strategy. *Interfaces*, 14(1):126–137, 1984.
Stewart C. Myers and James A. Read Jr. Real options and hidden leverage. *Journal of Applied Corporate Finance*, 34(1):67–80, 2022.
Michael J. Rogers, Anuj Gupta, and Costas D. Maranas. Real options based analysis of optimal pharmaceutical research and development portfolios. *Industrial & Engineering Chemistry Research*, 41(25):6607–6620, 2002.
René Rohrbeck and Marcus E. Kum. Corporate foresight and its impact on firm performance: A longitudinal analysis. *Technological Forecasting and Social Change*, 129:105–116, 2018.
René Rohrbeck, Cinzia Battistella, and Eelko Huizingh. Corporate foresight: An emerging field with a rich tradition. *Technological Forecasting and Social Change*, 2015. https://doi.org/10.1016/j.techfore.2015.11.002.
Elina Sakellariou and Raffaele Vecchiato. Foresight, sensemaking, and new product development: Constructing meanings for the future. *Technological Forecasting and Social Change*, 184:121945, 2022. https://doi.org/10.1016/j.techfore.2022.121945.
Jere Savolainen and Mikael S. Knudsen. Contrasting digital twin vision of manufacturing with the industrial reality. *International Journal of Computer Integrated Manufacturing*, 32(2):165–182, 2021. https://doi.org/10.1080/0951192X.2021.1972471.

Jan Oliver Schwarz, René Rohrbeck, and Benjamin Wach. Corporate foresight as a microfoundation of dynamic capabilities. *FUTURES & FORESIGHT SCIENCE*, 2(2), 2020. https://doi.org/10.1002/ffo2.28.

Sanjay Sinha. The exploration–exploitation dilemma: A review in the context of managing growth of new ventures. *Vikalpa*, 40(3):313–323, 2015. https://doi.org/10.1177/0256090915599709.

David Teece, Gary Pisano, and Amy Shuen. Dynamic capabilities and strategic management. *Strategic Management Journal*, 18(7):509–533, 1997.

David J. Teece. Explicating dynamic capabilities: The nature and microfoundations of (sustainable) enterprise performance. *Strategic Management Journal*, 28(13): 1319–1350, 2007. https://doi.org/10.1002/smj.640.

Victor Tiberius, Henning Schwarzer, and Salvador Roig-Dobón. Radical innovations: Between established knowledge and future research opportunities. *Journal of Innovation & Knowledge*, 6(3):145–153, 2021. https://doi.org/10.1016/j.jik.2020.09.001.

Lenos Trigeorgis and Jeffrey J. Reuer. Real options theory in strategic management. *Strategic Management Journal*, 38(1):42–63, 2017. https://doi.org/10.1002/smj.2593.

Lenos Trigeorgis and Aristotelis E. Tsekrekos. Real options in operations research: A review. *European Journal of Operational Research*, 270(1):1–24, 2018. https://doi.org/10.1016/j.ejor.2017.11.055.

Juha Uotila, Markku Maula, Thomas Keil, and Shaker A. Zahra. Exploration, exploitation, and financial performance: Analysis of s&p 500 corporations. *Strategic Management Journal*, 30(2):221–231, 2009. https://doi.org/10.1002/smj.738.

Pierre Wack. Scenarios: Uncharted waters ahead. *Harvard Business Review*, September 1985.

Kevin S. R. Warner and Manuel Wäger. Building dynamic capabilities for digital transformation: An ongoing process of strategic renewal. *Long Range Planning*, 52(3):326–349, 2019. https://doi.org/10.1016/j.lrp.2018.12.001.

Part II

Managing an AI Strategy

6

Creating Value by Combining AI and Other Open Technologies: Cloud Infrastructure as a Pivotal Asset

Hervé Legenvre, Erkko Autio, and Ari-Pekka Hameri

6.1 Introduction

Research on digital technologies and infrastructures has highlighted the importance of 'control points' for value creation and capture within digital infrastructures—i.e., bottleneck technologies and assets that exercise a disproportionate influence on the performance of a given system (Pagani 2013). We advance the concept of pivotal assets to describe the central role of cloud infrastructure as a shared value-creating resource within the digital landscape. The cloud infrastructure is composed of a proliferating stack of complementary technologies that support a wide array of digital resources and related computing services and make them

H. Legenvre (✉)
EIPM 59 Rue Antoine Rédier, 74160 Archamps, France
e-mail: herve.legenvre@eipm.org

E. Autio
Imperial College London, Exhibition Road, London SW7 2AZ, UK

A.-P. Hameri
Université de Lausanne, 1015 Lausanne, Switzerland

P. Aaltonen and E. Kurvinen (eds.), *Contemporary Issues in Industry 5.0*, Technology, Work and Globalization, https://doi.org/10.1007/978-3-031-74779-3_6

available to large user audiences (Piccoli et al. 2022). Specifically, we describe how digital incumbents and others have been strengthening the cloud infrastructure's ability to support supermodular complementarities in digital infrastructures (Henfridsson et al. 2018; Jacobides et al. 2018) by judiciously releasing open technologies such as open-source software, open datasets, pre-trained machine learning algorithms, open hardware designs, and other technical resources that can be accessed and harnessed with highly permissive licensing conditions. Such releases have not only helped build momentum into the cloud and AI and machine learning (AIML) ecosystems, but they have also boosted the capacity of the cloud infrastructure to support generative innovation and the creation and exploitation of supermodular complementarities.

Pagani (2013) described the dynamic evolution of control points within an industry structure as a shift in the positions where value and power accumulate. Pagani suggested that vertical industry structures tend to be weakened by mechanisms such as the entry of niche competitors, the difficulty for incumbents to address diverse market requirements, and the rigidities of their organization. This leads to a disaggregation of the industry structure. On the other hand, horizontal industry structures face forces that push toward a more vertical integration. These forces include technical advances achieved by some firms, which drove their market power and proprietary integration of specific subsystems. This resulted in the formation of strategic bottlenecks (Baldwin 2015) where the focal points of value creation and appropriation within the industry structure migrated toward the technical system's technical bottlenecks. Although Pagani (2013) comprehensively described a pervasive and continuous transformation dynamic of value creation and appropriation within industries due to digitalization, we have a limited understanding of the dynamic by which some technologies evolve to become technology bottlenecks within digital infrastructures and how the proprietary control of technical bottlenecks supports the creation of strategic bottlenecks within the corresponding industry structure. In this paper, we therefore investigate how specific control points not only emerge out of technical advantages and competitive forces but also through their relationship with other components within a complex technical system. More specifically, we analyze the emergence of cloud infrastructure by studying how such relationships are shaped and manipulated by the judicious release of open technologies.

This article starts by describing cloud infrastructure, its history, and its technical architecture. We then describe how different layers of the cloud infrastructures interrelate and generate value through supermodular complementarities. This allows us to characterize cloud infrastructure as a pivotal asset that resides at the crossing point of multilateral supermodular complementarities.

6.2 Digital Infrastructures, Cloud Infrastructure, and Cloud technology Ecosystems

In this section, our focus is on digital, cloud, and AI and machine learning (AIML) infrastructures and their related developer and technology provider communities. Digital infrastructure is a: *"shared, open (and unbounded), heterogeneous and evolving socio-technical system.consisting of a set of IT capabilities and their user, operations and design communities"* (Hanseth and Lyytinen 2010). Digital infrastructures enable the functioning of the economy and society, including firms and industries. Unlike specific information systems, digital infrastructures are not defined by a distinct set of functions, and unlike specific applications, they do not have strict boundaries (Bygstad 2010; Hanseth and Modol 2021). Instead, digital infrastructures are shared, constantly evolving, heterogeneous, and open sociotechnical systems of digital technologies and capabilities whose evolution is non-linear, path-dependent, and influenced by network effects and unbounded learning in user, operations, and design communities (Hanseth and Lyytinen 2010; Hanseth and Modol 2021). They are systems of systems, composed of heterogeneous digital capabilities and related technologies and their respective user, operator, and design communities. The easy combinability inherent in digital technologies means that different communities can be recursively related, and as such constitutes a potent enabler of generative innovation (Bygstad 2010; Henfridsson et al. 2018; Yoo et al. 2012).

Digital infrastructures are composites of more specialized technology infrastructures that form identifiable wholes and are composed of specialized technology stacks, or constellations of interrelated technologies. Relevant to our discussion is the cloud infrastructure and a distinct, identifiable whole within it, the AI and machine learning (AIML) infrastructure. The AIML infrastructure constitutes a distinct subset of the wider cloud infrastructure, yet it also constitutes a distinct technology stack that is embedded in the wider cloud infrastructure.

Finally, specialized technology stacks are nurtured by technology providers and developer communities. We denote the combination of a specialized technology stack and its developer community a technology ecosystem, an example of which is the AIML ecosystem. The AIML ecosystem partially overlaps with and is embedded within the wider cloud infrastructure.

6.3 Cloud Infrastructure: History and Technical Architecture

We review the emergence and evolution of cloud services from the early aspiration to offer computing as a utility service up to the dominance of AWS, Microsoft Azure, and Google Cloud as key providers of public cloud services. We describe the key characteristics of cloud services such as on-demand availability, the pay-per-use commercial model, and the provision of software and cloud infrastructure as a service. We then describe the technical architecture of cloud services and how it meshes diverse digital resources and organizations.

In the 1960s, Joseph Carl Robnett Licklider was a leading computer scientist and instrumental in the creation of the Advanced Research Projects Agency Network (ARPANET), a precursor to the modern Internet. Licklider saw the potential of connecting computers and people to create a global information and communication network. He envisioned a future where people could access information and computing resources from anywhere and collaborate in real time.

In 2002, Amazon Web Services (AWS) was launched to offer cloud-based storage to businesses. In 2006, it started allowing users to rent virtual computing resources on demand and established the model under which cloud providers offer a platform for developers to build on and deploy applications. In the following years, other major cloud providers such as Microsoft and Google entered the market, with their cloud-based service platforms. As a result, the adoption of cloud services accelerated rapidly, coinciding with the rapid growth in the use of mobile devices, the rise of big data, and eventually, the widespread adoption of machine learning technologies.

In 2009, a paper authored by researchers from the University of Berkeley summarized the key characteristics and advantages of cloud services (Armbrust et al. 2010). This paper was one of the first to describe cloud services, applications, and the underlying hardware as digital resources that were provided as a service. Organized this way, cloud infrastructures offer benefits, including access to infinite computing resources on demand, thereby eliminating the need to plan and provision these resources internally. Under the cloud as a service model, users can increase their access to computing resources when they need it without the need to make an upfront investment in an internal computing capacity. Instead, users of a cloud service pay for the use of cloud resources as they access them. Today, the cloud infrastructure has become a general-purpose technology that is driving digitalization within virtually all sectors.

Today, cloud services provide any organization with the capability to easily aggregate data from different sources, interconnect different stakeholders, technologies, and resources, and scale their operations as needed. By leveraging these capabilities, organizations can gain deeper insights into their data, improve their operations, and create new opportunities for innovation and growth. Cloud computing services have become central to digitalization and digital transformation.

The cloud services market is dominated by a few major players, including Amazon Web Services (AWS), Microsoft Azure, and Google Cloud Platform (GCP). These companies currently hold the largest market share in the cloud service market. This domination results from the investments these companies have made to expand their infrastructure including all their data centers, and the provision of a wide range of services and capabilities to their customers.

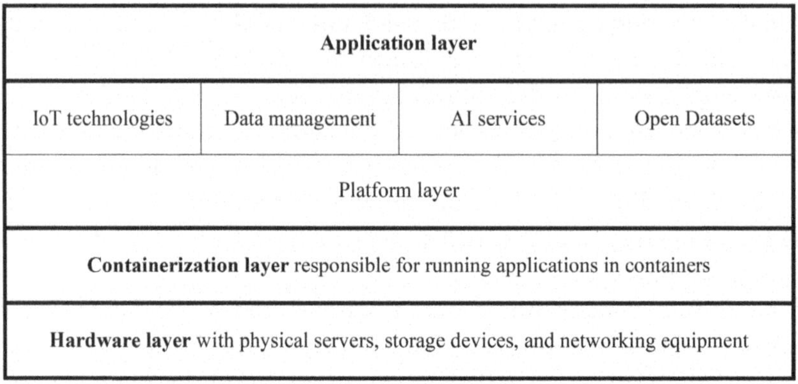

Fig. 6.1 Cloud technology ecosystem as a layered technical system

We describe a cloud infrastructure as a layered technical system starting with hardware at the bottom and ending with applications at the top (see Fig. 6.1).

At the bottom of the cloud technology stack is the hardware layer. This layer consists of physical servers including computing power, storage devices, and networking equipment. These components are housed in a data center, which is a large facility designed to provide space, power, and cooling for these devices.

Above the physical infrastructure, there is the containerization layer. This layer is responsible for running applications in software containers, which are lightweight and portable. Kubernetes is an open-source project and one of the most popular container orchestration platforms used in cloud infrastructures. It automates the deployment, scaling, and management of containerized applications.

Above the containerization layer, there is the platform layer. This layer provides pre-built services and tools that developers can use to develop, test, and deploy their applications. These services include databases and other data management tools such as Hadoop, Elasticsearch, MongoDB, and others, which are commonly used in this layer.

The platform layer of the cloud infrastructure also provides Internet of Things (IoT) services and technologies. IoT devices can communicate with cloud servers and services using various communication protocols.

In this layer, IoT devices can be connected to the cloud, and their data can be collected, stored, and analyzed to provide insights and drive decision-making. The platform layer of the cloud infrastructure stack can provide pre-built IoT services that developers can use to build IoT applications.

The platform layer of the cloud infrastructure also provides pre-built AI services that developers can use to build intelligent applications. AI models can be deployed using containerization or serverless technologies. Cloud providers also offer AI services such as speech recognition, natural language processing, image recognition, and computer vision that can be directly integrated into applications.

The platform layer of the cloud infrastructure also provides open datasets that can be stored and accessed in the cloud infrastructure. Cloud providers provide a curated list of open datasets that can be accessed by developers to further train and specialize pre-trained machine learning algorithms and AI models, generate insights, and drive decision-making.

Finally, at the top of the cloud infrastructure stack, there is the application layer. This layer is where the actual applications run. The applications are sometimes organized as 'digital resources'—i.e., algorithmically coded functionalities that can be accessed through a simple programmatic interface and bundled with other functionalities to create novel value offerings. These applications can be web-based, mobile, or desktop-based, and they can be developed using a variety of programming languages and frameworks.

6.4 Background: Appropriation Value in Digital Infrastructures

According to Pagani (2013), the migration of control points within an industry architecture prompts corresponding shifts in the concentration of power and value appropriation ability. Vertical industry architectures tend to be eroded by niche competition, sub-optimal ability to satisfy heterogeneous demand, and organizational rigidities. All these forces drive disaggregation within the industry architecture. Conversely, horizontal industry architectures tend to exhibit forces that tend toward greater vertical integration. These include technical advances, accumulation of market power, and proprietary integration of individual subsystems, each facilitating the formation of strategic bottlenecks (Baldwin 2015). Although Pagani describes a constant dynamic of shifting loci for value creation and appropriation within industries, we only have a limited understanding of how some assets and not others become central to an industry architecture during a period of industry disaggregation. While the ability to control bottleneck technologies (technologies that exercise a disproportionate effect on the user-perceived performance of a given technological system) plays a key role in the evolving dynamic of value creation and appropriation within industry structures, less is known about how some technologies end up becoming bottlenecks (Jacobides and Tae 2015). We suggest that technology bottlenecks are decided by the configuration of their relationships with other technologies and complementary assets. As described by (Asgari et al. 2017) during periods of technological discontinuity, a broad reconfiguration of the industry's capability base occurs as new complements are needed to enhance the collective value creation potential of a group of complementary and complementary, often co-specialized assets. In this article, we therefore extend the technology control argument by elaborating a logic of relationships and complementarities among technologies within the industry's technology base.

The concept of complementarity helps illuminate how value is created and captured within digital infrastructures. In economics, complementarities are defined as synergies that make a bundle of technology and complementary resource(s) more valuable in combination than what the combined value of these is in isolation. When complementary technologies are bundled into a system, the value of the system becomes superior to the sum of the values of individual parts. In such systems, value is usually not distributed equally among the providers of different components: those modules that exercise a disproportionate effect on user-perceived value allow their providers to appropriate a greater share of the value created by the system as a whole. Understanding the characteristics of complementarities and how they shape system-level performance is therefore important.

Helfat (2002) distinguished between core and complementary capabilities where a complementary capability can only exist because of the core resource it complements. A mobile application needs a platform (IoS or Android) to function. This represents a unilateral complementarity, as the platform can exist without many of the mobile applications, whereas individual applications always require a platform to run. Building on Teece (1986) and Helfat (2002), also distinguished between generalized and specialized complementary capabilities. Specialized complementary capabilities are applicable in specific settings only whereas generalized ones apply to a broad range of settings. A mobile application is typically focused on a specific setting while the mobile platform can support a broad range of settings.

The concept of supermodular complementarities helps uncover the impact of complementarities on value creation and appropriation within technical systems (Jacobides et al. 2018; Topkis 1978; Milgrom and Roberts 1990). A supermodular complementary refers to a situation where there exist increasing returns to the joint production and or consumption of the complements: As the perception of a smartphone operating system's value increases, a growing number of applications are developed; and the higher the number of open-source developers, the quality and perceived value of Linux grows in a nonlinear way. Supermodular complementarities are different from 'unique' and 'generic' complementarities. In the case of 'unique' complementarities, the value of the components is greater when consumed together, but there are no increasing returns: for example, a car represents the greater value when complemented with tires, but increasing the number of different tires does not generate significant additional value. Generic complementarities exist when two items are more valuable when jointly consumed, but the components can be consumed jointly with many other components as well (e.g., house and furniture).

In the digital sector, mobile operating systems, such as iOS and Android, provide a platform for third-party developers to create and distribute apps. The more users that use the platform, the more valuable the platform becomes for app developers, as the platform offers developers access to more potential customers for their apps. There therefore exists a supermodular relationship between the operating system and its application developers. However, the reverse relationship is not automatic. Although the value of the smartphone operating system for app developers increases in relationship with the size of its user base, the value of the mobile operating system for users may not increase in relationship with the number of apps available, as users may be indifferent to many of the available apps. This creates a unilateral supermodular complementarity between the platform and app developers. The platform's success depends more on its ability to attract and retain high-quality app developers rather than simply increasing the raw number of apps, and the proliferation of low-quality apps may even undermine the value of the smartphone operating system, as its perceived quality suffers in the eyes of users. The relationship between smart phone platforms and app developers may also change due to technical developments. Over time, as new developer tools such as React Native have emerged to support the easy portability of applications across smartphone platforms, this has reduced the dependency of individual developers upon any specific smartphone platform.

Cloud infrastructure constitutes a complex, multi-layered technology stack that exhibits a wide array of complementarities and various degrees of co-specialization among its constituent technologies and assets. It therefore provides a rich context for the study of how different kinds of complementarities emerge and evolve among varyingly co-specialized technologies and assets and how such developments affect both the system's value creation potential as a whole, as well as the ability of different participants to appropriate their share of the collectively created value. We next describe our research method.

6.5 Analysis of the Digital Technology Ecosystems

Since 2018, we have investigated different technology ecosystems that are part of the cloud infrastructure. We have investigated how open technologies shape competitive advantages in digital infrastructures (Legenvre et al. 2022; Autio et al. 2023) and how technology ecosystems combine distant capabilities for smart industries (Bernardes and Legenvre 2022). We have also explored how Alphabet has been building and driving ecosystem momentum within the AI and ML (AIML) technology ecosystem through the judicious release of previously proprietary technologies into the public domain (Autio et al. 2022). More recently, we have begun to explore open-source ventures and data ecosystems. Cloud infrastructure appears as a foundation technology in all our investigations. For the present discussion, we use data collected during our various research efforts to describe the complementarity dynamics that surround cloud infrastructure.

In this section, we review how some complementarity dynamics surrounding cloud infrastructure have unfolded over time. We start with the hardware layer before moving up the cloud technology stack.

6.5.1 Hardware Layer

Within the hardware layer, the Open Compute Project (OCP), initiated by Facebook, is an open hardware initiative that supports the design of data center hardware such as computer servers. By releasing and creating open hardware designs, companies active in the OCP community have enabled hyperscale companies including cloud computing platforms such as Google and Microsoft to build, expand, and enhance their data center infrastructure rapidly and flexibly. By using OCP-compliant servers, storage devices, and many other technologies, cloud providers also benefit from innovations that improve their performance and reduce their energy consumption and operating costs. In turn, companies' activities within the OCP take advantage of the growing demand generated by their clients. An open hardware initiative reduces transaction costs, as dependencies on suppliers are eliminated for companies who buy in large volumes. It also reduces search costs, as the community attracts innovators interested in taking part in industry development. The relationship between the OCP and cloud platforms is characterized by supermodular complementarity, as more progress on the OCP side makes cloud services more valuable.

Furthermore, an open hardware community such as the OCP creates further synergies among hardware technologies, as diverse and distant capabilities are meshed by this community. This supports diverse, concurrent, and mutually reinforcing super-modular complementarities across hardware capabilities within the OCP ecosystem. Collectively, these can be characterized as multilateral supermodular complementarities. The modular structure and widely adopted interface standards of the OCP ecosystem support the flexible creation and exploitation of new supermodular complementarities, as new technical advances can be rapidly co-opted throughout the system. For example, the introduction of a new cooling technology can be easily integrated across a range of complementary technologies within the OCP system. This is possible as the OCP has facilitated the emergence, around a modular and open architecture, of a community that drives innovation and generates value mostly captured by the companies who deploy data centers on a large scale. Companies such as Meta, Microsoft, and Google have unleashed and profited from innovation synergies among complementary and co-specialized capabilities on the hardware side. In a thriving ecosystem such as the OCP, ample business opportunities can be seized by ecosystem participants who also benefit from simple access to one another's capabilities and from sharing knowledge and resources.

6.5.2 Containerization Layers

In the containerization layer, Kubernetes and Apache Mesos are open-source container orchestration platforms that enable the efficient creation and management of cloud resources. The relationship between containerization technologies and cloud platforms is characterized by supermodular complementarity, as more of one makes the other more valuable.

By using these open-source solutions, organizations can deploy and scale applications in the cloud more easily, which can increase the value of cloud platforms. Moreover, the open-source nature of these solutions fosters innovation, as they are continually improved and adapted to the needs of the community. New projects and services continuously emerge from these open-source communities and enhance the value of the cloud platform as a whole. In turn, the success of cloud platforms attracts new developers to join and grow the open-source community and contribute to further innovation. This results in multilateral supermodular complementarities, as different projects can be mixed and matched to create value. Kubernetes is one of many open-source projects at the center of a broader developer community that surrounds the Cloud Native Computing Foundation CNCF. On the one hand, Kubernetes is a standard used by all cloud platforms. On the other hand, it is supported by a vibrant developer community of over 200,000 contributors and over 200 projects. This community produces generative spillovers and related use case innovation, as the CNCF community also counts hundreds of startups as currently active and contributing participants.

How Google Orchestrated the Emergence of the Kubernetes Ecosystem

In mid-2010 Google was lagging behind AWS and Microsoft in cloud services. To shake up the status quo, it open-sourced Kubernetes, the software containerization and data center management platform, to help clients more easily migrate into the cloud and potentially become customers of Google Cloud. With the 2015 release of Kubernetes, Google initiated an open-source developer community, and Kubernetes was handed over to the Cloud Computing Native Foundation (CNCF). Although this meant that Google lost proprietary control of Kubernetes, Google expected that the Kubernetes community would boost its capabilities and help establish Google as a recognized leader for Kubernetes and other cloud-native developments

The Kubernetes maneuver proved successful: in 2020, the Kubernetes developer community comprised 52,000 contributors, and in 2023, it reached 200,000. Kubernetes had dislodged open-source alternatives such as Mesosphere from their leadership positions, and in 2020, its adoption rate reached 91% of cloud-based container orchestration platforms. The Kubernetes maneuver proved successful, and Google's VP for Infrastructure commented in hindsight: *"Google had to make a bold move in the cloud space to be the long-term winner. Kubernetes has been a wonderful journey with highs and lows, but in the end, it has changed the game for cloud and computing at large."*

6.5.3 IoT Layer

IoT devices generate vast amounts of data, which is then processed and analyzed in the cloud to extract valuable insight and enable new applications and services. IoT technologies, by enabling access and communication of data, act as a complementary technology that enhances the value of cloud services. At the same time, by leveraging resources in the cloud, the value of IoT devices and technologies is enhanced, as cloud services help scale data processing capabilities and provide access to advanced functionalities. Moreover, cloud infrastructure provides IoT technologies and the data generated by IoT devices with numerous complementary capabilities, such as advanced analytics and machine learning that enhance their value and enable new applications. For example, by using cloud-based analytics and AI algorithms, IoT devices can detect anomalies, predict failures, and optimize operations. This ability to mesh numerous complementary technologies and capabilities supports multilateral supermodular complementarities across IoT, cloud infrastructure, data processing, and AI capabilities.

6.5.4 Data Management Layer

Cloud platforms, IoT, and other technologies have also benefited from the emergence of open-source software for data curation and data management. Tools like Apache Hadoop, MongoDB, Elasticsearch, and others have emerged as popular solutions for processing and analyzing large datasets in the cloud. The relationship between open-source software for data curation and data management and cloud platforms supports a supermodular complementarity. As more open-source tools are developed and deployed in the cloud, the value of cloud infrastructures increases for potential users, as the cloud technology ecosystem becomes more powerful and able to offer a more flexible platform for data processing and analysis across a wide range of use cases. Similarly, as cloud platforms become more powerful and flexible, the value of open-source tools increases, as they can take advantage of these resources to perform more complex data processing and analysis tasks. Then, as data curation and data management are dominated by open-source software, digital infrastructures can be easily integrated. Anyone can create new connectors that are made available to everyone to facilitate further integration. This ability to easily mix and match technologies facilitates the emergence of multilateral supermodular complementarities among data curation and data management tools. Also on a broader scale, these tools drive multilateral supermodular complementarities, as they enhance the value of all technologies connected to cloud platforms. For instance, open-source software available for data curation and data management has facilitated the development of IoT, AI, and machine learning technologies.

6.5.5 AI Layer

The rise of AI models and machine learning frameworks has enabled the creation of multilateral supermodular complementarities within cloud infrastructures, AI, and other adjacent technologies. The availability of pre-trained AI models for tasks like natural language processing and image recognition has accelerated the adoption of cloud infrastructures in an ever-increasing number of industries. This relationship between AI models and cloud infrastructures can be seen as supermodular complementarity, as more of one makes the other more valuable. For example, as more AI models are developed and deployed in the cloud, the value of cloud infrastructures increases for prospective users, as there are more resources available for training and deploying these models. Similarly, as cloud platforms become more powerful and scalable, the value of AI models and frameworks increases, as they can take advantage of these resources to perform more complex tasks and deliver better results. Beyond the relationship between AI technologies and cloud platforms, AI complements adjacent technologies as described already with IoT and data curation and management software.

How Google Orchestrated and Drove Ecosystem Momentum for AI Technologies AI frameworks and models have initially been released under source licenses by companies such as Google and Meta. In 2015, the academic community was making rapid progress in the development of AI technologies and applications, yet the technological base of the AI developer community remained fragmented. To address this fragmentation and drive momentum within the AIML ecosystem, Google released TensorFlow, an open-source machine learning framework that is used to train AIML models and design AIML applications. TensorFlow quickly gained popularity with academics and developers who could rapidly create and share AI models and develop complementary technologies. This led to the emergence of a large ecosystem of developers, online courses, books, open-source projects, complementary technologies, service providers, and AI startups, which was able to attract significant investment and client interest across all sectors. Google and Facebook, among others, continued to fuel this ecosystem by releasing rich datasets, pre-trained models, and other complementary resources under open-source licenses, further empowering the new generation of AIML computer scientists. This success was due to a deliberate technology-sharing strategy by companies like Google and Facebook, which made AI frameworks and complementary resources accessible to everyone. Part of the motivation of Google was associated with Google Cloud Platform which could now offer its clients an opportunity to develop and run their own AIML applications in the cloud. This was also one of the strategies used by Google to try to catch up with AWS as a cloud service provider

6.5.6 Access to Specialized Hardware

The emergence of AI has accelerated the need to establish access to specialized hardware for AIML model training. It has also created supermodular complementarities between specialized hardware and cloud infrastructures. Specialized hardware for AI adds value to cloud platforms by enabling the training and operation of AI and ML models in the cloud. AIML specialized hardware consists of custom-designed processors, and Tensor Processing Units (TPUs) that are optimized for the effective computation and training of machine learning algorithms and offer high performance while minimizing power consumption. The introduction of TPUs triggered a virtuous cycle where the increasing demand for AIML resources fuelled the development and deployment of more advanced hardware for AIML computation, which in return enhanced the capabilities of cloud platforms. As cloud providers integrate specialized hardware, they offer more valuable AIML services and attract more clients who want to use the cloud for machine learning workloads.

6.5.7 Open Datasets Layer

Open datasets act as complements that enhance the value of cloud platforms by allowing the development of new applications and use cases for users who can leverage the datasets available to train customized ML algorithms and thus improve their operations and decision-making capabilities. This relationship between open datasets and cloud infrastructure is characterized by supermodular complementarity: when open datasets become available on the platform, the value of cloud infrastructures increases, as there are more resources available for creating use-specific applications and training new specialized ML algorithms.

6.5.8 Questioning the Future of Cloud Infrastructure Supermodular Dynamics

The emergence of heterogeneous open technology ecosystems centered around cloud platforms has created a vast cloud technology ecosystem where all technologies can be easily accessed and assembled. This could threaten the ability of cloud service providers to capture extensive value beyond their core business over time. Today's supermodular complementarities could evolve into submodular ones when adding new technologies will create diminishing returns, and this synergistic effect will vanish. This could happen as technologies further standardize, as functionalities overlap, as the complexity of adding technology increases, and as the market enters a phase of saturation.

While, according to the data we collected, this is not yet the case today, we have seen already some of the cloud service providers maneuvering against their complement providers to try to capture more value out of complements themselves. For instance, Amazon Web Service started to compete with Elasticsearch, the open-source search and analytics engine, by launching its own managed service called Amazon Elasticsearch Service. The use of the word Elastic by Amazon Web Services was challenged in court. Amazon finally abandoned the use of the name Elastic, and the two companies settled their conflict and started cooperating again. This rapid change demonstrates that, for these two companies, harvesting benefits from supermodular complementarities was more productive than competing in markets and battling in courts.

Another maneuver of a cloud platform against its complement providers became visible after the launch of ChatGPT by OpenAI. Indeed, both Microsoft and Google now favor the adoption of a more proprietary approach for large language models. They justify it by the costs associated with the development of such models and by ethical considerations. A more proprietary approach is an opportunity for them to extract value from such compliments. In reaction, Meta, Amazon, and IBM now favor a more open-source approach to AI. This is a classic competitive dynamic; when leaders are tempted to go proprietary, followers coalesce and form open-source ecosystems to undermine their advantages. Simultaneously, we saw companies who own significant amounts of data that have been used to train large language models such as Twitter and Reddit charging for access to their API. So as Microsoft and Google turned against open-source complement providers, other platforms sided with them. We believe that open-source AI model providers will continue to challenge companies such as Microsoft and Google in the future thanks to both new technical advances and strong ecosystem momentum powered by supermodular complementaries. Such development will provide diversity from both technical and cultural perspectives. Adopting an open technology approach for AI models empowers communities around the world to develop and use AI in ways that reflect their unique cultural contexts and linguistic needs. We also believe that Microsoft and Google will keep contributing to the open-source AI movement as they do not want to upset academics, developers, and a large share of their complement providers. When supermodular complementarities have been reinforced by open-source forces, it can be difficult to return to more proprietary dynamics.

These two examples show that we are still in an era of supermodular complementarities for could technologies, but diminishing returns from adding complements could arise at some point in the future.

6.6 Discussion

We have described the cloud technology ecosystem and the sub-ecosystems it comprises. Our findings describe the cloud technology ecosystem as a nexus of diverse multilateral supermodular complementarities. Our findings show that cloud platforms occupy a pivotal position within digital architectures. Cloud infrastructures, according to the taxonomy of Helfat (2002), are a core and general technology that underpins all modern digital applications. Cloud platforms have benefited from supermodular complementarities with complementary technologies that help build and exploit them. They also benefited from supermodular complementarities within and among diverse technology ecosystems within the digital infrastructure. This is true within the OCP and CNCF communities. This is also true within and among IoT, data management, and AIML technology ecosystems.

Our findings lead us to define cloud platforms as pivotal assets that reside at the center of cloud infrastructures and related technology ecosystems. We call such an asset pivotal because of three characteristics. First, they occupy a central position within the overall cloud technology ecosystem, and, by extension, within the digital infrastructure of their users. They provide access to and interconnect diverse subecosystems of technologies. Second, the heterogeneous sets of technologies and resources that help create, build, and exploit cloud platforms exhibit multilateral supermodular complementarities, as all of them create value for cloud infrastructures and the platforms capture value. Such multilateral supermodular complementarities drive network effects at the technology level. The value of each technology increases as a result of the adoption and use of all complementary technologies within the ecosystem. Finally, we witnessed a significant share of open technologies among these complementary capabilities that allow cloud platforms to capture a large share of the value created within digital infrastructures. Open technologies not only reduce the costs of the technologies; they also facilitate the integration of technologies and the continuous emergence of innovation across complements (See Fig. 6.2).

Open technologies, as catalysts for innovation, provide a fertile ground for the emergence of new promising developments and spur cycles of resource diversification that reshape existing technological landscapes. This is not merely a quantitative expansion of resources that eliminates technical bottlenecks, but also a qualitative transformation in how these resources get combined and utilized. Through this process, the diverse technology ecosystems meshed thanks to cloud platforms continually adapt, evolve, and diversify in response to the opportunities and challenges posed within an open environment.

As resources diversify and networks of complementarities expand, open technology ecosystems become hotbeds for innovation. Novel recombination of resources gives rise to new solutions to old problems.

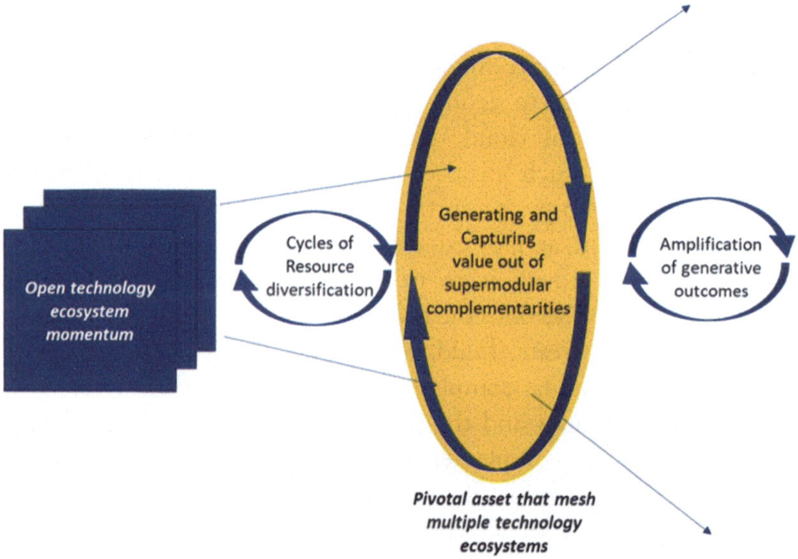

Fig. 6.2 Open technologies, pivotal assets, supermodular complementarities, and generativity

At the same time, transforming and combining existing resources creates functionalities that were previously unimagined. In this way, unexpected yet beneficial outcomes emerge from a generative process.

In this context, the role of supermodular complementarities becomes paramount. Supermodularity implies a synergistic relationship between resources, meaning the combined value of different modules is greater than the sum of the values of individual modules in isolation. Thanks to open technologies, this synergy amplifies generativity—the potential to create diverse outputs, including unexpected ones, from a set of inputs. The diversified resources, in their innovative configurations, form a complex network of complementary relationships, reinforcing each other and contributing to the overall value of the ecosystem.

Transitioning from a closed to an open technical system can precipitate large-scale shifts within the related technology ecosystem. This profound change can trigger a proliferation of diverse outcomes and trigger an explosion of innovation.

Centrality, heterogeneity, and openness enabled the emergence of supermodular complementarities for cloud platforms that act as the pivotal assets that mesh together diverse technology ecosystems.

6.6.1 Implications for Practitioners: The Strategy of Pivotal Asset Owner

Pivotal assets and their technology complements tend to exhibit strong supermodular complementarities that drive increasing returns to scale and benefit the owners of pivotal assets. This is achieved as pivotal asset owners facilitate the opening of the technology ecosystems that surround their assets. By doing so they attract new users and developers who all use and rely on the core and generic capabilities offered by their pivotal assets. Companies that control pivotal assets need to have the resources and capabilities to invest in developing open technologies. Thanks to the careful orchestration and stewardship of these diverse technology ecosystems they ensure that these technology ecosystems remain sustainable and that openness leads to beneficial outcomes for all stakeholders. As they do so, they can leverage their large networks of developers, customers, and partners to strengthen the complementarities between components on their platforms. This results in increasing returns to scale and winner-take-most dynamics markets structured around pivotal assets.

6.7 Conclusion

In conclusion, our research has highlighted the pivotal role of cloud platforms within the broader cloud technology ecosystem. These platforms occupy a central position and serve as access points that interconnect various sub-ecosystems of open technologies. We have identified three key characteristics that make them pivotal assets.

First, cloud technology ecosystems exhibit multilateral supermodular complementarities. The diverse open technologies and resources involved in creating, building, and leveraging cloud platforms generate value for cloud service providers and complement providers. The adoption and use of open complementary technologies result in network effects, where the value of each technology increases in conjunction with the adoption of other complementary technologies.

Second, a significant portion of such complementary capabilities is comprised of open technologies. Open technologies not only reduce costs but also facilitate the integration of technologies and drive continuous innovation across complements. They serve as catalysts for innovation, providing fertile ground for the emergence of new possibilities and diversification of resources. This diversification goes beyond mere quantitative expansion, transforming and combining resources in ways that reshape existing technological landscapes.

Lastly, the interplay between centrality, heterogeneity, and openness creates a generative process within open technology ecosystems. Supermodular complementarities play a paramount role in this process, as the combined value of resources surpasses the sum of their values. The diverse and innovative configurations of resources form a complex network of complementary relationships that reinforce each other and contribute to the overall value of the ecosystem sometimes in unexpected ways.

In the future, additional research could help further understand how diverse open technology ecosystems co-evolve to maintain generativity and continuously create value altogether. This could lead to a better understanding of how and why constraints that span different technology ecosystems emerge and how participants in complex interconnected technology ecosystems deal with these bottlenecks.

In summary, our findings emphasize the critical role of cloud platforms as pivotal assets within the cloud technology ecosystem. Their centrality, heterogeneity, and openness foster supermodular complementarity, driving innovation, and enabling the emergence of diverse and unexpected outcomes. By understanding and harnessing these dynamics, we can further enhance the value and potential of cloud platforms and their surrounding ecosystems.

Acknowledgements We extend our gratitude to Päivi Aaltonen and Emil Kurvinen for their editing of the book. Their valuable feedback and support have been instrumental in refining our work and enhancing the quality of our contribution. We are appreciative of their efforts throughout this project.

References

M. Armbrust, A. Fox, R. Griffith, A. D. Joseph, R. Katz, A. Konwinski, G. Lee, D. Patterson, A. Rabkin, I. Stoica, and M. Zaharia. A view of cloud computing. *Communications of the ACM*, 53(4):50–58, 2010.

N. Asgari, K. Singh, and W. Mitchell. Alliance portfolio reconfiguration following a technological discontinuity: Alliance portfolio reconfiguration and discontinuities. *Strategic Management Journal*, 38(5):1062–1081, 2017.

E. Autio, A. P. Hameri, and H. Legenvre. Open technology maneuvering in digital infrastructures. In H. Chesbrough, A. Radziwon, W. Vanhaverbeke, and J. West, editors, *The Oxford Handbook of Open Innovation*, chapter 30. Oxford University Press, 2023.

Erkko Autio, Hervé Legenvre, and Ari-Pekka Hameri. Driving infrastructural advantage: Google's strategic moves in ai digital technology commons. In *Academy of Management Proceedings*, volume 2022, page 16002. Academy of Management, 2022.

Carliss Y. Baldwin. Bottlenecks, modules and dynamic architectural capabilities. Finance Working Paper 15–028, Harvard Business School, 2015. Available at SSRN: https://ssrn.com/abstract=2512209.

E. Bernardes and H. Legenvre. Accessing and integrating distant capabilities in smart industry projects. In T. Bondarouk and M. R. Olivas-Luján, editors, *Advanced Series in Management*, pages 125–149. Emerald Publishing Limited, 2022.

B. Bygstad. Generative mechanisms for innovation in information infrastructures. *Information and Organization*, 20(3–4):156–168, 2010.

O. Hanseth and K. Lyytinen. Design theory for dynamic complexity in information infrastructures: The case of building internet. *Journal of Information Technology*, 25(1):1–19, 2010.

Ole Hanseth and Juan Rodon Modol. The dynamics of architecture-governance configurations: An assemblage theory approach. *Journal of the Association for Information Systems*, 22(1), 2021.

C. E. Helfat. The birth of capabilities: Market entry and the importance of pre-history. *Industrial and Corporate Change*, 11(4):725–760, 2002.

O. Henfridsson, J. Nandhakumar, H. Scarbrough, and N. Panourgias. Recombination in the open-ended value landscape of digital innovation. *Information and Organization*, 28(2):89–100, 2018.

M. G. Jacobides and C. J. Tae. Kingpins, bottlenecks, and value dynamics along a sector. *Organization Science*, 26(3):889–907, 2015. https://doi.org/10.1287/orsc.2014.0958.

M. G. Jacobides, C. Cennamo, and A. Gawer. Towards a theory of ecosystems. *Strategic Management Journal*, 39:2255–2276, 2018.

H. Legenvre, E. Autio, and A.-P. Hameri. How to harness open technologies for digital platform advantage. *MIS Quarterly Executive*, 21(1), 2022.

P. Milgrom and J. Roberts. Rationalizability, learning, and equilibrium in games with strategic complementarities. *Econometrica*, 58(6):1255–1277, 1990.

M. Pagani. Digital business strategy and value creation: Framing the dynamic cycle of control points. *Mis Quarterly*, pages 617–632, 2013.

G. Piccoli, J. Rodriguez, and V. Grover. Digital strategic initiatives and digital resources: Construct definition and future research directions. *MIS Quarterly*, 46 (4):2289–2316, 2022.

D. J. Teece. Profiting from technological innovation: Implications for integration, collaboration, licensing and public policy. *Research Policy*, 15(6):285–305, 1986.

D. M. Topkis. Minimizing a submodular function on a lattice. *Operations Research*, 26(2):305–321, 1978.
Y. Yoo, R. J. Boland, K. Lyytinen, and A. Majchrzak. Organizing for innovation in the digitized world. *Organization Science*, 23(5):1398–1408, 2012.

7

Analysis of Digital Twin-Related Competences in Manufacturing

Mira Timperi, Kirsi Kokkonen, Ilkka Donoghue, Lea Hannola, and Kalle Elfvengren

7.1 Introduction

Digital twin (DT) technologies are suitable for many purposes and offer various opportunities for companies. DTs have streamlined operations (Leung et al. 2022), enhanced resource efficiency (Golovina et al. 2020), provided foundations for novel businesses (VanDerHorn and Mahadevan 2021), and contributed to multiple sustainability aspects (Kamble et al. 2022; He and Bai 2021). To this day, DTs have been recognized as offering possibilities for various industries, for example, in aerospace (Jin et al. 2023), agriculture (Purcell et al. 2023), healthcare (de Boer et al. 2022), construction (Kan and Anumba 2019), and manufacturing (Kritzinger et al. 2018), where DT technology can provide value to production, maintenance, decision-making, safety, planning and design,

M. Timperi (✉) · K. Kokkonen · I. Donoghue · L. Hannola · K. Elfvengren
Department of Industrial Engineering and Management, School of Engineering Sciences, LUT University, Lappeenranta, Finland
e-mail: mira.timperi@lut.fi

P. Aaltonen and E. Kurvinen (eds.), *Contemporary Issues in Industry 5.0*, Technology, Work and Globalization, https://doi.org/10.1007/978-3-031-74779-3_7

training, remote access operations, and many other areas (e.g., Bao et al. 2019; Liu et al. 2021; Meierhofer et al. 2020).

DTs and other data-based digital technology solutions have garnered increasing attention in academia and the manufacturing industry for over a decade (e.g., Alnowaiser and Ahmed 2023; Liu et al. 2021) as their potential in terms of, for example, competitiveness (Lattanzi et al. 2021) and sustainability challenges (He and Bai 2021) have begun to be better understood. The importance of DT adoption is also recognized at the level of the European Union through EU and national funding initiatives. The research focus has increasingly turned from applying DTs mainly to product design to their role encompassing the entire business value chain and resulting in improved products, production processes, system performance, and services (Onaji et al. 2022). Previous research has studied, for example, technical and technological requirements (e.g., Damjanovic-Behrendt and Behrendt 2019; Liu et al. 2021; Semeraro et al. 2021) and business aspects (e.g., Lim et al. 2020; Minerva and Crespi 2021; Onaji et al. 2022), but the competences needed for DT adoption remain a rather unresearched area. Thus, this chapter investigates what competences are commonly needed to utilize DTs in manufacturing.

According to Nicoletti et al. (2020), the needed competences vary among digital technologies. They noted that the adoption of technologies is always, at some level, influenced by other factors, such as required investments and the regulatory barriers to market entry, which differ between technologies. Hence, single digital technologies should be examined separately as regards their enablers and prerequisites for adoption. One digital technology accelerator has been the Industry 4.0 (I4.0) revolution. I4.0 focuses on implementing connected and smart technology into different areas of the organization, such as production and product-service systems (PSS) (e.g., Frank et al. 2019; Pirola et al. 2020). The competence requirements stemming from the I4.0 wave have been studied by Kipper et al. (2021), according to whom professional education plays a pivotal role in securing the needed skills, and by Hernandez-de-Menendez et al. (2020), who concluded that future professionals must be able to exploit knowledge and add value in various collaborative domains. The successor of I4.0 is the Industry 5.0

(I5.0) revolution with sustainability and human perspectives. Due to the novelty and early stages of I5.0, only a few studies discuss its competence needs. One example of such a study is from Salminen et al. (2023), who found that the requirements vary depending on company size and the implemented technology. Also, the vast growth of artificial intelligence (AI)-based technologies is altering skill and competence needs at an accumulating pace (e.g., Morandini et al. 2023). All the abovementioned changes demand active assessment and vigilance from companies.

One commonly used approach to assess digital technology-related competence needs is the technology–organization–environment (TOE) framework. According to Baker (2012), the three context areas of TOE serve particularly the adoption and implementation of innovations. However, it has some recognized gaps: a review by Gangwar et al. (2014) summarized that the TOE framework does not consider sociological or cognitive variables, organizational learning, professionals' skills and experience, technology readiness, change management capabilities, security issues, or government- and country-related factors. Further, Horani et al. (2023) pointed out that it also leaves out individual characteristics, such as top management support. Considering the above, the research angle related to the needed competences in digital technology adoption is significant and topical—new and innovative solutions do not arise by themselves; rather, a wide variety of competences, skills, experts, and other resources are needed to design, develop, build, and maintain them. Thus, among competences, the required resources and collaboration perspectives are also explored. This study used a qualitative research method. The research was carried out through interviews and focus group workshops in selected companies in the manufacturing industry and their service providers. The chapter answers the following research question: *What competences are needed to utilize digital twins in the manufacturing industry?*

As a main contribution, this study provides a competence framework for DT and other digital technology adoption. The framework consists of four interdependent categories—technological, cognitive, soft, and managerial competences. Further, the results highlight that identifying competence and resource needs alone does not guarantee the successful adoption of DTs; many other aspects must be considered before the competences can be truly utilized, e.g., available financial and human resources. There are also many challenges in companies related to the concentration of skills in different functions and the lack of an all-encompassing vision. The researchers also noticed that ownership and responsibilities for DT projects in companies are not always clear, which requires comprehensive management of digital strategy and DT-related competences. Further, the adoption of DTs is seen to have impacts on companies' organizational structures.

7.2 Related Research

7.2.1 Digital Transformation Through Industrial Revolutions

DTs and other digital technologies are part of digital transformation and digitalization. Digital transformation is a pervasive, continual process depicting organization-wide change toward novel business models (e.g., Brunetti et al. 2020; Schallmo et al. 2017; Verhoef et al. 2021), whereas the term 'digitalization' refers to the transfer of analog information into digital data and the effect it generates. Digitalization helps to process information electronically, increase efficiency and flexibility, save process costs, and accelerate time-to-market (Köhler-Schute 2016). Interest in digital transformation and digitalization is evident. Previous research has found that digital transformation, digitalization, and digital technologies affect manufacturing business in various ways (e.g., Björkdahl 2020; Favoretto et al. 2022; Zangiacomi et al. 2020), for example, by powering industrial revolutions (Syam and Sharma 2018; Vrana and Singh 2021).

The ongoing industrial revolution, named I4.0, is steering the emergence of smart factories using cyber-physical systems and the IoT (Coelho et al. 2023). Following I4.0 is the concept of I5.0, which is based on the idea of merging sustainable development goals and digitalization provisions from the fourth industrial revolution through human-centric solutions, bio-inspired technologies, and cyber-safe data transmission (Farsi et al. 2021). The shortcoming of I4.0 is its limited impact on the socio-economic transition that is driven by both humans and technology (Jefroy et al. 2022). The focus of I5.0 is to correct these shortcomings. Thus, while I4.0 is focused primarily on economic objectives to be achieved through digital transformation and the automation of monotonous work processes, I5.0 will also bring in social and ecological objectives (Hein-Pensel et al. 2023).

According to a profound bibliographic analysis by Coelho et al. (2023), most of the papers associated with the fifth industrial revolution address how I5.0 will do what I4.0 did not achieve: promote a more just and sustainable society, where there are collaborative relationships between machines and humans. I5.0 enables more sustainable and technology-oriented workplaces through digitalization, AI, and robotics by optimizing human–machine–robot interactions and supporting the empowerment of humans rather than replacing them with industrial robots (Majerník et al. 2022). In addition, Hein-Pensel et al. (2023) identify the main elements of I5.0 as sustainability, resiliency, and human-centered design. According to Paschek et al. (2019) and Lachvajderová and Kádárová (2022), unsolved dilemmas for the future include questions of what skills are needed and are to be developed, what kind of rules for human and machine interaction must be defined, which impacts AI may have, and what conflicts may arise between humans and AI. Furthermore, the rapid development of innovative technologies, such as the DT, is affected by questions related to human and machine interactions, where the DT represents the real-world counterpart in a virtual environment. The accuracy of a DT depends on an AI algorithm and data quality as well as the physics and mathematical accuracy of the simulation model. The integration of both approaches creates a DT that can achieve accuracy close to the real-world counterpart. However, DTs based on AI and/or physics-based simulation call for new competences that organizations rarely have (Jaiswal et al. 2022).

7.2.2 Digital Twins in Manufacturing Industry

The concept of a DT is generally acknowledged as a promising and innovative research area, as well as a strategic way to improve current manufacturing processes (Lattanzi et al. 2021). Academic literature has provided numerous definitions of a DT (e.g., Bao et al. 2019; Liu et al. 2021; Negri et al. 2017; Wang et al. 2021). The term has been assigned various meanings and used for different purposes and application domains (Lattanzi et al. 2021). Originally, the concept of the DT was created in early the 2000s by Dr. Michael Grieves, who defined it as a virtual representation of a physical product or system that is upgraded constantly with data from the physical counterpart (Grieves, 2014). Over the years, definitions of DTs have evolved as research around the topic has expanded. For example, Lattanzi et al. (2021) summarized some significant definitions of DTs among their potential application areas in product lifecycles. Based on their study, DT concepts and technologies have gained increasing interest over the years in the industry. DT technology can have a significant impact on automation systems. Moreover, it may provide business value throughout the various product lifecycles in manufacturing. However, many research papers still focus on DT concept definitions, meaning that further research on DT systems in manufacturing is still needed to tackle the open challenges (Lattanzi et al. 2021).

Manufacturing companies use DTs to increase their flexibility and competitiveness and to forecast the health and performance of their products over their lifecycles (Lattanzi et al. 2021). Liu et al. (2021) have summarized the industrial application areas of DTs in respective lifecycle phases—they found out that most research papers on DTs focus on a single lifecycle phase, while only 5% of studies cover the entire lifecycle. Manufacturing (45%) and service phases (32%) are the most common areas of published DT research, while only 1% of research papers focus on the retirement or end-of-life phase (Liu et al. 2021). Li et al. (2022b) have analyzed the application areas of DTs in manufacturing through time dimensions, i.e., design, production, and operation & maintenance phases. In these lifecycle phases, DTs can serve specific purposes, e.g., simulation verification in the design phase, equipment monitoring in the production phase, and health maintenance in the operation and maintenance phases. The application areas of DTs in manufacturing (Li et al. 2022b; Liu et al. 2021) are summarized in Fig. 7.1.

The retirement or end-of-life phase is often not counted as an actual lifecycle phase, and knowledge about the behavior of a product or system

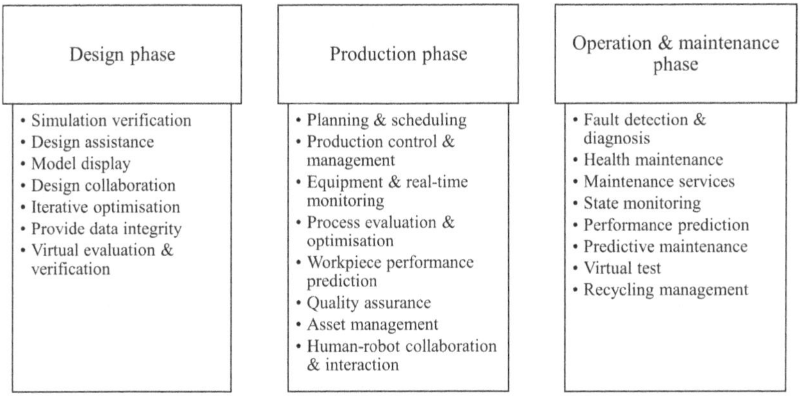

Fig. 7.1 Application areas of DTs in manufacturing (modified from Li et al. (2022b) and Liu et al. (2021))

is often lost when the solution is retired (Liu et al. 2021). Moreover, the small number of published research papers on DTs in the end-of-life phase or during the entire lifecycle indicates the need for further research, for example, regarding DTs' potential to solve sustainability challenges. In addition, the required competences and resources for DTs vary in different lifecycle phases and between various digital technologies, but there are only a few research papers covering the competence needs of DT utilization.

7.2.3 Competence Needs in the Adoption of New Digital Technologies

Companies create value by transferring different inputs into outputs (Grant 1996). The academic literature from the resource-based angle depicts these inputs as 'resources' (e.g., Grant 1996; Teece et al. 1997) that can be either tangible or intangible: tangible resources refer to assets that are property-based, such as financial and physical resources, whereas intangible resources are comprehended as skill- and knowledge-based organizational, human, and technological assets (Das and Teng 2000; Jancenelle 2021). The efficiency and effectiveness of resources depend not only on their existence but on how they are managed.

Hence, companies need competences and capabilities, i.e., activities and processes through which they deploy their resources (e.g., Grant 2010; Whittington et al. 2020).

The terms 'competence' and 'capability' have differing definitions in the academic literature; some academics see 'competence' as an upper-level ability to use resources and capabilities (e.g., Barney and Hesterly 2010; Sanchez 2008) while others use the term 'capability' to depict a longer-term ability to form competitive advantage which is based on different levels of resources (e.g., Brown and Eisenhardt 1999; Whittington et al. 2020). However, these terms are often used interchangeably to depict the deployment of resources in ways that help in achieving a company's goals in the competitive context. The present research also sees these terms as interchangeable, and for clarity, only the term 'competences' is used. Also, the term 'skills' is used to depict person-related specific know-how and talent, whereas competences are understood more as company-level skills.

Combining resources into competences is a complex process that is highly dependent on the types of resources that companies can draw on (e.g., Helfat and Peteraf 2015; Jancenelle 2021). Digital technologies are strongly complementary to other intangible resources of a company (e.g., Brynjolfsson et al. 2017; Khin and Ho 2018), such as workers' skills or managerial talent. This means that the factors related to competences are likely to play a specific role in the adoption of new digital technologies (Nicoletti et al. 2020). Several authors have stated that digital transformation entails the need for new kinds of skills and competences to ensure the efficient application and management of advanced technologies (e.g., Cimini et al. 2020; da Silva et al. 2022; Onaji et al. 2022). For instance, Cimini et al. (2020) argue that big data and related technologies play a prominent, disruptive role in today's digital transformation that requires machine operators to extend their skill set. Also, the increasing intelligence of technological systems and the generation of more complex data require more qualified workers for decision-making in very different areas (Cagliano et al. 2019; Jerman et al. 2020). In general, the increasing complexity of human–machine interconnection makes it necessary to study the new ways in which people work (Galati and Bigliardi 2019).

The requirement of new kinds of skills and competences in the adoption of digital technologies inevitably means that companies' competence profiles and the labor market need to adapt accordingly (da Silva et al. 2022; Liboni et al. 2019). Thus, the renewal of key competences for adapting existing jobs as well as establishing a competence profile for new jobs have been recognized as important elements in this development (e.g., Ana et al. 2019; Jerman et al. 2020). More specific know-how and new skills will be needed, e.g., from multiple new engineering areas. In their study of smart factories, Jerman et al. (2020) found those areas to be, e.g., in programming, IoT design, data analytics, robotics, bionics, and mechatronics. Onaji et al. (2022) also highlight that along with the development of interoperable production systems and ever-increasing uses of data, engineering skills need to become more interdisciplinary. As repetitive, easy activities are expected to be largely automated (e.g., da Silva et al. 2022), future competences are directed toward more strategic, coordinated, and creative activities. Jerman et al. (2020) argue that the role of soft competences, such as conflict management, leadership, emotional intelligence, and motivation, is expected to rise in the future. Moreover, the importance of continuous learning, flexibility, creativity, collaboration, problem-solving, and critical and analytical thinking has been emphasized in the development of I4.0 technologies (Gilli et al. 2023; Jerman et al. 2020).

Although the need for new competence profiles is widely recognized, and the significant disruptive impact of digital transformation on today's business and society is evident, the number of organizations that are ready to take full advantage of this development is still limited. Gilli et al. (2023) state that harnessing the opportunities of digital technologies is one of the great challenges companies are facing today. Most companies are well aware of the potential of new digital technologies, but they lack a clear path to bridge the gaps to reshape existing processes in line with emerging technologies (Gökalp and Martinez 2022). Khin and Ho (2018) also highlight that besides the importance of an orientation toward digital technology adoption, a company also needs to have competences to integrate digital technologies into its innovation processes. Li et al. (2022a) state that companies should not consider only technology diffusion and adoption; systematic improvement is needed in, e.g., the management of strategy, organization, business processes, and operation modes. Further, Hannola et al. (2021) have noted that it is important to match enabling technologies with the actual needs of users and customers. These statements are strengthened by Gilli et al. (2023), who highlight the importance of the role of leaders who grasp the opportunities of digitalization for their businesses and transform them into new business models.

When considering DTs, Broo and Schooling (2023) found the skills gap to be one of the most important underlying factors in the unsuccessful adoption of DTs; without a fundamental understanding of technologies throughout the organization, DT development cannot be achieved. According to Kober et al. (2022), there are only a few employees in manufacturing companies who already have the appropriate skills to develop, use, and evaluate DTs. Thus, extensive training or recruitment is necessary. Further, Gilli et al. (2023) state that many DT processes have failed not because of a lack of knowledge of the technology but because of a lack of leadership skills in orchestrating different expertise fields, renewing organizational structures and processes, and creating new business models. Kober et al. (2022) also note that one of the most underestimated hurdles is employee acceptance. Hence, more emphasis should be given to change management during the transformation process.

In addition, companies are filling their skills gap by forming different kinds of partnerships. The rapid development of DTs has boosted new solutions and service businesses, but at the same time, also the need for collaboration, as companies cannot provide all the needed skills and competences by themselves (e.g., Kokkonen et al. 2022; Meierhofer et al. 2020). Increasingly, DTs can be applied throughout product lifecycles from creation to reuse and modification, which enables collaborative management between all companies in the value chain (Fan et al. 2022). However, collaboration is not without problems either; in addition to the challenges related to the technological fit of several applications and systems, more open collaboration raises questions concerning, e.g., disadvantages of dependency on other companies, uncertainties regarding data sharing and management, differentiating goals of the companies involved, and the lack of appropriate governance models for collaborative relationships (Kokkonen et al. 2022; Reim et al. 2022). Hence, renewing collaboration models demands that companies adopt new kinds of openness and collaboration skills.

7.3 Methods

This study used a qualitative research approach consisting of semi-structured thematic interviews and focus groups. According to Carey and Asbury (2016), qualitative research is useful when exploring new topics and examining complex issues. Yin (2015) emphasizes that the advantage of qualitative research is that it enables in-depth studies on a broad array of topics. Miles et al. (2020) argue that qualitative data enable chronologizing a flow of events and consequences while deriving credible explanations. Moreover, a qualitative approach gives opportunities, e.g., to examine the phenomena in real-life contextual conditions, to contribute insights from existing or new concepts, and to acknowledge the potential relevance of multiple sources of evidence instead of a single source alone (Yin 2015).

According to Miles et al. (2020), the choice of methods is important when intending to obtain the best answers. Thus, attention should be given to the selection of the most suitable methods to produce them. The chosen methods for this research (semi-structured interviews and focus groups) were seen to serve this goal. Semi-structured interviews are conversational and reasonably informal (Longhurst 2010). They consist of open-ended and formulated questions that provoke free responses and provide a basis for discussion (McIntosh and Morse 2015). In relation to structured interviews, semi-structured interviews are more adaptable and flexible, which provides room for researchers to adjust their research and obtain more in-depth information (Ruslin et al. 2022). A focus group method was seen to complement and enrich the data gathered from semi-structured interviews. Krueger and Casey (2000) describe the focus group as an efficient method for obtaining data from multiple participants, thus increasing the overall number of participants in a study. In a focus group, a small group of people is engaged in an informal discussion around a particular topic or a set of issues. The discussion is usually based on general guideline questions. The researcher generally acts as a moderator for the group; posing the questions, keeping the discussion flowing, and enabling group members to participate (Carey and Asbury 2016; Silverman 2004). The idea of focus group work is not to reach a consensus but to collect deep, strongly held beliefs and perspectives (Carey and Asbury 2016). The combination of two research datasets was seen as forming an effective sample size; four precisely chosen interviews with professionals, and 12 focus group discussions with a wider group of people engaged in the researched theme areas, proved to saturate the research data. Although guidelines on sample sizes for saturation have been identified in the academic literature (see e.g. Hennink and Kaiser 2022), more essential is ensuring that the sample is adequate for the phenomenon studied, i.e., the collected data have captured the diversity, depth, and nuances of the issues studied (Francis et al. 2010; Hennink and Kaiser 2022).

The interviewees chosen for the thematic, semi-structured interviews were four professionals representing manufacturing and manufacturing consultancy companies. The focus group workshops were arranged as several company workshops with five companies over a longer period. Four of the companies operate in the manufacturing industry, and one company is a service provider for manufacturing companies. An overview of the interviewees and companies who participated in the workshops and the relevance of each participant and event for the study are presented in Table 7.1.

The interviews were carried out online via collaboration software. All the interviews were recorded and supported with comprehensive written notes. Some of the workshops were conducted as face-to-face meetings and some as online meetings. In the interviews and focus group workshops, the following themes were discussed: (1) the DT maturity level of the companies; (2) the business potential of DTs and new DT-enabled services; (3) skills and competences to adopt, deliver, implement, and maintain DTs; (4) availability and sources of DT-related skills and competences; and (5) resource needs and ownership of DT solutions. The results from company workshops were collected as slide-set

Table 7.1 Overview of interviews and workshops

		Company's business sector	Date	Relevance for the research
Interviews	Role of the interviewee			
Company A	R&D Programme Manager	Heavy equipment and technology engineering	March 2023	Industry insight on DT adoption
Company B	Development manager	On-site transport solutions	April 2023	Industry insight on DT adoption
Company C	Consultant	Product management consultancy	May 2023	Business insight on DT adoption and product management
Company D	Consultant	Product lifecycle management and business development consultancy	June 2023	Business insight on DT adoption and impact on customer business
Workshops				
Company A		Heavy equipment and technology engineering	November 2021–January 2022, April 2023	Industry insight on DT adoption
Company E		Power solutions	January 2023, April 2023	Industry insight on DT adoption
Company F		Robotics and automation	January 2023, April 2023	Industry insight on DT adoption
Company G		Bearing solutions	September–December 2021, April 2023	Business insight on DT adoption
Company H		Software solutions	October 2021, April 2023	Service provider insight on DT adoption

presentations and supported with written notes. The data obtained from the interviews and workshops were processed through thematic analysis. According to Braun and Clarke (2014), thematic analysis is useful, especially for applied research focusing on practical matters outside academia, such as in the manufacturing context in this case. The thematic analysis was executed using a four-level framework for classifying different competences needed in the adoption of digital technologies, especially DTs.

Previous academic literature presents several classifications and categorizations of competences and skills, including models with differing numbers of skill and competence levels (e.g., Janjua et al. 2012; Mumford et al. 2000), different competence domains (e.g., Hogan and Warrenfeltz 2003; Kauffeld 2006) and different competence hierarchies (e.g., Rifkin et al. 1999; Viitala 2005). The framework used in this study is based mainly on Mumford et al.'s (2000) classification into complex problem-solving skills, solutions construction skills, and judgment skills; Janjua et al.'s (2012) competence classification into functional, generic management, social, and cognitive skills, and personal characteristics; and Viitala's (2005) six-dimensional classification into technical, business, knowledge management, leadership, social, and intrapersonal competences. These theoretical frameworks are combined with the competence needs related to digital technology adoption identified in previous academic discussion (e.g., da Silva et al. 2022; Gilli et al. 2023; Jerman et al. 2020; Onaji et al. 2022).

The formed competence categories are as follows:

- *Technological competences*, comprising functional and technical competences in different engineering areas.
- *Cognitive competences*, comprising problem-solving skills, critical and analytical thinking, and solution construction skills.
- *Soft competences*, comprising social skills, collaborative skills, conflict management, emotional intelligence, and creativity.
- *Managerial competences*, comprising judgment skills, generic management skills, business know-how, knowledge management, and leadership.

The empirical results, classified in the abovementioned competence categories, are presented in the next section.

7.4 Research Results

The results of this study indicate that companies' situations as regards needed skills and competences vary based on the maturity level of their DT journey. Based on the collected data, there are categorizations that all companies need to consider if they are implementing DTs in their business, either as a supportive solution or as a part of a large-scale business transformation. The following subsections introduce the competences involved in DT adoption and other factors, such as needed resources, influencing the success of the transformation.

7.4.1 Required Competences for Digital Twin Utilization

The analysis of data from the expert interviews and workshops indicates that adopting, developing, building, and maintaining DTs and other digital technologies require an exceptional skill profile consisting of multiple competences. The results were classified into the four competence categories formed in the methodology section: technological, cognitive, soft, and managerial competences (see Fig. 7.2).

Due to the multi-technical nature of DTs, companies need professionals with strong **technological** skills and competences in various specialties to implement and keep the solution running. Examples of needed technological skills are strong proficiencies in information technology, programming, and system and software development, as well as expertise in simulation, design, and installation. The abovementioned competences are needed in all phases of designing, building, and testing the DT solution, whereas knowledge of electricity, dynamics, mechanics, and hydraulics is often required to merge the physical equipment with the DT. Other engineering competences are also needed, e.g., for the companies to launch products to the market.

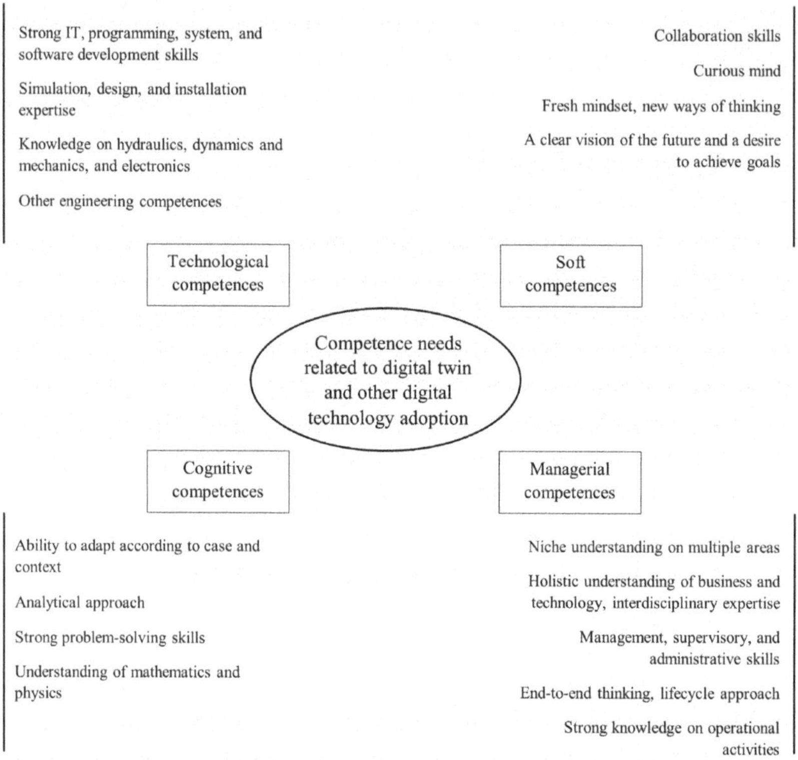

Fig. 7.2 Competence framework related to DT and other digital technology adoption

From a **cognitive** viewpoint, introducing DTs and other digital technologies involves the need for retrained, adaptable competences because resiliency according to case and context is essential in a fast-paced and changing operating environment; digital transformation alters the manufacturing business by introducing novel tools and new ways of working. An analytical approach, strong problem-solving skills, and more detailed competences, e.g., in mathematics and physics, play important roles in solving challenges, developing new operations, and reaching the best possible outcomes.

Utilizing digital technologies also requires **soft** competences, such as collaboration skills, a curious mind, and a fresh mindset. Collaboration is emphasized because DTs are rarely developed alone but in collaboration networks. However, the ownership of the solution, the basic skills and core competence to maintain and fine-tune the DT solution, and the ability to lead the development work must be inside the company itself. Regarding an open, curious mind and a fresh mindset, a big leap toward novel thinking is needed. Using a DT requires changes in operating methods—if such a solution is not already in use, it is difficult for companies to position themselves to exploit its full potential. Essential in solving this challenge is a willingness to solve things that do not fall directly under one's domain because the DT's domain has not yet been defined. The challenge is illustrated through an example: for a person working as a mechanical designer, it is usually clear what belongs to their field of tasks, i.e., what their work tasks and responsibilities are. If, on the other hand, a person is given a DT as their domain, they must penetrate the entire organization with all its silos and processes to maintain it. To conclude, the lack of a job description and domain causes a challenge in defining the necessary skills, thus highlighting the importance of a clear vision of the future and a desire to achieve goals.

In addition to technological, cognitive, and soft competence needs, there are also **managerial** competence needs. Managerial competences can be divided into detailed, certain niche areas, or more holistic entities. The holistic view is challenging, as it includes interdisciplinary needs for knowledge and skills. However, someone who handles both perspectives, technical and business, and understands what kind of technical solutions can be used and how to start a business is required to accelerate the development process. Overall, establishing a DT solution requires various management, supervisory, and administrative skills. Some examples of identified development areas are commercial product management and business development. An important example is the requirement to know the supply chain and the ways data can be used to improve the development of the offered product-service solutions. Another need seen was the competence development of senior management where the focus will be to lead a digital organization that is integrated end-to-end, through the value chains and related product lifecycles. Managerial competences should also include a strong knowledge of the company's operational activities.

According to the interviewees, the internal competence demands created by DTs may differ from the skill profile of existing staff, which means that companies must recruit new specialists. However, the recruiting process is often somewhat complicated because the competences needed depend vastly on the context and the intended use of the DT solution and because DTs cannot be mastered through a single subject or discipline one could study. The current state and maturity of the DT solution must be understood as well because according to the interviewees, competence needs are not stable and change over time: a company starting DT implementation requires different competences than a company that has been using DTs for a decade, meaning that competence needs are bound to the company's operational maturity and its ecosystem's maturity. Even so, the competence categories are interdependent, i.e., successful implementation of DT requires management of all areas, and thus, arranging competence areas in order of importance does not serve the purpose.

7.4.2 Tangible and Intangible Resource Needs and Ownership of DT Solutions

There are also other aspects to consider after recognizing the needed competences. These matters include tangible and intangible resources, e.g., human resources, required investments, technological assets, and ownership of DT solutions. According to the interviewees, it is a well-known problem that if a scheme does not have resources, it will progress quite slowly, if at all—planned actions should always be resourced and recognized at the management level. Too often, the DT development has not been allocated with specifically assigned human resources; instead, the development work is done alongside other tasks. This results in prioritization issues between different tasks, which results in other matters easily bypassing the DT implementation. In general, it requires a person who takes things forward: the development work depends on whether the company understands and agrees that the intended plan has potential worth investing in. After this agreement, the company is ready to allocate resources so that the development is preserved. Resources include not only workforce and time but also technological aspects, such as systems and software.

However, companies do not need competences or resources to build and run DTs if the DTs are not granted with required investments. Proving the actual value of the planned investment to the company's management can be challenging, and that is why it is necessary to explain what benefits the intended DT solution can bring. Is it a mandatory investment without which the company drops out of the business, or is it an investment that produces additional value, such as better competitiveness, lower costs, or more committed customers? The required and resulting changes must be described in detail, as well as how these changes correspond to company strategy.

Furthermore, competences, resources, or investments will not take the DT implementation far unless related ownership and responsibility issues have been clarified. The ownership of DTs was seen as a difficult question among the research participants because ownership requires knowledge of lifecycle management practices and technologies in ways that must be implemented to support the enterprise's products and services. In the traditional, siloed company structures still used in most manufacturing companies, there is not usually a natural position or owner for DTs—the difficulty is that a DT's domain spreads across the organization to different areas and departments without a responsible party. Solving this dilemma is critical because DTs will not live without an owner promoting their design and development and upholding the solution with a fresh mindset. According to the interviewees, there is no straightforward answer to the question of who owns or who should own the DT solution; ownership depends on the intended use and chosen business model. One possible answer to the ownership issue could be organizations establishing a concept owner role with an 'end-to-end' lifecycle management responsibility. The role should also define the positions needed in the industry context to achieve the goals from job descriptions, process development, and digital technology.

7.5 Discussion

The interview results are aligned with previously published research (e.g., Jerman et al. 2020; Onaji et al. 2022) in highlighting the need for DT-related technological and soft competences and skills. The interviewees also stressed the importance of managerial competences that require an understanding of how DTs impact the enterprise architecture of the company end-to-end, thus aligning with Gilli et al.'s (2023) statement about the significance of human and management factors. Moreover, the adoption of DTs requires new roles that own and are responsible for both the integrated physical product-service system and its digital counterpart. At the same time, as noticed earlier by Kokkonen et al. (2022) and Meierhofer et al. (2020), the rapid development of DTs drives companies toward collaborative business models, as they cannot provide all necessary competences by themselves. This development further highlights the importance of needed cognitive competences found in the research data, such as adaptability according to case and context.

The results of this study showed that one of the main obstacles to DT adoption is a siloed organizational structure. Hence, companies should take a step toward end-to-end thinking and focus on the smooth operation of an organization with clear roles and responsibilities. The implementation of DTs impacts company structures in multiple ways: it requires changes in organizational and process structures that result in both change management and employee retraining to achieve the skillsets. At the same time, this adjusts existing role descriptions and creates skill gaps within the organization's structure. However, the competences and skills needed in companies vary based on the case, and this variation influences how related gaps can be filled—that is, either through training existing employees or securing expertise from outside the company. Moreover, as noted earlier by Kober et al. (2022), the implementation of DTs in organizations requires the revision of existing training programs to include the needs placed on the companies from the implementation of DTs. All companies involved in this research saw that certain competences to manage and coordinate the work are needed internally, but more technical skills could be outsourced from a partner ecosystem. Moreover, along with the development of I5.0, the change in the working environment should be the removal of repetitive tasks from humans to AI and process automation. The goal should be for humans to excel in creative and other areas where DTs and AI have limitations, for example, the development of concepts and approval of new AI-based solutions. Organizations will move tasks from humans to AI, and the role and competences of humans should be developed with these goals in mind; the competence needed to maintain and develop this type of system requires technical and managerial competence in simulation, AI, and data analytics as well as the competence to integrate these domains into a working solution.

Competence needs are also dependent on goals that the company is trying to achieve, that is, incremental improvement versus business transformation. Focusing on incremental development and improvement are issues of a mature company, i.e., a company with strong operating models and significant investments in its organization and culture. This is realized through equipment and know-how that can be either documented or tacit knowledge. The idea of a sudden change in ways of working that DTs can create can be too much for the organization to adopt—this research result strengthens the previous findings of, e.g., Kober et al. (2022) and Gilli et al. (2023), on the importance of change management and employee acceptance when implementing changes to the organization's operations.

This research confirmed the previous notions of da Silva et al. (2022) and Liboni et al. (2019), according to whom companies' competence profiles should correspond to the requirements of implemented digital technologies. DTs, as noticed by, e.g., Liu et al. (2021), are by nature cross-disciplinary and thus require knowledge of a broader scope and the combination of these different fields horizontally rather than a deep vertical understanding of a narrow area. Moreover, the issues are amplified through education programs, for example, universities, offering education traditionally in specific, vertical areas, such as engineering, manufacturing, computer science, or business, focusing on narrow expertise even though the education and training offering of DTs should be holistic over the company's extended operating model and not siloed into domains or schools. The amount of uncertainty is further increased by the requirement to customize reskilling and training programs based on the needs of the company. The difficulty of DT is its natural end-to-end footprint across the organization from different departments to expertise domains, which brings the discussion to ownership and responsibility issues.

As stated earlier by, e.g., Li et al. (2022a), planned digital solutions must be aligned with company strategy, which requires efforts from management and ownership. At present, companies do not have managers or owners for a DT, which creates a problem in developing and maintaining it. DTs require an owner within the organization: without a responsible person or department, the DT falls victim to insufficient resources. However, nominating an end-to-end owner for a DT is often challenging, as it creates a new force in the organization with end-to-end influence and decision-making power that causes conflict in the existing organizational setup. The abovementioned structural issues are closely linked to the organization's leadership and management, how the company is run, and what management methods are used.

7.6 Conclusions

This chapter investigated the competences and resources commonly needed when adopting and utilizing DTs in the manufacturing industry. The literature review and data obtained from interviews and workshops answered the research question: **"What competences are needed to utilize digital twins in the manufacturing industry?"** In unveiling the competence demands, resource and collaboration perspectives were also touched on, as these are prerequisites for successful DT utilization.

As a **theoretical contribution**, this study provided a competence framework proposal related to digital technology adoption. The framework contains four main categories: technological, cognitive, soft, and managerial competences. The proposed framework combines previously published research into an applicable tool for analyzing digital technology- and DT-related competences when planning or adopting such technologies. This study fills a theoretical gap and increases existing knowledge on required DT-related competences in the manufacturing industry in all the abovementioned categories.

The research also provided **practical contributions** to manufacturing industry professionals. Managers can utilize the framework in estimating their company's situation and maturity level and in detecting possible competence shortages that require attention from all four categories. Moreover, managers may recognize development targets from managerial demands and realize the true potential of novel, pervasive, end-to-end thinking, which can motivate them to rethink traditional, inflexible, siloed organization structures hindering the development of DT solutions.

In addition to the four-field competence framework, the competences and skills that a company needs to benefit from the use of DTs can be divided into two separate areas. The first area is understanding of *the business case,* and holding the experience and skills to design and implement DTs at the required maturity level. This implementation capability should continue to evolve and be maintained as business needs grow. The second area is *the organization's ability* to effectively use DTs in its daily operations, as part of its operating model. To conclude, core competence and role in organizations is the cross-organizational DT concept and/or business owner, whose role is to define and drive the transformation caused by DT in the enterprise at the level that brings the most value with the correct level of investment and risk. The question is where to find and acquire this kind of expertise, and, on the other hand, if the company has the resources to hire such competent. One of the key success criteria, according to Onaji et al. (2022), is an end-to-end virtual product–process integration where data are captured continuously throughout the lifecycle. This end-to-end thinking is a significant leap forward for many organizations, one that places new demands on leadership and upper management.

However, the identification of competences and resources does not support the development of DT solutions very far without a radical change in ways of thinking. The senior management level of an organization must understand the benefits and risks related to a DT-centric operating model, in which case it can be granted sufficient competences and resources, and the development work and adoption of the solution become easier. DTs must be driven by a business strategy where goals are identified and short-term business benefits are defined because a clear vision helps organizations commit to DT development. Moreover, implementing a DT solution should not be done recklessly—resources and abilities for building these solutions must be in order: a DT solution cannot be implemented despite excellent competences if there is no system on which the solution is built. On the other hand, the system cannot be built without skilled competences either.

This study revealed that the competence and resource needs related to DTs and other digital technologies are relevant and topical for **further research** as well. This observation is supported by the novelty and rapid increase of the literature published on the topic. The significance and potential of these matters have been realized in academic discussions and manufacturing industries. After the competence and resource aspects, the next natural subject to study would be digital sustainability: digital transformation and the emerging I5.0 enhance sustainability in many ways, but sustainability in the implementation of DT solutions remains a rather unresearched area. Questions related to this research angle involve, for example, how to take care of sustainability issues from the beginning, in the implementation, and during the use of a DT solution; how companies can best develop their digital sustainability competences; and what kinds of ecosystems should be established for organizations to implement new, innovative DT solutions so that they can focus on the solutions' use and management and safely outsource those steps and tasks that fall outside their core business.

References

K. K. Alnowaiser and M. A. Ahmed. Digital twin: Current research trends and future directions. *Arabian Journal for Science and Engineering*, 48(2):1075–1095, 2023.

A. Ana, D. Meirawan, I. Kustiawan, N. Supriatna, E. Nugraha, A. D. Minghat, Muktiarni, and V. Dwiyanti. Future jobs in coming of industry revolution 4.0. *International Journal of Advanced Science and Technology*, 29(5):567–574, 2019.

J. Baker. The technology–organization–environment framework. In Y. Dwivedi, M. Wade, and S. Schneberger, editors, *Information Systems Theory:*

Explaining and Predicting Our Digital Society, volume 28 of *Integrated Series in Information Systems*, pages 231–245. Springer, New York, NY, 2012. https://doi.org/10.1007/978-1-4419-6108-2_12.

J. Bao, D. Guo, J. Li, and J. Zhang. The modelling and operations for the digital twin in the context of manufacturing. *Enterprise Information Systems*, 13(4):534–556, 2019.

J. B. Barney and W. S. Hesterly. *Strategic management and competitive advantage: Concepts*. Prentice Hall, 2010.

J. Björkdahl. Strategies for digitalization in manufacturing firms. *California Management Review*, 62(4):17–36, 2020.

V. Braun and V. Clarke. What can "thematic analysis" offer health and well-being researchers? *International Journal of Qualitative Studies on Health and Well-Being*, 9(1):26152, 2014.

D. G. Broo and J. Schooling. Digital twins in infrastructure: Definitions, current practices, challenges and strategies. *International Journal of Construction Management*, 23(7):1254–1263, 2023.

S. L. Brown and K. M. Eisenhardt. Patching: Restitching business portfolios in dynamic markets. *Harvard Business Review*, 77:72–82, 1999.

F. Brunetti, D. T. Matt, A. Bonfanti, A. De Longhi, G. Pedrini, and G. Orzes. Digital transformation challenges: Strategies emerging from a multi-stakeholder approach. *The TQM Journal*, 32(4):697–724, 2020.

E. Brynjolfsson, D. Rock, and C. Syverson. Artificial intelligence and the modern productivity paradox: A clash of expectations and statistics. In A. Agrawal, J. Gans, and A. Goldfarb, editors, *The Economics of Artificial Intelligence: An Agenda*, pages 23–60. University of Chicago Press, 2017.

R. Cagliano, F. Canterino, A. Longoni, and E. Bartezzaghi. The interplay between smart manufacturing technologies and work organization: The role of technological complexity. *International Journal of Operations and Production Management*, 39:913–934, 2019. https://doi.org/10.1108/IJOPM-01-2019-0093.

M. A. Carey and J. E. Asbury. *Focus group research*, volume 9. Routledge, 2016.

C. Cimini, F. Pirola, R. Pinto, and S. Cavalieri. A human-in-the-loop manufacturing control architecture for the next generation of production systems. *Journal of Manufacturing Systems*, 54:258–271, 2020. https://doi.org/10.1016/j.jmsy.2020.01.002.

P. Coelho, C. Bessa, J. Landeck, and C. Silva. Industry 5.0: The arising of a concept. *Procedia Computer Science*, 217:1137–1144, 2023. https://doi.org/10.1016/j.procs.2022.12.312.

L. B. P. da Silva, R. Soltovski, J. Pontes, F. T. Treinta, P. Leitão, E. Mosconi, L. M. M. de Resende, and R. T. Yoshino. Human resources management 4.0: Literature review and trends. *Computers & Industrial Engineering*, 168:108111, 2022. https://doi.org/10.1016/j.cie.2022.108111.

V. Damjanovic-Behrendt and W. Behrendt. An open source approach to the design and implementation of digital twins for smart manufacturing. *International Journal of Computer Integrated Manufacturing*, 32(4–5):366–384, 2019.

K. Das and B.-S. Teng. A resource-based theory of strategic alliances. *Journal of Management*, 26(1):31–61, 2000. https://doi.org/10.1016/S0149-2063(99)00037-9.

B. de Boer, C. Strasser, and S. Mulder. Imagining digital twins in healthcare. *Prometheus*, 38(1):67–81, 2022.

M. Hernandez-de-Menendez, R. Morales-Menendez, C. A. Escobar, and M. McGovern. Competencies for industry 4.0. *International Journal on Interactive Design and Manufacturing (IJIDeM)*, 14:1511–1524, 2020. https://doi.org/10.1007/s12008-020-00716-2.

Y. Fan, C. Dai, S. Huang, P. Hu, X. Wang, and M. Yan. A life-cycle digitaltwin collaboration framework based on the industrial internet identification and resolution. *The International Journal of Advanced Manufacturing Technology*, 123(7):2883–2911, 2022.

M. Farsi, R. K. Mishra, and J. A. Erkoyuncu. Industry 5.0 for sustainable reliability centered maintenance. In *Proceedings of the 10th International Conference on Through-life Engineering Service*, pages 1–6, University of Twente, The Netherlands, 2021.

Carlos Favoretto, Giovani H. D. S. Mendes, Mauro G. Filho, Mario Gouvea de Oliveira, and Gilberto M. D. Ganga. Digital transformation of business model in manufacturing companies: Challenges and research agenda. *Journal of Business & Industrial Marketing*, 37(4):748–767, 2022. https://doi.org/10.1108/JBIM-08-2021-0382.

J. J. Francis, M. Johnston, C. Robertson, L. Glidewell, V. Entwistle, M. P. Eccles, and J. M. Grimshaw. What is an adequate sample size? operationalising data saturation for theory-based interview studies. *Psychology & Health*, 25(10): 1229–1245, 2010. https://doi.org/10.1080/08870440903194015.

A. G. Frank, L. S. Dalenogare, and N. F. Ayala. Industry 4.0 technologies: Implementation patterns in manufacturing companies. *International Journal of Production Economics*, 210:15–26, 2019. https://doi.org/10.1016/j.ijpe.2019.01.004.

F. Galati and B. Bigliardi. Industry 4.0: Emerging themes and future research avenues using a text mining approach. *Computers in Industry*, 109:100–113, 2019. https://doi.org/10.1016/j.compind.2019.04.018.

H. Gangwar, H. Date, and A. D. Raoot. Review on it adoption: Insights from recent technologies. *Journal of Enterprise Information Management*, 27(4):488–502, 2014.

K. Gilli, M. Nippa, and M. Knappstein. Leadership competences for digital transformation: An exploratory content analysis of job advertisements. *German Journal of Human Resource Management*, 37(1):50–75, 2023.

M. Grieves. Digital twin: Manufacturing excellence through virtual factory replication. *White Paper*, 1(2014):1–7, 2014.

T. Golovina, A. Polyanin, A. Adamenko, E. Khegay, and V. Schepinin. Digital twins as a new paradigm of an industrial enterprise. *International Journal of Technology*, 11(6):1115–1124, 2020.

R. M. Grant. Prospering in dynamically-competitive environments: Organizational capability as knowledge integration. *Organization Science*, 7:375–387, 1996.

R. M. Grant. *Contemporary strategy analysis*. Wiley, 7th edition, 2010.

E. Gökalp and V. Martinez. Digital transformation maturity assessment: Development of the digital transformation capability maturity model. *International Journal of Production Research*, 60(20):6282–6302, 2022. https://doi.org/10.1080/00207543.2021.1991020.

L. Hannola, I. Donoghue, K. Kokkonen, K. Elfvengren, and J. Papinniemi. Identifying industrial needs for real-time simulation. In A. Mikkola, J. Ukko, M. Saunila, and J. Heikkinen, editors, *Creating value with sustainable production on real-time simulation*, pages 13–27. Routledge Taylor & Francis Group, 2021.

B. He and K. J. Bai. Digital twin-based sustainable intelligent manufacturing: A review. *Advances in Manufacturing*, 9:1–21, 2021.

F. Hein-Pensel, H. Winkler, A. Brückner, M. Wölke, I. Jabs, I. J. Mayan, A. Kirschenbaum, J. Friedrich, and C. Zinke-Wehlmann. Maturity assessment for industry 5.0: A review of existing maturity models. *Journal of Manufacturing Systems*, 66:200–210, 2023. https://doi.org/10.1016/j.jmsy.2022.12.009.

C. E. Helfat and M. A. Peteraf. Managerial cognitive capabilities and the microfoundations of dynamic capabilities. *Strategic Management Journal*, 36(6):831–850, 2015.

M. Hennink and B. N. Kaiser. Sample sizes for saturation in qualitative research: A systematic review of empirical tests. *Social Science & Medicine*, 292:114523, 2022.

R. Hogan and R. Warrenfeltz. Educating the modern manager. *Academy of Management Learning and Education*, 2(1):74–84, 2003.

O. M. Horani, A. S. Al-Adwan, H. Yaseen, H. Hmoud, W. M. Al-Rahmi, and A. Alkhalifah. The critical determinants impacting artificial intelligence adoption at the organizational level. *Information Development*, 0(0):Article 02666669231166889, 2023. https://doi.org/10.1177/02666669231166889.

N. Jefroy, M. Azarian, and H. Yu. Moving from industry 4.0 to industry 5.0: What are the implications for smart logistics? *Logistics*, 6(26):1–27, 2022. https://doi.org/10.3390/logistics6020026.

S. Jaiswal, E. Sanjuro, J. Cuadrado, J. Sopanen, and A. Mikkola. State estimator based on an indirect kalman filter for a hydraulically actuated multibody system. *Multibody System Dynamics*, 54(4):373–398, 2022.

V. E. Jancenelle. Tangible-intangible resource composition and firm success. *Technovation*, 108:Article 102337, 2021. https://doi.org/10.1016/j.technovation.2021.102337.

Y. S. Janjua, M. A. Naeem, and F. N. Kayani. The competence classification framework. a classification model for employee development. *Interdisciplinary Journal of Contemporary Research in Business*, 4(1):396–404, 2012.

A. Jerman, M. Pejić Bach, and A. Aleksić. Transformation towards smart factory system: Examining new job profiles and competences. *Systems Research and Behavioral Science*, 37(2):388–402, 2020. https://doi.org/10.1002/sres.2657.

J. Jin, J. Hu, C. Li, Z. Shi, P. Lei, and W. Tian. A digital twin system of reconfigurable tooling for monitoring and evaluating in aerospace assembly. *Journal of Manufacturing Systems*, 68:56–71, 2023.

S. S. Kamble, A. Gunasekaran, H. Parekh, V. Mani, A. Belhadi, and R. Sharma. Digital twin for sustainable manufacturing supply chains: Current trends, future perspectives, and an implementation framework. *Technological Forecasting and Social Change*, 176:Article 121448, 2022. https://doi.org/10.1016/j.techfore.2021.121448.

C. Kan and C. J. Anumba. Digital twins as the next phase of cyber-physical systems in construction. In *Computing in civil engineering 2019: Data, sensing, and analytics*, pages 256–264. American Society of Civil Engineers, 2019.

S. Kauffeld. Self directed workgroups & team competence. *Journal Of Occupational Psychology*, 79(1):1–21, 2006.

S. Khin and T. C. F. Ho. Digital technology, digital capability and organizational performance. a mediating role of digital innovation. *International Journal of Innovation Science*, 11(2):177–195, 2018. https://doi.org/10.1108/IJIS-08-2018-0083.

L. M. Kipper, S. Iepsen, A. J. Dal Forno, R. Frozza, L. Furstenau, J. Agnes, and D. Cossul. Scientific mapping to identify competencies required by industry 4.0. *Technology in Society*, 64:Article 101454, 2021. https://doi.org/10.1016/j.techsoc.2020.101454.

C. Kober, M. Fette, and J. P. Wulfsberg. Challenges of digital twin application in manufacturing. In *2022 IEEE International Conference on Industrial Engineering and Engineering Management (IEEM)*, pages 0162–0168. IEEE, 2022.

K. Kokkonen, L. Hannola, T. Rantala, J. Ukko, M. Saunila, and T. Rantala. Preconditions and benefits of digital twin-based business ecosystems in manufacturing. *International Journal of Computer Integrated Manufacturing*, 36(5):789–806, 2022.

W. Kritzinger, M. Karner, G. Traar, J. Henjes, and W. Sihn. Digital twin in manufacturing: A categorical literature review and classification. *Ifac-PapersOnline*, 51(11):1016–1022, 2018.

R. A. Krueger and M. A. Casey. *Focus groups: A practical guide for applied researchers*. Sage, 3rd ed. edition, 2000.

C. Köhler-Schute. *Digitalisierung und Transformation in Unternehmen: Strategien und Konzepte, Methoden und Technologien, Praxisbeispiele*. KS-Energy-Verlag, Germany, 2016.

L. Lachvajderová and J. Kádárová. Industry 4.0 implementation and industry 5.0 readiness in industrial enterprises. *Management and Production Engineering Review*, 13(3):102–109, 2022. https://doi.org/10.24425/mper.2022.142387.

L. Lattanzi, R. Raffaeli, M. Peruzzini, and M. Pellicciari. Digital twin for smart manufacturing: A review of concepts towards a practical industrial implementation. *International Journal of Computer Integrated Manufacturing*, 34(6):567–597, 2021. https://doi.org/10.1080/0951192X.2021.1911003.

E. K. Leung, C. K. H. Lee, and Z. Ouyang. From traditional warehouses to physical internet hubs: A digital twin-based inbound synchronization framework for piorder management. *International Journal of Production Economics*, 244:Article 108353, 2022. https://doi.org/10.1016/j.ijpe.2021.108353.

J. Li, J. Zhou, and Y. Cheng. Conceptual method and empirical practice of building digital capability of industrial enterprises in the digital age. *IEEE Transactions on Engineering Management*, 69(5):1902–1916, 2022a.

L. Li, B. Lei, and C. Mao. Digital twin in smart manufacturing. *Journal of Industrial Information Integration*, 26:Article 100289, 2022b. https://doi.org/10.1016/j.jii.2021.100289.

L. B. Liboni, L. O. Cezarino, C. J. C. Jabbour, B. G. Oliveira, and N. O. Stefanelli. Smart industry and the pathways to hrm 4.0: Implications for scm. *Supply Chain Management*, 24(1):124–146, 2019. https://doi.org/10.1108/SCM-03-2018-0150.

K. Y. H. Lim, P. Zheng, and C. H. Chen. A state-of-the-art survey of digital twin: Techniques, engineering product lifecycle management and business innovation perspectives. *Journal of Intelligent Manufacturing*, 31:1313–1337, 2020.

M. Liu, S. Fang, H. Dong, and C. Xu. Review of digital twin about concepts, technologies, and industrial applications. *Journal of Manufacturing Systems*, 58: 346–361, 2021. https://doi.org/10.1016/j.jmsy.2020.06.017.

R. Longhurst. Semi-structured interviews and focus groups. In N. Clifford, S. French, and G. Valentine, editors, *Key methods in geography*, pages 103–115. Sage Publications, 2010.

M. Majerník, N. Daneshjo, P. Malega, P. Drábik, and B. Barilová. Sustainable development of the intelligent industry from industry 4.0 to industry 5.0. *Advances in Science and Technology Research Journal*, 16(2):12–18, 2022. https://doi.org/10.12913/22998624/146420.

M. J. McIntosh and J. M. Morse. Situating and constructing diversity in semi-structured interviews. *Global Qualitative Nursing Research*, 2: 2333393615597674, 2015. https://doi.org/10.1177/2333393615597674.

J. Meierhofer, S. West, M. Rapaccini, and C. Barbieri. The digital twin as a service enabler: From the service ecosystem to the simulation model. In H. Nóvoa, M. Dragoicea, and N. Kühl, editors, *Exploring service science, Proceedings of 10th International Conference, IESS*, Lecture notes in business information processing, page 377. Springer, 2020.

M. B. Miles, A. M. Huberman, and J. Saldana. *Qualitative data analysis: A methods sourcebook*. Sage Publications, 4th ed. edition, 2020.

R. Minerva and N. Crespi. Digital twins: Properties, software frameworks, and application scenarios. *IT Professional*, 23(1):51–55, 2021.

M. D. Mumford, S. J. Zaccaro, M. S. Connelly, and M. A. Marks. Leadership skills: Conclusions and future directions. *Leadership Quarterly*, 11(1):155–170, 2000.

E. Negri, L. Fumagalli, and M. Macchi. A review of the roles of digital twin in cps-based production systems. *Procedia Manufacturing*, 11:939–948, 2017.

G. Nicoletti, C. von Rueden, and D. Andrews. Digital technology diffusion: A matter of capabilities, incentives or both? *European Economic Review*, 128: Article 103513, 2020. https://doi.org/10.1016/j.euroecorev.2020.103513.

I. Onaji, D. Tiwari, P. Soulatiantork, B. Song, and A. Tiwari. Digital twin in manufacturing: Conceptual framework and case studies. *International Journal of Computer Integrated Manufacturing*, 35(8):831–858, 2022.

D. Paschek, A. Mocan, and A. Draghici. Industry 5.0—the expected impact of next industrial revolution. In *Thriving on future education, industry, business and society: Proceedings of the MakeLearn and TIIM International Conference 2019*, 2019.

F. Pirola, X. Boucher, S. Wiesner, and G. Pezzotta. Digital technologies in productservice systems: A literature review and a research agenda. *Computers in Industry*, 123:Article 103301, 2020. https://doi.org/10.1016/j.compind.2020.103301.

W. Purcell, T. Neubauer, and K. Mallinger. Digital twins in agriculture: Challenges and opportunities for environmental sustainability. *Current Opinion in Environmental Sustainability*, 61:Article 101252, 2023. https://doi.org/10.1016/j.cosust.2022.101252.

W. Reim, E. Andersson, and K. Eckerwall. Enabling collaboration on digital platforms: A study of digital twins. *International Journal of Production Research*, 61(12):3926–3942, 2022.

K. I. Rifkin, M. Fineman, and C. H. Ruhnke. The human side: Developing technical managers—first you need a competency model. *Research-Technology Management*, 42(2):53–57, 1999. https://doi.org/10.1080/08956308.1999.11671273.

Ruslin, S. Mashuri, M. S. A. Rasak, F. Alhabsyi, and H. Syam. Semi-structured interview: A methodological reflection on the development of a qualitative research instrument in educational studies. *IOSR Journal of Research & Method in Education (IOSR-JRME)*, 12(1):22–29, 2022.

K. Salminen, J. Siivonen, L. Hillman, T. Rainio, M. Ukonaho, M. Ijas, M. Lantz, and M. Aho. Sustainable digital transformation of manufacturing industry: Needs for competences and services related to industry 5.0 technologies. In *2023 Portland International Conference on Management of Engineering and Technology (PICMET)*, pages 1–9. IEEE, 2023. https://doi.org/10.23919/PICMET59654.2023.10216871.

R. Sanchez. A scientific critique of the resource-based view (rbv) in strategy theory, with competence-based remedies for the rbv's conceptual deficiencies and logic problems. In R. Sanchez, editor, *Research in competence based management: A focused issue on fundamental issues in competence theory development*, pages 3–78. Emerald Group Publishing Limited, 2008.

D. Schallmo, C. A. Williams, and L. Boardman. Digital transformation of business models—best practice, enablers, and roadmap. *International Journal of Innovation Management*, 21(08):Article 1740014, 2017. https://doi.org/10.1142/S136391961740014X.

C. Semeraro, M. Lezoche, H. Panetto, and M. Dassisti. Digital twin paradigm: A systematic literature review. *Computers in Industry*, 130:Article 103469, 2021. https://doi.org/10.1016/j.compind.2021.103469.

D. Silverman. *Qualitative research: Theory, method and practice*. SAGE Publications, 2nd ed. edition, 2004.

M. Sofia, F. Fraboni, M. De Angelis, G. Puzzo, D. Giusino, and L. Pietrantoni. The impact of artificial intelligence on workers' skills: Upskilling and reskilling in organisations. *Informing Science: The International Journal of an Emerging Transdiscipline*, 26:39–68, 2023.

N. Syam and A. Sharma. Waiting for a sales renaissance in the fourth industrial revolution: Machine learning and artificial intelligence in sales research and practice. *Industrial Marketing Management*, 69:135–146, 2018.

D. Teece, G. Pisano, and A. Schuen. Dynamic capabilities and strategic management. *Strategic Management Journal*, 18:509–533, 1997.

E. VanDerHorn and S. Mahadevan. Digital twin: Generalization, characterization and implementation. *Decision Support Systems*, 145:Article 113524, 2021. https://doi.org/10.1016/j.dss.2021.113524.

P. C. Verhoef, T. Broekhuizen, Y. Bart, A. Bhattacharya, J. Q. Dong, N. Fabian, and M. Haenlein. Digital transformation: A multidisciplinary reflection and research agenda. *Journal of Business Research*, 122:889–901, 2021.

R. Viitala. Perceived development needs of managers compared to an integrated management competency model. *Journal of Workplace Learning*, 17(7):436–451, 2005.

J. Vrana and R. Singh. Digitization, digitalization, and digital transformation. In *Handbook of nondestructive evaluation 4.0*, pages 1–17. Springer, Cham, 2021.

K. J. Wang, Y. H. Lee, and S. Angelica. Digital twin design for real-time monitoring–a case study of die cutting machine. *International Journal of Production Research*, 59(21):6471–6485, 2021.

R. Whittington, P. Regnér, D. Angwin, G. Johnson, and K. Scholes. *Fundamentals of strategy*. Pearson Education, 5th ed. edition, 2020.

R. K. Yin. *Qualitative research from start to finish*. The Guilford Press, 2nd ed. edition, 2015.

A. Zangiacomi, E. Pessot, R. Fornasiero, M. Bertetti, and M. Sacco. Moving towards digitalization: A multiple case study in manufacturing. *Production Planning & Control*, 31(2–3):143–157, 2020.

8

Navigating the Innovation Process: Challenges Faced by Deep-Tech Startups

Johan Kask and Gabriel Linton

8.1 Introduction

Innovation is essential for industry and businesses, acting as the engine of societal advancement and harnessing rapid technological advances. Nonetheless, the journey of transforming a mere invention or idea into a market-ready innovation is laden with uncertainties and risks. As a result, many inventions fail to survive the commercialization stage. While innovation may vary in complexity, the process remains fraught with difficulty and high failure rates, especially when it involves complex and research-intensive technologies, also known as 'deep tech.' This research strives to bridge the gap in the literature by taking a systems perspective to understand the barriers facing deep-tech startups. This introduces

J. Kask (✉) · G. Linton
CREDS—Center for Research on Digitalization and Sustainability, University of Inland Norway, Kongsvinger, Norway
e-mail: johan.kask@inn.no

G. Linton
e-mail: gabriel.linton@inn.no

P. Aaltonen and E. Kurvinen (eds.), *Contemporary Issues in Industry 5.0*, Technology, Work and Globalization, https://doi.org/10.1007/978-3-031-74779-3_8

the scholarly field of innovation systems, which emphasizes the systemic nature and interdependencies involved in innovation processes (Edquist 1997; Chaminade and Edquist 2006; Rakas and Hain 2019). Artificial Intelligence, Robotics, Security, Radar, Sensors, the Internet of Things, and Energy, and Biotechnology exemplify deep-tech solutions with the potential to address global issues and revolutionize their sectors, underscoring their importance for societal development.

However, as the global pursuit of technological advancements continues, a fine grained understanding of the deep-tech innovation process has often been overlooked. Despite their transformative potential, deep-tech companies often encounter heightened challenges compared to 'shallow-tech' counterparts due to the research-intense nature of their technology, necessitating more knowledge, time, and resources for market introduction. This difference is partly due to deep-tech startups' nature of being more capital intensive, with associated significant risks concerning technology functionality, market existence, and funding for the entire innovation journey. Additionally, a more complicated technology can be harder to understand, requiring higher expertise levels from financiers, which, along with capital intensity and associated risks, makes these companies less attractive to investors than shallow-tech companies, where a new mobile app or service can be developed in just a few months, presenting quicker returns. The critical period from invention to commercialization is known as the 'Valley of Death' (Auerswald and Branscomb 2003), as the costs of development exceed the revenue, making it difficult to secure funding and resources. By engaging with literature on innovation systems and entrepreneurship, this chapter illustrates how these systemic challenges affect the survival of deep-tech startups. Deep tech's longer and more expensive commercialization process makes this valley particularly perilous, with greater chances of failure (Auerswald and Branscomb 2003). This makes it more likely that valuable deep-tech companies will not be able to secure the funding needed, resulting in bankruptcy and that other than the source country later capitalizing on the original investments.

To illustrate, the Swedish innovation system is today designed mainly for shallow tech such as mobile apps, meaning that there is a lack of specific support for deep-tech companies, making the Valley of Death especially taxing for them. Here, models and theories on national and regional innovation systems can provide insights into the specific challenges faced by countries in fostering environments conducive to deep-tech innovations (Nelson 1993; Lundvall and Rikap 2022). The problem is amplified when a product is developed but the commercialization process is incomplete, coupled with the growing difficulty in finding new financing sources. When a physical product is to be manufactured, an industrialization process (i.e., to be able to produce standardized) needs to be developed, which is more difficult the more complex the product is. At the same time, startups have already made full use of many different financing options and it is becoming more difficult to find new sources of funding. The difficulty grows when the industrialization process involves closely knit hardware and software. Moreover, current innovation systems rarely offer robust support to startups during the industrialization processes, with most of these processes taking place in large companies with greater and different resources.

This chapter aims to investigate the challenges faced by deep-tech startups in the innovation process, particularly concerning the commercialization of their potentially disruptive and revolutionary inventions. To this end, the chapter sheds light on the complexities of the Valley of Death for deep-tech startups, referencing the Swedish context, and examining the industrialization process for startups. This chapter's contribution lies in exploring the unique challenges that deep-tech companies, particularly startups, face during the innovation process. By exploring the distinctions between deep tech and shallow tech and investigating the reasons for disparities in support and success, this chapter provides insight for investors, policymakers, and scholars. The insights presented here can contribute to a broader understanding of the innovation system's current landscape and can guide strategies to support deep-tech startups.

Following this introduction, the next section provides a theoretical background, drawing upon existing literature to frame the unique challenges faced by deep-tech startups. Subsequent sections use a Swedish case, discussing the financing and support mechanisms for deep-tech startups, and practical considerations in navigating the Valley of Death. The chapter concludes with a synthesis of the insights gained, offering recommendations and outlining avenues for future research and policy intervention.

8.2 Theoretical Background

This theoretical background establishes a foundation for understanding the challenges faced by new companies, especially deep-tech startups. Research on the Valley of Death describes the phenomenon as the space between research and product development or as the space between opportunity discovery (invention) and the process of product development (innovation) (Markham et al. 2010). Sandberg and Aarikka-Stenroos (2014) reviewed the literature and found that a lack of competencies and unsupportive structures contribute to the Valley of Death. We, therefore, focus on startups' human capital and the innovation systems designed to navigate startups across the Valley of Death (Fig. 8.1).

In this research, we combine auxiliary theories from both micro-level dynamics, on human capital—which posits that the skills, knowledge, and experience of individuals are entral to organizational success (Becker

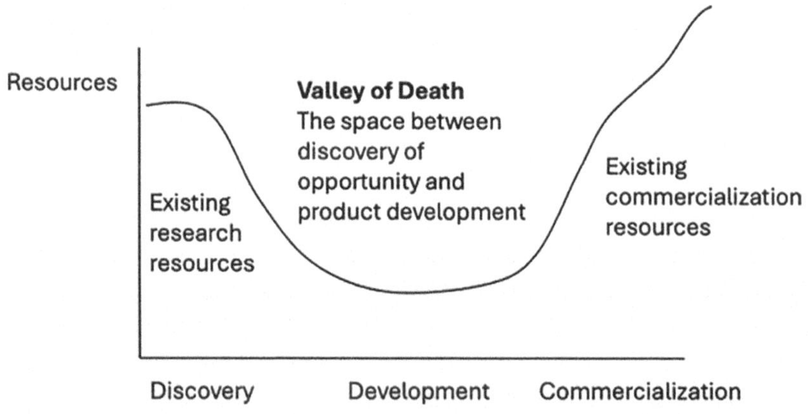

Fig. 8.1 Illustration of the Valley of Death (design based on Markham et al. 2010)

1964)—and supportive structures, i.e., innovation systems, that influence the trajectory of startups. Thus, in this chapter, we draw upon a systemic approach that combines perspectives rooted in both Becker (1964) and Lundvall (1992), aligning individual and in-house capabilities (e.g., human capital) with external support systems to provide a systemic, holistic view of the deep-tech startup landscape. On the one hand, the human capital strand of research can help us better understand how these elements are intertwined with the success of deep-tech startups. On the other hand, the systemic view of innovation systems helps us understand how external factors and support systems also play an important role in facilitating the innovation process. This dual focus allows us to explore how the internal and the external interact to either facilitate or hinder the commercial success of deep-tech startups. By combining these perspectives, we can also better understand this two-sided interplay in overcoming the barriers typically encountered in the Valley of Death (Auerswald and Branscomb 2003).

First, about the internal lack of competencies. Recent studies in entrepreneurship have increasingly highlighted the important role of human capital in startup success. It emphasizes the critical role of various knowledge domains, the importance of prior startup experience, the role of team dynamics, and the necessity of connecting with or acquiring missing competencies. The human capital of the founder/entrepreneur, as characterized by education, ability, knowledge, skill, and experience, has been fundamentally linked with a startup's likelihood of success in the market. Research consistently shows that individuals with higher levels of human capital are more likely to establish successful businesses, and more adept at attracting essential capital—a vital component for startup growth (Colombo and Grilli 2010; Ko and McKelvie 2018). For deep-tech startups, given the complexity of technology, the importance of human capital extends beyond mere knowledge to include adaptability. In the domain of deep tech, these human capital challenges are amplified by the nature of the technologies involved. Whereas shallow-tech startups might pivot quickly in the face of an obstacle, deep-tech startups often must navigate complex technical terrains.

Successful startups often require various types of knowledge: industry-specific insights; technical knowledge related to the product, marketing acumen; and knowledge of leading companies; and/or prior entrepreneurial experiences (Lim and Busenitz 2020). Those founders and entrepreneurs with higher levels of education, more work experience, particularly in the same sector, and more entrepreneurial human capital are equipped with better capacity for entrepreneurial assessment. This enriched knowledge base allows them to seize business opportunities and make effective strategic decisions essential for a new company's success (Colombo and Grilli 2010). These findings resonate with the theory of knowledge spillover, where the transfer and application of specific knowledge within an industry or sector result in innovation and growth (Audretsch and Keilbach 2007). However, Lim and Busenitz (2020) have illustrated that previous experience in management from large corporations might be less important for startups than previously assumed. Instead, their research points to the relevance of having previous startup experience in the entrepreneurial process. This is particularly important for companies that need to undergo industrialization. This observation aligns with Shane's (2000) notion of 'prior knowledge,' where specific experiences are viewed as critical to recognizing and exploiting entrepreneurial opportunities.

Moreover, and related, it's challenging for individuals to have comprehensive knowledge and experiences required. For deep-tech startups, where innovation is at the forefront, the urgency to supplement missing competencies is even more pronounced. This leads to an essential task for startup founders to find ways to supplement their existing competencies through various means. Previous studies have explored the role of mentoring and networks in enhancing the human capital of entrepreneurs (Wright et al. 2007), and the research has underscored the importance of team dynamics within the entrepreneurial process (Klotz et al. 2014), thereby contributing to success: The implication is that the more complicated the entrepreneurial process, as is the case with deep-tech startups, the greater the need for a comprehensive and diverse skill set within the company, or accessible from other actors surrounding it. This echoes the insights from team heterogeneity literature, suggesting that diverse teams may bring a richer variety of perspectives, thereby enhancing creativity and problem-solving (Hoogendoorn et al. 2013).

Next, we turn to the external barrier of unsupportive systems (Sandberg and Aarikka-Stenroos 2014). While startups inherently rely on human capital, they also depend on supportive external innovation systems and robust financial structures. The innovation systems framework, often rooted in the early works of Lundvall (1992), underscores the importance of networks, institutions, and policies in fostering an environment conducive to innovation. In particular, challenges related to financing have been well-documented in the innovation literature. The scarcity of private capital, especially in the face of long and costly commercialization processes, can pose major barriers to startups seeking funding (Winborg and Landström 2001). This is further compounded by the time required to realize a return on investment, which can diminish the appeal to investors.

In addition to emphasizing the importance of an efficient finance structure, the literature also highlights the importance of efficient and supportive innovation systems (Ferrary and Granovetter 2009). The evaluation of research and development activities can be challenging and frequently holds little practical value until a product is finished, creating obstacles for companies involved in protracted and expensive development (Hall et al. 2016). The theoretical concept of 'information asymmetry' further complicates financing scenarios; it occurs when companies have more insight into their investment returns than external investors, leading to higher costs or even inaccessibility of external financing, particularly when the assets possess low-security value (Carpenter and Petersen 2002).

These understandings provide essential insights for entrepreneurs and investors and set the stage for future research to explore methods by which startups can effectively bridge their competence gaps, and for policymakers how to organize efficient innovation systems. It can also help innovation systems and educational institutions set up curricula and support the specific needs of startups in fostering entrepreneurship. With this theoretical backdrop, we will further examine how these concepts play out specifically in the Swedish innovation system, shedding light on the unique challenges and opportunities in this context. These insights pave the way for a deeper understanding of deep-tech startups, highlighting the synergy between human capital, financial challenges, and the overarching innovation system. As we dig deeper into the Swedish context in the following sections, these foundational concepts will be used as a perspective.

8.3 Methods

The methodology adopted for this study is based on a case study approach, which is suitable for exploring the dynamics within the deep-tech startup and about the wider startup landscape to generate insights about the challenges of crossing the Valley of Death. The chosen method allows for an in-depth examination of individual cases within their real-life contexts, enhancing the robustness and relevance of the empirical findings (Eisenhardt 1989). However, by employing a *comparative* study across multiple cases (Eisenhardt and Graebner 2007), the research goes also beyond individual cases, facilitating a broader understanding of patterns and trends across deep-tech support systems, and thus allowing for theoretical generalizations. In this study, two main cases and a total of 17 Swedish robotics startups were covered.

As the study is designed to be explorative, the approach allows for an iterative process between theory and empirical data (Dubois and Gadde 2002). Thus, it is well-suited to the dynamic nature of startups and innovation systems, where pre-defined hypotheses may not fully capture the internal or contextual challenges of deep-tech startups. The explorative nature of the study also aligns with the systemic view discussed in the theoretical background, facilitating a comprehensive exploration of various factors affecting these startups.

Data collection involved a mix of qualitative techniques, primarily semi-structured interviews, and document analysis. The interviews were conducted with founders and key personnel from selected deep-tech startups, while relevant documents, such as annual reports and investment pitches, were reviewed to complement and corroborate interview data. That way, we got a rather thick case for each of the main startup cases. Silverman's (2021) recommendations on qualitative research were followed to ensure that the data analysis followed a systemic coding scheme and data collection methods were sensitive to contextual nuances (see also (Seale and Silverman 1997).

8.4 The Swedish Case

Sweden, known for its innovative environment and robust startup support system, provides a rich context to investigate the dynamics of deep-tech startups. Two of its growing robotics startups, Alpha Robotics and Beta Robotics, exemplify the challenges and opportunities in this space. These two Swedish startups exhibit typical traits of small startups and require long and capital-intensive development before a market can be reached. The entrepreneurs operate their companies on their own. Alpha Robotics is working on a robot that will assist people in living independently, with a primary focus on healthcare. Beta Robotics creates a multifunctional service robot that can be outfitted for specific tasks.

Both organizationally and business-wise, these two companies differ. Alpha Robotics has a product that the market is ready to buy if it can be sold at a suitable price. Therefore, a cost-effective manufacturing process is needed. Beta Robotics has less interest from the market but will be able to have a higher margin on the product. Regarding the organizations' proactivity, risk-taking, and innovativeness, Alpha Robotics can be described as very high, while Beta Robotics is more medium to medium–high. Acting entrepreneurially can be beneficial, but an excess of entrepreneurial propensity can become ineffective (Andersén 2010; Linton 2016). Beta Robotics has surrounded itself with advisors and a board of directors more comprehensively than Alpha Robotics. The market for Beta Robotics is niche and specific, whereas Alpha Robotics has a product that is standardized and could have a very large market if the price is right. Alpha Robotics has difficulty charging high margins on the product, but to bring down the price, the product needs to be further industrialized to reduce manufacturing costs. In contrast, for Beta Robotics, the price is not as decisive to the customer, and there is a greater margin. However, it has been more difficult to reach out to the market and to get people to take the step and buy the product. The cases of Alpha and Beta Robotics show the critical importance of human capital, as discussed earlier. Alpha Robotics, for instance, exemplifies the challenges faced by startups when the product needs further industrialization to reach a competitive price point, highlighting the practical implications of financing and innovation systems.

Alpha and Beta Robotics offer detailed insights into individual startup journeys. Yet, to gain a broader understanding of the entire robotics startup community, it was essential to cast a wider net. We, therefore, ventured beyond these two companies to explore the overarching landscape of robotics startups. This expanded exploration allows us to explore on a deeper level how the theoretical concepts discussed play out on a larger scale within a Swedish innovation system. To achieve this, a broader study was conducted focusing on startups linked to Robotdalen, a regional innovation system for robotics. A total of 23 startups were identified as interesting cases, and interviews were conducted with 17 of these startups. Presented below is a table listing the 17 companies with their latest reported annual turnover and the number of employees:

Table 8.1 offers a comprehensive overview of the financial performances of the 17 startups in focus. Notably, 9 out of the startups have achieved sales of over SEK 2 million in the last annual sales, and total turnover exceeded SEK 75 million, with 47 jobs created. The review of the annual reports reveals an encouraging trend: there is growth in almost every startup with sales above SEK 2 million mark. It is, therefore, reasonable to assume that turnover will increase in the coming years. This positive financial growth trend, especially in deep-tech startups, reaffirms the earlier discussed significance of supportive innovation systems and the role of efficient financial structures in ensuring startup success.

Our interviews uncover a wide variety of financing for these companies. A pre-dominant trend, however, is the extensive reliance on government grants. Institutions such as *Almi, Vinnova* and the *Swedish Agency for Economic and Regional Growth emerge* as major funders through their various grants. Besides institutional support, it is also clear that many entrepreneurs have made personal financial commitments, either by directly investing in their ventures or by securing private loans for this purpose. While venture capital and business angels represent a desired financing avenue, only 8 of the 17 startups have successfully secured such financing, illustrating the competitive nature of this type of funding. The

Table 8.1 Comparative analysis of selected Swedish deep-tech startups

Business	Sales (in thousand SEK)	Number of employees	Type of development	Venture capital
A	24,000	13	Product–Robot	Yes
B	13,000	4	Product–AI	No
C	12,000	6	Product–Robot	No
D	9000	11	Product–Sensors	Yes
E	7000	4	Product–Robot	Yes
F	4000	0	Product–Robot	Yes
G	3000	1	Application for Robot	No
H	2000	5	Service–AI	Yes
I	2000	0	Product–Robot	No
J	200	1	Product–Sensors	No
K	200	1	Product–Robot	Yes
L	100	1	Product–Robot	Yes
M	0	0	Product–Robot	No
N	0	0	Product–Robot	No
O	M&A	N/A	Product–Robot	No
P	M&A	N/A	Application for Robot	No
Q	M&A	N/A	Product–Robot	Yes

heavy reliance on government grants and especially personal financial commitments is indicative of the challenges faced by startups crossing the Valley of Death. It also underscores the importance of robust innovation systems, as highlighted in the theoretical background, where external support can significantly impact a startup's journey.

8.5 Findings

The findings of this study provide insights into the challenges and opportunities faced by deep-tech startups, primarily focusing on financing and product complexity, human capital, and the role of innovation systems.

Firstly, the critical aspect of financing was a prevalent theme throughout the study, revealing the layers of complexities involved in funding deep-tech startups. Entrepreneurs with prior experience in the startup process, especially in funding, tended not to view funding as a major hurdle, though they acknowledged its inherent complexities. The complex nature of financing extends beyond this, with many different types of financing available to companies. This complexity is exacerbated by the fact that long-term financing plans rarely hold and need constant revision, thus requiring more capital than initially anticipated. The Swedish case reveals a clear pattern: simpler products with straightforward industrialization processes typically have a shorter path to market. This is often related to the number of components and the inherent complexity of the product. For example, companies interviewed that developed applications using existing robots faced fewer complexities than those developing a robot from scratch. More complex innovations involve numerous different components and both software and hardware built from scratch increase the difficulties. Such hurdles show the challenge of the Valley of Death for deep-tech startups, where initial development stages recieve support, but the gap between product development and commercial viability poses substantial financial strain.

The complexities in financing are not limited to the product's nature but also extend to the overall financial planning. As the development process progressed, it was conveyed that it became more and more difficult to secure funding. In the beginning stages, it is relatively easy to get started and get grants that do not need repayment, and then expand with, for example, loans. However, as the process unfolds, it becomes increasingly more challenging to find further financing options. Consequently, many entrepreneurs invest their private funds or secure private loans for funding. They often sell equity in their companies, predominantly at advanced stages. But the longer the process takes, the less ownership is reasonable or possible to allocate. This underlines that the complexity of financing increases with the number of different stages, particularly as more complicated products demand greater capital over extended periods. Additionally, the fragmented approach to product development, where the process is divided into smaller stages, may lead to components not fitting together, underscoring the need for a more integrative view of the entire development process.

Next, the study explored the role of human capital and how deep-tech startups could access it and get assistance. Startups exhibited a wide variance in their human capital. While many founders possessed customer or user perspectives that are beneficial for understanding the needs in a good way, industry-specific knowledge and entrepreneurial experience were often lacking. The study indicates a trend where those with industry knowledge and previous experience performed somewhat better. While the data from the Swedish case does not conclusively affirm this, a notable trend emerges. Hence, our findings indicate, as assumed, that founders with higher human capital are more likely to establish successful companies, and we show that there is a strong correlation between the human capital of the founders and a startup's chance of success in the market.

Finally, a third important finding explores the role of innovation systems in supporting deep-tech companies. The lack of a focused strategy or program on the part of the innovation system to aid these companies was identified as a major concern. The study found that key components, such as an effective funding system and access to human capital, were not adequately developed in the innovation systems that supported the interviewed deep-tech startups. Private capital is hard to secure for prolonged and expensive commercialization processes, and challenges such as information asymmetry make external financing costly or even unattainable. This highlights the importance of accessing the right human capital, and it seems that close collaboration with innovation environments can help reduce information asymmetry and supplement the lack of human capital and specialized competencies in startups. Hence, we can conclude that it is critical to invest in innovation environments—where the innovation system may be a key actor—to better support deep-tech startups and the industrialization process. These environments should have a breadth and depth of knowledge in their networks, as well as contributions to research, publicity, and companies. This would allow them to identify any gaps in human capital and try to fill them. In addition, close cooperation with the startup company would help to reduce information asymmetry when compared to more traditional financial institutions. Given the prevalent lack of experience working with startups, innovation systems, and broader environments must aid in identifying suitable industrialization partners. Such collaboration can lead to a more solid foundation for these startups and emphasize the critical importance of specialized innovation systems in fostering growth.

As indicated earlier in the chapter, the interplay between financing, product complexity, human capital, and innovation systems presents a specific and difficult challenge for deep-tech startups. The Swedish cases' findings offer an outline for understanding these complexities and forging a path forward. Tailored support frameworks that align financial, human, and technological resources, grounded in strategic foresight, can reinforce the unique potential of deep-tech companies. The important question remains: How should we design this innovation system?

8.6 Discussion

This discussion underscores the need for a robust innovation system tailored for deep-tech startups, addressing their distinct challenges and leveraging their unique opportunities. Drawing on the study's findings, several key suggestions emerge for improving and designing future innovation systems to best support deep-tech startups.

Specialized innovation environments, tailored for deep tech, are essential. It is argued that traditional means of financial judgment often fall short when dealing with deep tech, due to inherent uncertainties and long developmental timelines. As such, a more nuanced approach is necessary, making capital more accessible through tailored financing models that understand the complexities of deep tech. This entails supporting funds through long development stages, not just earmarking finances for 'safe' shallow-tech projects. Support in the early stages through grants, investments, and seed capital is vital, and the separation of funding systems for entrepreneurial and non-entrepreneurial businesses helps target resources effectively. This study indicates that there are capital market imperfections, in line with Carpenter and Petersen (2002), and that deep-tech environment needs are context-specific.

Additionally, addressing information asymmetry in the financing journey is also underlined. Deep-tech startups often suffer from inaccessible private venture capital due to the complex nature of their offerings. Building on Shane's (2000) idea of prior knowledge, this can be addressed by the specialization of innovation systems in the domain of the deep tech in question. Such systems can articulate the startup's potential to investors, enhancing financing ability.

Thirdly, the mobilization of necessary human capital is pinpointed as crucial. Deep-tech startups need a well-rounded team, encompassing not just technical skills but also commercial and legal expertise. Intellectual capital, especially relational capital, is important for securing financing for startups (Nigam et al. 2021), and our study indicates that this is even more important for deep-tech startups. Investment in education and training to develop a skilled workforce is key to meeting the demands of the deep-tech sector. This calls for an innovation system connecting startups with seasoned professionals who can guide growth stages. Previous research has highlighted how the human capital of founders, such as education and industry experience, is an important aspect of favorable outcomes for startups (Kato et al. 2015). Our research extends this by suggesting how human capital can be developed through targeted training and education in the innovation system. Connections to a broader network, providing continual resources and expertise, become important to success. This reinforces the need for a support system that is dynamic and can develop human capital for deep-tech startups.

Another aspect revolves around network building. Deep-tech startups must access a comprehensive network providing knowledge and resources. This necessitates building collaborative networks that bridge startups with other entities, reducing information asymmetry and facilitating information flow. Emphasis is placed on focusing more on technological specialization rather than regional limitations. A well-orchestrated network aids in rapid feedback, broad resource access, and essential connections. Through a system of innovation perspective (Edquist 1997) our research extends Lundvall and Rikap (2022) research on national and corporate innovation systems. Our results indicate that strategic focus on specialized networks is needed for deep-tech startups, whereas Lundvall and Rikap (2022) highlight the national and corporate level networks.

Finally, the advancement of an entrepreneurial mindset within the innovation system is seen as critical. The dynamic nature of deep tech necessitates a bold, forward-thinking approach—one that focuses on potential and is unafraid of possible failures. This mindset unlocks the full potential of deep-tech startups, focusing on broader possibilities of market disruption and radical innovation. Previous research has highlighted the need for an entrepreneurial mindset of technology leaders and scientists (Iafelice et al. 2022). Our research suggests this a bit differently, it is perhaps not the scientists that need to be more entrepreneurial, rather it is the whole innovation system, not only leaders, but every member of the innovation system.

These five insights are instrumental in guiding stakeholders and policymakers in crafting frameworks that recognize the unique attributes of deep-tech companies. Close collaboration between innovation environments and startups is necessary to facilitate information flow and reduce asymmetry, as is integration with larger industrialization partners, and effective utilization of government grants and policies. Investing in education and training to foster a skilled workforce is also key to meeting the demands of the rapidly growing deep-tech sector. The varied challenges faced by deep-tech startups highlight the critical role of specialized innovation systems in fostering a thriving innovation system. The concerted effort that aligns financial, human, and technological resources, anchored by a clear vision and long-term strategic planning, becomes the path forward (Fig. 8.2).

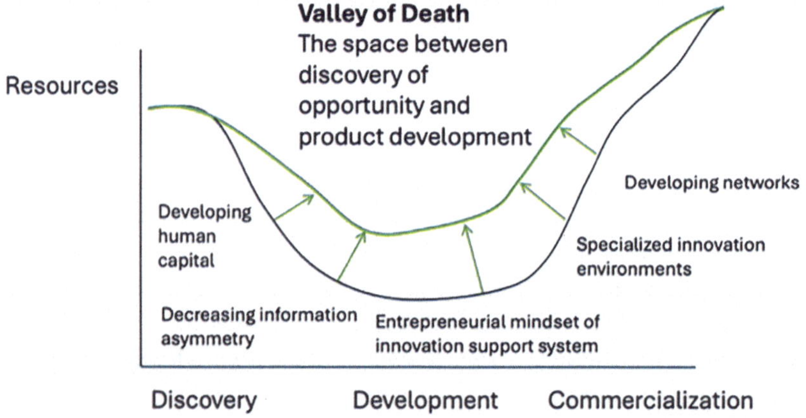

Fig. 8.2 Illustration of the Valley of Death (design based on Markham et al. 2010)

The findings align with our previous work (Kask and Linton 2023), demonstrating principles that serve as critical pillars to the endeavor of nurturing deep-tech startups. It underlines the argument that the tailored support system is not merely preferable but necessary for the rapidly growing deep-tech sector. Future research might also research-specific mechanisms to implement these suggested principles in various regional and technological contexts.

8.7 Conclusion and Implications

In conclusion, deep-tech startups can cross the valley and thrive under a varied approach, diverging from conventional methods. By applying the insights from this research, the success path of deep-tech startups can be paved. This involves understanding deep tech's complexities, reducing financial information asymmetry, mobilizing the right human capital, developing specialized networks, and developing an entrepreneurial mindset in sync with deep tech's ambition. Together, these principles forge a pathway that promotes the growth of individual deep-tech startups and enhances the broader technological landscape, offering novel solutions that have the power to revolutionize industries and enrich society.

This research contributes to the research stream on the Valley of Death by analyzing challenges that deep-tech startups face during early phases. We illustrate how different approaches to the innovation process influence the startups' ability to secure financing, as also highlighted in previous research on Valley of Death (Wessner 2005). The research draws on Romme et al. (2023) and Barr et al. (2009) to propose educational frameworks suitable for deep-tech innovation. Our research also relates to Ellwood et al. (2022) study, who detail the stages of crossing the Valley of Death through specific innovation processes, our research offers a more systemic approach by combining an analysis of human capital and support from the innovation system.

Investors, particularly venture capitalists, need to recalibrate their evaluation metrics to prioritize long-term value creation and technological breakthrough potential (Carpenter and Petersen 2002). Moving beyond mere calculable returns, they should also consider the transformative potential of deep-tech startups. This implies shifting from traditional investment evaluation metrics to those that also capture the long-term disruptive potential and the inherent value of technological advancements. Policy-makers play an essential role in shaping the innovation landscape and are challenged to create policies that adopt specialized funding, network building, and expertise mobilization (Audretsch and Keilbach 2007). This approach highlights the need to focus on technological domains rather than geographical regions, thereby leveraging sector-specific networks to optimize resource use (Chaminade and Edquist 2006), redefining how innovation systems are frequently organized today.

Building on this, the principles shed light on new perspectives, notably in redefining innovation financing, emphasizing the nuanced mobilization of human capital, and introducing a novel perspective on building technologically specialized networks. This approach necessitates a move beyond 'safe' investment paradigms and emphasizes a cohesive blend of various proficiencies, extending human capital theory within complex technology domains. Reorienting networks around technologically specialized, as opposed to regionally confined, provides a fresh understanding of deep-tech innovation. An entrepreneurial approach within innovation systems also reflects a new take on organizational culture, stressing that the system must emulate the dynamism and disruptive potential akin to the startups it supports (Iafelice et al. 2022).

These insights mark a large step toward understanding and fostering deep-tech innovation, with potentially far-reaching effects across industries, economies, and societies. They offer both practical and theoretical insights, enriching the fields of innovation financing, human capital, network theory, and entrepreneurial culture. The complexity of deep-tech innovation requires an adaptable and sophisticated approach, challenging traditional paradigms and inspiring new methodologies. This leads us to a thought: Are our current innovation systems, (too) often bound by geographical borders and conventional risk assessment, fundamentally misaligned with the visionary and disruptive nature of deep-tech innovation? While the answer remains a subject of debate, this research pushes the boundary, suggesting that traditional systems may not be fully equipped for the unique demands of deep-tech innovation. The insights gained from this research present a challenge to traditional theories of innovation management, particularly those that emphasize risk minimization and localized network building. The principles laid out here require a rethinking, shifting the focus from risk-averse investment strategies to ones that embrace the unknown and uncertain potentials. This shift undermines the traditional economic principles of calculable return on investment that still dominate existing financing models. The emphasis on aligning networks based on technological specialization, instead of geography, challenges traditional perspectives found in economic geography and innovation clusters. The call to go beyond local or even national borders, organizing innovation systems by technological fields, represents a departure from regional innovation systems theory.

Future research could consider case studies that compare and contrast traditional innovation systems with those reoriented around deep-tech principles. Comparative analyses can show the tangible benefits of the latter. Qualitative interviews with managers, policymakers, and especially investors established in the deep-tech space can offer further insight into practical challenges and strategies to navigate them.

Finally, promoting an entrepreneurial mindset within innovation systems prompts a reevaluation of traditional management practices, which often favor short-term gains over long-term disruptive potential. This perspective challenges prevailing organizational behavior theories, suggesting a need for frameworks that integrate entrepreneurial thinking into innovation system design. These advancements open new avenues for exploration and debate, inviting researchers to engage with these concepts and question established paradigms. Thus, future research could expand our understanding of innovation in the deep-tech sector and offer a novel perspective on theories and practices that guide our approach to technological advancement. This reorientation toward a potential-driven model suggests a promising shift in innovation support practice. As we venture into an era dominated by deep tech, it becomes urgent to realign our strategies, theories, and practices, ensuring they resonate with the dynamism and promise this sector holds.

References

Jim Andersén. A critical examination of the eo-performance relationship. *International Journal of Entrepreneurial Behaviour & Research*, 16(4):309–328, 2010.

David B. Audretsch and Max Keilbach. The theory of knowledge spillover entrepreneurship. *Journal of Management Studies*, 44(7):1242–1254, 2007.

Philip E. Auerswald and Lewis M. Branscomb. Valleys of death and darwinian seas: Financing the invention to innovation transition in the united states. *The Journal of Technology Transfer*, 28(3):227–239, 2003.

Stephen H. Barr, Theodore Baker, Steven K. Markham, and Angus I. Kingon. Bridging the valley of death: Lessons learned from 14 years of commercialization of technology education. *Academy of Management Learning & Education*, 8(3): 370–388, 2009.

Gary S. Becker. *Human capital: A theoretical and empirical analysis, with special reference to education*. National Bureau of Economic Research, New York, 1964.

Robert E. Carpenter and Bruce C. Petersen. Capital market imperfections, high-tech investment, and new equity financing. *The Economic Journal*, 112(477):F54–F72, 2002. https://doi.org/10.1111/1468-0297.00683.

Cristina Chaminade and Charles Edquist. From theory to practice: the use of the systems of innovation approach in innovation policy. In *Innovation, Science, and Institutional Change: A Research Handbook*, pages 141–163. Oxford University Press, 2006.

Massimo G. Colombo and Luca Grilli. On growth drivers of high-tech startups: Exploring the role of founders' human capital and venture capital. *Journal of Business Venturing*, 25(6):610–626, 2010. https://doi.org/10.1016/j.jbusvent.2009.01.005.

A. Dubois and L. E. Gadde. Systematic combining: an abductive approach to case research. *Journal of Business Research*, 55(7):553–560, 2002.

Charles Edquist. *Systems of innovation: Technologies, institutions, and organizations*. Pinter, London, 1997.

K. M. Eisenhardt. Building theories from case study research. *Academy of Management Review*, 14(4):532–550, 1989.

K. M. Eisenhardt and M. E. Graebner. Theory building from cases: Opportunities and challenges. *Academy of Management Journal*, 50(1):25–32, 2007.

Paul Ellwood, Christopher Williams, and James Egan. Crossing the valley of death: Five underlying innovation processes. *Technovation*, 109:102162, 2022. https://doi.org/10.1016/j.technovation.2021.102162.

Michel Ferrary and Mark Granovetter. The role of venture capital firms in silicon valley's complex innovation network. *Economy and Society*, 38(2):326–359, 2009. https://doi.org/10.1080/03085140902786827.

Bronwyn H. Hall, Pietro Moncada-Paternò-Castello, Sandro Montresor, and Antonio Vezzani. Financing constraints, r&d investments and innovative performances: New empirical evidence at the firm level for europe. *Economics of Innovation and New Technology*, 25(3):183–196, 2016. https://doi.org/10.1080/10438599.2015.1076194.

Sander Hoogendoorn, Hessel Oosterbeek, and Mirjam van Praag. The impact of gender diversity on the performance of business teams: Evidence from a field experiment. *Management Science*, 59(7):1514–1528, 2013. https://doi.org/10.1287/mnsc. 1120.1674.

Brian Iafelice, Thomas Kovijanic, and Marshall W. Condry. Acquiring an entrepreneurial mindset for technology leaders and scientists. *IEEE Engineering Management Review*, 50(3):96–102, 2022. https://doi.org/10.1109/EMR.2022.3192933.

Johan Kask and Gabriel Linton. Five principles for overcoming obstacles in deeptech startup journeys. *Journal of Small Business and Enterprise Development*, 30 (1):1–3, 2023. https://doi.org/10.1108/JSBED-07-2022-0291.

Masatoshi Kato, Hiroyuki Okamuro, and Yuji Honjo. Does founders' human capital matter for innovation? evidence from japanese start-ups. *Journal of Small Business Management*, 53(1):114–128, 2015. https://doi.org/10.1111/jsbm.12091.

Anthony C. Klotz, Keith M. Hmieleski, Bret H. Bradley, and Lowell W. Busenitz. New venture teams: A review of the literature and roadmap for future research. *Journal of Management*, 40(1):226–255, 2014. https://doi.org/10.1177/0149206313493325.

Eun-Jeong Ko and Alexander McKelvie. Signaling for more money: The roles of founders' human capital and investor prominence in resource acquisition across different stages of firm development. *Journal of Business Venturing*, 33(4):438–454, 2018. https://doi.org/10.1016/j.jbusvent.2018.01.003.

Jason Y.-K. Lim and Lowell W. Busenitz. Evolving human capital of entrepreneurs in an equity crowdfunding era. *Journal of Small Business Management*, 58(1): 106–129, 2020. https://doi.org/10.1111/jsbm.12499.

Gabriel Linton. *Entrepreneurial orientation: Reflections from a contingency perspective*. Örebro University, Örebro, 2016.

Bengt-Åke Lundvall. *National Systems of Innovation: Towards a Theory of Innovation and Interactive learning*. Pinter, London, 1992.

Bengt-Åke Lundvall and Cecilia Rikap. China's catching-up in artificial intelligence seen as a co-evolution of corporate and national innovation systems. *Research Policy*, 51(1):104395, 2022. https://doi.org/10.1016/j.respol.2021.104395.

Steven K. Markham, Steven J. Ward, Lynda Aiman-Smith, and Angus I. Kingon. The valley of death as context for role theory in product innovation. *Journal of Product Innovation Management*, 27(3):402–417, 2010. https://doi.org/10.1111/j.1540-5885.2010. 00724.x.

Richard R. Nelson. *National innovation systems: a comparative analysis*. Oxford University Press, Oxford, 1993.

Nandita Nigam, Samir Mbarek, and Anis Boughanmi. Impact of intellectual capital on the financing of startups with new business models. *Journal of Knowledge Management*, 25(1):227–250, 2021. https://doi.org/10.1108/JKM-06-2020-0460.

Marija Rakas and Daniel S. Hain. The state of innovation system research: What happens beneath the surface? *Research Policy*, 48(9):103787, 2019. 10.1016/ j.respol.2019.103787.

A. Georges L. Romme, Jason Bell, and Gerrit Frericks. Designing a deep-tech venture builder to address grand challenges and overcome the valley of death. *Journal of Organization Design*, pages 1–21, 2023. https://doi.org/10.1007/s41469-023-00113-2.

Birgitta Sandberg and Leena Aarikka-Stenroos. What makes it so difficult? a systematic review on barriers to radical innovation. *Industrial Marketing Management*, 43(8):1293–1305, 2014. https://doi.org/10.1016/j.indmarman.2014.08.003.

Clive Seale and David Silverman. Ensuring rigour in qualitative research. *The European Journal of Public Health*, 7(4):379–384, 1997. https://doi.org/10.1093/eurpub/7. 4.379.

Scott Shane. Prior knowledge and the discovery of entrepreneurial opportunities. *Organization Science*, 11(4):448–469, 2000. https://doi.org/10.1287/orsc.11.4.448.14602.

David Silverman. *Doing qualitative research*. Sage, London, 2021.

Charles W. Wessner. Driving innovations across the valley of death. *Research-Technology Management*, 48(1):9–12, 2005. https://doi.org/10.1080/08956308.2005.11657292.

Joakim Winborg and Hans Landström. Financial bootstrapping in small businesses: Examining small business managers' resource acquisition behaviors. *Journal of Business Venturing*, 16(3):235–254, 2001. https://doi.org/10.1016/S0883-9026(99)00055-5.

Mike Wright, Keith M. Hmieleski, Donald S. Siegel, and Michael D. Ensley. The role of human capital in technological entrepreneurship. *Entrepreneurship Theory and Practice*, 31(6):791–806, 2007. https://doi.org/10.1111/j.1540-6520.2007.00202.x.

9

AI Adoption Challenges in Family-Owned Firms: A Case Study

Maija Worek and Päivi Aaltonen

9.1 Introduction

Digital transformation is currently reshaping organizations, individuals, ecosystems, and societies simultaneously on many levels (Dąbrowska et al. 2022a), forcing firms to adopt and apply new technologies (George et al. 2020) such as AI, which currently shutters many traditional industries dominated by long-lived family firms (Kammerlander and Ganter 2015). AI indeed provides a remarkable opportunity for family firms' growth (Lannon et al. 2023; Liu et al. 2020) but it is not yet widely applied: less than 5% of German family firms apply AI in their daily business (Soluk and Kammerlander 2023). Traditionally, technology adoption has been examined through models such as TOE

M. Worek (✉)
FHWien der WKW University of Applied Sciences for Management and Communication, Währinger Gürtel 97, 1180 Vienna, Austria
e-mail: maija.worek@fh-wien.ac.at

P. Aaltonen
Business School, LUT University, Lappeenranta, Finland

P. Aaltonen and E. Kurvinen (eds.), *Contemporary Issues in Industry 5.0*, Technology, Work and Globalization, https://doi.org/10.1007/978-3-031-74779-3_9

(technology, organization, and environment) (Tornatzky 1990; Arpaci et al. 2012) and TAM (technology acceptance model) (Davis 1989). However, evidence suggests that these theories do not apply to AI due to its complexity, and its lack of individual aspects such as talent, trust, and human collaboration (Frankiewicz and Chamorro-Premuzic 2020; Glikson and Wooley, 2020). Family firms, which are the most ubiquitous company form in the world (Villalonga and Amit 2020), have even more factors in play and are significantly slow to adopt new technologies (Chrisman et al. 2015; McElheran et al. 2024; Ulrich et al. 2023). Thus, empirical evidence on family firms' AI adoption would highlight the challenges faced by multiple traditional industry firms. Technology adoption has been discussed from various operational perspectives such as individual, organizational, technological, and environmental (Alsheibani et al. 2018), and by classifying findings on different levels of analysis (Bagozzi et al. 2022; Bertani et al. 2021; Dąbrowska et al. 2022b; Michael et al. 2019). To grasp the nuances of the social context and individual perspectives, informal routines, and organizational legacy (Geels 2002), family firms offer a fruitful base for subsequent theorizing AI adoption. While there is a long tradition of AI research in fields like operations management and information systems (Lee 2020), other management fields have only recently taken an interest in its organizational impacts (Michael et al. 2019; Iansiti and Lakhani 2020). This research ranges from organizational challenges and opportunities to AI's impact on functions such as marketing, human resources, and management and decision-making (Davenport and Ronanki 2018; Andreas and Michael 2019; Tambe et al. 2019). AI technologies introduce several novel challenges—but also potential for an emergent competitive edge. Potential benefits include positive economic value, the emergence of new organizational roles and functions, promotion of interactivity, increased comprehension, and instantaneous feedback (Kellogg et al. 2020), and organizations can maximize these benefits by balancing between AI augmentation and automation (Raisch and Krakowski 2021).

A growing body of literature examines new technology adoption and digitalization in family firms. These contributions assess when and how family firms adopt new technologies (Soluk and Kammerlander 2023 2021; König et al. 2013; Dressler and Paunovic 2021; Soluk 2022;

Souder et al. 2017), human and cultural resources (Ano and Bent 2022), socioemotional wealth aspects (Basly and Hammouda 2020), managerial attention as a precursor (Kammerlander and Ganter 2015), changes in work environment (Dressler and Paunovic 2021) and related topics such as business model innovation (BMI) (Brenk et al. 2019) as well as external triggers, such as crises, that push the companies toward digital adoption (Kraus et al. 2020; Soluk 2022; Soluk and Kammerlander 2021) and also the possible barriers for such implementation processes (Soluk and Kammerlander 2021 2023). The idiosyncratic nature that also impacts their technology adoption can take many forms. For example, due to the concentrated ownership structures, family firms pursue efficient decision-making processes. This can be a source of competitive advantage but also a barrier if the family is hesitant toward digital transformation (Soluk and Kammerlander 2023). What is more, the family influence and the non-financial goals (Kotlar et al. 2022) strongly impact the company's strategic preferences (Chrisman et al. 2015). Further features include family firms' risk aversion toward new technologies (König et al. 2013), which might further shape family firms' adoption of disruptive technologies.

Building on theoretical arguments, it is proposed that the influence of family in the business and the managerial aspect leads to specific challenges due to their idiosyncratic nature discussed above (König et al. 2013). There are only a few contributions examining the specific barriers that family firms experience, concentrating generally on digital transformation (Soluk and Kammerlander 2021), yet not the next evolution of AI technologies (Xu et al. 2021). Considering the potential opportunities AI can offer for family firms' growth (Liu et al. 2020) we posit that there is a need for further research on AI adoption in family firms (as also called by (Lannon et al. 2023)). To examine this, we adopt the following research question: RQ) *What kind of challenges do family-owned businesses experience in AI adoption and implementation?*

The purpose of this study is to empirically examine the challenges and eventual responses emerging in a new technology, namely the AI adoption process in five family-owned businesses. This study contributes to the literature on new technology adoption in family firms by highlighting specific challenges family firms experience in AI adoption and how they attempt to respond to these. Second, we contribute to the literature on new technology adoption in general by building specific categories describing the challenges the case companies face. Building on this, we form propositions to be tested and developed for further studies on technology adoption in family firms.

9.2 Theoretical Framework

9.2.1 AI Adoption in Industry 5.0

Artificial intelligence (AI) in current literature refers to a group of technologies and their functional applications, or a general level of technological maturity (Lichtenthaler 2020; Lee 2020). The focal points can be for example in the general operations and impacts of the applications (Glaser et al. 2021; Kellogg et al. 2020), or in the temporal development of industrial sectors, inspiring such terms as Intelligent Industry, Industry 4.0. or Industrial AI, or in the more detailed functionalities of algorithms technologies and uses, such as Cyber-Physical Systems (CPS), Internet of Things (IoT), and cloud computing (Lee 2020; Xu et al. 2021). Studies on the impact of such advanced technologies emphasize the interplay between technology, organization, and environment (TOE) (Tornatzky 1990), or novel technology acceptance (UTAUT) (Venkatesh 2022). However, currently, the availability of technology is no longer an issue and calls have been made to include the "human" perspective in the studies (Frankiewicz and Chamorro-Premuzic 2020; Agostini and Nosella 2019). The term Industry 5.0 further credits the impact of technology development on society as a whole, increasing resilience, prosperity, and increasing employee well-being—the society of human–machine work symbiosis (Xu et al. 2021). Further, this increasing maturity of AI technologies illustrates the industrial divergence between needs, strategies, and international expansion pathways due to an increasing variety of application usage. Technology-intensive industries utilizing AI in their operations differ from current empirical studies on AI adoption—such as the operations of plat-form giants such as Uber and Netflix (Iansiti and Lakhani 2020), and the general conceptualization of AI driving productivity and innovation across diverse indus-tries and companies (Brynjolfsson and McElheran 2016; Brynjolfsson and Mcafee 2017; Liu et al. 2020; Wamba-Taguimdje et al. 2020). Recent studies emphasize individual cognitive elements such as trust (Glikson and Wooley, 2020, Mubarak and Petraite 2020) and argue that understanding AI adoption is beyond simply using existing technology adoption models (Wang et al. 2021). A multilevel empirical perspective would create a solid base for subsequent theorizing (Dąbrowska et al. 2022b) by including TOE—perspectives on the human side of AI (similarly e.g. Davenport and Ronanki 2018; Frankiewicz and Chamorro-Premuzic 2020). Thus, to assess how Industry 5.0 technologies impact firm operations, a holistic view of technology, organization, the market, and *people* should be taken into consideration.

9.2.2 Technology Adoption in Family Firms

The literature on new technology adoption in family businesses is scattered over various disciplines, such as family firm innovation (review by (Calabrò et al. 2019)) and BMI (Brenk et al. 2019; Brinkerink et al. 2020). Findings from current studies show that the idiosyncratic characteristics, such as ownership and decision-making structures (Soluk and Kammerlander 2023), family influence, succession process (Lannon et al. 2023), and non-financial goals of family firms (Kotlar et al. 2022), may create barriers and drivers that hinder the technology adaption process, specifically its organization and management (De Massis et al. 2012). In this vein, Bruque and Moyano (2007) find that personnel issues, such as difficulties in finding a qualified workforce needed for the specific technology can pose a barrier to such an adoption process in the family firm. Furthermore, internal power structures and culture can pose further challenges (Bruque and Moyano 2007; López-Fernández et al. 2016). From a theoretical perspective, König et al. (2013) develop a model proposing that family influence weakens the forces that influence the adoption of discontinuous technologies. Forces such as formalization, need for external capital, and political resistance strengthen the sources of organizational paralysis, ties to existing assets, and rigidity of mental models. They argue that the influence of a family results in different challenges in new technology adoption than those that apply to nonfamily firms for these reasons. Kammerlander and Ganter (2015) highlight the meaning of managerial support (along with (Cassia et al. 2012; Niehm et al. 2010)), which is essential in new technology adoption. In this vein, managerial non-economic goals (Kotlar et al. 2022) need to be aligned with adoption processes. Without managerial support, especially from the owner-manager-family, AI adoption will not reach support in the family company (Soluk and Kammerlander 2023). In addition, Cassia et al. (2012) found that other managerial factors such as commitment and time orientation potentially have a positive impact generally on innovation adoption. New technology can generally be viewed as risky for the family firms' internal landscape such as socioemotional wealth, which may even challenge the family stability when new methods and potentially new employees are introduced (Gómez-Mejía et al. 2007). Family firms generally protect their wealth by avoiding risky innovations (Muñoz-Bullón and Sanchez-Bueno 2011). A few studies state socioemotional wealth as central to new technology adoption (Souder et al. 2017), finding that family firms are more reluctant regarding new technology adoption, especially among family firms with minority family influence. To sum up, current findings on new technology adoption in family firms have found that family firms might face specific challenges in such processes due to their idiosyncratic nature. While such contributions exist, the focus of current studies lies on innovation or digital transformation in general. Only scarce evidence exists regarding AI adoption specifically; more is being called for, especially regarding the challenges in AI adoption (Lannon et al. 2023; Soluk and Kammerlander 2023). This is surprising considering the specific challenges they may have, such as the lack of necessary (for family firm preferably internal) human resources (Soluk and Kammerlander 2023), which makes them dependent on external knowledge and resources. To protect the socioemotional wealth (Gómez-Mejía et al. 2007; Souder et al. 2017), family firms may withhold from adopting disruptive technologies altogether. These findings show that family firms may handle new technology adoption processes differently than nonfamily firms and that they may face particular challenges in such transitions. For practitioners and family managers to support and manage such processes, more evidence is needed on family firms' new technology adoption, especially AI.

9.3 Methods

To understand the complexity of established family-owned companies in their process of adopting and implementing new technology, a qualitative case study setting with an abductive approach and systematic combining (Dubois and Gadde 2002) was applied. This setting was chosen, as our interest was to find interdependencies between the cases, generating reasonable justifications (in the vein of (Eisenhardt 1989; Eisenhardt and Graebner 2007)).

9.3.1 Cases Selection and Data Collection

All of the case companies are part of a joint research project, where multiple rounds of primary data collection were applied over the years 2021–2023. The project aimed at developing automated solutions for manufacturing and AI, so all of the companies already have adopted AI in their products and processes. We obtain primary data from interviews, workshops, and secondary data from publicly available company reports, such as annual reports and press releases. Several interviews and workshops were conducted with key persons responsible for the AI implementation in each company. Altogether more than 16 h of primary data from 12 different individuals were analyzed. Secondary data encompasses the last 10 years (2012–2022) of annual reports, press releases, and official documents for each company, as well as some additional data, such as publicly available company videos and podcasts. Our sampling criteria ensure that all interviewees have first-hand experience on the topic and have an interest in developing solutions concerning new technology adaptation. Additionally, wide gathering of secondary data ensures data triangulation and inclusion of additional viewpoints that were not covered in the interviews as well as early identification of communication of the topic in the company documents. An overview of the data is presented in Table 9.1.

Table 9.1 Types of data per company

Case	4 h workshop	Additional interviews	Positions	Hrs	Additional data
A	4 persons	NA	CEO, systems developer, AI systems developer, head of engineering	4	Annual reports 2012–2022, press releases
B	2 persons	1	Product group manager, project lead	5	Annual reports 2012–2022, press releases, website reports, podcast, video
C	No	5	Data science managers, Head of people flow op timization, Head of Ana lytics, Head of (X) devel opment	5	Annual reports 2012–2022, web site reports, press releases
D	No	1	Director, Data-driven services	1	Annual reports 2012–2022, website reports, press releases
E	1 person	1	Product group manager	1	Annual reports 2012–2022, website reports, press releases

Table 9.2 Key characteristics of case companies

Company	Year founded	Last available revenue (*t*€)	Family ownership (%)	Last available nr of employees
A	1963	79.790	86.40	550
B	1970	755.123	61.93	1800
C	1910	10.906	62.28	61,380
D	2005	4.088	74.53	11,500
E	1908	158.324	18.96	802

9.3.2 Case Companies

Details of the case companies are displayed in Table 9.2. All of the companies are based in Finland but operate in global business internationally and have international subsidiaries except for Company A. In all of the companies, the majority of the shares are held by the family. Except for Company A, all of them are publicly listed companies.

9.3.3 Data Analysis

The data was analyzed with a content analysis based on the themes arising from the raw primary and secondary data (Eisenhardt 1989; Eisenhardt and Graebner 2007), the overarching research question as a central theme. In the first step, central themes but also other related topics that the interviewees mentioned as relevant were highlighted in the raw data applying open coding. This gave us an understanding that there were many simultaneous topics discussed on AI, such as cultural issues, the process, the status where the company currently is or was, and the barriers and drivers. It was decided to concentrate on the challenges on many levels, as these seemed to be present in many interviews and workshop discussions. Axial coding was applied here in the interviewee's statements regarding challenges. These were organized into first-order themes that were as close to the original statements as possible (Corley and Gioia 2004). The second-order themes were formed based on the first-order themes, as we organized the first-order themes in thematic categories. Thus, the aggregate dimensions are the most abstract ones, compared to the original statements. After this, this categorization was compared with suitable literature on technology adoption challenges (Dąbrowska et al. 2022b). Based on this comparison with the literature and the aggregate dimensions, categories of challenges identified in the data are built. The categories and dimensions are presented in Figure 1. In the figure, the column on the left represents the themes highlighted in the raw data. From these themes, conceptual categories are developed. Finally, the conceptual categories are further organized in aggregate dimensions of people, organization, and environment. The aggregate dimensions represent the most abstract form of the challenges. Figure 9.1 summarizes the analysis.

9.4 Findings

Several categories of challenges can be found in the data. Three main categories are people, organization, and environment (POE), which are further divided into more detailed subcategories, as presented in Figure 1. In the following, the categories are described, enriched with a few examples from the data, and reflected in the theory. Further examples from the data with a connection to theory are presented in Tables 9.3, 9.4, and 9.5.

9.4.1 People Level

The challenges related to human resources in the organization include themes such as talent attraction/job concerns, communication/motivation, and involvement, summarized in Table 9.3. Examples of addressing these challenges are different ways of motivating and involving people, addressing their fear of being useless, and the possibilities of incentivizing their innovative initiatives regarding AI. Below, we discuss each of these challenges in this category, presenting examples from the data and finally reflecting our findings with current literature.

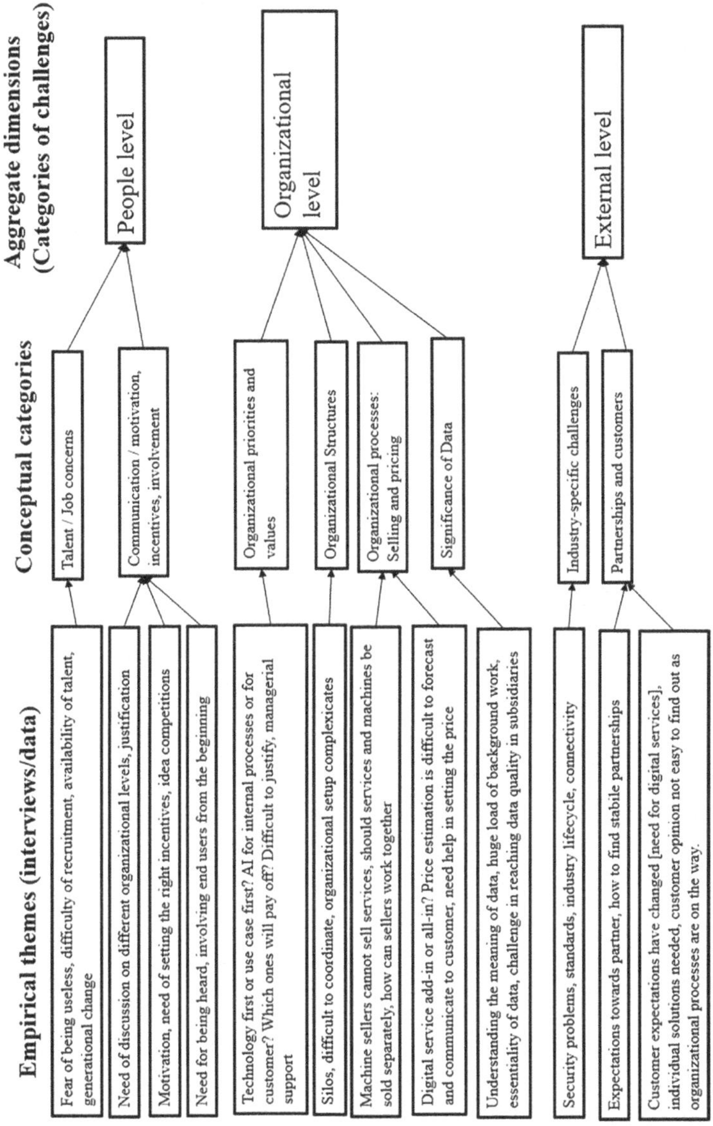

Fig. 9.1 Data structure

Table 9.3 Main findings: people

Challenge	Selection of quotes	Theoretical concepts
Talent attraction, Job concerns	"People fear for their jobs, that an algorithm will replace them" (Company D) "It comes to the recruitment of people and availability of talent and skills"… there was no way of getting people to location X". (Company B)	Talent attraction (Bruque and Moyano 2007; Frankiewicz and Chamorro-Premuzic 2020); importance of tacit knowledge (Hadjimichael and Tsoukas 2019)

Challenge	Selection of quotes	Theoretical concepts
Communication, Motivation	"need of discussion is in higher management level and then sales, marketing and after marketing" (Company B) "When they get something from you, they will deliver the stuff you want… If you put it like that, it motivates people. But if you just ask them or make them deliver data, it's a no go." (Company D) "You need to find the words to motivate each type of personnel and tell them why we need their input, if you force or give them instructions, it's a no-go it won't work" (Company D)	Employee resistance and the lack of formalization (Soluk and Kammerlander 2021); negative associations (Tong et al. 2021); new forms of motivation and control (Kellogg et al. 2020), increase visibility in organizations to combat the fear of losing jobs (Haefner et al. 2021; Senoner et al. 2022)
Involvement	"It is very important to involve the service area managers and service personnel themselves already at the beginning to make them feel heard and important so that they don't feel that this is not kind of absurd order with black magic like AI, which may create all kinds of unnecessary resistance." (Company C)	AI requires humans to change their behavior (Krakowski et al. 2023), Collaborating with AI is different than with humans (Anthony et al. 2023; Kellogg et al. 2020), AI requires humans to improve or 'be better' (Allen and Choudhury 2022; Anthony et al. 2023; Tong et al. 2021)

Table 9.4 Main findings: organization

Challenge	Selection of quotes	Theoretical concepts
Priorities and values	"If they don't see that a customer would be ready to pay for this, it is often difficult to justify an investment for the managers." (Company C) "It's a question of how they are prioritized as the budget is monetary, resources are restricted… a clear organizational process does not exist." (Company C) the difficulty in digital services is that they don't necessarily deliver direct monetary value, but instead they impact reputation, brand image, customer satisfaction, usability, the problem is how to convert this to a currency… we don't knowthis yet" (Company C)	Managerial support is essential for the implementation of discontinuous technologies (Kammerlander and Ganter 2015; Porfírio et al. 2021); Experimentation with AI is not reported transparently (Rammer et al. 2022)
Structures	"Lack of knowledge, lack of assigned, clear roles and diverse responsibilities… It is more of an organizational challenge." (Company C) "It's probably the biggest learning and challenge in how we can offer simple valuecreating solutions for the customer when our setup is very complex". (Company D) "… the how can we present new things for the customer when there are a couple of more hurdles in between compared to like, Spotify. We cannot communicate directly with the customer through the system…" (Company D)	Change and organizational design (Dąbrowska et al. 2022b), Adopting new organizational structures and forms (Lanzolla et al. 2020), and cross-functional collaboration (Dremel et al. 2017) is essential; Less centralization and formalities of organizational structures (Craig and Moores 2006), new forms of control (Kellogg et al. 2020), reduction of production variance (Craig and Moores 2006): AI enables new forms of control (Kellogg et al. 2020)

(continued)

Table 9.4 (continued)

Challenge	Selection of quotes	Theoretical concepts
Pricing and selling	"The customers strongly assume that the digital services are included in the price" (Company B). "We have needed help... one needs much knowledge about the existing offering in the market and about their prices and quality" (Company B). "We are not where we want to be in how to set the price... and how to communicate the promise of the value to the customer". (Company D) "you will need to build a new business unit, own sellers and customer responsibility" (Company F) "I quite often give access to digital service for free for a few months to let the customer try it out and see the benefits and then to charge for them after the period (Company B)	The focal point is on research and long term orientation, also paving the way to increasing number of custom solutions and expertise (Aaltonen et al. 2023a); AI leverages annual sales (Rammer et al. 2022)
Significance of data	"Data is usually not a mystical IT-thing; it means whether we know what is happening in the company or not" (Company C) "It is central to clear for people that they know how the data is connected to what their job and what happens to the data after that" (Company B) "the culture needs to change regarding why we need data, why it is important, why do we need to see that it is of high quality. There are a lot of discussions on this, as we are in a traditional industry." (Company C)	Data quality and accuracy should be an organizational priority (Al Badi et al. 2022; Merhi 2023); Data drives learning from AI and networks development (Brynjolfsson and McElheran 2016); Data analytic capabilities reflect on innovation capabilities (Wu et al. 2021)

Table 9.5 Main findings: environment

Challenge	Selection of quotes	Theoretical concepts
Industry, legislation	"There must come something also to the EU side or government side or global rules for how the things can be done" (Company A). "(...) they might need a very specific thing (standard fulfilled) in China, but at the same time, to enter the US market, we need to fill a standard and make a change in hardware". (Company C) "The most critical technology enabler for us is connectivity and satellites" (Company B)	Government and industry characteristics generally impact innovation performance (Collinson and Liu 2019), Ai has an impact on wage inequality (Domini et al. 2022)

Challenge	Selection of quotes	Theoretical concepts
Partners	"We need to find the right partners in these projects (...) expect the partner to have experience which can be utilized" (Company B) "They have not even seen this type of equipment at some places. (Company A) "We started developing it with the other part, other (product) guys, and we did it with remote connections or that stuff... It was a long process to do" (Company A)	Constant need to increase AI applications (Berente et al. 2021; Haenlein and Kaplan 2019), ability to manage partnerships and IS sourcing as central (Peppard andWard 2004), Data role in networks (Gregory et al. 2021)
Customers	"The customers strongly assume that the digital services are included in the price" (Company B). "We have needed help... one needs much knowledge about the existing offering in the market and about their prices and quality" (Company B). "We are not where we want to be in how to set the price... and how to communicate the promise of the value to the customer". (Company D)"It is essential to have the customer involved" (Company B). "Customers' strong opinion is that the digital services should be included in the hardware price" (Company B) "It's essential howto present it to the customer and make it into something valuable instead of offering some complicated analysis" (Company D) "development together with a customer is slower and a lot is going on so it is more difficult to introduce more stuff" (Company D)	Digital Transformation changes customer expectations (Aaltonen et al. 2023b; Kurvinen et al. 2024), opens up ways for organizations to develop their offerings (Gregory et al. 2021), changes in customer acquisition (Krakowski et al. 2023)

9.4.1.1 Talent Attraction and Job Concerns

Some case companies experience challenges regarding talent when implementing AI. On the other hand, in attracting the right personnel in the right locations and on the other hand in keeping talent while addressing their concerns regarding AI. Due to the tradition and the nature of its industry, Company B's headquarters is located far away from major cities. To address this, they had to establish a new subsidiary through the acquisition of a software company to get the resources they needed. This shows that companies located far away from central areas need to find creative ways to attract personnel needed for AI implementation and development. A representative of Company B describes this as follows:

> "it comes to the recruitment of people and availability of talent and skills"... "(we only had) RandD locations in X and Y (far away from the major cities). We faced problems and that's also in the background of opening this site, especially automation software talents, there was no way of getting people to location X." (Company B)

Another challenge in the people category is related to the concerns that the personnel may have when parts of it can be given over to AI and automatized processes, as a representative from company D describes:

> "People fear for their jobs, that an algorithm will replace them" (...) "this has appeared also in surprising connections" (...) "people worry about that what will happen to them when even this kind of ape work will be taken away." (Company D)

In this case, the company had developed an internal AI-based solution to automatize a simple, monotonous task, facing resistance from worried employees who were nervous about the changes in their tasks and the possibility of AI replacing them altogether. Ways to address this challenge are similar to addressing the motivation and involvement, which are discussed below.

9.4.1.2 Communication/Motivation and Incentives

Related to the fears described above, in many cases the interviewees mentioned the difficulties in the high need for discussion and with getting employees on board with the change on different organizational levels. With AI implementation, many actors needed to be convinced about the significance of data and the automation that AI implementation had on these particular actor's daily tasks. Generational issues and differences in organizational levels were mentioned. In the course of AI implementation, the interviewees described that it was also a cultural change in the organization, the whole company needing to change the direction toward an "AI culture." To communicate the change and to get people on board with it, companies described different ways to involve and incentivize personnel:

> "The same thing applies for service personnel and internal personnel as for our customers; once they see the added benefit they'll get, they'll work with you to give you the stuff you want." (–) "You need to find the words to motivate each type of personnel and tell them why we need their input, if you force or give them instructions, it's a no-go, it won't work." (Company D).

> "It is very important to involve the service area managers and service personnel themselves already at the beginning to make them feel heard and important so that they don't feel that this is not kind of absurd order with black magic like AI, which may create all kinds of unnecessary resistance." (Company C)

Generally, the cruciality of the human aspect is highlighted in the process of new technology adoption, both in general DT literature (Davenport and Redman 2020) as well as in family firms adopting new technologies (Ano and Bent 2022; Bruque and Moyano 2007). The aspect of talent attraction is also found a barrier in the earlier literature on family SMEs in new technology adoption (Bruque and Moyano 2007). Our data underlines that it is important to find ways to motivate and communicate with each type of employee group to reduce resistance. In line with these findings, Soluk and Kammerlander (2021) also found that one of the barriers to introducing digital technologies in Mittelstand firms is employee resistance. One way to reduce such resistance is to share success stories on the topic among both internal and external stakeholders. This can benefit new technology adoption in the organization. Such experiences can help to justify and effectively demonstrate the value and the potential benefits for the organization as well as for the individuals and lower their resistance to the adoption. Such conscious communication supports the new technology adoption, but family firms might struggle with this due to the lack of formalization, especially in smaller firms (De Massis et al. 2012; König et al. 2013). In the literature on digital transformation, aspects of human resources and talent are also seen as crucial for new technology adoption (Davenport and Redman 2020). Based on this, we propose:

P1 Employee resistance can pose a barrier to the AI adoption and implementation process in family firms; involving and motivating employees early by showing the potential benefit of their work contributes to success.

9.4.2 Organizational Level

The challenges found on the organizational level category include barriers in organizational structures and values as well as the specific organizational processes such as pricing and selling AI-based solutions. The significance of data is presented as a further challenge, as in case it is not acknowledged by key stakeholders, it hinders the AI adoption and implementation process. Below we discuss each of these challenges in this category, presenting examples from the data, and reflecting our findings with DT and family firm literature, summarized in Table 9.4.

9.4.2.1 Organizational Priorities and Values

The challenges in organizational priorities regard to the decisions on which digital projects to support and invest in an organization, oftentimes without knowing which ones will be beneficial and which ones not. Furthermore, whether AI should be developed and implemented to smoothen the company's internal processes whether they should concentrate on the processes of the customer, and whether there should be the technology first or a use case first are central dilemmas of priorities. These quotations reflect the challenges in setting the organization's priorities for certain projects, where the lack of process poses a barrier to the justification:

> it's a question of how to create these innovations in digital products and services and how they are prioritized as the budget is monetary, resources are restricted..." (...) "For this, a clear organizational process does not exist." "If they don't see that a customer would be ready to pay for this, it is often difficult to justify an investment for the managers. (Company C)

In the literature, the alignment of the AI implementation process with the organization's goals and metrics such as key performance indicators (KPIs) is essential to justify the resources needed for the projects. The lack of formal processes in initiating AI-based innovations can hinder the implementation process, especially if the organization lacks a clear vision of AI altogether (Bérubé et al. 2021). A further barrier to the internal priority setting is the nature of AI products and the difficulty of evaluating their monetary value:

> Before the digital era, we could calculate just how fast it (the product) works (and calculate the investment) but now the difficulty in digital services is that they don't necessarily deliver direct monetary value, but instead, they impact reputation, brand image, customer satisfaction, usability, the problem is how to convert this to a currency... we don't know this yet (Company C)

Lack of managerial support in combination with a lack of internal structures and processes is presented as a further barrier to the development:

> "Our highest manager may communicate to all of us and encourage us to boldly try out new things (with data), but it's not an incentive, it's just a pep talk. This kind of encouraging talk is not worth much or there is none. It would be great to try out new stuff, but if our technology just is not on a certain level, it makes no sense to develop something temporary just to try out new improvements for example with an algorithm (Company C).
>
> it was great that our owners realized that we need to invest in lifecycle and digital services to attract investors. And I was like, yeah, finally we start connecting the pieces of the puzzle, this is how it should go" (…) "As I talked to our CEO about whether we will now become a software company, he said it's not what our owners want, it's not our DNA. But if it's what our customers need it's fine, then the owners also understand it (Company B).
>
> It's not easy in any way (to get data development projects on the way), we talked a lot about it internally, and finally, we got the CEO convinced, he talked about it in the board meetings and then things started rolling, but we still weekly discuss on how to proceed internally with these things" (Company B)
>
> Finally, the organization's own identity can stand in the way of AI implementation, as in case B:
>
> "We just kept hearing (internally) that 'but we are machine producing company!'(…) We can't be just a machine producing company anymore or we will lose in this competition." This reflects the need for a cultural change crucial to the implementation, as discussed above in the people category of challenges as well.

To sum up, challenges regarding organizational priorities and values relate to the difficulties in getting support for initiated AI projects due to a lack of organizational processes, a lack of (honest) managerial support, or difficulties in articulating the possible monetary value of digital products. Specifically, regarding managerial support, in the literature, Kammerlander and Ganter (2015) highlight the need for managerial support as essential for the implementation of discontinuous technologies. In family firms, this challenge may be particularly relevant due to their characteristic of exercising favoritism in recruiting and toward peers, resulting in a lack of high-quality managers (De Massis et al. 2012). For the implementation of complex new technologies such as AI, that require significant changes in organizational structures and processes, human capital is particularly relevant. The rigidity of certain managerial models connected to family influence hinders the adoption of discontinuous technologies (König et al. 2013). Based on this, we propose:

P2 (a) Organizational priorities and values can pose a barrier to AI implementation in the family firm if the organization's identity is not in line with the proposed developments.

P2 (b) Lack of honest managerial support can pose a challenge for AI implementation in family firms.

9.4.2.2 Organizational Structures

General structural themes that emerged from the interviews include silos, which make cross-functional cooperation more difficult. Oftentimes, the anticipated need for a new process or structure was mentioned. Compared to business-to-customer software development, business-to-business software was experienced as more difficult to test the application as the "way to reach the end user" is not as straightforward, as interviewees from companies C and D describe:

> Lack of knowledge, lack of assigned, clear roles, and diverse responsibilities. If we have roles in service development where one silo is responsible for portfolio management, one for selling spare parts, one in service development concepts, and one in service contracts, then you suddenly have six or seven teams, and developing something new would require a combination of these teams, it is difficult to coordinate (Company C)

> It's probably the biggest learning and challenge of how we can offer simple value-creating solutions for the customer when our setup is very complex. (Company D)

Organizational structure relates to the formalization and management structures of family firms and is also related to innovation development in family firms: less formality and decentralized structures enabled innovation development (Craig and Moores 2006; Kraus et al. 2020). In line with this, AI implementation triggers various changes in organizational processes and structures and strategic alignment (Cennamo et al. 2020; Dąbrowska et al. 2022b), which is essential to successfully implement new technologies. As is reflected in the quotation of Company C above, establishing cross-functional teams may smoothen technology adoption in the whole organization, but to make such teams work, they need to be coordinated efficiently and they need an established structure. In line with this, we propose:

P3 Lack of suitable or too complex organizational structures and silos can hinder AI implementation processes in family firms. Flexible structures are needed to address this.

9.4.2.3 Organizational Processes: Selling and Pricing

Challenges mentioned in processes such as selling the product include difficulties in combining the capabilities of sellers that are used to selling the "traditional" hardware product that is each of the case company's core products. When software is added, the added value for the customer needs to be packaged, priced, and also sold in a new way, as new needs of the customer are met, and new solutions can be offered. Some companies result in adding more sellers sharing responsibilities, one concentrating on traditional products and the other one on digital services. This, however, results in organizational silos, where sellers compete on the same incentives and also confusion from the customer side. Regarding pricing, it is experienced difficult to justify and set a price for an added AI service. Especially where the core product may be similar to the rivalries but where the digital product adds a certain value. This value is difficult to demonstrate and predict the direct value for the customer. These challenges are reflected in the following quotes:

> We have needed help in pricing these services and calculating the business cases, it's by no means easy, as one needs much knowledge about the existing offering in the market and about their prices and quality. (Company B)

> We are not where we want to be in how to set the price in predictive maintenance and how to communicate the promise of the value to the customer. (Company D)

> If you want to grow with this kind of new business, then you will need to build a new business unit, own sellers, and customer responsibility. If you just put slides into the bag of a machine seller, it'll never work. (Company F)

These findings are similar to the study of Langley and Truax (1994), finding that the technology adoption process is linked to the organization's other internal processes, showing that various process models contribute to the understanding of such adoption processes. AI adoption creates new products, product bundles, and changes as well as the way value is created. Although there are no findings specifically addressing organizational processes in family firms' technology adoption, their change processes may be more unstructured due to the lack of formalization (De Massis et al. 2012). Technological champions, people pushing for change (Bruque and Moyano 2007), might also help integrate processual changes.

9.4.2.4 Significance of Data

Challenges regarding the significance of data regard the understanding of the meaning of quality as essential; the prognosis and usability of AI depend on the basic data input. If the basic data is not entered in a certain way, it might not be possible for the algorithm to handle and apply. As this means a certain background work where an employee might not understand why and where the data is used, there might well be discrepancies and misunderstandings, especially in case companies with many international subsidiaries. Furthermore, certain industry standards pose challenges for the data. These quotations reflect this challenge:

> It is central to clear for people that they know how the data is connected to what their job is and what happens to the data after that. That's what we have been concentrating on and this is still ongoing. (Company B)

> Data is usually not a mystical IT thing; it means whether we know what is happening in the company or not. It usually opens one's eyes, like, true; if we don't even know where our (service) guys currently are, it's probably not a good thing. (Company C)

Data accuracy should be a priority (Merhi 2023) and is listed as a top challenge for AI implementation in other studies (Al Badi et al. 2022; Weber et al. 2023). Weber et al. (2023) suggest a set of specific organizational capabilities to be developed to address the complexity of AI challenges. They suggest a specific Data Management system to address this challenge.

9.4.3 Environmental Level

Organizational environments, such as networks, partnerships, and geographical locations impact the potential of AI solution adoption. The main findings on this topic are summarized in Table 9.5 and discussed here in more detail.

9.4.3.1 Industry-Specific Challenges

Industry-specific challenges regard the specific, sometimes data security-related or legal environment that constrains or sets some rules for the technology application. Company A states that they would need "something from the EU side or government or global rules for how things can be done" (...) "It's good to develop new things but I think that the ecosystem is not ready to take (certain) action yet." Besides the business environment, the physical one can pose challenges for the technical implementation of AI:

> You might have snow or rain or whatever and even these forest canopy leaves affect those sensors heavily. (Company B).

and

> I think one challenge, other than just placing sensors to the boom structure, is that our attachment, or the bucket that is used for grabbing the material, can be quite large and it's hard to see behind it and it's gonna be swinging in front of the lidar view. (Company A).

These findings are in line with the literature, which suggests that the characteristics of both industry and the government impact innovation performance (Collinson and Liu 2019). Such external shocks can indeed trigger digital transformation in family firms (Soluk 2022), which impacts other technologies as well.

P4 Family firms experience industry- and legalization-specific challenges when implementing AI technologies.

9.4.3.2 Partnerships and Customers

Partnership and customer challenges include the challenges regarding the specific challenges that arise when digital services are developed together with the customer and/or partners and how they are presented. Regarding partnerships, challenges include difficulties in finding and identifying partners with the needed experience and establishing stable partnerships. Regarding customers, findings show that the customers might have very individual needs, where co-creation is essential and an explicit wish from the customer side:

> "Internally, there is a stronger will for the application" (...) "but it's not because they would be afraid of AI, but because the development together with the customer is slower and a lot is going on so it's more difficult to introduce more stuff." (Company D)

Customer involvement is seen as essential in AI product and service creation; however, it is slower due to both organizational and technological hurdles. While the literature finds chances for companies to co-developing solutions and offerings with their customers (Collinson and Liu 2019), it also poses challenges by intensifying and reorganizing the inter-organizational collaboration and competition dynamics (Cennamo et al. 2020). The case companies express the need to collaborate with new kinds of companies and even competitors in new ways. Family firm literature states that family firms seek to build social capital with their stakeholders by cooperating more with other firms, seeking inputs for their innovation (Llach and Nordqvist 2010) especially the closeness to customers promotes innovation. Such long-lasting relationships provide stability in turbulent times (Gómez-Mejía et al. 2007), like introducing new technologies, like Company A states:

> We do have very long partnerships. I think that also part of the family business approach, that this is kind of from one generation to the next kind of thing. One of our first customers in Finland, (company name), will have 50 years of co-operation with them next year, and with some of our dealers, they started almost 20 years ago, when we just started manufacturing there. We do try to always find partners with whom there is longevity in the partnership. (Company A)

Family firms may experience such challenges when creating AI solutions together with their customers, however, the background of the challenges seems to stem from their structures and processes and not from the partnerships per se. In line with the literature, and as reflected in the quotations, family firms do collaborate with partners and customers to smoothen their innovation adoption (Hausman 2005; Kim et al. 2004) and seek stable relationships with their stakeholders (Miller and Le Breton-Miller, 2005). This experience of connectedness and long-term relationships contribute to the formation of the company identity of the firm (Gómez-Mejía et al. 2007). Collaborative innovation efforts help family firms tackle their barriers to gaining technological inputs (Feranita et al. 2017). In line with above, we propose:

P5 Family firms experience challenges in identifying and establishing the right partnerships essential for new technology adoption; customer-centered development is found important but slow.

9.5 Discussion

This study empirically examines new technology adoption processes and challenges in five family-owned manufacturing companies. All case companies have adopted AI technologies but are in somewhat different stages in the implementation. We found many categories of challenges which we categorized into the people-organization-environment (POE) framework. The people level encompasses challenges mainly with the employees and their jobs, such as talent and job concerns, incentives, and involvement of employees and managers in the implementation process. Here, employee resistance is found to be a central challenge, as we posit in P1. This is supported by the literature as well: attracting and keeping talent is found to be a central barrier to new technology adoption in family firms (Bruque and Moyano 2007). AI adoption can indeed create insecurity in the organizational environment. Also, managerial talent is essential in engaging personnel and thus lowering political resistance (König et al. 2013). Attracting the right talent is essential for AI strategy (Frankiewicz and Chamorro-Premuzic 2020), which is not always easy for family firms, as future talents perceive them slower in new technology adoption (Ceja Barba and Tàpies 2009). It can be summarized that the challenges in the people category seem more contextual and individual, which makes them more difficult to address. The challenges presented here may not have a source in family firm nature but can be found in many organizations.

Second, the challenges on the organizational level are for example the organization's priorities and values that are not aligned with the technology adoption, as we posit in proposition P2a. Especially in the case of new and emerging technologies, it is not always clear from the start which projects will be profitable and which not, which makes prioritization difficult. In large companies changing metrics for KPIs and other measurements just for the sake of a technology adoption is seldom a fast process. Our proposition P2b posits the need for managerial support (Kammerlander and Ganter 2015; Kotlar et al. 2022; Niehm et al. 2010), which is essential for a project to get resources and internal priority in the company and for the employees to accept the technology. Regarding the organization's structures, if the organization's "setup is too complex", as mentioned by company D in the data, it can be difficult to establish communication flows needed for the technology adoption. The lack of suitable organizational structures and the establishment of silos make the cooperation between organizational units and customers bureaucratic and time-consuming. This is reflected in P3. Therefore, adopting new organizational forms might be necessary (Lanzolla et al. 2020). Along with the technology adoption, there might be new products and services that need to be priced and sold differently than the original products the companies are manufacturing (Duch-Brown et al. 2022). Also, the significance of data should be seen on an organizational level as a priority (Al Badi et al. 2022; Merhi 2023) as "it (data) should not be seen as a mystical IT-thing" (Company C). Finally, the challenges on the environmental level regard the industry level as well as the global and institutional environment, as we posit in the P4. The family companies examine difficulties in the business environment if it does not adapt to the technological change. On the institutional level, they express the need to get a kind of legal network for technology development. On the global level, only recently institutional actors are starting to give guidance to companies on how to apply it and the data (as the AI act of the European Parliament). Also, the stakeholders such as customer- and partnership-related challenges are considered here. It is found that developing the technology together with the customer is essential but also more costly and difficult regarding the organizational structures; data developers may not have direct customer contact according to the structure even if it would be needed in a certain project. Developing the technology together with the customer changes the customer expectations and extends the possibilities for further digital offerings. It is difficult for the family firms to find the right, stable partnerships for technology development, as posited in P5, however, it is essential for innovation (Feranita et al. 2017).

9.5.1 Implications for Theory and Practice

Our findings contribute to both family business and AI/DT literature. We extend the current theory on AI by suggesting a POE framework for assessing AI implementation in organizations and by categorizing AI adoption challenges and possible responses to these. We contribute to the growing body of AI theories which, stemming from information systems research, mostly concentrates on the technological areas of digital transformation (Yoo et al. 2012). We show that neglecting the human and individual aspects and other firm-related aspects of such technology adoption processes can hinder the adoption process and success (Soluk and Kammerlander 2021; De Massis et al. 2012). Second, we contribute to the literature on technology adoption in family firms, showing specific challenges when family firms implement AI, which has been scarcely examined in existing literature (Soluk and Kammerlander 2021). Managers working in family firms as well as practitioners supporting family firms in processes of technology adoption will gain insights in recognizing the influence of family-specific strategic preferences, as these may impact the adoption process and raise challenges. Practitioners are advised not to assume the universal applicability of technology adoption processes for the case of family firms. Family owners gain insights for self-reflection for ongoing and upcoming technology adoption processes.

9.5.2 Limitations and Future Research

As with all studies, also this one has its shortcomings. As our sample consists only of family companies, a comparison between family and nonfamily firms is not possible. Therefore, we only can show possible challenges in our sample and not assess whether they would apply to nonfamily firm samples as well. Further empirical evidence is needed to examine this. Furthermore, as our data does not encompass interviews with all companies' managing families, identifying the family influence is not always clear and possible. This is a shortcoming that further studies examining specifically the family influence could tackle. Table 9.6 summarizes further suggestions for future research.

9.6 Conclusions

This study empirically examined family firms' challenges in technology adoption and implementation. Our findings show that family firms experience challenges in AI adoption in three main areas, namely people, organization, and environment (POE). We, therefore, propose this POE framework applicable for AI adoption instead of the TOE (Tornatzky 1990) applied in the current literature on digital transformation. POE aspects encompass also the human and talent aspects essential for AI adoption in organizations, where TOE falls short. We conclude that the subcategories found under these aspects may vary depending on industries and even geographical areas and may differ in nonfamily firms, but adding the people aspect to the framework is important when developing AI theories further. Even though our findings highlight the specific features of family firms, certain challenges are most likely to be universal for many companies adopting and implementing AI technologies.

Table 9.6 Future research directions

People	
Talent and knowledge	Understanding the significance of the human capital in AI transformation (Ano and Bent 2022; Davenport and Redman 2020), Talent attraction barriers and enablers (Bruque and Moyano 2007; Frankiewicz and Chamorro-Premuzic 2020), Role and impact of tacit knowledge (Hadjimichael and Tsoukas 2019)
Resistance and collaboration	Overcoming employee resistance (Soluk and Kammerlander 2021), Understanding AI resistance and changing working conditions (Man Tang et al. 2022, Anthony et al. 2023; Hafermalz and Riemer 2021; Krakowski et al. 2023), Efficient channeling of new forms of motivation (Kellogg et al. 2020), Redesigning practices for collaboration and lessening the demand for individual change (Anthony et al. 2023; Man Tang et al. 2022, Allen and Choudhury 2022)
Organization	
AI values	Integration of managerial support to changing employment environment (Kammerlander and Ganter 2015; Porfírio et al. 2021), Harnessing positive AI efficiency to strategy and vision (Yang et al. 2019; Rammer et al. 2022; Hunt et al. 2022)
Structures and processes	New structures and processes to ease AI integration (Lanzolla et al. 2020; Craig and Moores 2006), Changes in current practices to improve AI utilization (Kellogg et al. 2020; Dixon et al. 2021)
Data	Data processes integration to operations (Al Badi et al. 2022; Merhi 2023), Data processes utilization for networks and innovation capabilities (Wu et al. 2021, Brynjolfsson and McElheran 2016; Brynjolfsson and Mcafee 2017; Gregory et al. 2021)
Environment	
Industry and legislation	Response capabilities to AI induced changes (Collinson and Liu 2019; Hunt et al. 2022), AI in relation to minorities and inequality (Domini et al. 2022)
Partnerships and collaboration	Changing demands in partnership collaboration due to AI (Berente et al. 2021; Haenlein and Kaplan 2019; Peppard and Ward 2004), Methods and levels for intra-organizational collaboration with AI (Dremel et al. 2017; Gregory et al. 2021)
Customers	Novel product creation with the help of AI in line with changed customer expectations and networks (Krakowski et al. 2023; Gregory et al. 2021), Using data and AI for service improvement and efficiency (Senoner et al. 2022)

References

Päivi Aaltonen, Laavanya Ramaul, Emil Kurvinen, Antero Kutvonen, and Andre Nemeh. *Organizational barriers and enablers in reaching maturity in digital twin technology*. CRC Press, 1 st edition, 2023a.

Päivi Aaltonen, Laavanya Ramaul, Emil Kurvinen, Antero Kutvonen, and Andre Nemeh. *Handbook of Digital Twins*. Palvgrave Macmillan, 1 edition, 2023b.

Lara Agostini and Anna Nosella. The adoption of industry 4.0 technologies in smes: results of an international study. *Management Decision*, 58(4):625–643, 2019.

F. K. Al Badi, K. A. Alhosani, F. Jabeen, A. Stachowicz-Stanusch, N. Shehzad, and W. Amann. Challenges of ai adoption in the uae healthcare. *Vision*, 26(2): 193–207, 2022.

R. Allen and P. Choudhury. Algorithm-augmented work and domain experience: The countervailing forces of ability and aversion. *Organization Science*, 33(1): 149–169, 2022a.

S. Alsheibani, Y. Cheung and C. H. Messom. Artificial intelligence adoption: AI-readiness at firm-level. *PACIS*, 4(2018): 231–245, 2018.

Kaplan Andreas and Haenlein Michael. Siri, siri, in my hand: Who's the fairest in the land? on the interpretations, illustrations, and implications of artificial intelligence. *Business horizons*, 62(1):15–25, 2019.

Benoit Ano and Rody Bent. Human determinants influencing the digital transformation strategy of multigenerational family businesses: a multiple-case study of five french growth-oriented family firms. *Journal of Family Business Management*, 12(4):876–891, 2022.

C. Anthony, B. A. Bechky, and A. L. Fayard. "collaborating" with ai: Taking a system view to explore the future of work. *Organization Science*, 34(5):1672–1694, 2023.

Ibrahim Arpaci, Yuksel C. Yardimci, Selcuk Ozkan, and Ozgur Turetken. Organizational adoption of information technologies: A literature review. *International Journal of eBusiness and eGovernment Studies*, 4(2):37–50, 2012.

Richard P. Bagozzi, Michael K. Brady, and Ming-Hui Huang. Ai service and emotion. *Journal of Service Research*, 25(4), 2022.

Sami Basly and Amine Hammouda. Family businesses and digital entrepreneurship adoption: A conceptual model. *The Journal of Entrepreneurship*, 29(2):326–364, 2020.

Nicholas Berente, Bin Gu, Jan Recker, and Radhika Santhanam. Managing artificial intelligence. *MIS quarterly*, 45(3):1433–1450, 2021.

Francesco Bertani, Linda Ponta, Marco Raberto, Andrea Teglio, and Silvano Cincotti. The complexity of the intangible digital economy: an agent-based model. *Journal of Business Research*, 129:527–540, 2021.

Sven Brenk, Dirk Lüttgens, Konstantin Diener, and Frank Piller. Learning from failures in business model innovation: solving decision-making logic conflicts through intrapreneurial effectuation. *Journal of Business Economics*, 89:1097–1147, 2019.

Jasper Brinkerink, Emanuela Rondi, Cristina Benedetti, and Unai Arzubiaga. Family business or business family? organizational identity elasticity and strategic responses to disruptive innovation. *Journal of Family Business Strategy*, 11(4): 100360, 2020.

Sebastian Bruque and Juan Moyano. Organisational determinants of information technology adoption and implementation in smes: The case of family and cooperative firms. *Technovation*, 27(5):241–253, 2007.

Erik Brynjolfsson and ANDREW Mcafee. Artificial intelligence, for real. *Harvard business review*, 1:1–31, 2017.

Erik Brynjolfsson and Kristina McElheran. The rapid adoption of data-driven decision-making. *American Economic Review*, 106(5):133–39, 2016.

Marc Bérubé, Tara Giannelia, and Gregory Vial. Barriers to the implementation of ai in organizations: Findings from a delphi study. *Hawaii International Conference on System Sciences*, 2021. 09981331.

Andrea Calabrò, Mariangela Vecchiarini, Johanna Gast, Giovanna Campopiano, Alfredo de Massis, and Sascha Kraus. Innovation in family firms: A systematic literature review and guidance for future research. *International Journal of Management Reviews*, 21(3):317–355, 2019.

L. Cassia, A. de Massis, and E. Pizzurno. Strategic innovation and new product development in family firms: An empirically grounded theoretical framework. *International Journal of Entrepreneurial Behavior & Research*, 18(2):198–232, 2012.

Luis Ceja Barba and Josep Tàpies. Attracting talent to family-owned businesses: the perceptions of mba students, 2009.

Carmelo Cennamo, Giovanni B. Dagnino, Alberto Di Minin, and Gianvito Lanzolla. Managing digital transformation: Scope of transformation and modalities of value co-generation and delivery. *California Management Review*, 62(4):5–16, 2020.

James J. Chrisman, Jess H. Chua, Alfredo de Massis, Federico Frattini, and Mike Wright. The ability and willingness paradox in family firm innovation. *Journal of Product Innovation Management*, 32(3):310–318, 2015.

Simon Collinson and Yi Liu. Recombination for innovation: performance outcomes from international partnerships in china. *R&D Management*, 49(1):46–63, 2019.

Kevin G. Corley and Dennis A. Gioia. Identity ambiguity and change in the wake of a corporate spin-off. *Administrative Science Quarterly*, 49(2):173–208, 2004.

Justin B. L. Craig and Ken Moores. A 10-year longitudinal investigation of strategy, systems, and environment on innovation in family firms. *Family Business Review*, 19(1):1–10, 2006.

Thomas H. Davenport and Thomas C. Redman. Digital transformation comes down to talent in 4 key areas. *Harvard Business Review*, 2(6), 2020.

Thomas H. Davenport and Rajeev Ronanki. Artificial intelligence for the real world. *Harvard Business Review*, 96(1):108–116, 2018.

Fred D. Davis. Technology acceptance model: Tam. In *Information Seeking Behavior and Technology Adoption*, pages 205–219, 1989.

Alfredo De Massis, Pramodita Sharma, Jess H. Chua, and James J. Chrisman. *Family Business Studies: An Annotated Bibliography*. Edward Elgar Publishing, 2012.

J. Dixon, B. Hong, and L. Wu. The robot revolution: Managerial and employment consequences for firms. *Management Science*, 67(9):5586–5605, 2021.

G. Domini, M. Grazzi, D. Moschella, and T. Treibich. For whom the bell tolls: The firm-level effects of automation on wage and gender inequality. *Research Policy*, 51(7):104533, 2022.

C. Dremel, J. Wulf, M. M. Herterich, J. C. Waizmann, and W. Brenner. How audi ag established big data analytics in its digital transformation. *MIS Quarterly Executive*, 16(2), 2017.

Markus Dressler and Igor Paunovic. Sensing technologies, roles and technology adoption strategies for digital transformation of grape harvesting in sme wineries. *Journal of Open Innovation: Technology, Market, and Complexity*, 7(2):123, 2021. https://doi.org/10.3390/joitmc7020123.

A. Dubois and L. E. Gadde. Systematic combining: An abductive approach to case research. *Journal of Business Research*, 55(7):553–560, 2002. https://doi.org/10.1016/S0148-2963(00)00195-8.

Néstor Duch-Brown, Estrella Gomez-Herrera, Frank Mueller-Langer, and Songül Tolan. Market power and artificial intelligence work on online labour markets. *Research Policy*, 51(3):104446, 2022.

Justyna Dąbrowska, Aggeliki Almpanopoulou, Alexander Brem, Henry Chesbrough, Valentino Cucino, Alberto Di Minin, Ferran Giones, Henri Hakala, Claudio Marullo, and Anne-Laure Mention. Digital transformation, for better or worse: a critical multi-level research agenda. *R&D Management*, 52(5):930–954, 2022a.

Justyna Dąbrowska, Argyro Almpanopoulou, Alexander Brem, Henry Chesbrough, Valentina Cucino, Alberto Di Minin, Ferran Giones, Henri Hakala, Cristina Marullo, Anne-Laure Mention, Letizia Mortara, Sladjana Nørskov, Petra Nylund, Calogero Oddo, Agnieszka Radziwon, and Paavo Ritala. Digital transformation, for better or worse: A critical multi-level research agenda. *R&D Management*, 53 (5):930–954, 2022b.

E. Glikson and A. W. Woolley. Human trust in artificial intelligence: Review of empirical research. *Academy of Management Annals*, 14(2), 627–660, 2020.

Kathleen M. Eisenhardt. Building theories from case study research. *Academy of Management Review*, 14(4):532–550, 1989. https://doi.org/10.5465/amr.1989.4308385.

Kathleen M. Eisenhardt and Melissa E. Graebner. Theory building from cases: Opportunities and challenges. *Academy of Management Journal*, 50(1):25–32, 2007. https://doi.org/10.5465/amj.2007.24160888.

F. Feranita, J. Kotlar, and A. de Massis. Collaborative innovation in family firms: Past research, current debates and agenda for future research. *Journal of Family Business Strategy*, 8(3):137–156, 2017.

B. Frankiewicz and T. Chamorro-Premuzic. The post-pandemic rules of talent management. *Harvard Business Review*, 13, 2020.

Frank W. Geels. Technological transitions as evolutionary reconfiguration processes: a multi-level perspective and a case-study. *Research Policy*, 31(8-9):1257–1274, 2002.

Gerard George, Karim Lakhani, and Phanish Puranam. What has changed? the impact of covid pandemic on the technology and innovation management research agenda. *Journal of Management Studies*, 2020.

Vern L Glaser, Neil Pollock, and Luciana D'Adderio. The biography of an algorithm: Performing algorithmic technologies in organizations. *Organization Theory*, 2(2): 26317877211004609, 2021.

Luis R. Gómez-Mejía, Kevin T. Haynes, Manuel Núñez-Nickel, Kathyrn J. L. Jacobson, and José Moyano-Fuentes. Socioemotional wealth and business risks in family-controlled firms: Evidence from spanish olive oil mills.

Administrative Science Quarterly, 52(1):106–137, 2007. https://doi.org/10.2189/asqu.52.1.106.

Robert Wayne Gregory, Ola Henfridsson, Evgeny Kaganer, and Skolkovo Harris Kyriakou. The role of artificial intelligence and data network effects for creating user value. *Academy of Management Review*, 46(3):534–551, 2021.

D. Hadjimichael and H. Tsoukas. Toward a better understanding of tacit knowledge in organizations: Taking stock and moving forward. *Academy of Management Annals*, 13(2):672–703, 2019.

Niklas Haefner, Joakim Wincent, Vinit Parida, and Oliver Gassmann. Understanding ai adoption: an analysis of german technology acceptance. In *The Digital Transformation of Labor (Open Access)*, pages 299–320. Routledge, 2021.

Michael Haenlein and Andreas Kaplan. A brief history of artificial intelligence: On the past, present, and future of artificial intelligence. *California Management Review*, 61(4):5–14, 2019. https://doi.org/10.1177/0008125619864925.

E. Hafermalz and K. Riemer. Productive and connected while working from home: What client-facing remote workers can learn from telenurses about 'belonging through technology'. *European Journal of Information Systems*, 30(1):89–99, 2021.

A. Hausman. Innovativeness among small businesses: Theory and propositions for future research. *Industrial Marketing Management*, 34(8):773–782, 2005.

W. Hunt, S. Sarkar, and C. Warhurst. Measuring the impact of ai on jobs at the organization level: Lessons from a survey of uk business leaders. *Research Policy*, 51(2):104425, 2022.

Marco Iansiti and Karim R Lakhani. *Competing in the age of AI: strategy and leadership when algorithms and networks run the world*. Harvard Business Press, 2020.

Nadine Kammerlander and Markus Ganter. An attention-based view of family firm adaptation to discontinuous technological change: Exploring the role of family ceos' noneconomic goals. *Journal of Product Innovation Management*, 32(3): 361–383, 2015.

Katherine C Kellogg, Melissa A Valentine, and Angele Christin. Algorithms at work: The new contested terrain of control. *Academy of Management Annals*, 14 (1):366–410, 2020.

D. Kim, D. Kandemir, and S. T. Cavusgil. The role of family conglomerates in emerging markets: What western companies should know. *Thunderbird International Business Review*, 46(1):13–38, 2004.

Josip Kotlar, Alfredo de Massis, Federico Frattini, Christopher B. Bingham, and Hanqing Fang. Family management and family governance: A configurational approach. *Journal of Business Research*, 139:1198–1212, 2022.

S. Krakowski, J. Luger, and S. Raisch. Artificial intelligence and the changing sources of competitive advantage. *Strategic Management Journal*, 44(6):1425–1452, 2023a.

Sascha Kraus, Mikko Pohjola, Anssi Koponen, and Sami Aaltonen. Digital transformation in family-owned mittelstand firms: A dynamic capabilities perspective. *Journal of Business Research*, 140:505–515, 2020.

E. Kurvinen, A. Kutvonen, P. Aaltonen, J. Salakka, and B. Ghalamchi. Physics-based digital twins leveraging competitive edge in novel markets. In *Handbook of Digital Twins*, pages 185–199. CRC Press, 2024.

Anne König, Nadine Kammerlander, and Albrecht Enders. The family innovator's dilemma: How family influence affects the adoption of discontinuous technologies by incumbent firms. *Academy of Management Review*, 38(3):418–441, 2013. https://doi.org/10.5465/amr.2011.0168.

A. Langley and J. Truax. A process study of new technology adoption in smaller manufacturing firms. *Journal of Management Studies*, 31(5):619–652, 1994.

F. Lannon, R. Lyons, and C. O'Connor. Generation ai and family business: a perspective article. *Journal of Family Business Management*, 2023.

G. Lanzolla, A. Lorenz, E. Miron-Spektor, M. Schilling, G. Solinas, and C. L. Tucci. Digital transformation: What is new if anything? emerging patterns and management research. *Academy of Management Discoveries*, 6(3), 2020.

Jay Lee. *Industrial AI: Applications with Sustainable Performance*. Springer, 2020.

Ulrich Lichtenthaler. Five maturity levels of managing ai: From isolated ignorance to integrated intelligence. *Journal of Innovation Management*, 8(1):39–50, 2020.

Jun Liu, Huihong Chang, Jeffrey Yi-Lin Forrest, and Baohua Yang. Influence of artificial intelligence on technological innovation: Evidence from the panel data of china's manufacturing sectors. *Technological Forecasting and Social Change*, 158:120142, 2020.

J. Llach and M. Nordqvist. Innovation in family and non-family businesses: A resource perspective. *International Journal of Entrepreneurial Venturing*, 2(3-4): 381–399, 2010.

M. Concepción López-Fernández, Ana M. Serrano-Bedia, and Manuela Pérez-Pérez. Entrepreneurship and family firm research: A bibliometric analysis of an emerging field. *Journal of Small Business Management*, 54(2):622–639, 2016. https://doi.org/10.1111/jsbm.12161.

Kristina McElheran, Jie Feng Li, Erik Brynjolfsson, Zachary Kroff, Emel Dinlersoz, Lucia Foster, and Byron Zolas. Ai adoption in america: Who, what, and where. *Journal of Economics & Management Strategy*, 2024.

M. I. Merhi. An evaluation of the critical success factors impacting artificial intelligence implementation. *International Journal of Information Management*, 69: 102545, 2023. https://doi.org/10.1016/j.ijinfomgt.2023.102545.

Haenlein Michael, Kaplan Andreas, Tan Chee-Wee, and Zhang Pengzhu. Artificial intelligence (ai) and management analytics. *Journal of Management Analytics*, 6 (4):341–343, 2019.

D. Miller and I. Le Breton-Miller. Management insights from great and struggling family businesses. *Long Range Planning*, 38(6), 517–530, 2005.

Mohammad Fikri Mubarak and Modesta Petraite. Industry 4.0 technologies, digital trust and technological orientation: What matters in open innovation? *Technological Forecasting and Social Change*, 161:120332, 2020. https://doi.org/10.1016/j.techfore.2020.120332.

Fernando Muñoz-Bullón and María J. Sanchez-Bueno. The impact of family involvement on the r&d intensity of publicly traded firms. *Family Business Review*, 24(1):62–70, 2011. https://doi.org/10.1177/0894486510396870.

Linda S. Niehm, Keisha Tyner, Mack C. Shelley, and Mary A. Fitzgerald. Technology adoption in small family-owned businesses: Accessibility, perceived advantage, and information technology literacy. *Journal of Family and Economic Issues*, 31: 498–515, 2010. https://doi.org/10.1007/s10834-010-9225-4.

J. Peppard and J. Ward. Beyond strategic information systems: Towards an is capability. *The Journal of Strategic Information Systems*, 13(2):167–194, 2004.

J. A. Porfírio, T. Carrilho, J. A. Felício, and J. Jardim. Leadership characteristics and digital transformation. *Journal of Business Research*, 124:610–619, 2021.

Sebastian Raisch and Sebastian Krakowski. Artificial intelligence and management: The automation–augmentation paradox. *Academy of Management Review*, 46(1): 192–210, 2021.

Christian Rammer, Gastón P Fernández, and Dirk Czarnitzki. Artificial intelligence and industrial innovation: Evidence from german firm-level data. *Research Policy*, 51(7):104555, 2022.

J. Senoner, T. Netland, and S. Feuerriegel..Using explainable artificial intelligence to improve process quality: Evidence from semiconductor manufacturing. *Management Science*, 68(8):5704–5723, 2022.

J. Soluk and N. Kammerlander. Digitale transformation und künstliche intelligenz in familienunternehmen. In *Handbuch Digitale Wirtschaft*, pages 1–17. Springer Fachmedien Wiesbaden, 2023.

Jan Soluk. Organisations' resources and external shocks: Exploring digital innovation in family firms. *Industry and Innovation*, 29(6):792–824, 2022. https://doi.org/10.1080/13662716.2022.2029418.

Jan Soluk and Nadine Kammerlander. Digital transformation in family-owned mittelstand firms: A dynamic capabilities perspective. *European Journal of Information Systems*, 30(6):676–711, 2021. https://doi.org/10.1080/0960085X.2021.1877126.

David Souder, Ajay Zaheer, Harry Sapienza, and Rebecca Ranucci. How family influence, socioemotional wealth, and competitive conditions shape new technology adoption. *Strategic Management Journal*, 38(9):1774–1790, 2017. https://doi.org/10.1002/smj.2410.

Prasanna Tambe, Peter Cappelli, and Valery Yakubovich. Artificial intelligence in human resources management: Challenges and a path forward. *California Management Review*, 61(4):15–42, 2019.

P. Man Tang, J. Koopman, S. T. McClean, J. H. Zhang, C. H. Li, D. De Cremer, and C. T. S. Ng. When conscientious employees meet intelligent machines: An integrative approach inspired by complementarity theory and role theory. *Academy of Management Journal*, 65(3):1019–1054, 2022.

Shuang Tong, Ning Jia, Xuan Luo, and Zheng Fang. The janus face of artificial intelligence feedback: Deployment versus disclosure effects on employee performance. *Strategic Management Journal*, 42(9):1600–1631, 2021.

Louis G. Tornatzky. *The Processes of Technological Innovation.* Lexington/DC Heath & Company, 1990.

Patrick Ulrich, Verena Frank, and Ricardo Buettner. Artificial intelligence in small and medium-sized family firms: An empirical study on the impact of family influence. *Corporate Governance and Organizational Behavior Review*, 7(1): 72–80, 2023.

Viswanath Venkatesh. Adoption and use of ai tools: A research agenda grounded in utaut. *Annals of Operations Research*, 308(1):641–652, 2022. 10.1007/ s10479-020-03918-9.

Belen Villalonga and Raphael Amit. Family ownership. *Oxford Review of Economic Policy*, 36(2):241–257, 2020.

Serge-Lopez Wamba-Taguimdje, Samuel Fosso Wamba, Jean Robert Kala Kamdjoug, and Chris Emmanuel Tchatchouang Wanko. Influence of artificial intelligence (ai) on firm performance: the business value of ai-based transformation projects. *Business Process Management Journal*, 26(7):1893–1924, 2020.

Michael Weber, Michael Engert, Nils Schaffer, Julian Weking, and Helmut Krcmar. Organizational capabilities for ai implementation—coping with inscrutability and data dependency in ai. *Information Systems Frontiers*, 25(4):1549–1569, 2023. https://doi.org/10.1007/s10796-021-10170-3.

Wu Yu, Shanhong Guo, Yulin Shi, and Jianbo Guo. Digital transformation in emerging markets: What is ahead? *Technological Forecasting and Social Change*, 167:120653, 2021.

Xun Xu, Yuqian Lu, Birgit Vogel-Heuser, and Lihui Wang. Industry 4.0 and industry 5.0—inception, conception and perception. *Journal of Manufacturing Systems*, 61:530–535, 2021.

Yifan Yang, Eric W. K. See-To, and Savvas Papagiannidis. You have not been archiving emails for no reason! using big data analytics to cluster b2b interest in products and services and link clusters to financial performance. *Industrial Marketing Management*, 86:1–14, 2019.

Y. Yoo, R. J. Boland, K. Lyytinen, and A. Majchrzak. Organizing for innovation in the digitized world. *Organization Science*, 23(5):1398–1408, 2012.

Part III

Prospects of Distributed AI Experimentation

10

Exploring the Role of Individual Learning for Human–AI Empowered Sustainability Transitions: An Integrative Review of Literature

Ellen Saltevo, Antero Kutvonen, and Marko Torkkeli

10.1 Introduction

Sustainability transitions (STs) involve the purposeful transformation of sociotechnical systems (i.e., system innovation) underlining key societal functions (e.g., mobility, energy, housing, and food) in a normatively guided direction (i.e., what is considered sustainable) (Geels 2005; Kemp and Martens 2007). STs are characterized by interdependent and complex development processes between multiple elements, dimensions, and actors; long-term change processes of overcoming forces that maintain incumbent systems and facilitating forces that contribute to the institutionalization of emerging systems; as well as uncertainty over the best courses of action and open-mindedness of objectives according to evolving understanding (Köhler et al. 2019). Due to these attributes, STs require experimental operationalization and reflexive governance

E. Saltevo (✉) · A. Kutvonen · M. Torkkeli
School of Engineering Sciences, Industrial Engineering and Management, LUT University, 34 Yliopistonkatu, 53850 Lappeenranta, Finland
e-mail: ellen.saltevo@lut.fi

P. Aaltonen and E. Kurvinen (eds.), *Contemporary Issues in Industry 5.0*, Technology, Work and Globalization, https://doi.org/10.1007/978-3-031-74779-3_10

approaches, in which learning plays a crucial role in directing the development and adaptation of the system (Loorbach 2010; Kemp et al. 2007). Notably, STs and artificial intelligence (AI) share fundamental characteristics as learning-based systems. AI refers to "a systems' ability to interpret external data correctly, to learn from such data, and to use those learnings to achieve specific goals and tasks through flexible adaptation" (Kaplan and Haenlein 2019). While the complete integration of these two systems so far appears to be a techno-utopian aspiration, the synergistic development of human and artificial learning is on its way. However, the effective utilization of AI in this context necessitates a comprehensive and detailed understanding of learning in STs to determine how synergies can best be achieved.

Despite the acknowledged importance of learning in established theories and management principles in the field of STs, relatively limited research has been specifically dedicated to this area (Truffer et al. 2022). Recently, scholars such as Van Mierlo and Beers (2020), Van Poeck et al. (2020), Goyal and Howlett (2020), Luederitz et al. (2017a), and Rauschmayer et al. (2015) have highlighted conceptual underdevelopment, theoretical fragmentation, and methodological challenges in the field. Furthermore, much of the existing literature on learning in STs focuses on collectives, overlooking the research significance of the individual perspective (Lähteenoja et al. 2022). In multi-minded social systems, individuals exhibit purposefulness and capacity for making choices that influence the system's trajectory (Gharajedaghi 2011), which is why it is important not to overlook the micro-foundations that exert influence on the system's development.

Consequently, calls for further research on several areas relating to individual learning in STs have been made: the role of individual learning (Rauschmayer et al. 2015), the determinants influencing learning (Van Poeck et al. 2020), individual learning's impact on collective learning (Van Mierlo and Beers 2020), and ways of bridging the current separation of micro–macro analysis levels (Köhler et al. 2019).

These point to a research gap in understanding the role of individual learning in connection to the whole and defining the underlying factors and mechanisms that influence individual learning contributions in STs. This research aims to bridge this gap through an integrative literature review that provides a conceptual framework, which further enables a discussion on the synergy points of human–artificial learning for facilitating the twin (green and digital) transition. The relevance of this research is highlighted by the European Union's strategic focus on Industry 5.0 development, which aims for human-centric change, putting central emphasis on empowering the workforce with technologies that complement human capabilities and in the microfoundations of development (e.g., up- and re-skilling) for facilitating a just and more balanced twin transition (European Commission et al. 2021).

10.2 Key Concepts and Theories

Multi-actor processes in STs are complicated due to varying agencies, interests, strategies, and capabilities (Köhler et al. 2019). Agency and capability are interdependent concepts; agency is the ability to pursue one's objectives, while capability is the ability to act effectively to achieve those objectives (Sen 1999). Individual agencies and the subsequent assembly of individual capabilities give rise to collective agency and capability through learning (Pelenc et al. 2015; Pahl-Wostl 2006). In the field of STs, the dominant theoretical framework is the multilevel perspective, and the primary management frameworks are transition management and strategic niche management. These theories and concepts assume different learning entities (who learns), processes (how learning occurs), and functions (what is the role of learning), which will be elaborated on next.

The multilevel perspective outlines system innovation evolution as a dynamic interplay among three nested levels (niches, regime, and landscape) interlinking various dimensions, elements, and actors into sociotechnical systems. System innovations emerging from niches may gradually grow to pose an alternative configuration able to disrupt existing regime structures when landscape changes render the incumbent system suboptimal, creating takeover opportunities for the emerging system (Geels 2002 2004 2005 2010). Transitions are shaped by structuration [based on Giddens (1984)], and learning is an iterative process of multi-agency interaction with existing and emerging structures that inform the innovation's trajectory forward (Geels 2002 2019).

Transition management is a policy-driven approach for the multiphase (including pre-development, take-off, acceleration, and stabilization) adaptive governance of transitions (Rotmans et al. 2001). The entity in focus is the system in transition, commonly characterized as a complex adaptive system (Loorbach 2010), which consists of diverse agents interacting, adapting, learning, and self-organizing into emergent structures, properties, and phenomena without designated management (Holland 1995, 1998). Transition management relies on the inherent change dynamics of complex systems (Rotmans and Loorbach 2009; Loorbach 2010), but pursues to influence them through collaborative learning in cyclical transition management processes, influencing interaction patterns and thus directing the system's course (Turnheim et al. 2015; Kemp et al. 2007).

Strategic niche management focuses on niches as platforms for innovation incubation and experimentation and assumes that through the strategic creation, development, and sequencing of these spaces, niches can grow into disruptive innovation trajectories (Markard et al. 2012; Hoogma et al. 2002; Kemp et al. 1998 2001). Niches operate in an ecosystemic manner, consisting of interdependent groups of actors centered around a shared vision of radical innovation that co-develops resources and aligns capabilities, creating value for the whole (Schot and Geels 2008; Geels and Raven 2006; Moore 1993; Adner 2017; Adamides and Mouzakitis 2009). Learning in strategic niche management is a central process for testing and iterative development to reshape visions for guiding the direction (global niche) and operational configuration further (local niche) (Geels and Raven 2006; Schot and Geels 2008; Kemp et al. 1998). While niches involve diverse actors, special emphasis is attributed to companies due to their function in innovation creation. In the context of STs, this refers primarily to sustainability-oriented innovation that is directed at "realizing social and environmental value in addition to economic returns" on a systemic level (Adams et al. 2016).

Companies, as differentiated entities guided by strategic visions, learn through dynamic capabilities, referring to "the firm's ability to integrate, build, and reconfigure internal and external competencies to address rapidly changing environments" (Teece et al. 1997). Recent research has started exploring dynamic capabilities in sustainability-oriented innovation (e.g., Inigo and Albareda 2019; Cavalcanti Barros Rodrigues and Gohr 2022).

The aforementioned focus is on collective entity learning in STs. However, education for sustainable development is an emerging policy-driven learning-specific research field, focusing on individual competency development through educational innovation to facilitate individual agency for sustainability (Zhang and Wang 2022; UNESCO 2017). Individual learning is construed as a socio-emotional-cognitive-behavioral process that builds competencies that both enable and empower individual development and action for sustainability and thus indirectly contribute to generating change across domains (UNESCO 2017). Prominent contributions in the field include the development of competency frameworks, e.g., the "GreenComp" (Bacigalupo and Punie 2022).

Learning also plays a fundamental role in AI and is the very function that distinguishes AI from explicitly human-programmed expert rule-based systems (Kaplan and Haenlein 2019). Modern AI usually refers to machine learning, which withholds different learning algorithms and subsequent models (e.g., deep, reinforcement, transfer, ensemble, and evolutionary) that can be used to build systems for a variety of purposes (e.g., analytical, robotics, natural language processing, and predictive modeling systems) applicable across sectors (Sarker 2021; Banzhaf and Machado 2024). The potential of artificial intelligence to contribute meaningfully to sustainability transitions depends on its successful coupling with actor empowerment and transformative practices (Mäkitie et al. 2023), and the emerging field of augmented/integrated intelligence explores how AI systems can be harnessed to enhance and elevate human capabilities (Zhou et al. 2021; Lichtenthaler 2018).

10.3 Material and Methods

This study adopts an integrative approach to reviewing the current literature on learning and competency building in STs. An integrative literature review is a suitable research approach for examining topics in which, despite a body of existing literature, conceptual integration is still lacking and evidence from different disciplines and types of studies can be gathered for a critical evaluation and synthesis of the literature in pursuit of building a comprehensive understanding of the topic to further theory development and the generation of new insights (Snyder 2019; Torraco 2005). Data for the literature review was gathered from two scientific databases by necessitating a combination of search terms for the title and the abstract referring to the sought-after phenomena ("transition" or "sociotechnical"), the processes or outcomes under investigation ("learning" or "competency"/ "competencies" or "capability"/ "capabilities"), and the overarching context ("sustainable"/ "sustainability") in this study. AI literature was not included in the search query due to the recognition that research on AI in this context is extremely limited. Therefore, the approach of this study is to first construct a foundational understanding of learning in STs through literature review synthesis in the results section, and then, in connection with relevant AI literature, explore opportunities for synergies of human-AI learning in the discussion section to generate new insights. This approach allows for targeted and meaningful engagement with all the key elements relevant to this study and a human-centric exploration approach to AI integration. Table 10.1 further details the sample generation for the integrative literature review.

In integrative literature reviews, the application of an underlying theoretical or conceptual structuring of some kind is preferred to analyze the literature in a coherent and structured way (e.g., Torraco 2005; Rocco and Plakhotnik 2009). Accordingly, a well-established analytical framework known as "Coleman's boat" (Coleman 1986 1987 1990) from the field of sociology is applied in this study. Given that the field of sustainability transitions is heavily influenced by sociology (Köhler et al. 2019), it can be considered justifiable to draw from it for further development as

Table 10.1 Sample generation for the literature review

SEARCH	
Search time	May 2023
Search filters	Journal articles + English language
Search database and query	1. Scopus database: (TITLE (transition OR sociotechnical) AND ABS (learning OR competence* OR capability*) AND ABS (sustainability*)) 2. Web of Science database: ((TI = ((transition OR sociotechnical))) AND AB = ((learning OR competence* OR capability*))) AND AB = ((sustainability*))
Search results	488 articles (after elimination of duplicates)
SEARCH	
Phase 1	Exclusion of articles from journals with an SJR ranking below one (quality criterion)
Phase 2	Inclusion of articles with abstracts referring to transitions of socio-ecological-technical–economic nature and addressing explicitly learning (relevance criterion)
Phase 3	The remaining articles were reviewed in their entirety and included in the final sample if they were assessed to potentially contribute theoretical, empirical, or conceptual value to the research questions
Final sample	32 articles (indicated by asterisks in the reference list)

well. By employing the set categories and relationships from the framework as a baseline, the thematic organization, evaluation, and synthesis of data are enabled in a structured way.

The framework, based on Coleman's theory of social structure (Coleman 1986 1987 1990), illustrates the interconnections of macro- and micro-level phenomena and, as such, provides a general representation of how individual agents' and their actions are shaped by the collective contexts they are embedded in and how, as a result, they further contribute to the restructuring of these contexts. The framework consists of four distinct states: the collective state at the macro-level, the individual agent's state of being at the micro-level, the individual agent's state of action at the micro-level, and the collective state's outcome at the macro-level (Coleman 1986 1987 1990). However, macro-level

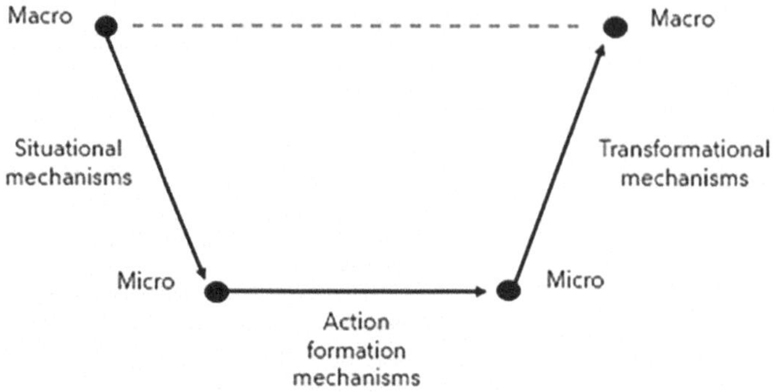

Fig. 10.1 An illustration of the framework, integrated from Coleman (1986 1987 1990) and Hedström and Swedberg (1998)

outcomes are considered characteristically unpredictable and often left unspecified in the framework (Ylikoski 2021); hence, their exclusion also from this research and only general reference going forward. These states interlink through mechanisms further conceptualized by Hedström and Swedberg (1998) as situational (macro–micro), action formation (micro-micro), and transformational (micro–macro), detailing the influence of social structures on individuals and vice versa, but not implying causality (Ylikoski 2021). Situational mechanisms explain how social structures shape an individual's state of being and thinking; action formation mechanisms explain how individual state of being influences action; and transformational mechanisms explain how individual action and interaction generate social structures (Hedström and Swedberg 1998). Figure 10.1 illustrates the framework and the connecting mechanisms. The continued relevance of the framework is demonstrated by its recent applications, for example, in management (Cowen et al. 2022) and policy learning (Dunlop and Radaelli 2017).

10.4 Literature Review Synthesis

According to the structure of the previously defined analytical framework, we have analyzed the sampled literature for analogous states and mechanisms depicting learning in STs.

10.4.1 The Macro-State and Its Connection to Micro-State

Sustainable development has prompted a shift in the underlying assumptions of what constitutes favorable socioeconomic development, as well as the methods and approaches through which it is pursued. The literature underscores several key pillars indicative of this shift: (1) the direction of socioeconomic change is not defined solely by economic growth but also encompasses normative justice- and ethics-based imperatives; (2) the occurrence of change is an actively assisted future-oriented transformation rather than a passive phenomenon subject to historical research; (3) the problems underlying change have become increasingly complex, interconnected, and systemic by nature; (4) the realization of change is not to be enacted by the powerful few but by multi-actor coalitions combining perspectives and efforts of many domains and disciplines; (5) the change dynamics have shifted from rivalry and dominance to coopetition, collaboration, and coevolution; (6) change is not a process to be controlled but rather one that should be influenced continuously in a reflexive and adaptive manner (Beers et al. 2014; Bos and Brown 2012; Bögel et al. 2019; Cuppen et al. 2019; Luederitz et al. 2017a b; Oliver et al. 2021; Rauschmayer et al. 2015; Safarzyńska et al. 2012; Singer-Brodowski 2023; Svare et al. 2023; Turnheim et al. 2015; Van Poeck et al. 2020; Van de Kerkhof and Wieczorek 2005; Von Wirth et al. 2019; Voß and Bornemann 2011; Wittmayer and Schäpke 2014; Öztekin and Gaziulusoy 2019). This sustainability transition paradigm at the macro level provides an overarching framework for guiding change.

Situational mechanisms link macro- and micro-levels, translating the sustainability transition paradigm into practice across levels. These mechanisms embed the paradigm in the daily activities of agents, contextualizing the paradigm locally and further informing the individual. The literature highlights a variety of mechanisms for this transcontextualizing, as noted by Beers et al. (2014), Luederitz et al. (2017a), and Cuppen et al. (2019), are key, with Luederitz et al. (2017a) identifying four main narratives: green economy, low-carbon transformation, ecotopian solutions, and transition movements, which guide systemic interventions. Furthermore, Loorbach (2010) multilevel governance model is frequently cited (e.g., Kemp et al. 2007; Bos and Brown 2012; Raven et al. 2010), outlining strategic (vision development, strategic discussions, long-term goal formulation), tactical (agenda building, negotiating, networking, and coalition building), and operational (experimentation, project building, implementation) as means of procedural governance through which the transition paradigm is intentionally put forward across different levels. Most commonly, however, these mechanisms manifest in various initiatives such as policy frameworks and programs (e.g., Scholz and Methner 2020; Svare et al. 2023), research and innovation projects (e.g., Beers et al. 2019) business development activities (Bögel et al. 2019), community-based initiatives (e.g., Öztekin and Gaziulusoy 2019; Affolderbach and Schulz 2016; Von Wirth et al. 2019; van Oers et al. 2023), educational or scientific reforms (Wittmayer and Schäpke 2014; Singer-Brodowski 2023), which materialize the sustainability agenda in localized contexts.

10.4.2 The Micro-State

As noted by Svare et al. (2023), "a theory of learning in STs (sustainability transitions) needs to consider the learning needs of the learners, how these relate to shifting perceived challenges and to what extent the resulting learning is useful in dealing with these challenges." Learning needs thus arise from a reflected discrepancies between current abilities and those needed to effectively perform tasks or roles in a specific setting (Van Mierlo and Beers 2020; Singer-Brodowski 2023). The identification of learning needs is enabled by uncertainty awareness that makes way for cognitive dissonance (Broto et al. 2014) and the activating processes of reflexivity, autonomy, and empowerment (Svare et al. 2023). Identifying learning needs can be a challenge due to limited rationality, bias, and resistance to change (Safarzyńska et al. 2012; Van Mierlo and Beers 2020). The learning needs of individuals are diverse and dependent on the heterogeneous contextual properties of agents. Contextual factors interact in diverse variations, shaping the emergent learning process and consequently its outcomes (Van Poeck et al. 2020). The literature provides an abundance of contextual factors that can be considered influential in determining individual learning needs, which are classified into three distinct categories, which together form the learner's metacontext.

Firstly, intracontextual factors encompass a wide array of elements within a specific entity (e.g., individual, organization, system). These factors direct learning according to each person's current schemata and competencies, both explicitly, to the extent that the person is aware of them (Wittmayer and Schäpke 2014), and inexplicitly, where unconscious priorities shape decisions (Van Poeck et al. 2020), based on Wertsch (1998). Van Poeck et al. (2020) identify a spectrum of individual factors (e.g., cognition, emotion, values, and experiences) alongside entity embeddedness components (e.g., culture and paradigms), which influence the learning process. Further, Van Mierlo and Beers (2020) determine the diversity of intracontextual factors as a source of embeddedness in societal context on four distinct levels, drawing from different theoretical domains; in collaborative learning contexts individual diversity is attributed to cognitive differences inside groups; in organizational learning contexts, diversity is attributed to the differences in competencies, roles, routines, and values of the practitioners in the organization; in ecology learning contexts stakeholder diversity is attributed to differences in knowledge, past experiences, values, and roles determined in networks; in economy learning contexts diversity is attributed to larger entities differing in terms of competencies, culture, and reasoning frameworks determined in sectoral or cross-sectoral systems (e.g., the innovation system). Notably, in the context of sustainability transitions, the concept of intracontextual factors takes on additional complexity. Bögel et al. (2019) specifically highlight the notion of institutional plurality, which refers to the coexistence and concurrent influence of multiple institutional logics (e.g., norms, values, regulations, cultures, and beliefs) within transitions, which exemplifies the multifaceted nature of intracontextual factors where various embedded logics interact.

Secondly, inter-contextual factors can have a significant influence on directing individual learning, encompassing interactions both between individuals (interpersonal interactions) and among individuals in an entity (dynamics). These factors encompass relational practices, as highlighted by Van Poeck et al. (2020), and a variety of roles that carry specific expectations, responsibilities, and capabilities. Direct impacts on individual learning can arise from roles within one's community, as illustrated by Wittmayer and Schäpke (2014) in identifying various roles for researchers in sustainability transitions (e.g., change agents, knowledge brokers, reflective scientists). Indirect impacts on individual learning can come from organizational roles within the wider system, as exemplified by Bos and Brown (2012) in categorizing roles like "champions," who lead and innovate, and "bridging organizations," which serve as connectors and integrators, thus determining individual learning priorities. Thirdly, extra-contextual factors, which bind different entities together in a common context in which transitions evolve, include spatial (natural, immaterial, and anthropogenic), temporal, and material artifacts (Affolderbach and Schulz 2016; Van Poeck et al. 2020).

10.4.3 Connection From Micro-State to Micro-Action

At the micro-level, individual learning needs shape individual action through the mechanism of learning. This learning process involves both the creation of the new and the discarding of the old (van Oers et al. 2023; Van Mierlo and Beers 2020). The components that influence this learning process will be detailed in the following sections.

10.4.3.1 Learning Space

Learning in STs is generally described as occurring across various domains, levels, and collective entities. However, Beers et al. (2019) suggest that the effectiveness of learning processes in STs is fundamentally contingent upon their congruence with the elements of the specific learning space. In a similar vein, Singer-Brodowski (2023) advocates for the shaping of suitable learning spaces rather than directly intervening in the learning process itself. Consequently, it is important to delineate and increase focus on the different learning spaces, both actual and conceptual, that are prevalent within STs.

Among the literature, different learning spaces have been outlined, each with a unique focus depending on the originating discipline. In transition management, Beers et al. (2019) refer to arenas that emphasize learning within and between local and global loci, each space consisting of differentiated learning about knowledge, constituencies, values, activities, interests, goals, and roles. In sustainability science, Wittmayer and Schäpke (2014) describe societal learning spaces as co-constructed collaboratives where science and society join forces to address sustainability issues, create solutions and actionable experiments, and gain new knowledge, with a focus on learning about the ownership, and nature of sustainability, power relations, and action goals. In design science, Öztekin and Gaziulusoy (2019) suggest a three-tiered embedded learning space, comprising specific, community, and global contexts, which interplay through learning about concrete actions, theoretical codes, meanings, and purposes. In innovation studies, Bos and Brown (2012) define creative spaces as platforms of radical ideas where stakeholders come together to learn about new ideas, visions, and agendas. In urban studies, Von Wirth et al. (2019) describe urban arenas as co-creative collaborative spaces in cities for engaging with the local community for systemic sustainable innovation design and testing. In educational sciences, Singer-Brodowski (2023), and in policy sciences, Voß and Bornemann (2011), describe the creation of discursive spaces as informal and individual-accessible platforms for societal discussion to learn about the diverse normativity-base of action propositions of collective concern.

Across these diverse spaces in STs, individual learning is often considered implicit, and thus the true effectiveness of learning is difficult to establish. However, there's a growing recognition of supplementing implicit individual learning with explicit formal and professional education in these settings (e.g., Bögel et al. 2019; Von Wirth et al. 2019; Van Poeck et al. 2020; Van Mierlo and Beers 2020).

10.4.3.2 Learning Approaches

The existing body of literature provides a clear shared understanding that experiential (i.e., learning from experiences) and social (i.e., learning from interaction) are the two primary approaches to learning in sustainability transitions. In deep interplay, the two approaches result in cognitive (e.g., new solutions, mental models, knowledge, skills) and relational (e.g., relationships, trust, empathy) capital (Van Mierlo and Beers 2020; Scholz and Methner 2020; Beers et al. 2014). Despite the integral nature of the two, due to the differences in nature and consequent reliability of feedback from the two approaches, for analytical purposes, it is best to maintain a separation of the two approaches.

Experiential learning, influenced by Dewey's (1916/1997) pragmatic learning theory and encompassing learning by doing and reflective practice, is essential in transition management, emphasizing learning from experiments and reflection at different stages (Vande Kerkhof and Wieczorek 2005; Luederitz et al. 2017b; Svare et al. 2023; Turnheim et al. 2015; Van Poeck et al. 2020; Van Mierlo and Beers 2020). Experimentation can take various forms, such as larger transition initiatives (e.g., Bos and Brown 2012), smaller bounded-sociotechnical experiments (e.g., Brown and Vergragt 2008), urban living labs (e.g., Von Wirth et al. 2019), and innovation experiments (e.g., Beers et al. 2014). In experiential learning for the individual, extending reflection beyond the mere outcomes of experimentation to actor-relevant attributes, such as legitimacy and relevance, is key (Turnheim et al. 2015).

Social learning–drawing from Wenger's (2000) community of practice theory, Bandura's (1977) social learning theory, and Nelson and Winter's (1982) evolutionary theory of economic change involves learning from each other (observation, sharing of knowledge, and imitation) and learning with each other (creating shared or divergent understanding and meaning-making) in a connected social setting (e.g., Kemp et al. 2007; Rauschmayer et al. 2015; Van de Kerkhof and Wieczorek 2005; Beers et al. 2014; Svare et al. 2023; Van Mierlo and Beers 2020; Scholz and Methner 2020; Beers et al. 2019; Voß and Bornemann 2011; Brown and Vergragt 2008; Safarzyńska et al. 2012).

Social learning is informed by the diverse values, knowledge, and interests of the multistakeholder environment (Van Mierlo and Beers 2020). Learning with each other can either serve the role of integrating perspectives and creating interdependence among actors for acting in concert or embracing the diversity of perspectives for innovation and generating alternative pathways for transitions; however, the general perception is that STs require balancing between consensus and conflict, as both elements serve a purpose (Van Mierlo and Beers 2020; Scholz and Methner 2020). Beers et al. (2019) emphasize that effective social learning is a shared process among contextually diverse entities that, through externalization, internalization, negotiation of common meaning, and integration (based on Beers et al. 2006), focuses more on translating perspectives than merely transferring them. Conflicts, if harnessed appropriately, can provide significant learning opportunities, whereas unaddressed, might lead to divided and differentiated learning among conflicting communities (Cuppen et al. 2019; Beers et al. 2014). Effective conflict management strategies include, for example, Schön and Rein (1994) frame reflection to clarify underlying perspectives and their impact on actionable issues for critical examination and reframing (Voß and Bornemann 2011; Brown and Vergragt 2008) and Rip (1986) approach of using controversy as an informal technology assessment and leveraging diverse viewpoints for further exploration in a widened social setting for more informed and deeper social learning (Voß and Bornemann 2011; Cuppen et al. 2019).

Social learning is fundamentally a process of learning in interaction, where individual and collective understanding is constructed in dynamic interplay (Scholz and Methner 2020) based on Reed et al. (Brown and Vergragt 2008; Van Mierlo and Beers, 2020; 2010). As learning is differentiated among collectives (Safarzyńska et al. 2012), including transition arenas (e.g., Brown and Vergragt 2008; Beers et al. 2014; Scholz and Methner 2020), businesses and organizations (e.g., Bögel et al. 2019; Duygan et al. 2021), and networks (Goyal and Howlett 2020), individual learning can be considered contingent on the differentiated community it is connected to, thus making collective composition and its internal dynamics, influential factors for learning. Furthermore, Beers et al. (2014) demonstrate the importance of extending social learning beyond collectives to the wider social environment. Relating to this, transition management has faced criticism for overlooking the specificities of internal (e.g., power and politics) and outer dynamics (e.g., democratic legitimacy) (Rauschmayer et al. 2015). Voß et al. (2009) illustrate the importance of social learning-related procedural issues in enabling constructive learning dynamics—such as inclusivity, diversity, representativeness, power balance, and transparency—essential for legitimizing learning outcomes and, subsequently, the reflexive governance approach directing STs. Additionally, effective social learning in STs is often considered to necessitate some form of subtle guidance, making the inclusion of a facilitator (e.g., project monitor, researcher, knowledge broker) instrumental (Wittmayer and Schäpke 2014; Van de Kerkhof and Wieczorek 2005; Lähteenoja et al. 2022).

10.4.3.3 Learning Forms

Scholars in the field almost unanimously refer to different forms of learning, drawing on Argyris and Schön (1978), and Bateson (1972) conceptualizations of multiple loops of learning (e.g., Van de Kerkhof and Wieczorek 2005; Broto et al. 2014; Van Mierlo and Beers 2020; Van Poeck et al. 2020; Lähteenoja et al. 2022). In its most basic form, learning is zero-loop learning, characterized by automatic, conditional responses to situations. First-loop learning is a feedback-based reflective adjustment of responses within existing frames of reference. Second-loop learning involves deeper reflection and questioning of the current frames themselves, leading to a possible reconfiguration of responses based on new interpretations of situations. Third-loop learning includes meta-level reflection, such as learning about learning and learning how to transform the frames that generate learning. Thus, the learning loops represent a progression from conditioned learning to incremental, extended, and transformative change in the frames that generate responses to a given situation (Argyris and Schön 1978; Bateson 1972). Van Mierlo and Beers (2020) [based on Senge (1990)] note that feedback is a key challenge to learning in transitions, as in complex settings, feedback often comes from the immediate results of actions, neglecting the indirect, long-term, or elsewhere realized consequences, thereby possibly misrepresenting the reality of reflection.

In STs, first- and second-loop learning are prominent. First-loop focuses on acquiring solution-based knowledge via cognitive analysis, while second-loop learning, critical for breaking path dependency and lock-in, delves into understanding problems and solutions through normative analysis (Van de Kerkhof and Wieczorek 2005; Van Mierlo and Beers 2020). Third-loop learning, while less explored in ST studies, focuses on changing the underlying operative theories within organizations, which guide decision-making and behaviors (Argyris and Schön 1978; Bateson 1972). Singer-Brodowski (2023), based on Mezirow's (1978) transformative learning, argues for the importance of extending the focus beyond organizational frames to the frames of individuals influencing in various informal collectives (e.g., multiprofessional networks) and thus facilitating more systemic learning in STs.

Empirical research on learning in STs, though limited (Van Poeck et al. 2020), mainly confirms the prevalence of first- and, to some extent, second-loop learning (e.g., Lähteenoja et al. 2022; Broto et al. 2014; Brown and Vergragt 2008; Svare et al. 2023). Third-loop learning, while generally considered essential for sustainability transitions (Singer-Brodowski 2023), lacks extensive empirical support. In this literature review, only two studies confirmed empirically the existence of third-loop learning (see Bos and Brown 2012; Svare et al. 2023). Consequently, Lähteenoja et al. (2022) caution against favoring one learning form over others based on generalized assumptions, as the effectiveness of learning in transitions ultimately depends on the specific context (e.g., transition phase and timing) and the involved actors (e.g., existing competencies).

10.4.4 Micro-Action

A fundamental objective of transition activities is to equip and enable all members of society to contribute to the advancement of sustainability within their respective realms (Rauschmayer et al. 2015) based on Loorbach (2007) and Luederitz et al. (2017b). Van de Kerkhof and Wieczorek (2005) note that while diversity among actors in transitions fosters learning, a degree of homogeneity is considered crucial for effective coordination. Homogeneity can be considered in terms of competencies to outline generalizable learning outcomes that enable individuals to influence the evolution of the transition. Research has generated various competencies in the context of transitions [e.g., Raven et al. 2010; Loorbach 2010; Luederitz et al. 2017b; Svare et al. 2023) based on (Wiek et al. 2011; Redman and Wiek 2021; Rauschmayer et al. 2015)], which can be synthesized as the ability to: (1) reflect on the guiding principles and objectives for the system's target state, (2) envision long-term scenarios and identify uncertainties, (3) understand system dynamics, structures, and connections, which comprise the systemic functioning of the whole, (4) innovate and use creativity to generate new solutions, (5) build relational capital for collective action, (6) integrate diverse perspectives and logics across the system, (7) construct, experiment, and implement change strategies, (8) monitor, evaluate, and adjust to system evolution, (9) exercise agency within one's relative realm, (10) self-reflect, learn, and adjust one's position and role within the system.

Competencies empower individuals to exercise agency effectively (Duygan et al. 2021). The effectiveness of competencies relies on an individual's ability to appropriately employ a set of competencies to address a particular situation (Svare et al. 2023), the correspondence of those actions with others in an interdependent environment (Safarzyńska et al. 2012), the activation of essential supportive resources for a specific practice (Duygan et al. 2021), as well as pairing competencies with a suitable form of agency. Individual agency is distributed across the system and manifests in various forms in transitions, ranging from the informal agency (e.g., lifestyle choices) (Rauschmayer et al. 2015) to the formal agency (e.g., institutional entrepreneurship) (Duygan et al. 2021). Furthermore, (Partzsch 2017) suggests agency in STs takes predominantly three forms: "power with" is agency empowered by the collective to act by shared values; "power to" is self-empowered agency to unidirectionally inflict change by one's values; and "power over" is relationally empowered agency to shape the actions of others.

10.4.5 Connection from Micro-Action to Macro-State

Based on the literature, the role of individual agency in influencing processes that structure and inform the functioning of the system in transformation is based on two types of complementary mechanisms: (1) co-evolutionary mechanisms of variation, selection, and retention, as well as (2) relational mechanisms of diffusion, mutation, migration, and scaling.

A co-evolutionary perspective suggests that change in one part of the system influences another, which leads to gradual evolution across levels, driven by changes within and among various interconnected entities at each level (Kemp et al. 2007). Although co-evolution focuses on the broad strokes of change, individual changes are ground zero for realized impact across the system, as exemplified by Safarzyńska et al. (2012): individual exploration and learning foster a variety of practices that become selected for their utility to both individuals (i.e., individual selection) and collectives (i.e., group selection), which evolve into Meso-level rules that disrupt existing coordination and to new macro-level interaction patterns, resulting in simultaneous decoordination and recoordination of structures that create realignment and propel the system toward self-organization and coevolution ultimately culminating in structural changes and the emergence of novel system properties (Safarzyńska et al. 2012) based on Dopfer, (2006). Moreover, with growing interest in the deliberate construction of knowledge and learning systems in STs (e.g., Oliver et al. 2021; Luederitz et al. 2017b; Svare et al. 2023), the individual agency can be seen to have an increasing part in shaping these evolutionary processes through the aggregation of inputs and the design of such systems.

A relational perspective to change in transitions is proposed by Affolderbach and Schulz (2016), where individual actors act as practice carriers across entities, places, and levels within sustainability transitions, and through the interactions and inter-connectedness of individuals in larger sociospatial contexts (e.g., cities) diffuse and mutate into unique "assemblages of innovation." This underscores the importance of individual agency in spreading variations across the system by diffusing them deeper into surrounding contexts, migrating them into other contexts, and scaling them into broader contexts (Öztekin and Gaziulusoy 2019; Von Wirth et al. 2019; Bos and Brown 2012).

10.5 Discussion

Societies currently find themselves amid multiple parallel STs initiated to respond to the urgent need for sustainable change on a massive scale. AI is seen as possibly the single most potential technology to accelerate sustainable development (Gupta et al. 2021; Van Wynsberghe 2021), but an understanding of where and how that impact is realized in the system is lacking. Most works on the subject are sectoral studies of various AI tools utilized in improving sustainability outcomes, e.g., food (Camaréna 2020) or energy systems (Nizetic et al. 2023). As STs are predicated on the function of human learning systems that are social systems with high levels of human agency, they have so far been generally dismissed as impregnable to meaningful AI integration. The dominant frameworks used in conceptualizing and managing sustainability transitions focus on the macro- and meso-levels of the system and collective change and, as such, arguably cannot fully respond to the need to effectively manage these transitions or to discover how AI could help. This research has opened up the multiple tiers in these frameworks, all the way down to the foundational micro-level processes of learning that drive STs, and related them to the macro-level. In doing so, an integrative multilevel framework is provided that reveals the factors and mechanisms inside the complex adaptive learning systems found in transitions toward more sustainable paradigms and thus enables further exploration into possible human-AI learning synergies.

The paradigm is carried by situational mechanisms (narratives, governance, and initiatives) across nested levels to individuals. As the individual becomes instilled with new cues of values, processes, and actions, reframing ways of being and doing things, discrepancies may arise. These discrepancies, depending on the individual's metacontext, bring forth different kinds of learning needs in practicing agency. Learning is an action-formation mechanism to alleviate those discrepancies, as individual agency is empowered by competencies. Learning processes are formulated in a combination of spaces, approaches, and forms of learning, leading to different learning outcomes. When individuals practice agency across the system, through transformational mechanisms (evolutionary and relational), learnings accrue into emergent transition capabilities of the whole, which further shape the trajectory of the system.

Opening up the mechanisms underlying the learning in STs illuminates further opportunities for facilitating transitions. Once individual learning is triggered, it can be effectively fostered by the creation of fitting conceptual and actual conditions, i.e., learning spaces. AI deep learning generative models, i.e., multi-layered non-linear learning and syncretization of novel data (Bian and Xie 2021), could be utilized in the re-arrangement of conceptual learning spaces to process, integrate, and subsequently re-interpret existing disciplinarily separate research and data from conceptual learning spaces into potentially improved configurations that frame learning in STs. The de facto use of AI in learning extends the actual learning spaces into the digital sphere, which brings possibilities for creating more structured conditions for learning via evidence-based monitoring and assistance to individual learning. However, as evidenced by AI-enabled adaptive learning platforms developed for educational settings, the effective utilization of such platforms requires considerable design effort to result in fit-for-purpose benefits (Kabudi et al. 2021). However, if digital learning spaces are modeled successfully, it would enable the scalability of such spaces more effectively.

Within STs, competencies are developed primarily through experiential or social learning. Effective experiential learning requires systematic data collection, analysis, and contextual reflection on the initiatives and experiments conducted, which can often be neglected (Sætra 2023). AI has tremendous potential to support this by managing the collection, linking, cross-referencing, preliminary analysis, and contextualization of data in connection to STs, thereby addressing some of the problems in establishing effective feedback (Camaréna 2020; Sætra 2023; Pan and Nishant 2023). For social learning approaches, on the other hand, direct intervention by AI remains too challenging for current AI solutions, but they should instead be used to facilitate appropriate social interaction processes and connections (Pan and Nishant 2023). This could be enacted, e.g., by using AI evolutionary learning through swarm intelligence tools to foster participatory and negotiation-like social learning, which, via real-time human input and AI optimization, has shown improved intelligence in business contexts (Metcalf et al. 2019).

AI can also "move the goalposts" in terms of the general competencies for sustainability that should be achieved. Most of the currently targeted competencies can be directly supported or elevated by the thoughtful application of different AI tools, thereby accelerating the achievement of a functional level of competence by the individual. This would have an empowering effect on the broader learning system, as with the support of AI, an even higher share of the agents within the system will be able to independently evaluate and align their activities correctly by relying on narrative and metacontextual cues to produce co-evolutionary systemic change without direct management from the top-down—in essence, transforming larger portions of the whole into a true complex adaptive system state. This would bolster the correctness and effectiveness of selection at the level of transformative mechanisms, granting agents the possibility to better evaluate beneficial variations to solidify at the macro level.

It is evident that AI–human-empowered learning systems in STs are currently set to primarily operate through the decentralized application of AI tools harnessed independently by individual agents embedded in different group, organizational, and network contexts at the micro-level, as envisioned in some sectoral studies (e.g., Camaréna 2020; Nizetic et al. 2023). As with other sustainability competencies, we will undoubtedly need to learn through experimentation and iteration to discover the optimal combination of different AI models that can tap into the complex essence of learning in STs for each agent. Therefore, as we progress, the utilization of AI ensemble learning, i.e., a combination of learning models for improved fit (Zounemat-Kermani et al. 2021), seems appropriate, as there is no "one size fits all" solution to be discovered in pursuing human-centric AI implementation for meta contextually differing individual learners. The application of AI to the critically important learning system for STs is not without risks. With the emergence of AI-empowered agencies, transparency, and consciousness over deployed AI tools and their underlying algorithms are imperative. It is vital to ensure that AI's role in influencing individual agency forms promotes "power to" and "power with" by providing individuals with accurate knowledge and suitable tools for acting on their own and shared values and objectives, instead of contributing to "power over" AI manipulation. This is also echoed by increasing research interest in the development of explainable and trustworthy AI in domains where AI-empowered agencies could have profound societal implications (e.g., Markus et al. 2021). AI as a technology paradoxically can capture many of the flaws distinct to human learning, and as such, it stands to exacerbate issues with power, politics, and democratic legitimacy already problematic in STs. Due to how AI works, it has a documented tendency to reinforce path dependencies, replicate and even strengthen the embedded patterns of bias within the data and decisions it learns from, and result in preferential outcomes (Camaréna 2020; Vinuesa et al. 2020; Pan and Nishant 2023). As AI helps to solve sustainability issues, its development and application also generate new ones (Gupta et al. 2021), e.g., a greenhouse gas produced in training AI models (Strubell et al. 2019) or widening the digital divide between developed and developing nations (Vinuesa et al. 2020). Therefore, further integration of AI into human learning requires an additional AI literacy competency for individuals to assess the extent to which AI tools can be used effectively, reliably, and ethically to facilitate learning (Miao et al. 2021).

The integration of AI into the human learning system is likely to happen in stages, where the adoption of much of the first generation of AI-empowered learning systems is already possible. The first generation of AI-empowered learning will result from the diffusion of generic-purpose AI among individual learners, such as advanced generative AI tools (e.g., ChatGPT 4.0) that are already able to provide significant algorithmic assistance to most knowledge-related tasks (Ritala et al. 2024) and provide much of the needed functionality. Such AI excels and functions largely on first-loop learning and becomes less applicable the more sensemaking and higher-order learning are required (Pan and Nishant 2023), naturally leading us to the discussion on how responsibilities and roles in human–AI collaborative learning systems would be shared in the second and further generations of human–AI collaborative learning.

10.6 Conclusions

In this integrative literature review, we have illuminated the significance of individual learning in the multilevel embedded context of STs and delineated the underlying influential factors and mechanisms for a more concise theoretical understanding. The employed methodology limits the study to the material in the literature sample, and as such, future studies are invited to empirically relate these findings in different ST contexts to bridge theory and practice.

The analytical framework we have outlined, and the possible AI-human synergy points elaborated, offer a valuable baseline to which distinct STs (e.g., hydrogen economy or regenerative industry) can build to further analyze context-specific learning and design more explicit knowledge and learning systems—an emerging interest in transition practice and research.

Moreover, as human–AI integration deepens, there is an exciting opportunity for research to explore how this convergence alters roles (e.g., how does AI impact the role of individual learning in different tasks) and learning dynamics (e.g., how does the integration of AI impact social learning dynamics) within STs and, as such, contributes to the emergence of potentially new influential factors and mechanisms. During these initial stages of human–AI-empowered sustainability transitions, much remains to be discovered, underscoring the essential need for continued research to map and elucidate the realized effects of augmented intelligence for the agents involved and for the dual transition in progress.

In summation, human–AI empowered learning systems are only as effective as the paradigms and models they are conceptualized and trained by, the individual learners and data points from which the system extrapolates information to appropriately direct its trajectory, as well as the structural connectors and algorithms that underpin the system's capacity for self-organization of the whole and co-evolutionary development among its parts. The interplay of these elements highlights the imperative to thoughtfully navigate human–AI collaborative learning by leveraging both systemic (macro) and individual (micro) perspectives for transparency throughout processes to ensure the identification of limiting factors for managing inherent risks and enabling factors for creating synergy benefits. This facilitates the optimized division and merging of roles and responsibilities between humans and AI for an improved learning function to steer sustainability transitions.

References

E. D. Adamides and Y. Mouzakitis. Industrial ecosystems as technological niches. *Journal of Cleaner Production*, 17(2):172–180, 2009.

R. Adams, S. Jeanrenaud, J. Bessant, D. Denyer, and P. Overy. Sustainability-oriented innovation: A systematic review. *International Journal of Management Reviews*, 18(2):180–205, 2016.

R. Adner. Ecosystem as structure: An actionable construct for strategy. *Journal of Management*, 43(1):39–58, 2017.

J. Affolderbach and C. Schulz. Mobile transitions: Exploring synergies for urban sustainability research. *Urban Studies*, 53(9):1942–1957, 2016*.

C. Argyris and D. A. Schön. *Organizational learning: A theory of action perspective*. Addison-Wesley, 1978.

M. Bacigalupo and Y. Punie, editors. *GreenComp—The European sustainability competence framework, authored by Bianchi, G., Pisiotis, U., and Cabrera Giraldez, M.* Publications Office of the European Union, 2022. https://doi.org/10.2760/13286.

A. Bandura. *Social learning theory*. Prentice Hall, 1977.

W. Banzhaf and P. Machado. Fundamentals of evolutionary machine learning. In W. Banzhaf, P. Machado, and M. Zhang, editors, *Handbook of Evolutionary Machine Learning (Genetic and Evolutionary Computation)*. Springer, 2024.

G. Bateson. *Steps to an ecology of mind: Collected essays in anthropology, psychiatry, evolution, and epistemology*. University of Chicago Press, 1972.

P. J. Beers, H. P. Boshuizen, P. A. Kirschner, and W. H. Gijselaers. Common ground, complex problems and decision making. *Group Decision and Negotiation*, 15: 529–556, 2006.

P. J. Beers, F. Hermans, T. Veldkamp, and J. Hinssen. Social learning inside and outside transition projects: Playing free jazz for a heavy metal audience. *NJAS- Wageningen Journal of Life Sciences*, 69:5–13, 2014*.

P. J. Beers, J. A. Turner, K. Rijswijk, T. Williams, T. Barnard, and S. Beechener. Learning or evaluating? towards a negotiation-of-meaning approach to learning in transition governance. *Technological Forecasting and Social Change*, 145: 229–239, 2019*.

Y. Bian and X.-Q. Xie. Generative chemistry: drug discovery with deep learning generative models. *Journal of Molecular Modeling*, 27(3):71–71, 2021.

J. J. Bos and R. R. Brown. Governance experimentation and factors of success in socio-technical transitions in the urban water sector. *Technological Forecasting and Social Change*, 79(7):1340–1353, 2012*.

V. C. Broto, S. Glendinning, E. Dewberry, C. Walsh, and M. Powell. What can we learn about transitions for sustainability from infrastructure shocks? *Technological Forecasting and Social Change*, 84:186–196, 2014*.

H. S. Brown and P. J. Vergragt. Bounded socio-technical experiments as agents of systemic change: The case of a zero-energy residential building. *Technological Forecasting and Social Change*, 75(1):107–130, 2008*.

P. Bögel, K. Pereverza, P. Upham, and O. Kordas. Linking socio-technical transition studies and organisational change management: Steps towards an integrative, multi-scale heuristic. *Journal of Cleaner Production*, 232:359–368, 2019*.

S. Camaréna. Artificial intelligence in the design of the transitions to sustainable food systems. *Journal of Cleaner Production*, 271:122574, 2020.

B. Cavalcanti Barros Rodrigues and C. F. Gohr. Dynamic capabilities and critical factors for boosting sustainability-oriented innovation: Systematic literature review and a framework proposal. *Engineering Management Journal*, 34(4):591–619, 2022.

J. S. Coleman. Social theory, social research, and a theory of action. *American Journal of Sociology*, 91(6):1309–1335, 1986.

J. S. Coleman. Microfoundations and macrosocial behavior. In J. C. Alexander, B. Giesen, R. Münch, and N. J. Smelser, editors, *The micro-macro link*, pages 153–173. University of California Press, 1987.

J. S. Coleman. *Foundations of social theory*. The Belknap Press of Harvard University Press, 1990.

A. P. Cowen, F. Rink, I. R. Cuypers, D. A. Grégoire, and I. Weller. Applying coleman's boat in management research: Opportunities and challenges in bridging macro and micro theory. *Academy of Management Journal*, 65(1):1–10, 2022.

E. Cuppen, U. Pesch, S. Remmerswaal, and M. Taanman. Normative diversity, conflict and transition: Shale gas in the netherlands. *Technological Forecasting and Social Change*, 145:165–175, 2019*.

K. Dopfer. Evolutionary economics: A theoretical framework. In K. Dopfer, editor, *The evolutionary foundations of economics*, pages 3–55. Cambridge University Press, 2006.

C. A. Dunlop and C. M. Radaelli. Learning in the bath-tub: The micro and macro dimensions of the causal relationship between learning and policy change. *Policy and Society*, 36(2):304–319, 2017.

M. Duygan, A. Kachi, T. D. Oliveira, and A. Rinscheid. Introducing the endowmentpractice-institutions (epi) framework for studying agency in the institutional contestation of socio-technical regimes. *Journal of Cleaner Production*, 296:126396, 2021*.

Directorate-General for Research European Commission, Innovation, M. Breque, L. De Nul, and A. Petridis. *Industry 5.0—Towards a sustainable, human-centric and resilient European industry*. Publications Office of the European Union, 2021. https://doi.org/10.2777/308407.

F. Geels and R. Raven. Non-linearity and expectations in niche-development trajectories: ups and downs in dutch biogas development (1973–2003). *Technology Analysis & Strategic Management*, 18(3-4):375–392, 2006.

F. W. Geels. Socio-technical transitions to sustainability: A review of criticisms and elaborations of the multi-level perspective. *Current Opinion in Environmental Sustainability*, 39:187–201, 2019.

F.W. Geels. Technological transitions as evolutionary reconfiguration processes: a multi-level perspective and a case-study. *Research Policy*, 31(8-9):1257–1274, 2002.

F.W. Geels. From sectoral systems of innovation to socio-technical system: insights about dynamics and change from sociology and institutional theory. *Research Policy*, 33(6-7):897–920, 2004.

F.W. Geels. Processes and patterns in transitions and system innovations: refining the co-evolutionary multi-level perspective. *Technological Forecasting and Social Change*, 72:681–696, 2005.

F.W. Geels. Ontologies, socio-technical transitions (to sustainability), and the multi-level perspective. *Research Policy*, 39:495–510, 2010.

J. Gharajedaghi. *Systems thinking: Managing chaos and complexity: A platform for designing business architecture*. Elsevier, 2011.
A. Giddens. *The constitution of society: Outline of the theory of structuration*. University of California Press, 1984.
N. Goyal and M. Howlett. Who learns what in sustainability transitions? *Environmental Innovation and Societal Transitions*, 34:311–321, 2020*.
S. Gupta, S. D. Langhans, S. Domisch, F. Fuso-Nerini, A. Felländer, M. Battaglini, M. Tegmark, and R. Vinuesa. Assessing whether artificial intelligence is an enabler or an inhibitor of sustainability at indicator level. *Transportation Engineering*, 4: 100064, 2021.
P. Hedström and R. Swedberg. Social mechanisms: An introductory essay. In P. Hedström and R. Swedberg, editors, *Social mechanisms: An analytical approach to social theory*, pages 1–31. Cambridge University Press, 1998.
J. Holland. *Emergence: From Chaos to Order*. Oxford University Press, 1998.
R. Hoogma, R. Kemp, J. Schot, and B. Truffer. *Experimenting for sustainable transport*. Taylor & Francis, 2002.
E. A. Inigo and L. Albareda. Sustainability oriented innovation dynamics: Levels of dynamic capabilities and their path-dependent and self-reinforcing logics. *Technological Forecasting and Social Change*, 139:334–351, 2019.
Holland J. *Hidden Order: How Adaptation Builds Complexity*. Addison-Wesley, 1995.
T. Kabudi, I. Pappas, and D. H. Olsen. Ai-enabled adaptive learning systems: A systematic mapping of the literature. *Computers and Education: Artificial Intelligence*, 2:100017, 2021.
Andreas Kaplan and Michael Haenlein. Siri, siri, in my hand: Who's the fairest in the land? on the interpretations, illustrations, and implications of artificial intelligence. *Business Horizons*, 62(1):15–25, 2019.
R. Kemp and P. Martens. Sustainable development: how to manage something that is subjective and never can be achieved? *Sustainability: science, practice and Policy*, 3(2):5–14, 2007.
R. Kemp, J. Schot, and R. Hoogma. Regime shifts to sustainability through processes of niche formation: the approach of strategic niche management. *Technology Analysis & Strategic Management*, 10:175–195, 1998.
R. Kemp, A. Rip, and J. Schot. Constructing transition paths through the management of niches. In R. Garud and P. Karnoe, editors, *Path dependence and creation*, pages 269–299. Lawrence Erlbaum Associates, 2001.
R. Kemp, D. Loorbach, and J. Rotmans. Transition management as a model for managing processes of co-evolution towards sustainable development. *The*

International Journal of Sustainable Development & World Ecology, 14(1):78–91, 2007*.

F. W. Köhler, Geels, F. Kern, J. Markard, E. Onsongo, A. Wieczorek, F. Alkemade, F. Avelino, A. Bergek, F. Boons, L. Fünfschilling, D. Hess, G. Holtz, S. Hyysalo, K. Jenkins, P. Kivimaa, M. Martiskainen, A. McMeekin, M. S. Mühlemeier, and P Wells. An agenda for sustainability transitions research: State of the art and future directions. *Environmental Innovation and Societal Transitions*, 31:1–32, 2019.

U. Lichtenthaler. Substitute or synthesis: The interplay between human and artificial intelligence. *Research-Technology Management*, 61(5):12–14, 2018.

D. Loorbach. *Transition management: New mode of governance for sustainable development*. International Books, 2007.

D. Loorbach. Transition management for sustainable development: a prescriptive, complexity-based governance framework. *Governance*, 23(1):161–183, 2010.

C. Luederitz, D. J. Abson, R. Audet, and D. J. Lang. Many pathways toward sustainability: not conflict but co-learning between transition narratives. *Sustainability Science*, 12:393–407, 2017a*.

C. Luederitz, N. Schäpke, A. Wiek, D. J. Lang, M. Bergmann, J. J. Bos, and F. R. . . . Westley. Learning through evaluation–a tentative evaluative scheme for sustainability transition experiments. *Journal of Cleaner Production*, 169:61–76, 2017b*.

S. Lähteenoja, S. Hyysalo, J. Lukkarinen, T. Marttila, H. Saarikoski, M. Faehnle, and L. Peltonen. What does it take to study learning in transitions? a case of citizen energy in finland. *Sustainability: Science, Practice and Policy*, 18(1):651–664, 2022*.

J. Markard, R. Raven, and B. Truffer. Sustainability transitions: An emerging field of research and its prospects. *Research Policy*, 41(6):955–967, 2012.

A. F. Markus, J. A. Kors, and P. R. Rijnbeek. The role of explainability in creating trustworthy artificial intelligence for health care: a comprehensive survey of the terminology, design choices, and evaluation strategies. *Journal of biomedical informatics*, 113:103655, 2021.

L. Metcalf, D. A. Askay, and L. B. Rosenberg. Keeping humans in the loop: pooling knowledge through artificial swarm intelligence to improve business decision making. *California management review*, 61(4):84–109, 2019.

J. Mezirow. Perspective transformation. *Adult Education Quarterly*, 28(2):100–110, 1978.

F. Miao, W. Holmes, R. Huang, and H. Zhang. *AI and education: Guidance for policy-makers*. UNESCO, 2021. URL https://unesdoc.unesco.org/ark:/48223/pf0000376709.

J. F. Moore. Predators and prey: A new ecology of competition. *Harvard Business Review*, 71(3):75–83, 1993.

T. Mäkitie, J. Hanson, S. Damman, and M. Wardeberg. Digital innovation's contribution to sustainability transitions. *Technology in Society*, 73:102255, 2023.

R. R. Nelson and S. G. Winter. *An Evolutionary Theory of Economic Change*. Harvard University Press, 1982.

S. Nizetic, M. Müslüm Arıcı, and A. T. Hoang. Smart and sustainable technologies in energy transition. *Journal of Cleaner Production*, 389:135944, 2023.

T. H. Oliver, L. Benini, A. Borja, C. Dupont, B. Doherty, M. Grodzińska-Jurczak, and L. Tarrason. Knowledge architecture for the wise governance of sustainability transitions. *Environmental Science & Policy*, 126:152–163, 2021*.

C. Pahl-Wostl. The importance of social learning in restoring the multifunctionality of rivers and floodplains. *Ecology and Society*, 11(1), 2006.

S. L. Pan and R. Nishant. Artificial intelligence for digital sustainability: An insight into domain-specific research and future directions. *International Journal of Information Management*, 72:102668, 2023.

L. Partzsch. 'power with' and 'power to' in environmental politics and the transition to sustainability. *Environmental Politics*, 26(2):193–211, 2017*.

J. Pelenc, D. Bazile, and C. Ceruti. Collective capability and collective agency for sustainability: A case study. *Ecological Economics*, 118:226–239, 2015.

F. Rauschmayer, T. Bauler, and N. Schäpke. Towards a thick understanding of sustainability transitions: Linking transition management, capabilities and social practices. *Ecological Economics*, 109:211–221, 2015*.

R. Raven, S. Van Den Bosch, and R. Weterings. Transitions and strategic niche management: Towards a competence kit for practitioners. *International Journal of Technology Management*, 51(1):57–74, 2010*.

A. Redman and A. Wiek. Competencies for advancing transformations towards sustainability. *Frontiers in Education*, 6:785163, 2021.

M. S. Reed, A. C. Evely, G. Cundill, I. Fazey, J. Glass, A. Laing, and L. C. Stringer. What is social learning? *Ecology and Society*, 15(4), 2010.

A. Rip. Controversies as informal technology assessment. *Science Communication*, 8(2):349–371, 1986.

P. Ritala, M. Ruokonen, and L. Ramaul. Transforming boundaries: How does chatgpt change knowledge work? *Journal of Business Strategy*, 45(3):214–220, 2024.

T. Rocco and M. Plakhotnik. Literature reviews, conceptual frameworks, and theoretical frameworks: Terms, functions, and distinctions. *Human Resource Development Review*, 2009.

J. Rotmans and D. Loorbach. Complexity and transition management. *Journal of Industrial Ecology*, 13(2):184–196, 2009.

J. Rotmans, R. Kemp, and M. Van Asselt. More evolution than revolution: Transition management in public policy. *Foresight*, 3(1):15–31, 2001.

K. Safarzyńska, K. Frenken, and J. C. Van Den Bergh. Evolutionary theorizing and modeling of sustainability transitions. *Research Policy*, 41(6):1011–1024, 2012*.

I. H. Sarker. Machine learning: Algorithms, real-world applications and research directions. *SN Computer Science*, 2:160, 2021.

G. Scholz and N. Methner. A social learning and transition perspective on a climate change project in south africa. *Environmental Innovation and Societal Transitions*, 34:322–335, 2020*.

J. Schot and F. W. Geels. Strategic niche management and sustainable innovation journeys: Theory, findings, research agenda, and policy. *Technology Analysis & Strategic Management*, 20(5):537–554, 2008.

D. Schön and M. Rein. *Frame Reflection: Toward the Resolution of Intractable Policy Controversies*. BasicBooks, 1994.

A. K. Sen. *Development as Freedom*. Oxford University Press, 1999.

P. M. Senge. *The Fifth Discipline: Art and Practice of the Learning Organization*. Doubleday, 1990.

M. Singer-Brodowski. The potential of transformative learning for sustainability transitions: Moving beyond formal learning environments. *Environment, Development and Sustainability*, pages 1–19, 2023*.

H. Snyder. Literature review as a research methodology: An overview and guidelines. *Journal of Business Research*, 104:333–339, 2019.

E. Strubell, A. Ganesh, and A. McCallum. Energy and policy considerations for deep learning in nlp, 2019.

H. Svare, M. D. Gjefsen, A. den Boer, and K. Kok. Learning systems and learning paths in sustainability transitions. *Ecology and Society*, 28(1), 2023*.

H. Sætra. The ai esg protocol: Evaluating and disclosing the environment, social, and governance implications of artificial intelligence capabilities, assets, and activities. *Sustainable Development*, 31:1027–1037, 2023.

David J. Teece, Gary Pisano, and Amy Shuen. Dynamic capabilities and strategic management. *Strategic Management Journal*, 18(7):509–533, 1997.

R. J. Torraco. Writing integrative literature reviews: Guidelines and examples. *Human Resource Development Review*, 4(3):356–367, 2005.

B. Truffer, H. Rohracher, P. Kivimaa, R. Raven, F. Alkemade, L. Carvalho, and G. Feola. A perspective on the future of sustainability transitions research. *Environmental Innovation and Societal Transitions*, 42:331–339, 2022.

B. Turnheim, F. Berkhout, F. Geels, A. Hof, A. McMeekin, B. Nykvist, and D. van Vuuren. Evaluating sustainability transitions pathways: Bridging analytical approaches to address governance challenges. *Global Environmental Change*, 35: 239–253, 2015*.

UNESCO. *Education for Sustainable Development Goals: Learning Objectives.* UNESCO Publishing, 2017. URL https://doi.org/10.54675/CGBA9153.

M. Van de Kerkhof and A. Wieczorek. Learning and stakeholder participation in transition processes towards sustainability: Methodological considerations. *Technological Forecasting and Social Change*, 72(6):733–747, 2005*.

B. Van Mierlo and P. J. Beers. Understanding and governing learning in sustainability transitions: A review. *Environmental Innovation and Societal Transitions*, 34: 255–269, 2020*.

L. van Oers, G. Feola, H. Runhaar, and E. Moors. Unlearning in sustainability transitions: Insight from two dutch community-supported agriculture farms. *Environmental Innovation and Societal Transitions*, 46:100693, 2023*.

K. Van Poeck, L. Östman, and T. Block. Opening up the black box of learning-by-doing in sustainability transitions. *Environmental Innovation and Societal Transitions*, 34:298–310, 2020*.

A. Van Wynsberghe. Sustainable ai: Ai for sustainability and the sustainability of ai. *AI and Ethics*, 1(3):213–218, 2021.

R. Vinuesa, H. Azizpour, I. Leite, M. Balaam, V. Dignum, S. Domisch, and F. Fuso Nerini. The role of artificial intelligence in achieving the sustainable development goals. *Nature Communications*, 11(1):233, 2020.

T. Von Wirth, L. Fuenfschilling, N. Frantzeskaki, and L. Coenen. Impacts of urban living labs on sustainability transitions: Mechanisms and strategies for systemic change through experimentation. *European Planning Studies*, 27(2):229–257, 2019*.

J. P. Voß and B. Bornemann. The politics of reflexive governance: Challenges for designing adaptive management and transition management. *Ecology and Society*, 16(2), 2011*.

J. P. Voß, A. Smith, and J. Grin. Designing long-term policy: Rethinking transition management. *Policy Sciences*, 42:275–302, 2009*.

E. Wenger. Communities of practice and social learning systems. *Organization*, 7 (2):225–246, 2000.

J. V. Wertsch. *Mind as Action*. Oxford University Press, 1998.

A. Wiek, L. Withycombe, and C. L. Redman. Key competencies in sustainability: A reference framework for academic program development. *Sustainability Science*, 6(2):203–218, 2011.

J. M. Wittmayer and N. Schäpke. Action, research and participation: Roles of researchers in sustainability transitions. *Sustainability Science*, 9:483–496, 2014*.

Petri K. Ylikoski. Understanding the coleman boat. In Gianluca Manzo, editor, *Research Handbook on Analytical Sociology*, pages 49–63. Edward Elgar, 2021.

X. Zhang and P. Wang. Detecting the historical roots of education for sustainable development (esd): A bibliometric analysis. *International Journal of Sustainability in Higher Education*, 23(3):478–502, 2022.

L. Zhou, S. Paul, H. Demirkan, L. Yuan, J. Spohrer, M. Zhou, and J. Basu. Intelligence augmentation: Towards building human-machine symbiotic relationship. *AIS Transactions on Human-Computer Interaction*, 13(2):243–264, 2021.

M. Zounemat-Kermani, O. Batelaan, M. Fadaee, and R. Hinkelmann. Ensemble machine learning paradigms in hydrology: A review. *Journal of Hydrology*, 598: 126266, 2021.

E. E. Öztekin and A. I. Gaziulusoy. Designing transitions bottom-up: The agency of design in formation and proliferation of niche practices. *The Design Journal*, 22 (1):1659–1674, 2019*.

11

Machine Learning Promoting Sustainable Customer Behavior and Product Pricing

Katayoon Pourmahdi, Anna-Greta Nyström, and Amin Majd

11.1 Introduction

A more sustainable approach to marketing strategies helps firms protect the environment ecologically and leads to better organizational performance (Håkansson et al. 2005).

Sustainability concerns have become a highlighted topic influencing the marketing strategies of companies, particularly as regards product pricing strategies. Sustainable marketing is defined as a process involving the planning, implementation, and control of pricing, promotion, and distribution of products that reconciles ecological and economic factors (Fuller 1999; Sheth and Parvatiyar 1995). Although pricing strategies

K. Pourmahdi (✉) · A.-G. Nyström
Faculty of Social Sciences, Business and Economics, and Law, Åbo Akademi University, Turku, Finland
e-mail: katayoon.pourmahdi@abo.fi

A. Majd
Faculty of Engineering and Business, Turku University of Applied Sciences, Turku, Finland

P. Aaltonen and E. Kurvinen (eds.), *Contemporary Issues in Industry 5.0*, Technology, Work and Globalization, https://doi.org/10.1007/978-3-031-74779-3_11

are currently attracting attention from marketers and policymakers, few academic investigations specifically focus on pricing strategies. This topic has not been as extensively theoretically developed as other marketing subjects, such as promotion, product, and distribution (Hinterhuber 2004; Ingenbleek 2014; Liozu et al. 2012; Liozu and Hinterhuber 2013). Empirical studies show that only a few academic articles published in leading marketing journals have incorporated pricing strategies (Hinterhuber 2004; Liozu et al. 2012). Nevertheless, the pricing strategies of firms are becoming an important buying criterion for price-sensitive consumers (Belz and Peattie 2014; Hinterhuber 2004); in times of increasing energy prices and a focus on saving fuel energy, products are awarded labels indicating their energy efficiency levels, corresponding to different prices (Fuller 1999).

To address concerns regarding sustainable product pricing and price-sensitive customers' behavior, big data analytics powered by artificial intelligence (BDA-AI) is being used to assist companies in identifying influential factors affecting customer purchase decision-making (Dubey et al. 2020). More precisely, adapting Machine Learning (ML) methods offers a powerful tool for marketers to analyze and identify interactions within large quantities of data. Consequently, this chapter focuses on pricing decisions and sustainable consumer behavior, employing descriptive and predictive analytics using ML methods to visualize patterns and predict sustainable customer behavior. We aim to answer the following research questions:

What factors, in addition to price, influence customers' decision-making process when choosing sustainable food products that address sustainability concerns in their production processes? What is the likelihood of customers choosing sustainable food products over regular food products? The first research question aims to develop a theory-driven model for studying the topic, whereas the second research question showcases how descriptive and predictive analytics using ML methods can be deployed. From a theoretical standpoint, we review behavior theories to identify the main components affecting customer behaviors, such as attitudes, intentions, and habits. Then, using these theories, we propose a study model that showcases the inputs, exogenous factors, and hypothetical constructs of sustainable customer behavior that inform the empirical analysis. Finally, we develop a data-driven model utilizing descriptive and predictive analytics using ML methods, specifically visualization and logistic regression, to explore customers' purchasing behavior regarding sustainable products.

11.2 Consumer Purchase Behavior and Pricing Strategies: An Overview of Previous Research

This section presents an overview of theories related to consumer behavior in purchase decision-making, and pricing strategies. The review aims to explain the decision-making process, which will subsequently be examined using ML methods.

11.2.1 Consumer Behavior in Purchase Decision-Making

Success in creating a sustainable marketplace depends on developing a comprehensive understanding of consumer intention, their perception of purchasing sustainable products, and the barriers consumers encounter during the decision-making process to prevent sustainable consumption. By delving into the realm of consumer attitude, intention, habit, and behavior, researchers have endeavored to construct and evaluate models that forecast the drivers and barriers influencing sustainable consumer behavior (Ma et al. 2018). The following explanation of related theories gives a flavor of some important concepts related to consumer behavior.

According to the theory of planned behavior, the main determinant of consumer behavior is intention. Theoretically, a particular human behavior can be predicated by its intention, which is influenced by three core components: the subjective norm, the individual's behavioral attitudes (values, beliefs, and norms), and perceived behavioral control (Ajzen 1991). This theory was developed to predict an individual's intention to engage in a certain behavior at a specific place and time. Alphabet theory offers a detailed description of the relationship between habits, intentions, and the actual behavior of consumers. This theory was formulated through the synthesis of two environmental behavior theories: attitude–behavior–context theory and value–belief–norm theory. According to alphabet theory, knowledge, information-seeking, demographics, and context are the main components that affect human attitudes (Martínez-Carrasco Martínez et al. 2023; Sadeli et al. 2023; Taghikhah et al. 2021; Zepeda and Deal 2009). The rational choice theory is an early theory clarifying the understanding of the social, environmental, and economic behavior of customers. It has been used to describe the link between perception and human behavior in different contexts. According to this theory, an individual conducts a cost–benefit analysis before making an actual purchase decision (Zepeda and Deal 2009).

Inspired by the theories of planned behavior, alphabet theory, and rational choice theory, Fig. 11.1 illustrates a framework for capturing consumer behavior in purchase decision-making. Consequently, the components affecting individual attitudes are demographics, knowledge, information seeking, and context, while attitudes, habits, and context affect intention, intention, and habit subsequently affect behavior.

11.2.2 Capturing Consumer Behavior for Sustainable Product Purchases

Several theories and models, such as the Nicosia, Eagle, Kollat, and Blackwell models, have been proposed to explain consumer behavior and its influence on marketing strategies (Juan et al. 2017). A commonly used theory is the Howard–Sheth model, according to which consumer behavior theory, input, and external factors can provide various messages that can be crucial in customer purchasing decisions (Howard and Sheth 1969; Sheth 2011). The model claims that the effects of attitude on purchases are only possible through intention (Howard and Sheth 1969; Juan et al. 2017) and suggests three levels of consumer decision-making. These three categories are extensive problem-solving,

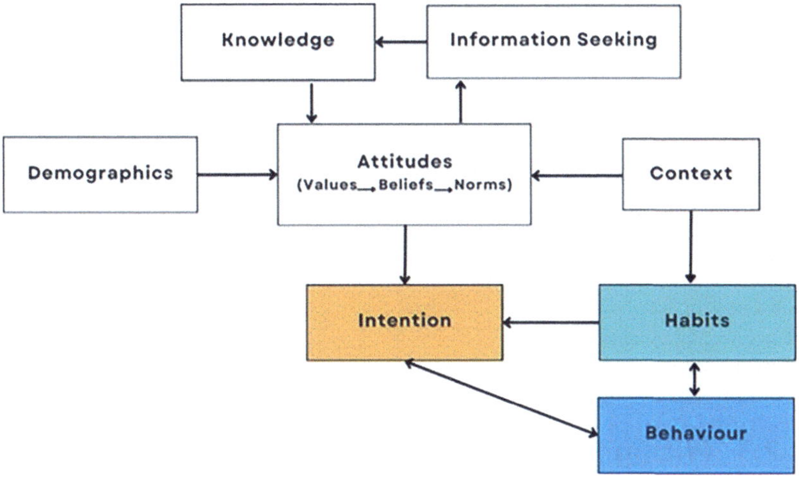

Fig. 11.1 Overview of consumer behavior in purchase decision-making

limited problem-solving, and habitual response behavior. These categories comprise four components of consumer behavior: input variables, hypothetical constructs, exogenous variables, and output variables. The input variables consist of three stages: significative, symbolic, and social. The output variables occur in a logical sequence, beginning with attention, brand comprehension, attitudes, and intentions, and ending with purchase. Hypothetical factors affect inputs and outputs' learning and perception constructs (Juan et al. 2017; Sheth 2011).

In line with consumer behavior theories and the logic of the Howard–Sheth model, we adopted four sets of dimensions in our study: input variables (product characteristics), hypothetical construct (customers' intentions, attitudes, and habits toward sustainable products), output variables (sales performance of sustainable products), and exogenous variables, which are not directly involved in decision making (demographic information). This study model simulates the real world and aims to attain a comprehensive understanding of the factors influencing sustainable consumer behavior. In Fig. 11.2, we identify the demographic information, product characteristics, and customer intentions, attitudes, and habits as determinants affecting sustainable consumer behavior.

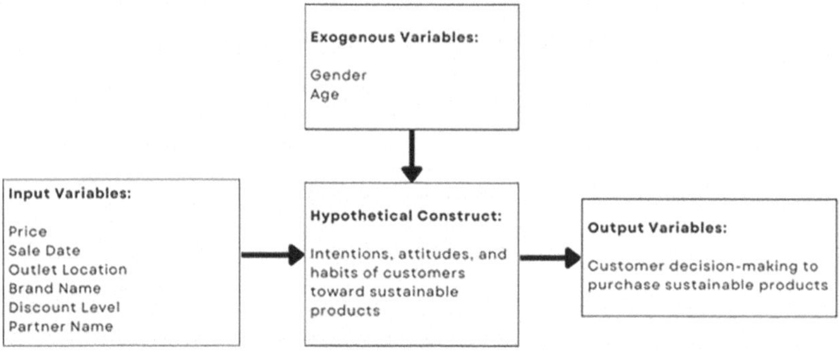

Fig. 11.2 Study model of customer behavior of sustainable product purchase

11.2.3 Pricing Strategies

Setting optimal pricing strategies requires the company to commit to objectives, actions, and operational strategies and to employ a set of control and review procedures. The marketing process of a company involves strategic choices that impact the type of pricing employed by the firm. Factors such as customer demographics, behavior, and product details all influence pricing. It is important to acknowledge the input required from departments such as accounting, research and development, sales, marketing, and manufacturing to implement optimal pricing strategies (Kotler and Keller 2016; Lancioni 2005). Moreover, the implementation of optimal pricing strategies is influenced by several key concepts, including market segmentation (Daraboina et al. 2024; Tynan and Drayton 1987), price elasticity of demand (Bijmolt et al. 2005; Whitaker 1988), and the concept of premium pricing (Anselmsson et al. 2014; Ashraf et al. 2017; Juan et al. 2017).

11.2.3.1 Pricing Strategy Development Based on Market Segmentation

Market segmentation enables marketers to address the diversity of consumers and their behaviors (Tynan and Drayton 1987). Sustainability market segmentation, in turn, divides heterogeneous markets into smaller ones. Thus, marketers vary their offerings to meet the evolving needs of customers regarding sustainable products. The four major variables used for market segmentation are geographic (customer's place of residence), behavioral (final decision to purchase), demographic (age, gender, and family size), and psychographic variables (attitude, intention, and habit) (Fuller 1999; Tynan and Drayton 1987). Considering consumers' perception of sustainability, which in turn influences their attitudes, intentions, and behaviors, the implementation of different pricing strategies based on the four major variables of sustainability market segmentation can create a win–win-win situation for consumers, firms, and society (Hempel 2024; Zhang and Zheng 2022). To clarify, traditionally, customers and businesses have been considered two parties in a competitive transactional game. In business transactions, price is a tentative quotation offered by the seller to a potential customer, which can be either accepted or refused. However, from a new competitive perspective, sustainable marketing considers the environment as a new party. All parties underpin transactions and aim for mutual success, making the integration of environmental costs into product prices a vital step (Fuller 1999).

11.2.3.2 Price Elasticity of Demand

By considering the price elasticity of products, decision-makers can calculate customers' willingness to pay for the product at different price points (Bijmolt et al. 2005). According to the price elasticity of demand devised by Marshall (2011), the formula for the coefficient of price elasticity of demand for products X_i (1, 2) is, $e_{(R)} = \frac{\frac{dQ}{Q}}{\frac{dP}{P}}$, where $\frac{dQ}{Q}$ represents the percentage change in demand for the good, and $\frac{dP}{P}$ is the percentage change in the price of the good. Although the demand for products generally moves in the opposite direction from their price, the impact of price changes can vary. The demand for some products is not significantly affected by changes in their prices, while the demand for others is highly responsive to price changes. The price elasticity of the demand for a product measures the percentage change in demand divided by the percentage change in its price. Products with high elasticity are considerably sensitive to price changes, whereas products with low elasticity are less responsive to price fluctuations (Auer and Papies 2020; Bijmolt et al. 2005; Ma et al. 2018; Marshall 2011; Whitaker 1988). The elasticities change according to the retailers, the manufacturer brand, location, time trend, stage of the product life cycle, household disposable income, inflation rate, and, importantly, the product category (Bijmolt et al. 2005).

11.2.3.3 Premium Pricing

From a sustainability perspective, the prices of sustainable products are higher than those of unsustainable products under normal competitive conditions (Ingenbleek 2015). The higher prices reflect the environmental costs, aiming to reduce the destruction and waste caused by production. This pricing strategy is known as *premium pricing*. Premium pricing refers to the practice of a retailer pricing a product or service above the market price in the same marketplace (Allsopp 2005; Fuller 1999; Juan et al. 2017).

According to Ottman (1993), customers are more likely to be receptive to green product prices when their primary needs for affordability, convenience, quality, and functionality are met. Additionally, as customers become more aware of environmental issues, the ecological attributes of products can influence their final purchase decisions and motivate them to pay premiums (Fuller 1999; Juan et al. 2017). In a typical market setting, customers seek products and services that meet their needs. It is important to recognize that a clean and habitable ecosystem is also a legitimate need; thus, customers must be aware of and prioritize the relationships between consumption decisions and environmental quality. To obtain environmental benefits, the five eco-cost drivers that may impact the unit cost structures are as follows: (1) product inputs of raw materials and energy; (2) process, facility, and management; (3) fugitive emission clean-up; (4) environmental legal action; and (5) routine regulatory compliance (Fuller 1999).

Primarily, the significance of the concepts above becomes even more important when considering sustainable products, which often have higher prices compared to regular products (Fuller 1999; Ingenbleek 2015). In this chapter, our results show that customers need to be segmented according to their needs and preferences. Companies must consider their profitability, costs, and external competitive dynamics. Additionally, product elasticity is measured to facilitate the implementation of optimal pricing decisions. Finally, customers must be convinced that the higher prices of sustainable products are a legitimate need, not only for our generation but also for future generations (Kotler and Armstrong 2010). To achieve this goal, in the following section, we analyze real-world retail data using ML methods to extract the significant features and position them effectively. We assume that ML methods assist in making effective pricing decisions by considering significant behavioral, demographic, and product features.

11.3 Descriptive, Predictive, and Prescriptive Analytics

The integration of ML in business analytics takes place through three distinctive analytical classifications (see Fig. 11.3): descriptive, predictive, and prescriptive analytics (Greasley 2019). While descriptive analytics (i.e., business intelligence) focuses on understanding past patterns and events, predictive analytics and prescriptive analytics are oriented toward the future, aiming to predict an outcome with a certain likelihood of accuracy. Concerning model development and analysis, both predictive and prescriptive analyses can be defined as methods utilizing historical data and using this data to make predictions. After importing the training dataset into ML algorithms, the prediction model can make predictions on new data. These analytics enable decision-makers to address questions such as "What will happen?" and "What next?" considering historical datasets and data-driven predictions. One should, however, note that descriptive analytics mainly deals with structured data, which is data that is processed by humans. Predictive and prescriptive analytics process and analyze both structured and unstructured data using computer algorithms (El Morr and Ali-Hassan 2019; Lone and Sofi 2022). The integration of ML into business operations provides a powerful tool for optimizing processes, solving complex problems, and making informed decisions within complex systems (Fishwick 1992). Interest in integrating ML algorithms into business operations has generated a new stream of literature highlighting the importance of developing specific capabilities in an organization before ML adoption. For instance, Keegan et al. (2022) highlight that firms face challenges preceding ML adoption in marketing. One specific challenge is the need to gain access to large high-quality datasets and acquire the necessary technological infrastructure for processing such data (procurement process). Furthermore, AI readiness and AI enablers have been proposed as core concepts in developing ML capabilities. For instance, Baabdullah et al. (2021) developed a conceptual model based on the technology-organization-environment framework (TOE) for understanding the impact of AI readiness and AI enablers on the acceptance of AI practices in the context of business-to-business small and medium enterprises.

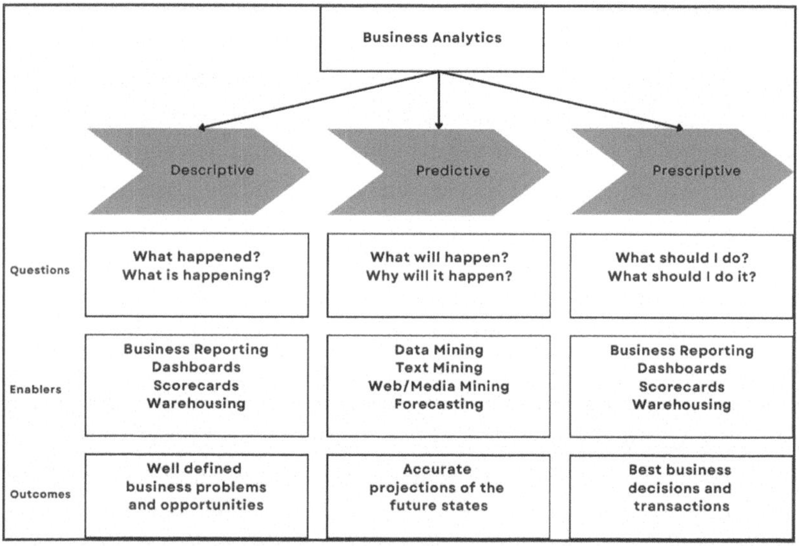

Fig. 11.3 Using ML in business analytics

The application of ML in the *food industry* effectively simulates its intangible aspects, including continuous feedback on the decision-making process despite limited information. This is particularly evident in the context of food policymaking, which requires long-term strategic decision-making regarding consumer preferences and future scenarios (Kler et al. 2022).

Integrating ML algorithms into the *retail industry* enables retailers to collect, curate, and analyze vast amounts of customer data and purchasing patterns. With this integration, retailers can predict demand patterns accurately. Furthermore, it enhances inventory management, demand forecasting, pricing optimization, and supply chain development. An overview of data analysis types, such as numeric, text, voice, and image/video data analysis, allows retailers to utilize and benefit from ML. The strategic adoption of ML in the retail industry is thus important for decision-makers but requires an understanding of how ML can specifically benefit their operations and customers rather than following trends or integrating ML into their businesses simply for public relations purposes (Shankar 2018).

Decision-making through ML algorithms and computational methods has been demonstrated by, for instance, Huiru et al. (2018), who employed experiments and mathematical analysis to show how customers shift their decisions toward other original alternatives when there is another option. Furthermore, realizing the benefits of AI requires interactive collaboration among suppliers, customers, and AI in the development of value co-creation practices. This involves adopting service-dominant logic and expanding critical capabilities in business-to-business (B2B) marketing (Paschen et al. 2021).

To summarize, the primary motivation for employing ML methods in the context of sustainable consumer behavior is the ability of these methods to capture the complexities arising from interactions among multiple agents (Huiru et al. 2018). However, in our study, the objective of the data-driven model is to examine customer decision-making using ML algorithms and explore how organizations can influence their customers' behavior to purchase sustainable products rather than unsustainable protein-based substitutes. The focus of this model is on predicting the demand of consumers for sustainable products while changes in prices and the consumers' perception of greenness occur in the system.

11.4 Descriptive Analysis of Retail Data: Vegetarian/Vegan Versus Meat-Based Purchases

Based on the overview of pricing strategies, consumer behavior, and especially the identified factors illustrated in Figs. 11.1 and 11.2, this section develops a framework for further elucidating the factors influencing sustainable food purchasing decisions and subsequently sustainable consumption. To exemplify how ML methods can aid in decision-making, we assume that customers plan to purchase protein-based products, which can be either vegetarian/vegan, or meat-based products. A protein-based food dataset from a food retailer was then used, including information on customer clusters and their sales performance over 5 years for two types of products, and the occurrence of nearly one million sales. There are fifteen customer clusters and two protein-based product types: vegetarian/vegan (P1) and meat-based (P2). In this study, the sustainability concerns are limited to the production process of vegetarian/vegan products, i.e., the product, its production process, or the packaging highlighting green consumerism and sustainable action. When consumers, acting as autonomous entities, arrive at the marketplace, they find both P1 and P2 items available in the retail store. Each consumer has a product preference that reflects their perception of sustainable consumption. During the decision-making phase, consumers decide whether to buy P1 or P2 items and consider various factors, such as the price. First, we evaluated the likelihood of each customer cluster purchasing each product category. Then, logistic regression modeling was applied to historical sales performance data to predict the purchase performance of new customers. This analysis aims to provide insights into purchasing patterns among different customer groups and forecast future trends in sustainable food consumption based on the developed framework of descriptive and predictive-analytic methods.

As depicted in Fig. 11.4, the prices of protein-based products have increased over time, and the upward slope of meat-based products is sharper than that of vegetarian/vegan products. However, the average price for vegetarian/vegan products is higher than their meat-based counterparts. Additionally, it is observed that the demand for meat-based products is higher than for vegetarian/vegan products. To understand demand and price changes, we refer to the price elasticity of demand for a product, which measures the degree of demand response to changes in an economic factor. Contrary to common belief, it does not mean that a lower price is more appealing to customers (Bijmolt et al. 2005). Therefore, it is assumed that consumers can be persuaded to purchase protein-based products at higher prices, considering factors such as income level, family size, living location, educational level, age, and gender.

The distribution of fifteen customer clusters across five popular outlets is depicted in Fig. 11.5, illustrating the dominant customer clusters in the market. Figure 11.6 and Fig. 11.7 illustrate the comprehensive purchasing trends of each customer group for these two products during

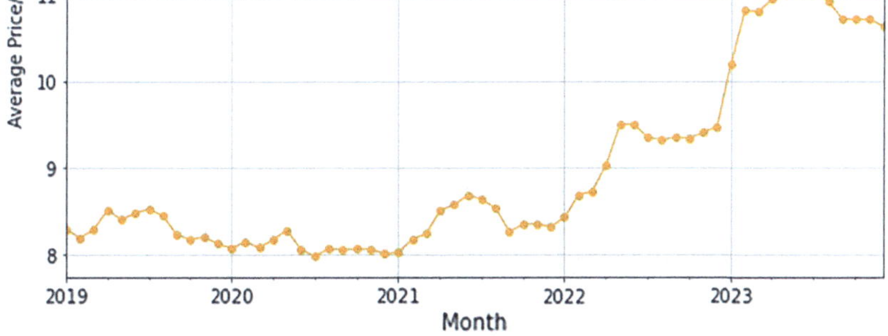

Fig. 11.4 Price changes for meat-based and vegetarian/vegan products over time

five time periods. There is a higher likelihood that females aged 25–44 are interested in vegetarian/vegan products. Thus, when measuring the correlation between customer groups, including age and gender, and sales performance, their correlation coefficient is 0.297, indicating a positive correlation. Additionally, the p-value is significantly less than 0.05, suggesting strong evidence that there is a correlation between the customer group and the sales performance of vegetarian/vegan products (Table 11.1).

The sales performance of vegetarian/vegan products has declined over time, which suggests that the higher prices of vegetarian/vegan products during this period must have affected price-sensitive customers. We can describe this trend in customer purchase performance by employing the salience theory established by Bordalo et al. (2012). The assumption is that there are two types of consumers in the market: one type of consumer is more sensitive to price while the other is more sensitive to greenness and these decision-makers assign higher importance to the product's salient attribute (Balcombe et al. 2021; Bordalo et al.

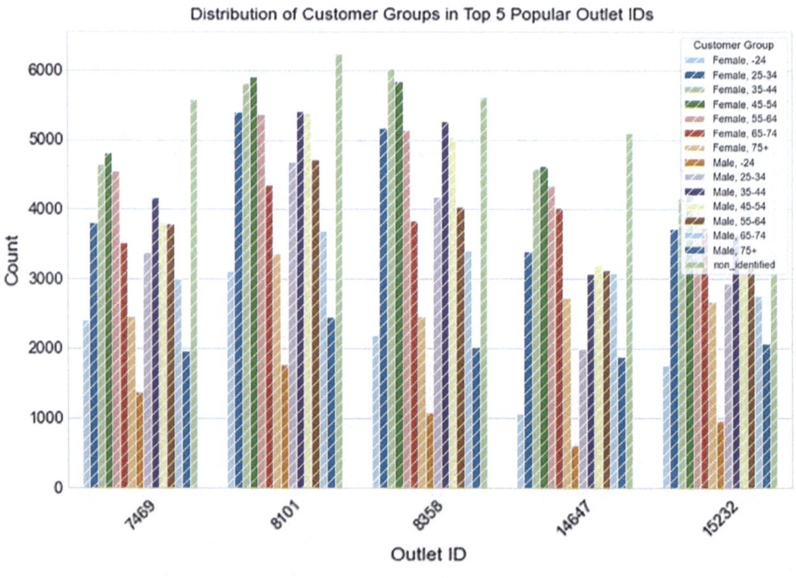

Fig. 11.5 Distribution of customer groups in the top five popular outlet IDs

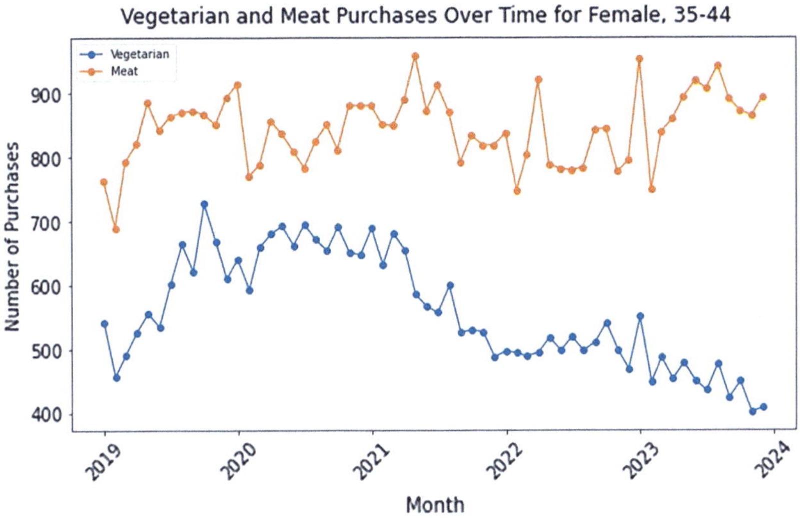

Fig. 11.6 Monthly sales performance of product types for females aged 35–44

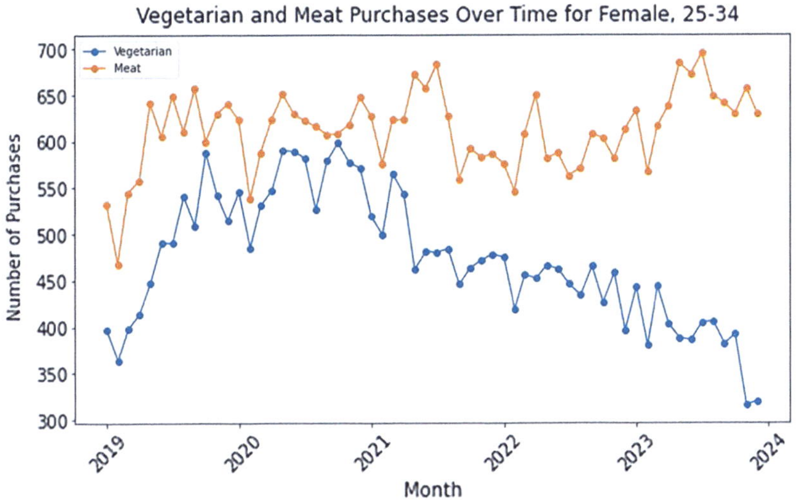

Fig. 11.7 Monthly sales performance of product types for females aged 25–34

Table 11.1 Sample generation for the literature review

Customer group	Meat-based purchase (%)	Vegetarian/vegan purchase (%)
Female, – 24	64.41382	35.58618
Female, 25–34	62.35827	37.64173
Female, 35–44	65.9257	34.0743
Female, 45–54	70.14261	29.85739
Female, 55–64	72.65657	27.34343
Female, 65–74	74.59792	25.40208
Female, 75 +	79.20754	20.79246
Male, – 24	80.66654	19.33346
Male, 25–34	70.07245	29.92755
Male, 35–44	70.81305	29.18695
Male, 45–54	75.3744	24.6256
Male, 55–64	80.35555	19.64445
Male, 65–74	80.77859	19.22141
Male, 75 +	86.04237	13.95763

2012). Type one (p_k) gives a higher weight to price in their decision-making process, while greenness receives the top ranking for type two (q_k). According to the salient thinker, the evolution of weight given by a customer's utility (U^{LT}) for greenness and price over time can be described using the following utility formulas: (1) price-sensitive and (2) green-sensitive customers. (1) $U^{LT}\ (q_k) = \theta_1 \left(\frac{\delta}{\delta\theta_1+\theta_2}\right) q_k - \theta_2 \left(\frac{1}{\delta\theta_1+\theta_2}\right) p_k$ and (2) $U^{LT}\ (q_k) = \theta_1 \left(\frac{1}{\theta_1+\delta\theta_2}\right) q_k - \theta_2 {}_{-} \left(\frac{\delta}{\theta_1+\delta\theta_2}\right) pk$. In this context, θ_1 and θ_2 denote the utility weights, and their sum is equal to 1. δ captures the degree of consumers' salient thinking: δ ($0 < \delta < 1$). The smaller δ, the higher the level of consumers' salient thinking. If customers prefer greenness, the provided equations indicate that the weight of greenness increases over time as $\hat{\theta}_1^k = \theta_1\left(\frac{1}{\theta_1+\delta\theta_2}\right) > \theta_1$, and simultaneously, the weight of the price decreases over time as $\hat{\theta}_2^k = \theta_2\left(\frac{\delta}{\theta_1+\delta\theta_2}\right) < \theta_2$, (Meng et al. 2022). Subsequently, consumers' decisions can change over time based on changes in various factors, including their perception of the salient attributes of the products (Herweg and Müller 2021). To validate the factors that have a statistically significant impact on sales performance (Y) (see Fig. 11.2), factor analysis was

Table 11.2 Influential factors that affect sales performance

	Exogenous variables	Analysis method	*P*-value
X1	Customer group (age, gender)	ANOVA	0.0000
	Input variables	Analysis method	*P*-value
X2	Sale date	ANOVA	4.79e-53
X3	Outlet location	ANOVA	6.40e−37
X4	Brand name	ANOVA	0.0000
X5	Discount level	ANOVA	0.0000
X6	Name of partnering entity	ANOVA	0.0000
X7	Consumer package size	Linear Regression	0.0000
X8	Price	Linear Regression	0.0000

employed to analyze the reliability of each factor in the given dataset. Analysis of Variance (ANOVA) is used for categorical variables, and linear regression is used for numerical variables in the provided code. Based on the results of the P-values, it concludes that variables X1 to X8 have a significant impact on the sales performance of sustainable products (see Table 11.2).

11.4.1 Predictive Analytics on Purchase Data: Logistic Regression Development

In the past few years, the logistic regression model has been widely employed to examine sales performance and customer decision-making (Fadlalla 2005). Logistic regression utilizes a binary dependent variable (sales performance, 0 or 1) to determine whether each customer group, in a specific scenario, comes to the marketplace and makes a final decision to purchase vegetarian/vegan (0) or meat-based products (1). It attempts to predict the probability of this binary outcome. Here, logistic regression offers a powerful tool for predicting our binary target, the named sales performances of vegetarian/vegan or meat-based products. In our analysis, the data set has been separated into inputs and targets. We employed logistic regression to predict the binary target, which is the sales performance, based on the input variables (X1:X8) that have higher P-values extracted from the dataset within the previous five time periods. After feature selection, the extracted independent observations include price, consumer package size, customer group (including age and gender), discount class, brand name, outlet location, partner name, and sale date. To divide the data, 80% of the one million sales performances were used for training, while the remaining 20% was reserved for testing which would evaluate the model's performance on unseen data. In our analysis, 20% of the one million sales performances were set aside as unseen data, meaning they were not used during the training phase.

The classification report on logistic regression (see Table 11.3) demonstrates that the model achieved high precision, recall, and an F1-score for both classes (0 and 1), with an overall accuracy of 91%. The model attempts to predict the decision of new customers entering the market. When we input the information on the relevant features of the new customer, such as the customer group, the consumer package size, and the discount class into the trained model, it will predict the probability of the customer belonging to each class of the binary dependent variable (e.g., sales performance being 0 or 1). To analyze a practical scenario, we considered a male customer aged thirty-five who enters a marketplace at a certain location. He notices a product priced at 9.50 euros, which provides an example for our analysis. The product is not on discount and has a specific brand name. The male customer decides to behave as code 1, meaning he buys the meat-based product (among other goods purchased in the retail store). The logistic regression model predicts that 30.31% of male customers aged thirty-five are to be classified as class 0, meaning that roughly a third of new customers in the chosen demographic target group decide to purchase vegetarian/vegan products, while the future sales for the meat-based products are indeed more than twice the percentage (60.31%) predicted for class 0.

In Fig. 11.8, the Receiver Operating Characteristic Curve (ROC) visualizes the logistic regression of this study, proving the model's accuracy in

Table 11.3 Classification report of logistic regression

Class	Precision	Recall	F1-score	Support
0	0.88	0.86	0.87	63,779
1	0.93	0.94	0.93	120,506
Accuracy			0.91	

classifying the data. The ROC score of 0.98% represents the performance of the model in classifying the positive and negative samples.

In addition, the coefficient of the price variable for the given dataset is approximately − 0.18. This shows that as the average kilogram price of a product increases, the likelihood of a positive sales performance decreases. In our case study, this implies that consumers are indeed price-sensitive, meaning they are influenced by changes in the price of both sustainable and unsustainable products, but only if the price changes by 0.18%. To summarize the predictive analysis, Table 11.4 presents an example of the predictive results of customer sales performance concerning sustainable food products, with a focus on the most popular outlet and a female customer group aged 55–64. The results indicate that customers visiting stores in different locations make different decisions. The accuracy of this prediction is nearly 92%. It is concluded that customers are evolving in their perception of the salient attributes of

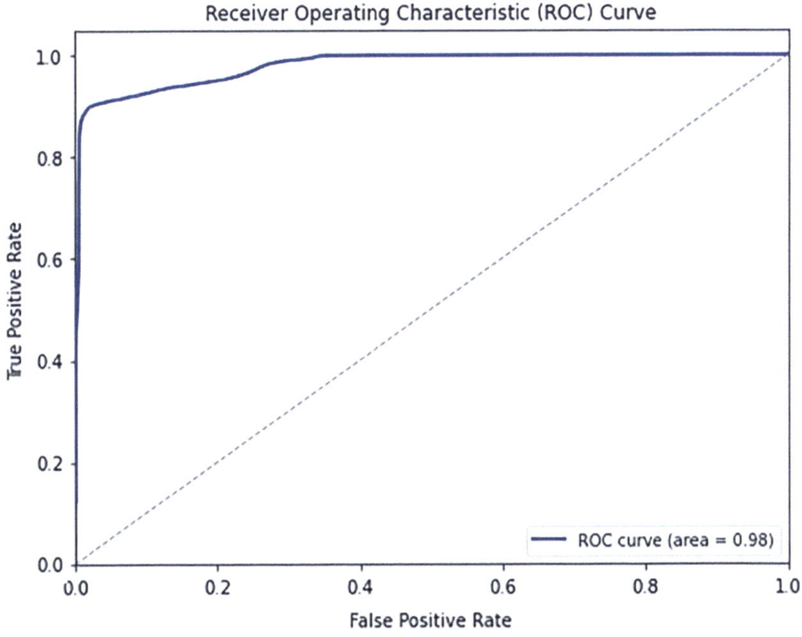

Fig. 11.8 ROC curve of study model

Table 11.4 Predicted sales performance results for female customers aged 55–64 at a popular outlet

	Predicted 0 (%)	Predicted 1 (%)
Actual 0	41.10	3.20
Actual 1	4.65	51.15

products. As can be seen in Table 11.3, the difference between selecting meat-based products and vegetarian/vegan is narrow in this outlet, whereas Table 11.2 indicates that, overall, customers have a greater preference for meat-based products than this difference suggests. Based on the given dataset, this prediction implies that customer behavior varies across outlets based on their perceptions of sustainability, as well as other factors such as prices, age, and income.

11.5 Concluding Discussion

This chapter links three distinct research areas that have not been previously synthesized in a modeling study, namely: (1) optimal pricing decisions for sustainable products, (2) sustainable consumer behavior, and 3) ML methods in marketing. This chapter explores decision-making based on a data-driven model and examines how a retailer, taking a pricing strategy and other features into account, can analyze and predict customers' purchase behavior when choosing sustainable products over unsustainable protein-based substitutes. We applied this model in the context of food-purchasing behavior, providing insights into consumers' sustainable choices and preferences. We rooted our descriptive and predictive analysis model on a wide understanding of consumer behavior, purchase decision-making toward sustainable customer behavior, and pricing decisions to identify factors that impact the choice of a product (green product versus non-green product, or vegetarian/vegan versus meat-based products). We make an important contribution to the modeling of pricing strategies based on ML, aiming to facilitate the understanding of how to utilize big data to predict purchase decisions; thus demonstrating how to facilitate managerial decision-making and impact pricing strategies to nudge consumer purchases toward sustainable consumption and green consumerism (Sharma and Joshi 2017). To summarize, this study underlines the complexity of promoting and predicting sustainable consumer behavior based on historical data. We have demonstrated how descriptive and predictive analytics using ML methods aid in identifying both current and future purchase trends and provided an extensive overview of the antecedents for those purchases to take place. We contribute to marketing research by bringing pricing strategies to the fore and using ML as the basis for empirical analysis of sustainable consumption within the food retail industry.

We suggest that future studies should focus on the behavioral factors that impact consumers' decision-making process when selecting sustainable products over unsustainable ones, even when the former is more costly. In addition to product specifications and consumer demographics, identifying and measuring intentions, attitudes, habits, and, subsequently, customer behavior will give marketers a comprehensive understanding of the company and customers' positions. Thus, data on individual characteristics and attitudes toward sustainability will help marketers achieve more detailed descriptions and predictions using ML methods. Eventually, data analyzed using ML methods may assist decision-makers, and as our case suggests retailers, to persuade customers that it is worth paying a higher price premium for sustainable products (Anselmsson et al. 2014; Ashraf et al. 2017), especially when ecological concerns are highlighted in their marketing.

Acknowledgements Katayoon Pourmahdi acknowledges Åbo Akademi University and the Turun Kauppaopetussäätiö research Grant No. 2023031, Turku, Finland.

References

Icek Ajzen. The theory of planned behavior. *Organizational Behavior and Human Decision Processes*, 50(2):179–211, 1991. https://doi.org/10.1016/0749-5978(91)90020-T.

James Allsopp. Premium pricing: Understanding the value of premium. *Journal of Revenue and Pricing Management*, 4(2):185–194, 2005. https://doi.org/10.1057/palgrave. rpm.5170138.

Johan Anselmsson, Niklas Vestman Bondesson, and Ulf Johansson. Brand image and customers' willingness to pay a price premium for food brands. *Journal of Product & Brand Management*, 23(2):90–102, 2014. https://doi.org/10.1108/JPBM-10-2013-0414.

Sajid Farooq Ashraf, Cheng Li, and Bilal Mehmood. A study of premium price brands with special reference to willingness of customer to pay. *International Journal of Academic Research in Business and Social Sciences*, 7(7):619–639, 2017. https://doi.org/10.6007/IJARBSS/v7-i7/3126.

Jens Auer and Dominik Papies. Cross-price elasticities and their determinants: A meta-analysis and new empirical generalizations. *Journal of the Academy of Marketing Science*, 48(3):584–605, 2020.

Abdullah M. Baabdullah, Ali A. Alalwan, Emma L. Slade, Rohit Raman, and Khaled F. Khatatneh. Smes and artificial intelligence (ai): Antecedents and consequences of ai-based b2b practices. *Industrial Marketing Management*, 98: 255–270, 2021. https://doi.org/10.1016/j.indmarman.2021.09.003.

Kelvin Balcombe, Iain Fraser, and Aditi Sharma. An econometric analysis of salience theory. *Bulletin of Economic Research*, 73(4):545–554, 2021. https://doi.org/10.1111/boer. 12264.

Frank-Martin Belz and Ken Peattie. *Sustainability Marketing, A Global Perspective*. John Wiley & Sons, second edition, 2014.

Tammo H. A. Bijmolt, Harald J. Van Heerde, and Rik G. M. Pieters. New empirical generalizations on the determinants of price elasticity. *Journal of Marketing Research*, 42(2):141–156, 2005. https://doi.org/10.1509/jmkr.42.2.141.62296.

Pedro Bordalo, Nicola Gennaioli, and Andrei Shleifer. Salience in experimental tests of the endowment effect. *American Economic Review*, 102(3):47–52, 2012. https://doi.org/10.1257/aer.102.3.47.

Ravi Daraboina, Orhan Cooper, and Mehdi Amini. Segmentation of organic food consumers: A revelation of purchase factors in organic food markets. *Journal of Retailing and Consumer Services*, 78:103710, 2024.

Rameshwar Dubey, Angappa Gunasekaran, Stephen J. Childe, David J. Bryde, Mihalis Giannakis, Cyril Foropon, David Roubaud, and Benjamin T. Hazen. Big data analytics and artificial intelligence pathway to operational performance under the effects of entrepreneurial orientation and environmental dynamism: A study of manufacturing organisations. *International Journal of Production Economics*, 226:107599, 2020. https://doi.org/10.1016/j.ijpe.2019.107599.

Christo El Morr and Hossam Ali-Hassan. Descriptive, predictive, and prescriptive analytics. In *Analytics in Healthcare*, pages 31–55. Springer International Publishing, 2019. https://doi.org/10.1007/978-3-030-04506-7_3.

Adam Fadlalla. An experimental investigation of the impact of aggregation on the performance of data mining with logistic regression. *Information & Management*, 42(5):695–707, 2005. https://doi.org/10.1016/j.im.2004.04.005.

Paul A. Fishwick. An integrated approach to system modeling using a synthesis of artificial intelligence, software engineering and simulation methodologies. *ACM Transactions on Modeling and Computer Simulation*, 2(4):307–330, 1992. https://doi.org/10.1145/149516.149530.

Donald A. Fuller. *Sustainable Marketing: Managerial-Ecological Issues*. SAGE Publications, 1999. https://doi.org/10.4135/9781452220611.

Andrew Greasley. *Simulating Business Processes for Descriptive, Predictive, and Prescriptive Analytics*. Pearson Education, 2019.

Carl Hempel. A segmentation and characterization of consumers affected by rising food prices. *Appetite*, 194:107192, 2024.

Fabian Herweg and Daniel Müller. A comparison of regret theory and salience theory for decisions under risk. *Journal of Economic Theory*, 193:105226, 2021. https://doi.org/10.1016/j.jet.2021.105226.

Andreas Hinterhuber. Towards value-based pricing—an integrative framework for decision making. *Industrial Marketing Management*, 33(8):765–778, 2004. https://doi.org/10.1016/j.indmarman.2003.10.006.

John A. Howard and Jagdish N. Sheth. *The Theory of Buyer Behavior*. John Wiley & Sons, New York, 1969.

Wang Huiru, Song Jinhui, Feng Jianying, Fan Huiru, Zhao Zhijian, and Mao Weisong. An agent-based modeling and simulation of consumers' purchase behavior for wine consumption. *IFAC-PapersOnLine*, 51(17):843–848, 2018. https://doi.org/10.1016/j.ifacol.2018.08.089.

Håkan Håkansson, Debbie Harrison, and Alexandra Waluszewski. *Rethinking Marketing: Developing a New Understanding of Markets*. Wiley, 2005. Available at: https://books.google.fi/books?id=42zYx0E8OWsC.

Paul Ingenbleek. The theoretical foundations of value-informed pricing in the service-dominant logic of marketing. *Management Decision*, 52(1):33–53, 2014. https://doi.org/10.1108/MD-03-2013-0128.

Paul Ingenbleek. Price strategies for sustainable food products. *British Food Journal*, 117(2):915–928, 2015. https://doi.org/10.1108/BFJ-02-2014-0066.

Yi-Kai Juan, Yuan-Hsiang Hsu, and Xiaoling Xie. Identifying customer behavioral factors and price premiums of green building purchasing. *Industrial Marketing Management*, 64:36–43, 2017. https://doi.org/10.1016/j.indmarman.2017.03.004.

Brendan J. Keegan, Ana I. Canhoto, and Dorothy A. Yen. Power negotiation on the tango dancefloor: The adoption of ai in b2b marketing. *Industrial Marketing Management*, 100:36–48, 2022. https://doi.org/10.1016/j.indmarman.2021.11.001.

Rahul Kler, Galal Elkady, Kailash Rane, Aman Singh, Md. Shahin Hossain, Deepak Malhotra, Suman Ray, and Kamal K. Bhatia. Machine learning and artificial intelligence in the food industry: A sustainable approach. *Journal of Food Quality*, 2022:1–9, 2022. https://doi.org/10.1155/2022/8521236.

Philip Kotler and Gary Armstrong. *Principles of Marketing*. Pearson Education, 13th edition, 2010.

Philip Kotler and Kevin Lane Keller. *Marketing Management*. Pearson, 15th edition, 2016.

Richard A. Lancioni. A strategic approach to industrial product pricing: The pricing plan. *Industrial Marketing Management*, 34(2):177–183, 2005. 10.1016/j. indmarman.2004.07.015.

Stephan M. Liozu and Andreas Hinterhuber. Pricing orientation, pricing capabilities, and firm performance. *Management Decision*, 51(3):594–614, 2013.

Stephan M. Liozu, Andreas Hinterhuber, Richard Boland, and Sheri Perelli. The conceptualization of value-based pricing in industrial firms. *Journal of Revenue and Pricing Management*, 11(1):12–34, 2012. https://doi.org/10.1057/rpm.2011.34.

Khursheed Lone and Shabir Ahmad Sofi. Descriptive, predictive, and prescriptive analytics in healthcare. In *Data Science for Effective Healthcare Systems*, pages 89–103. Chapman and Hall/CRC, 2022.

Pan Ma, Chao Zhang, Xiao Hong, and Huan Xu. Pricing decisions for substitutable products with green manufacturing in a competitive supply chain. *Journal of Cleaner Production*, 183:618–640, 2018. https://doi.org/10.1016/j.jclepro.2018.02.152.

Alfred Marshall. *Principles of Economics*. The Online Library of Liberty, 2011.

Laura Martínez-Carrasco Martínez, Margarita Brugarolas Mollá-Bauzá, and José Antonio Sánchez-Zapata. In search of a sustainable alternative for meat production: Understanding the purchase intention of meat from transhumance origin. *Renewable Agriculture and Food Systems*, 38(e20), 2023. https://doi.org/10.1017/S1742170523000121.

Zhiyi Meng, Na Zhao, Bin Shen, and Chang Zhai. Optimal pricing strategy for green products under salience theory. *Economic Research-Ekonomska Istraživanja*, 35(1):2960–2983, 2022. https://doi.org/10.1080/1331677X.2021.1985572.

Jacquelyn A. Ottman. *Green Marketing*. NTC Business Books, 1993. https://cir.nii.ac.jp/crid/1130282272598906368.

Jeannette Paschen, Ulrich Paschen, Erol Pala, and Jan Kietzmann. Artificial intelligence (ai) and value co-creation in b2b sales: Activities, actors and resources. *Australasian Marketing Journal*, 29(3):243–251, 2021. https://doi.org/10.1016/j.ausmj.2020.06.004.

Agriani H. Sadeli, Tomy Perdana, Yosini Deliana, and Bhakti S. Onggo. Consumers' purchase behavior in short food supply chains using social commerce in indonesia. *Journal of Cleaner Production*, 386:135812, 2023. https://doi.org/10.1016/j.jclepro.2022.135812.

Venkatesh Shankar. How artificial intelligence (ai) is reshaping retailing. *Journal of Retailing*, 94(4):vi–xi, 2018. https://doi.org/10.1016/S0022-4359(18)30076-9.

Aasha Sharma and Seema Joshi. Green consumerism: Overview and further research directions. *International Journal of Process Management and Benchmarking*, 7(2): 206, 2017. https://doi.org/10.1504/IJPMB.2017.083106.

Jagdish N. Sheth. *Models of Buyer Behavior: Conceptual, Quantitative, and Empirical*. Marketing Classics Press, 2011.

Jagdish N. Sheth and Atul Parvatiyar. The evolution of relationship marketing, 1995. Unpublished work or replace with publication details if available.

Firouzeh Taghikhah, Tatiana Filatova, and Alexey Voinov. Where does theory have it right? a comparison of theory-driven and empirical agent based models. *Journal of Artificial Societies and Social Simulation*, 24(2), 2021. https://doi.org/10.18564/jasss.4573.

A. Caroline Tynan and Jennifer Drayton. Market segmentation. *Journal of Marketing Management*, 2(3):301–335, 1987.

John K. Whitaker. The distribution theory of marshall's principles. In A. Asimakopulos, editor, *Theories of Income Distribution*, pages 105–132. Springer Netherlands, 1988. https://doi.org/10.1007/978-94-009-2661-5_5.

Lydia Zepeda and David Deal. Organic and local food consumer behaviour: Alphabet theory. *International Journal of Consumer Studies*, 33(6):697–705, 2009. https://doi.org/10.1111/j.1470-6431.2009.00814.x.

Qing Zhang and Yini Zheng. Pricing strategies for bundled products considering consumers' green preference. *Journal of Cleaner Production*, 344:130962, 2022. https://doi.org/10.1016/j.jclepro.2022.130962.

12

Role of Industrial Artificial Intelligence in Advancing Human-Centric Sustainable Development of Industry 5.0

Nampuraja Enose Kamalabai, Lea Hannola, and Ilkka Donoghue

12.1 Introduction

Manufacturing value chains have traditionally followed a linear model, characterized by a sequential series of distinct activities focused on the forward flow of materials. This is typically based on a TAKE-MAKE-WASTE economic model, also known as the linear economy (Lopes de Sousa Jabbour et al. 2018), which operates on a continuous cycle of material supply, where natural resources are retrieved from the environment and converted into manufactured products that are disposed at end of their useful life (Neves and Marques 2022). It focuses primarily on the production of goods, overlooking environmental and economic inefficiencies and the long-term consequences to the ecosystem. On the other hand, technological advancements and the Industrial Revolution have reshaped current patterns of production and consumption (Lopes

N. Enose Kamalabai (✉) · L. Hannola · I. Donoghue
Industrial Engineering and Management, LUT University, Lappeenranta, Finland
e-mail: nampuek@gmail.com

P. Aaltonen and E. Kurvinen (eds.), *Contemporary Issues in Industry 5.0*, Technology, Work and Globalization, https://doi.org/10.1007/978-3-031-74779-3_12

de Sousa Jabbour et al. 2018), of goods and services, resulting in the generation of more waste as a byproduct of consumption and production activities. Beyond the waste generated, the linear model also results in inefficiencies due to its non-circular design and use of unsustainable materials. These inefficiencies lead to underutilized capacities and suboptimal product lifecycles, largely resulting from insufficient information exchange, poor integration and collaboration, and inadequate visibility into product lifecycles and closed-loop processes. In the face of intensifying global challenges, this poses significant concerns regarding resource scarcity, waste generation, and environmental impacts. Addressing these issues effectively, requires coordinated and sustainable practices in the transition from a linear value chain model to a more sustainable and circular one, necessitating a notable change in mindset, operations, and strategic approaches.

The advent of Industry 4.0 holds the potential to reshape the way things are made, fundamentally changing how manufacturing value chains are implemented (Rosa et al. 2020; Dantas et al. 2021; Zheng et al. 2021). It signifies a profound shift in a traditional value chain, characterized by enhanced flows of goods and information, with each influencing the other significantly. It also entails a shift in communication patterns, transitioning from one-way to two-way flows among all participants in the value chain, including suppliers, producers, distributors, and consumers, allowing increased collaboration of physical and computational components in a value creation process. Yet, the initial implementations of Industry 4.0 have revolved around extensive digitalization with a techno-centric focus. This approach has often overlooked the core principles of sustainability, urging industries to broaden their perspectives and better understand sustainable outcomes beyond the focus on productivity, and profitability (Ejsmont et al. 2020; Beltrami et al. 2021; Saniuk et al. 2022). Therefore, there is a clear necessity to move Industry 4.0 beyond a narrow technology purview and strive for a balance between economic progress and social and environmental responsibility. Furthermore, the current understanding of the circular economy founded on broad concepts and different contexts, makes it difficult to reach a consensus over an exact definition of circular economy (Reike et al. 2018; An Andrade et al. 2021). Nevertheless, there is consensus on the core principles and objectives of the circular economy, all directed toward achieving sustainable development. There is also agreement on the necessity for fundamental systemic shifts to advance the transition to a circular economy, moving away from current practitioner efforts focused on incremental adjustments toward a potentially revolutionary approach (Kirchherr et al. 2023). Additionally, it's recognized that the foundational principles of Industry 4.0 will still serve as the basis for transitioning toward a more sustainable and regenerative economic model (Nascimento et al. 2019; Khan et al. 2021). The consensus emphasizes the importance of taking a comprehensive perspective toward sustainability that addresses every stage of the process and fosters a more interconnected and adaptive system (Ghobakhloo et al. 2023a b). Consequently, the Industry 4.0–Circular Economy nexus, is garnering attention due to their potential to implement systematic shifts and contribute to sustainable development (Rajput and Singh 2019; Tseng et al. 2018; Dantas et al. 2021; Lopes de Sousa Jabbour et al. 2018). This leads the transformation from a technocentric approach, in Industry 4.0, focusing solely on technological advancements to a value-centric paradigm (Enang et al. 2023; Atif 2023) in Industry 5.0. While a standard approach to managing these complexities continues to evolve, artificial intelligence (AI) holds the potential to serve as the backbone of intelligent closed-loop systems operating alongside humans. The European Commission has incorporated the adoption of a human-centric approach to digital technologies, with a specific focus on artificial intelligence, as a pivotal policy initiative in its endeavor to achieve the vision of Industry 5.0 (Breque et al. 2021). This is a critical enabler for realizing the transformative vision, centered on a resilient, sustainable, and human-centric approach (Leng et al. 2022).

This chapter therefore structured into four main sections. Following the introduction, Section 12.2 explores the theoretical background to provide a comprehensive understanding of the underlying concepts and principles aimed at capitalizing on existing circularity principles. It examines inherent circularities within individual stages of the value chain, emphasizing their potential to drive closed-loop practices and influence the transition to a circular economy. The section also elucidates key concepts of Industry 4.0, that enhance circularity as foundational to a circular value chain. Building on these foundational insights, Section 12.3 introduces a new paradigm aiming to engineer end-to-end circularity by integrating independent circular processes. It introduces concepts such as "vertical circularity," "horizontal circularity," and "closed-loop circularity," illustrating innovative approaches to value creation. Additionally, this section emphasizes the importance of socio-technical evolution in fostering a sustainable, resilient, and human-centric economy. It proposes leveraging artificial intelligence for cognitive coordination between humans and intelligent systems, crucial for managing the complexities of this transformation and supporting intelligent closed-loop systems. Finally, Section 12.4 summarizes the chapter, highlighting the urgency of accelerating this transition amidst global challenges. It underscores the strategic imperative of embracing these advancements as a cornerstone for Industry 5.0, advocating for co-innovation, co-design, and co-creation of personalized products and services within a circular economy framework.

12.2 Theoretical Background

12.2.1 Manufacturing Value Chain Processes and Their Inherent Circularities

The manufacturing value chain encompasses multiple stages of product management focused on optimizing material and resource utilization while minimizing waste. This is achieved through individual value-creation processes across the asset's lifecycle that are interconnected to form a value chain. Typically, a manufacturing value chain encompasses three primary value creation processes: Product Development, Production Operations, and Product Services. While both traditional and future value chains involve structured operational activities aimed at achieving specific objectives in the value creation process, they differ significantly in how individual processes network and interact. Traditionally, value chains have been unidirectional and acyclic from a lifecycle perspective, whereas future value chains show the potential to become cyclic, repeating lifecycle sequences multiple times. Several factors naturally promote the adoption of closed-loop principles within these value-creation stages and accelerate their integration. This section therefore aims to uncover these principles and evaluate their effectiveness, crucial for understanding their role in fostering a circular value chain. The objective is to capitalize on existing circularity principles within individual value chain stages and propose a holistic approach to establishing circular value chains.

12.2.1.1 Inherent Circularity within Product Development

Product development has evolved significantly, with the integrated design approach now being pivotal to modern product design strategies. Advancements in embedded systems and the integration of various technical disciplines are driving products toward becoming complex systems (Kagermann et al. 2013; Mosterman and Zander 2016). The advent of cyber-physical systems has further complicated product design, spanning multiple lifecycles encompassing embedded software, application software, hardware, networking, and cybersecurity (Monostori et al. 2016). Global competition and industry dynamics are accelerating the pace of product lifecycles, necessitating faster development times despite rising product demands. This necessitates a multidisciplinary and holistic approach in systems engineering to rethink how they conceive, design, and engineer such products, manage them across their lifecycle, and develop new applications and services (Kagermann et al. 2013; Mosterman and Zander 2016).

Consequently, "Systems Engineering" approaches have emerged to establish comprehensive system specifications integrating considerations across disciplines from the onset of development. Model-Based Systems Engineering (MBSE) has become a prominent industrial practice and uses models to design and analyze complex systems (Nguyen et al. 2017). This integrated engineering approach ensures all product requirements are met while considering functionality across the entire lifecycle, facilitating efficient and collaborative development with minimal errors and delays.

Emphasizing iterative design, collaboration across diverse disciplines and lifecycle stages, and continuous improvement, MBSE utilizes the concept of system lifecycle and closed-loop systems engineering to optimize the design of complex multidisciplinary systems. Figure 12.1 illustrates a typical closed-loop design employed in product development for integrated modeling of system architectures.

Such closed-loop systems engineering has inherent circularity fundamentals and is aligned with the thinking of building circularity into products. The evolution of intelligent technical systems for Industry 4.0 applications (Cyber Physical Systems), further emphasizes the need for

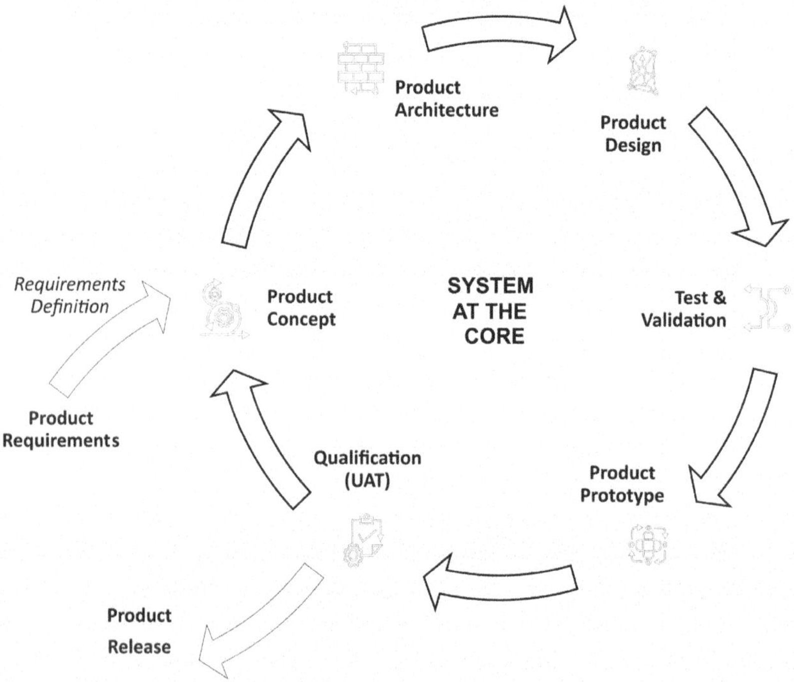

Fig. 12.1 Typical closed-loop system engineering approach for integrated modeling of system architectures

innovative modeling and systems engineering practices (Kagermann et al. 2013). These practices support Product Lifecycle Management (PLM) to effectively manage a complex product from design through production, use, and end-of-life. Future PLM implementations would therefore integrate System Engineering capabilities to model and simulate product behaviors in an integrated way and incorporate feedback from different disciplines, in making lifecycle decisions from a system perspective (Penciuc et al. 2016). Integrating product lifecycle management into circular economy practices is essential for achieving R-cycle management from a product lifecycle perspective. This approach serves as the fundamental basis for closing design-production-usage loops, which is highly dependent on choices made in early product development (Arekrans 2023). It goes a long way the integrate product, production, and service management that involves the collaboration and integration of different areas and functions within an organization to create a seamless development process for products and manufacturing systems (Disselkamp et al. 2023). The digital product passport (DPP) is in these lines and is seen as a decisive enabler in the circularisation of products, components, and materials in the manufacturing industry (Berg et al. 2021). The inherent circularities in product development therefore play a crucial role in advancing a sustainable circular economy and effectively managing the environmental impacts of products across the entire value chain.

12.2.1.2 Inherent Circularity within Production Operations

The foundational concept behind original industrial production design is centered on closed-loop systems. The processes and their respective control systems are accordingly designed to continuously monitor and adjust processes based on feedback, ensuring that the actual output aligns closely with the desired condition. The expected condition of the output is constantly compared with the actual conditions and necessary adjustments to minimize the difference or error. Such closed-loop systems are self-regulating processes operating through a feedback mechanism that regulates input–output relationships, enhancing accuracy, stability, and efficiency in applications such as temperature, motion, and process control. The operation of such a system is primarily described by a functional relationship between its input and output variables. The overall objective is a closed-loop production system optimizing resource usage (resource efficiency), by effectively managing personnel, equipment, materials, and physical assets while minimizing waste. Figure 12.2 illustrates a typical closed-loop control system, also known as a feedback control system, which features one or more feedback loops connecting its output and input.

Resource optimization is typically supported by the Manufa acting Operation Management System (or Manufacturing Execution System) which manages functions using resources to produce products during operations. These systems optimize control systems that coordinate materials, personnel, and equipment across production, maintenance, inventory, and quality functions, including test labs. ISA-95, based on the Purdue Reference Model, standardizes information exchange between control functions and enterprise functions, detailing interrelationships across different levels of manufacturing systems. With the rise of Cyber-Physical Production Systems (CPPS), Industry 4.0 implementations deploy autonomous and cooperating computational entities, or subsystems. These entities maintain close connections with the physical

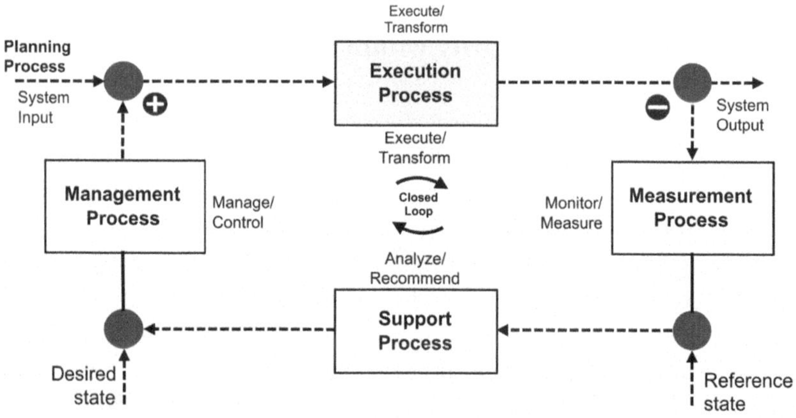

Fig. 12.2 Typical closed-loop production control design

world, including machines and ongoing production processes (Monostori et al. 2016). These subsystems possess the capability to interact with one another based on contextual demands, spanning all levels of production to leaner production systems (Berg 2021). Such closed-loop production systems aim for sustainability by improving economic and environmental goals simultaneously (Winkler 2011) facilitating the transition toward more resource-efficient and sustainable production practices.

12.2.1.3 Inherent Circularity within Product Services

Although service businesses for product companies have existed for many years, they are currently undergoing significant transformation. The rapid increase in intelligent industrial assets is reshaping the economy, promising improved quality of service with fewer resources. "Servitization," or long-term service contracts, has become a central theme for manufacturers, especially with the rise of Industry 4.0. This shift is primarily driven by the potential to leverage digital technologies and connectivity (Alcayaga et al. 2019) to create new business models and value propositions along the entire product lifecycle (Kiel et al. 2017; Favoretto et al. 2022). Technologies such as IoT (Internet of Things), cloud and edge computing, mobile applications, and data analytics have contributed to the popular concept of "anything-as-a-service" or "everything-as-a-service," (Kiel et al. 2017) enabling advanced service models by providing the right data at the right time. Consequently, product service providers are moving away from traditional break-fix and other transactional models, experimenting with new methods to create and deliver value. Therefore, closed-loop service management is evolving and aims to enhance integration within the service management process and between product development and service teams. Emerging service models address not only the operational phase but extend across the entire value chain, emphasizing closed-loop approaches that facilitate new circular business models (Berg et al. 2021).

The closed-loop approach, illustrated in Fig. 12.3, explicates the vital connection across products and lifecycle phases, linking the as-designed, as-implemented, as-operated, and as-used stages. This interconnection facilitates design changes based on field data, ensuring that products and services are developed with end-use in mind, embodying a true end-to-end lifecycle approach. This principle also forms the foundation for the concept of the digital twin, which continuously updates to reflect changes in the physical entity based on feedback from its digital counterpart. Such an approach enhances the service value proposition by integrating circularity parameters in several ways: designing systems according to customer and field requirements, shifting toward a more service-based manufacturing model, minimizing environmental impacts, and managing the lifecycle to become more eco-efficient. It provides product vendors with valuable insights into real-world field conditions, which is crucial for closing the quality loop. This aims to enhance product performance and longevity (extending lifetime), incorporate R-cycles (Winquist et al. 2023), and more. It aligns with the principles of sustainable production and consumption, focusing on "dematerializing" the economy by reducing material flows and creating products and services that deliver the same performance level with a significantly lower environmental burden (Mont 2002). The goal is to continuously "keep material in the loop," ensuring it is reprocessed and reused while providing value-added services that elevate performance levels and improve economic outcomes (Geissdoerfer et al. 2020).

12.2.1.4 Leveraging Existing Circularity Principles from Individual Value Stream Processes

The current ways of designing, producing, and using products inherently incorporate principles of circularity. The aforementioned details illustrate how these principles have effectively been applied in individual value stream processes. However, these implementations are highly fragmented, as they have been applied from different perspectives and have operated in silos. This presents significant opportunities to leverage in the transition toward a circular economy, offering a chance to integrate, collaborate, innovate, and create value. Emerging technologies and their

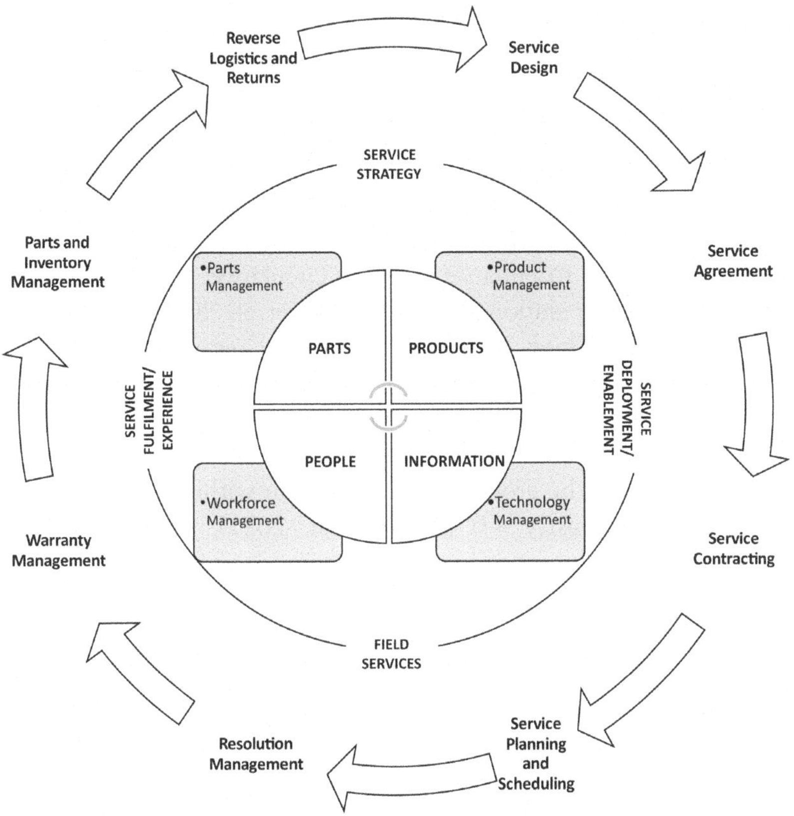

Fig. 12.3 Closed-loop approach in service lifecycle management

advance ing capabilities hold promise for extending the existing fragmented approach with a more systematic implementation strategy aimed at translating circular principles into tangible and sustainable impacts. This strategic approach requires a system-thinking perspective to achieve systemic change, integrating processes (Walmsley et al. 2019; Barnabè and Nazir 2022), closed-loop ecosystems (Kara et al. 2022; Camilleri 2019), and a lifecycle approach (Mohan and Katakojwala 2021), mutually reinforcing with Industry 4.0 design principles and the principles of circular economy.

12.2.2 Industry 4.0 and the Circular Economy

Since its inception, Industry 4.0 has revolved around value creation within a circular economy (Kagermann 2015; Blunck and Werthmann 2017). It is therefore evident that the foundational principles of Industry 4.0, even if not fully utilized are inevitable and will drive the future of a circular economy (Nascimento et al. 2019; Khan et al. 2021). In its ability to enhance resource circularity within production and consumption operational systems (Kiel et al. 2017; Müller et al. 2018; Rajput and Singh 2019), a closed-loop, regenerative economic model has increasingly emerged as the preferred industrialization model for attaining sustainable growth. Academic literature acknowledges the synergies between Industry 4.0 and Circular economy (da Silva and Sehnem 2022) and the growing transformation within the global value chains through Industry 4.0 (Awan et al. 2022). This represents a significant shift in how products, components, and materials will be circulated within the closed-loop manufacturing value chain (Berg et al. 2021) paving the way for substantial value creation at scale. It also involves fostering co-innovation, co-design, and co-creation of personalized products and services enabling mutual cognitive coordination between humans and intelligent systems (Leng et al. 2022). This section aims to explore the concepts of Industry 4.0 and its impact on the circular economy by focusing on its foundational design principles and implementation strategies. These principles, as outlined in Fig. 12.4, are pivotal in guiding manufacturers toward sustainable economic, environmental, and social development within the broader business ecosystem (Ghobakhloo 2020).

12.2.2.1 System Thinking and System Integration

Recent literature studies underscore Industry 4.0 as a data-centric paradigm centered on cyber-physical systems characterized by a complex architecture and heterogeneous components (Rajput and Singh 2019; Klingenberg et al. 2021). Adopting a systems thinking approach and

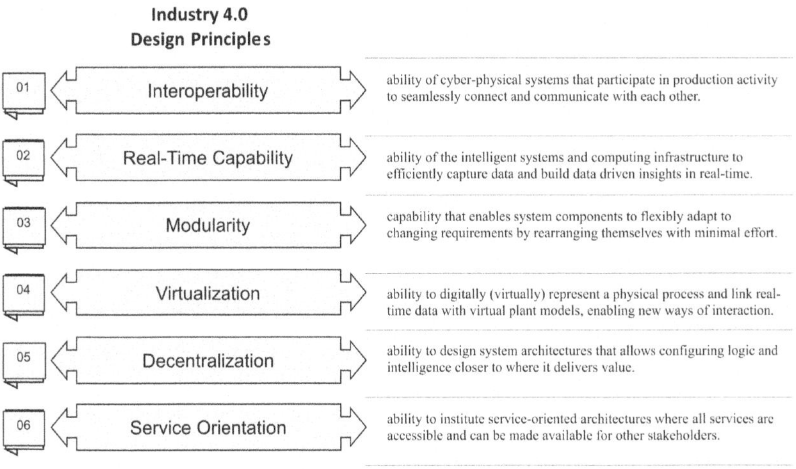

Fig. 12.4 Industry 4.0 design principles

integrating systems for achieving information interoperability is therefore essential (Büchi et al. 2020; Sanchez et al. 2020). Over the past decade, industrial manufacturing has transitioned significantly from factory-centric operations to interconnected digital production systems embedded within digital-physical networks (Laskurain-Iturbe et al. 2021). This evolution fosters collaboration across manufacturing operations, and business processes, and extends to supply chain partners and broader business ecosystems (Chen et al. 2023). The core objective of this transformation is to facilitate information exchange, enabling seamless interconnection and interoperability while leveraging comprehensive data analysis and real-time automated decision-making. This is outlined by three dimensions of integration, vertical integration, and networked manufacturing systems, horizontal integration through the value networks, and end-to-end digital integration across the value chain (Kagermann et al. 2013).

Vertical Integration

Vertical integration or vertical networking in Industry 4.0, aims to flatten the automation pyramid by reducing the layers between decision-making and system control within a single business. This connects all levels of an enterprise control system, from the field and control levels at the bottom to the supervisory and plant management level, right through to the enterprise planning level, thus enabling real-time data flow. This establishes a secure and reliable data exchange platform between plant-floor and enterprise applications, integrating production with broader business functions like supply chain management, product lifecycle management, and logistics. Real-time data flows across plant floors; from sensors, controllers, and mixed platform process control, right through to management, aiming at "global" interoperability. The goal is to achieve an interoperable "systems of systems" approach. A key challenge of vertical integration has been in the convergence of two distinct types of networks: the industrial communication network for industrial automation termed as operation network (OT network), and the traditional office network (IT network) that connects the enterprise. However, technologies like Unified Architecture (e.g., OPC UA) based on Open Platform Communications have significantly progressed in overcoming this challenge (Givehchi et al. 2017). OPC UA facilitates global interoperability across different platforms and manufacturers by enabling standardized data exchange between industrial devices and software applications, regardless of underlying protocols. This integration establishes a cohesive system across industrial ecosystems, facilitating real-time coordination and collaboration among stakeholders. Consequently, it sets up an integrated system closing loops in industrial ecosystems, enabling components and stakeholders to coordinate and collaborate in real-time (Sanchez et al. 2020). Overall, vertical integration transforms the traditional automation pyramid to a platform-independent service-oriented architecture, facilitating seamless data exchange and enhancing operational efficiency in Industry 4.0 environments.

Horizontal Integration

While vertical integration focuses on integrating processes within a single business entity, horizontal integration involves connecting the factory to various participants in the value chain through a well-designed, secure, and integrated workflow. In the context of Industry 4.0, the objective is to enhance inter-organizational interoperability, enabling vertically integrated organizations to share information more effectively across the supply chain. This often necessitates incorporating data from external entities such as suppliers, subcontractors, partners, and sometimes customers. It complements vertical integration by incorporating external relationships, integrating supplier and customer networks, information, and management systems, among other elements (Pérez-Lara et al. 2020). Horizontal integration extends to multisite operations and engaging third-party partners both upstream and downstream, thereby fostering opportunities for new business models and innovation through collaborative efforts. The objective is to achieve deeper alignment and transparency, thereby enhancing visibility, flexibility, and productivity, while also increasing levels of automation throughout the supply chain (Tiwari 2021). Through collaborative networks, enterprises combine resources, share risks, and swiftly adapt to market changes, seizing new opportunities (Brettel et al. 2014; Kagermann et al. 2013). Complete digital integration spans the entire supply chain, encompassing suppliers, manufacturing, logistics, distribution, and customer interactions. This necessitates organizational adjustments, interdisciplinary collaboration, and addressing social challenges throughout the transformation process (Veile et al. 2020). Both vertical and horizontal integration are therefore essential for achieving seamless communication across the value chain.

End-To-End Digital Integration Across the Value Chain

End-to-end integration in a value chain is primarily the extension of horizontal integration by encompassing all the stages providing comprehensive support across the entire lifecycle, from product development to manufacturing system engineering, production, and services (Kagermann et al. 2013). It entails integrating and connecting all processes, systems, and stakeholders involved in the lifecycle. For products, this means linking product design, development, planning, engineering, manufacturing, and services. Likewise, process plants, involve integrating engineering, construction, and operational phases, starting from functional specification requirements. This integration spans manufactured products and the manufacturing process, achieving a seamless convergence of the digital and physical worlds (Kagermann et al. 2013). Achieving this requires logical, end-to-end digital integration across stages of value creation and product (or plant) lifecycles, encompassing product ranges and their corresponding manufacturing systems (Kagermann et al. 2013). Beyond technical aspects, it extends beyond traditional business domains by adopting a business lifecycle approach. This is the basis for an end-to-end engineering approach across the entire value chain, a major part of the concept of Industry 4.0 (Bartodziej 2017). Figure 12.5 illustrates the concepts of Vertical, Horizontal, and End-to-end digital integration within the Industry 4.0 framework.

This therefore closely aligns with the principle of lifecycle thinking in sustainability. Incorporating such an integrated approach to Industry 4.0 (horizontal, vertical, and end-to-end) is crucial for enabling circular flows and realizing circular systems (Stahel 2016; Gebhardt et al. 2022). It forms the foundation for a cradle-to-cradle cycle (end-to-end), moving beyond the traditional 'end-of-life' approach (Halse and Jæger 2019), and plays a pivotal role in driving the transition toward a circular economy.

12.2.2.2 Lifecycle View of Industry 4.0

Lifecycle management is a crucial enabler of Industry 4.0, a central repository for all product-related data spanning from inception and production to sales and services. This integration of physical products and cyber services throughout their entire lifecycle (Machado Carla Gonçalves and da Silva 2020), offers a comprehensive approach to understanding, assessing, and improving economic, environmental, and

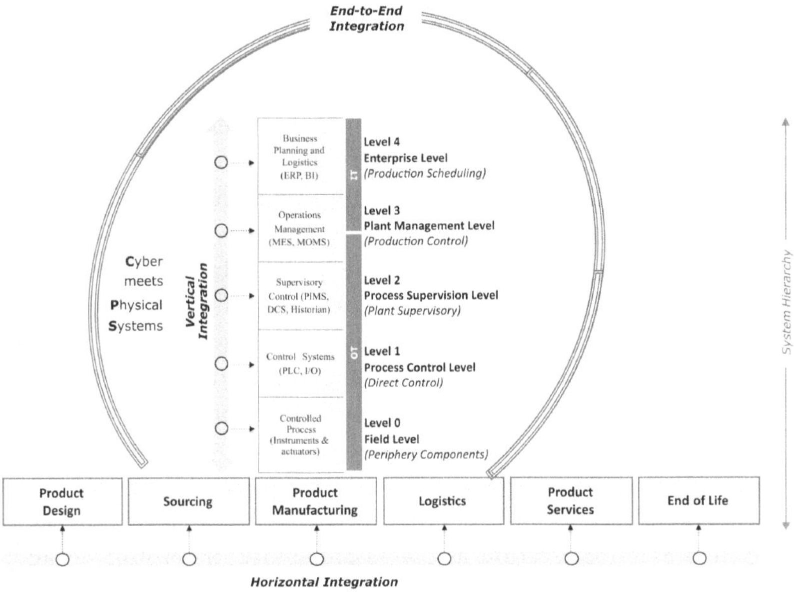

Fig. 12.5 Vertical, horizontal and end-to-end digital integration in industry 4.0

social dimensions. Industry 4.0 technologies, systems, and processes collaborate to enhance lifecycle management, promising significant advancements across the lifecycle of production equipment. During the design phase, it facilitates resource conservation, while in the operational phase, it delivers benefits such as improved performance, simplified system reconfiguration, reduced energy consumption, minimized pollution, and streamlined maintenance. These aspects not only facilitate the translation of technological innovations into products and services but also contribute to reducing total lifecycle costs, addressing environmental and economic considerations (Javaid et al. 2022). Such a lifecycle-driven business model is essential for sustainability strategies, where products (and associated services) are designed for circular economy principles, aiming for extended lifecycles and sustainable value creation across all lifecycle stages. This approach includes sustainable design, resource-efficient production processes, and the adoption of circular and symbiotic production systems (Machado Carla Gonçalves and da Silva 2020).

This is achieved through a three-step integration process aimed at positively and cohesively impacting all dimensions of sustainability. Initially, internal integration within a company (vertical integration) is established to familiarize the organization with the technology and ensure data availability and consistency. Many companies have successfully implemented Industry 4.0 technologies on the manufacturing shop floor, focusing on digital use cases that support sustainable practices such as eco-friendly product design, waste reduction, energy efficiency improvements, and water conservation. Subsequently, this integration extends to include adjacent stakeholders in the value chain (horizontal integration), such as third-party logistics providers and direct suppliers upstream, as well as distributors downstream, fostering enhanced data exchange. This collaborative approach identifies new opportunities for innovation and facilitates value creation across sustainability dimensions by leveraging access to supply chain information that was previously unavailable. This is where modern supply chains face unprecedented challenges, particularly due to their growing complexity involving multiple stakeholders across global locations, intricate logistics networks, and the imperative to share data beyond organizational boundaries. The ultimate step involves the integration of data across pertinent lifecycles and processes crucial for comprehensive end-to-end integration. However, the complexity involved amplifies integration challenges, particularly in dynamically collaborating across value streams and different product lifecycle chains. Advocating for closed-loop lifecycles and cradle-to-cradle approaches becomes essential in addressing these complexities. When effectively implemented, it extends beyond enhancing productivity and resource efficiency to enabling collaboration throughout the value chain, promoting closed-loop production systems, circular product lifecycles, sustainable product services, and circular economy business models, contributing positively to the development of the circular economy (Ghobakhloo 2020; Dantas et al. 2021; Khan et al. 2021).

Lifecycle Modelling in Industry 4.0

Reference Architecture Model for Industry 4.0 (RAMI4.0) framework provides a structured approach for lifecycle modeling in the context of Industry 4.0 (Moghaddam et al. 2018). It serves to establish a unified understanding among stakeholders and guides organizations in representing, managing, and optimizing assets throughout their entire lifecycle. This framework integrates essential elements of Industry 4.0 into a three-dimensional model, offering a structured and comprehensive approach. A crucial development in RAMI4.0 is the inclusion of a generalized lifecycle axis, based on IEC 62890, represented along the horizontal axis, which can also serve as the foundation for circular strategies. This axis covers the lifecycle and value stream of products, distinguishing between different stages from conception to disposal, critical for lifecycle modeling across various dimensions. This distinction is articulated through the definitions of "Type" and "Instance" to delineate the lifecycle stages of assets within Industry 4.0. A "Type" represents the initial concept of a product, evolving through subsequent development stages (Rojko 2017). When a "Type" progresses to an "Instance," it signifies the transition from prototype to actual production, with instances ultimately delivered to customers. This lifecycle progression from "Type" to "Instance" and vice versa can iterate multiple times over a product's lifecycle. Due to these interlinked lifecycles involving multiple stakeholders, individual component lifecycles are no longer viewed in isolation but as interconnected entities involving all stakeholders—from component suppliers to end customers. Hence, every object, whether it be a product, machine, or material, can be distinctly designated as a "Type" or "Instance."

In terms of information modeling, each "Object Type" is assigned a unique identifier linked to a specific entity within a system, (Zezulka et al. 2016), facilitating the assignment of generic metadata and specific data tailored for particular purposes based on standardized information management specifications across the value chain and involved stakeholders. This can be based on standard (industry) specifications for information management that works across the value chain. An "Object Instance," meanwhile, is an occurrence of an Object Type characterized by its instance identifier. Consequently, the lifecycles of Object Types and Object Instances can be independently managed within a value stream alongside value-adding processes. RAMI4.0's lifecycle and value stream axis illustrate how process layers operate within the product lifecycle and value stream context. The lifecycle of a product or system thus encompasses both Object Type and Object Instance lifecycles. The Object Type lifecycle initiates during the conceptual stage, extending through operations, maintenance, and customer usage phases, whereas the lifecycle of the product or system instance begins from manufacturing and proceeds through operations, maintenance, and customer usage stages. Architecturally, this is an interesting approach that supports the introduction of product lifecycle concepts spanning development, implementation, usage, maintenance, and eventual disassembly or disposal stages. This holistic approach is instrumental in realizing circular economy principles by facilitating a systematic and regenerative lifecycle model and managing information flows throughout an object's lifecycle. It also promotes the transformation of output from one product's lifecycle into input for another (R-cycle), ensuring continuous value creation within the value loop.

Linking of Value Streams in Industry 4.0

The manufacturing value chain comprises distinct value-creation processes spanning the lifecycle of an asset. Despite their variances, both traditional and future value chains adhere to a structured approach involving operational activities aimed at achieving specific objectives in the value creation process. Consequently, digitization and networking of all activities across value streams throughout lifecycle stages into integrated value networks becomes crucial, as it creates an integrated view and drives value creation for Industry 4.0. The availability of all relevant information in real-time through the networking of all value creation instances provides a comprehensive view of all the value-adding processes and enables control over the entire value stream across a product's lifecycle (Wolfgang 2016). Historically, companies have encountered challenges in maintaining and managing the integrity of the overall value chain, necessitating consistent linkage and management of data across multiple processes and their interrelationships.

Integrated product development revolutionizes conventional thought patterns by integrating product development trajectories and service innovation to establish a robust transformation pathway based on the service value chain (Liu and Zhao 2022). Within production processes, integrated production planning and control serve as the nervous system for optimizing operational efficiency (Chen et al. 2023). A networked manufacturing system orchestrates the efficient utilization of resources, people, and systems through planning, coordination, sequencing, scheduling, monitoring, and control of production activities to transform raw materials into finished products or components optimally (Oluyisola et al. 2022). This seamless integration involves embedding digital technologies across manufacturing facets to enhance value creation. Thus, the value-adding processes must be considered holistically alongside the lifecycle, rather than in isolation within a single factory, encompassing all factories and stakeholders involved, ranging from engineering through component suppliers to customers (Adolphs et al. 2015). The emphasis is therefore on optimizing material utilization and minimizing waste across core value creation processes: development, production, and services through cyclic and recycling processes (Wolfgang 2016).

System Composition for Lifecycle Implementation in A Circular Economy

The circular economy system diagram, known as the butterfly diagram, serves as a valuable tool for comprehensively understanding and practically applying the Circular Economy model. It highlights three key participants in the ecosystem: the Parts Manufacturer (responsible for product design), the Product Manufacturer (handling production), and the Service provider (managing services). Conceptually, these roles align intriguingly with the three business partners described in RAMI4.0: the component supplier, machine manufacturer, and factory operator.

Expanding lifecycle assessment and value stream mapping for decision-making purposes, therefore allows for exploring the extension of Industry 4.0 principles of "lifecycle and value stream" to the circular economy. The objective is to integrate the design and development process, manufacturing processes, and service management systematically and objectively. This approach facilitates a bi-directional flow of information (R-Cycles), where usage data can inform product updates returned to the manufacturer.

This iterative process improves the "Object Type" based on field results and updates its design specifications. The revised "Type" then informs the development of subsequent "Instances," with updated specifications reflected in the "object instance" during production. This integrated approach supports sustainable development aligned with circular economic objectives.

Transitioning toward a circular economy necessitates more than just resource efficiency; it requires a broader set of principles and practices encompassing circular product design, production management, and service management. While each of these components has been leveraging Industry 4.0 technologies, most of the lifecycle management initiatives remain isolated and fragmented. Challenges persist in breaking down entrenched silos within and across value chains, hindering effective coordination and alignment. Given the interdisciplinary nature of the circular economy, these silos pose significant obstacles. A crucial step toward realizing a circular economy involves organizing and bridging the fragmented landscape of multidisciplinary industries, fostering system-level disruptive innovation. This entails integrating (smart) product design, (smart) production, and (smart) services into a holistic and interconnected ecosystem spanning the entire product lifecycle. Such integration unlocks opportunities for advancing circular economy principles and implementations effectively.

12.3 The Approach

12.3.1 Establishing End-To-End Circularity Leveraging Industry 4.0 Principles

This section introduces an innovative approach aimed at achieving comprehensive end-to-end circularity. It emphasizes the utilization of inherent circular processes within the value chain while leveraging foundational principles and technological capabilities of Industry 4.0. The approach seeks to bridge gaps between isolated circular practices and advocates for a holistic perspective. By extending circularity principles from individual processes to encompass the entire value chain, this methodology transforms linear value chains into closed-loop value loops. These synergies between inherent circular systems promote circularity within traditionally linear industrial frameworks, significantly influencing the transition to a circular economy. This transition is crucial and holds substantial potential to impact our shift toward a circular economy. The introduction of concepts such as "vertical circularity,"horizontal circularity," and "end-to-end circularity" establish new avenues for value creation in a circular economy context. This represents a significant shift in how products, components, and materials are circulated within the closed-loop manufacturing value chain (Berg et al. 2021) paving the way for value creation at scale. It marks a significant transition from a technocentric focus (Industry 4.0) to a value-centric paradigm (Industry 5.0). As a critical enabler, it facilitates the realization of the transformative vision of Industry 5.0, emphasizing resilience, sustainability, and human-centric approaches (Berg et al. 2021; Leng et al. 2022).

12.3.1.1 Vertical Circularity

Vertical circularity refers to a closed-loop approach within individual processes of a linear value chain. This integrated workflow operates within an organization's value-creation processes, as firm-level and industry-level innovations (Kirchherr et al. 2023). It focuses on eliminating waste and optimizing processes without extending forward or backward integration to external value chain participants. This approach can significantly enhance organizational efficiencies by focusing on eliminating waste and optimizing processes, following a cradle-to-grave development model typical of a linear economy. The promising advancement of CPS, can enable efficient operations and design systems, effectively overcoming internal integration complexities Fig. 12.6, illustrates the implementation of vertical circular processes within each value creation process segment of the value chain, ensuring that resources and materials are continuously reused or recycled within the individual processes, thereby minimizing waste, and maximizing efficiency.

Nevertheless, to achieve effectiveness throughout the entire value chain, the industry must progress beyond mere efficiency. This strategic approach involves extending beyond optimizing internal processes to ensure alignment with value chain goals and objectives. By doing so, organizations can achieve "efficient effectiveness," a concept that maximizes efficiency through continuous feedback loops between process components. This holistic perspective not only enhances individual process perfor mance but also fosters seamless integration within the value chain, driving overall value and sustainability.

12.3.1.2 Horizontal Circularity

Horizontal circularity refers to the closed-loop systems established between individual vertical circular processes across the value chain. The primary objective is to integrate these closed loops (vertical circularities) of individual processes with a horizontal loop, enabling the reuse of materials and information across the entire value chain, as illustrated in the figure below. This concept translates the principles of closed-loop process management into value chain management, creating a comprehensive cognitive closed-loop system aimed at continuous improvement and cradle-to-cradle development within a circular ecosystem approach. Rather than extracting data from one process and feeding it into the next, this system establishes an all-inclusive, synergistic, and eco-effective approach for sustainable development across the value chain. This approach elevates the concept of effectiveness, redefining the relationship

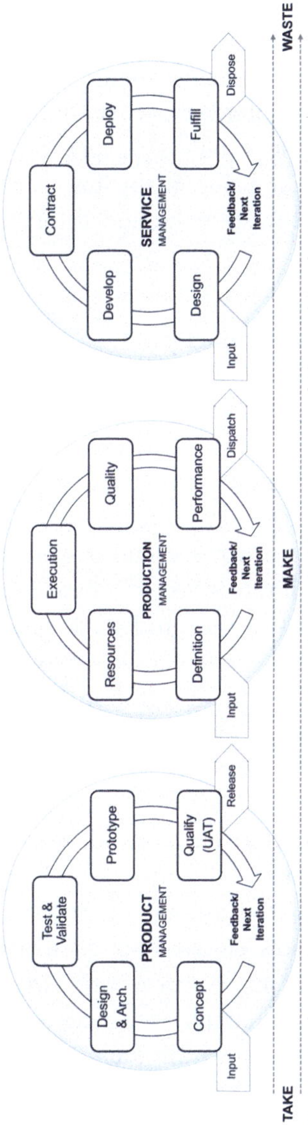

Fig. 12.6 Vertical circularity-circular process within the individual process of the value chain

between individual businesses (vertical) and the ecosystem (horizontal). Unlike efficiency, which focuses on mitigating risks within an organization, this strategy ensures that strategic planning and commitment are geared toward effectiveness, aiming to generate positive impacts and co-regenerate with larger ecosystems. Figure 12.7 illustrates horizontal circularity, occurring at the interface between individual vertical circular processes. This involves the seamless integration of circular practices across different stages of the value chain, fostering a holistic approach to resource utilization and waste reduction throughout the entire value chain.

12.3.1.3 Closed-Loop Circularity

Closed-loop circularity extends horizontal circularity by adopting a holistic cradle-to-cradle perspective encompassing the entire ecosystem associated with products, manufacturing systems, services, and all interconnected processes. This approach integrates various aspects of vertical and horizontal circularity to achieve end-to-end circularity. It can be envisioned as a system of interconnected closed loops, combining individual closed-loop systems (such as product design, manufacturing, and services) into a comprehensive circular closed-loop system (closed loop of individual closed loops). This integration links design and production with use and end-of-life management, establishing true end-to-end circularity. As processes become more complex and multifaceted, ensuring real-time, end-to-end transparency through effective bipartite information exchange is crucial. Standardization plays a key role in setting up a "single source of truth" for lifecycle data, facilitating seamless information exchange among designers, producers, and end-users. Figure 12.8 illustrates closed-loop circularity, emerging at the convergence of horizontal and vertical circularities. It illustrates the comprehensive integration of circular practices across different stages of the value chain (horizontal) and within each segment (vertical), ensuring a synergistic approach to sustainable resource management and waste reduction throughout the entire production process.

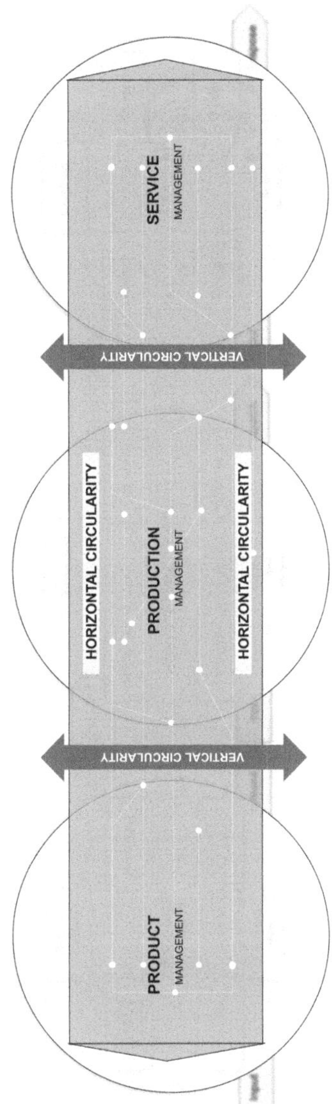

Fig. 12.7 Horizontal circularity—at the integration of the individual vertical circular processes

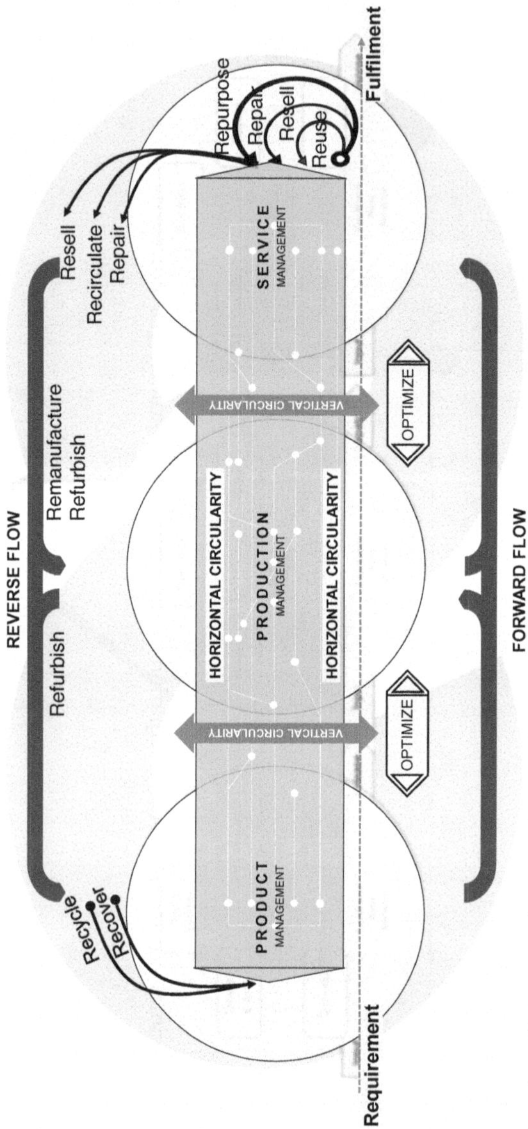

Fig. 12.8 Closed-loop circularity at the integration of horizontal and vertical circularities

A single enterprise cannot autonomously implement and efficiently operate a closed circular economy (Winkler 2011). Such an integrated approach to the circular economy therefore transcends fragmented methods, aiming for a holistic and impactful transformation. It encompasses circular systems engineering, lifecycle design, closed-loop product lifecycle management, human-centered design, human-in-the-loop manufacturing, circularity-integrated Digital Twins, end-to-end closed loops, product service systems, and other pragmatic approaches. The collaborative flow of information and materials creates a dynamic and efficient ecosystem that drives circular thinking. This approach facilitates the expansion of circular economy solutions, creating opportunities for all stakeholders and aligning with an economic model aimed at enhancing sustainability across environmental, economic, and social dimensions. It also complements the existing Industry 4.0 paradigm by promoting a human-in-the-loop closed-loop control system, which facilitates assisted decision-making where individuals actively participate in decision points within an otherwise automated process flow (Turner et al. 2022). Nevertheless, this implies higher complexity compared to linear transactional value chains and is viewed as a complex system requiring fundamental macro-level changes (Kirchherr et al. 2023). This sets the path to realizing the vision of Industry 5.0, an evolution designed to leverage the creativity of human experts collaborating alongside efficient, intelligent, and accurate machines (Maddikunta et al. 2022).

12.3.2 Leveraging AI to Accelerate Industry 5.0 in a Circular Economy

The concept of a Circular Economy, Economy may seem intuitively straightforward and easy to understand, however, realizing it in practice is a complex issue (Domenech et al. 2019). Yet, AI emerges as a pivotal tool in facilitating this transformative shift. It can accelerate the transition to a circular economy as it can help solve complex problems faster. AI, as a subset of the technologies driving the emergence of the Industry 4.0 era, occupies a prominent position in advancing the values of the circular economy that deals with models and systems that execute functions typically linked with complexity, reasoning, and learning functions, related to human intelligence (Acerbi et al. 2021). Industry 5.0 builds on the foundation laid by Industry 4.0, expanding and adapting its features to address emerging requirements. While Industry 4.0 primarily emphasized industrial automation, Industry 5.0 shifted toward a more inclusive, human-centric approach. This is the sociotechnical evolution wherein humans play a vital role, placing the operator at the core of manufacturing and production systems (Valette et al. 2023). It therefore advocates a forward-looking vision, by specifically putting research and innovation at the service of the transition to a sustainable, human-centric, and resilient industry (Breque et al. 2021). This transition involves adapting traditional linear operating models to reflect circular business practices and adopting a circularly interconnected perspective. It necessitates enabling mutual cognitive coordination between human and artificial intelligence, fostering co-innovation, co-design, and co-creation of personalized products and services (Leng et al. 2022). AI plays a significant role by autonomously and remotely monitoring efficiency throughout the manufacturing process and during the end-of-life phase of products (Ghoreishi 2019). The European Commission has incorporated a human-centric approach to digital technologies, with a particular focus on AI, as one of its key policy initiatives in the pursuit of Industry 5.0 (Breque et al. 2021).

While manufacturing organizations have started with AI for proven use cases, Generative AI (GenAI) holds tremendous promise for Industry 5.0 paradigms by assisting humans to perform effectively. Unlike traditional AI, which focuses on pattern detection, decision-making, analytics gathering, and data classification, GenAI is more collaborative in creating new content, guided responses, generative designs, and data synthesis. It aims to collaboratively create desired outputs, responses, recommendations, and solutions to complex problems. An increasing number of initiatives are exploring how AI can generate fresh opportunities within a circular economy. When strategically deployed, AI can accelerate the transition to a circular economy and toward Industry 5.0 by harnessing its capabilities across various dimensions, including AI-based Circular

Product Design, AI-based Circular Service Management, and AI-based Circular Production Management.

12.3.2.1 AI-Assisted Circular Product Design

While product design is inherently complex and time-consuming, the interdisciplinary nature of circular products amplifies this complexity, rendering them even more intricate systems. Circular products are typically designed based on three primary circular design principles: eliminate, circulate, and regenerate. These principles extend to various design aspects such as durability, reliability, maintainability, repairability, upgradability, adaptability, compatibility, reassembly, and recyclability (Ghoreishi 2019). Moreover, the advancement of CPS necessitates a redefinition of design processes to accommodate escalating levels of system complexity and the challenge of fully understanding the system's nature or potential failure modes (Hehenberger et al. 2016). Concrete challenges are also highlighted to underscore the necessity for a novel methodological approach to ensure successful CPS design, with particular emphasis placed on post-deployment system integration hurdles (Mosterman and Zander 2016). The introduction of the Human–Cyber–Physical System (HCPS) and Human-in-the-Loop CPS, which are composite intelligent systems consisting of humans, cyber systems, and physical systems, is engineered to achieve specific goals at an optimized level (Zhou et al. 2019). This development is significant in the transition to Industry 5.0, leveraging the creativity of human experts collaborating alongside intelligent systems.

As discussions around circular economy implementation evolve, the requirements for circular designs have expanded to encompass a broader range of functional and non-functional considerations. A limitation of sustainable systems engineering today is its inability to properly reason about value retention loops, i.e., to introduce systematic circularity into the engineering practice. This is due to the lack of ability to combine end-to-end process networks with bipartite systems and method sustainability. This limitation, in turn, motivates the convergence of Model-Based Systems Engineering (MBSE) and Product Lifecycle Management (PLM) toward true Model-Based Engineering (MBE) to realize a lifecycle-model-based approach that integrates data and supports end-to-end lifecycle processes. Navigating these complexities involves managing vast amounts of data and iterating through cycles while coordinating within intricate networks. AI, therefore, has the potential to handle complexity and make sense of abundant data more effectively. It can accelerate the design of new circular products, components, and materials fit for a circular economy through iterative machine learning-supported design procedures, facilitating swift prototyping and testing. The intent is to transition to a sustainable Industrial Revolution.

Consequently, product design engineering is transitioning from informal, conceptual approaches toward data-driven design methodologies (Wang et al. 2022), with AI poised to facilitate this systematic shift. AI holds immense potential in expediting prototyping and learning processes by integrating field performance data into iterative design cycles. AI techniques have proven immensely beneficial for sustainability efforts, particularly in managing vast volumes of data within digital thread-based engineering practices. The data-centric approach employed in the implementation of cyber-physical systems for design, modeling, simulation, and integration has been instrumental in this regard (Hehenberger et al. 2016). AI systems aim to respond in real-time to process issues, with advanced AI even self-monitoring and self-controlling in an autonomous style (Aphirakmethawong et al. 2022). AI has been applied to analyze data and make decisions for operating systems to reduce impacts on cost and quality. AI-enabled digital twins are well-positioned to govern end-to-end processes (Heithoff et al. 2023), offering opportunities for efficient data harvesting and rich decision support based on modeling and simulation. Given the multi-systemic nature of sustainability, multi-paradigm modeling (Vangheluwe et al. 2002), multi-view modeling (Cicchetti et al. 2019), and user-friendly, flexible modeling approaches, such as blended modeling (David et al. 2023), can provide solid foundations for the next generation of circular modeling frameworks and tools. AI-generated product design can use artificial intelligence to create new product designs and generate innovative concepts. Tools like DALL-E, the AI-powered image generation tool from OpenAI, use neural networks to create images based on provided descriptions, serving as an excellent resource for product designers to generate futuristic concepts that do not yet exist. Given the immensely complex nature of circular product design, modern machine learning, and AI methods will inevitably become integral to the toolbox of circular systems engineering.

12.3.2.2 AI-Assisted Circular Production Operations

Circular production or circular manufacturing signifies a major departure from traditional manufacturing practices. Its aim extends beyond merely creating sustainable products; it encompasses the adoption of circular methodologies throughout manufacturing processes. The objective is to minimize negative environmental impacts by manufacturing products designed for circular use, optimizing resource utilization, and extending product lifespans within a closed-loop supply chain ecosystem. Intelligent use of production assets, resources, and materials during production operations lies at the core of a circular economy (Rantala et al. 2023). Manufacturing operations, which consume considerable amounts of material resources, can effectively minimize energy consumption, material usage, and waste when operating within a closed-loop system (Schöggl et al. 2023). Transitioning from conventional methods to circular production management requires significant adaptation and innovation. This shift not only addresses numerous challenges but also presents opportunities to overcome them simultaneously (Winquist et al. 2023). It involves collaborating with efficient, intelligent, and precise machines, embodying the essence of Industry 5.0. This profound leap forward places humans at the center of manufacturing evolution, envisioning a symbiotic relationship between human workers and advanced technologies, fostering co-existing production operations management system (Rožanec et al. 2023). This transformation maps out human–machine relationships along a 5C evolution journey, progressing from Coexistence, Cooperation, and Collaboration to a future of Compassion and Coevolution (Lu et al. 2022). Among human–machine collaboration approaches, mutual learning stands out, highlighting the reciprocal collaboration between humans and machines as they jointly undertake tasks (Rožanec et al. 2023). The intricacies of contemporary manufacturing operations underscore the need to integrate advanced technologies such as artificial intelligence (AI) for optimal performance. The rise of digitalization in production equipment and operational processes signifies the adoption of advanced manufacturing technologies to manage complex, high-dimensional problems and data (et al. 2020). Existing literature findings underscore the growing importance of AI across various domains within smart production, including production operations, maintenance management, quality enhancement, supply chain management, inventory management, predictive maintenance, and autonomous operations (Cioffi et al. 2020; Srivastava et al. 2023). AI-driven analytics can identify operational inefficiencies, uncover bottlenecks, and find potential market opportunities by utilizing data generated by algorithms and data models (Zong and Guan 2024). AI leverages large datasets to analyze data generated during production processes. Using sensors and data analytics, AI predicts potential equipment failures and identifies maintenance needs before they occur, thereby extending product lifecycles and ensuring products remain functional, relevant, and sustainable for extended periods. Predictive maintenance systems powered by AI can proactively detect equipment failures, decrease downtime, and extend asset lifespans, enhancing operational efficiency and reducing costs. AI-based digital twins provide 3D virtual representations of real and complex operations, enabling improved design, health and safety, operations, maintenance, and services, leading to overall resource efficiency (Kolasani 2024).

AI-driven intelligent factories can move beyond conventional automation dependent on individual industrial robots toward interconnected CPS. This transformation revolutionizes production plants, facilitating communication among machinery and overarching factory systems through an IoT configuration. Robotic Process Automation can handle repetitive, high-volume tasks such as updating records, addressing queries, and performing calculations. Furthermore, AI enhances collaboration between suppliers, manufacturers, and other stakeholders for a more integrated manufacturing. Collaborative production is vital for establishing a circular economy, involving the coordination and cooperation of various stakeholders within the manufacturing value chain. Together, they drive sustainable production efforts. Human-in-the-loop manufacturing combines artificial intelligence and automation in the manufacturing process. AI and human–machine collaboration in manufacturing brings together the strengths of AI and human expertise to optimize various aspects of the manufacturing process, simulating human intelligence and acting without explicit instruction (Ciccarelli et al. 2024). Consequently, AI is recognized as the primary driver of the Fourth Industrial Revolution, driven by new ways of interaction between humans and machines. The integration of AI in circular production operations has significant implications, serving as a pivotal component in the progression of the Fourth Industrial Revolution and holding considerable potential in advancing circular manufacturing practices and fostering sustainable innovation.

12.3.2.3 AI-Assisted Circular Product Services

Since the greatest source of value lies in product usage, advancing circular productservice management emerges as a primary strategy for promoting a resource-efficient economy. It seeks to add value to products, extend their lifecycle through repair and maintenance, and enhance performance via refurbishment and upgrades during their end-of-life phase. Circular service management thus emphasizes an integrated approach by adopting closed-loop product-service systems for sustainable development (Camilleri 2019). This creates an efficient service ecosystem focused on the entire service lifecycle, from creation to end-of-life, aiming to reduce environmental impact, enhance resource efficiency, and promote sustainability based on real-time insights. Circular service management therefore represents a significant opportunity to extend the principles of the circular economy into the realm of service delivery. While intelligent product-service systems, as part of the digital servitization paradigm, have rapidly developed, literature reviews highlight the obstacles and practical challenges encountered by manufacturing firms. These include difficulties in diverging from entrenched business models, offerings, routines, and capabilities (Brekke et al. 2024; Ren and Zheng 2024; Naeem et al. 2024). Despite its growing significance, the circular economy remains an uncharted area in transformative service research (TSR), with a limited understanding of how the circular economy can support change for greater well-being among individuals and collectives (Sönnichsen et al. 2024). This necessitates intelligent design modifications to accommodate product services, digitally enabled methods for delivering new services, data-driven capabilities and innovation, customized service-based augmented innovation, service delivery systems, and innovative approaches to managing service outcomes (Brekke et al. 2024).

Since the greatest source of value lies in product usage, advancing circular product-service management emerges as a primary strategy for promoting a resource-efficient economy. This approach aims to add value to products, extend their lifecycle through repair and maintenance, and enhance performance via refurbishment and upgrades during their end-of-life phase. Circular service management thus empha sizes an integrated approach by adopting closed-loop product-service systems for sustainable development (Camilleri 2019). This creates an efficient service ecosystem focused on the entire service lifecycle, from creation to end-of-life, aiming to reduce environmental impact, enhance resource efficiency, and promote sustainability based on real-time insights. Circular service management therefore represents a significant opportunity to extend the principles of the circular economy into the realm of service delivery.

While intelligent product-service systems, as part of the digital servitization paradigm, have rapidly developed, literature reviews highlight the obstacles and practical challenges encountered by manufacturing firms. These include difficulties in diverging from entrenched business models, offerings, routines, and capabilities (Brekke et al. 2024; Ren and Zheng 2024; Naeem et al. 2024). Despite its growing significance, the circular economy remains an uncharted area in transformative service research (TSR), with a limited understanding of how the CE can support change for greater well-being among individuals and collectives (Sönnichsen et al. 2024). This necessitates intelligent design modifications to accommodate product services, digitally enabled methods for delivering new services, data-driven capabilities and innovation, customized service-based augmented innovation, service delivery systems, and innovative approaches to managing service outcomes (Brekke et al. 2024).

AI-enabled circular service management approaches, integrated with other digital technologies, have the potential to fundamentally reshape the conventional methods by which firms generate, deliver, and capture value (Mariani et al. 2023). Leveraging advanced technologies such as networking (e.g., Web 3.0), digitalization (e.g., mixed reality), and intellectualization (e.g., AI-generated content), product-service systems can revolutionize business innovation and service delivery to customers (Ren and Zheng 2024). By harnessing these advanced technologies, product-service systems can offer more dynamic and personalized experiences, enhance efficiency, and drive innovation across various industries. In the B2B context, firms have widely accepted the influence of AI on servitization while shifting from a product-centric to an "Everything as a Service" (XaaS) business model and logic (Abou-Foul et al. 2023; Nicoletti and Appolloni 2023).

Research indicates that proactive interaction in design, incorporating symbiosis between humans and smart-connected products, as well as AI-enabled collaborative intelligence, emerges as a novel design feature for innovative services, aligning with the human-centric and personalized themes of Industry 5.0 (Nicoletti and Appolloni 2023; Ren and Zheng 2024). An AI-based integrated business model considering digital servitization allows manufacturers to gain a competitive advantage through product-service innovation (Naeem et al. 2024). AI has the potential to amplify the competitive advantage of circular economy business models, such as product-as-a-service and leasing, by integrating real-time and historical data from products and users. This integration enhances product circulation for as long as possible, as they are reused, repaired, refurbished, remanufactured, and circulated among users with diverse and evolving needs. This will further motivate manufacturers to seek more sophisticated solutions leveraging deep learning and AI-based capabilities (Kohtamäki et al. 2022). Therefore, there is a consensus that organizations willing to leverage advanced technologies, including artificial intelligence, need to restrategize their business and operating models and realign operations to transform their operating models and reconfigure business architecture across the enterprise (Nicoletti and Appolloni 2023).

12.4 Conclusions

As global challenges intensify and value chains become increasingly interconnected, it's evident that the traditional linear economic model is inadequate. However, within these traditional models lie inherent capabilities and opportunities that can be effectively leveraged through advanced technologies. One such opportunity is the existence of inherent circularities within linear processes, providing pathways to transition toward more sustainable and circular practices. This chapter explores the inherent circularities within individual stages of the value chain, illustrating their potential to drive closed-loop practices and influence the transition to a circular economy. It also elucidates key concepts of Industry 4.0, detailing design principles and implementation strategies that enhance circularity as foundational to a circular value chain. By building on these foundational insights, it presents the nexus between Industry 4.0 and the Circular Economy—an evolution driven by technological advancements and sustainability imperatives, aiming to engineer end-to-end circularity. This approach not only enhances efficiencies and competitiveness in production operations but extends beyond, fostering innovation in sustainable product design and service delivery. Nevertheless, the journey toward achieving end-to-end circularity is complex and challenging. This complexity has catalyzed the emergence of the concept of Industry 5.0, which emphasizes deeper integration of human intelligence with advanced technologies like AI to foster sustainability and human-centric development. Organizations must therefore overcome organizational, technological, and cultural challenges to change the way they integrate, collaborate, innovate, and create value systematically in the transition toward sustainable and human-centric development. Overall, Industry 5.0 represents a paradigm shift toward more inclusive, sustainable, and resilient industrial practices, where AI and advanced technologies empower humans to drive meaningful change toward a circular economy and sustainable future.

References

Mohamad Abou-Foul, Jose L Ruiz-Alba, and Pablo J López-Tenorio. The impact of artificial intelligence capabilities on servitization: The moderating role of absorptive capacity-a dynamic capabilities perspective. *Journal of business research*, 157:113609, 2023.

Federica Acerbi, Dai Andrew Forterre, and Marco Taisch. Role of artificial intelligence in circular manufacturing: a systematic literature review. *IFAC-PapersOnLine*, 54(1):367–372, 2021.

Peter Adolphs et al. Status report-reference architecture model industrie 4.0 (rami4.0). Technical report, VDI-Verein Deutscher Ingenieure eV and ZVEI-German Electrical and Electronic Manufacturers Association, 2015.

Andres Alcayaga, Melanie Wiener, and Erik G Hansen. Towards a framework of smart-circular systems: An integrative literature review. *Journal of cleaner production*, 221:622–634, 2019.

Carlos An Andrade, Sandrine Selosse, and Nadia Maïzi. *Thirty years since the circular economy concept emerged: has it reached a consensus*. Working paper, Chaire Modélisation prospective au service du développement durable, 2021.

Janjira Aphirakmethawong, Erfu Yang, and Jorn Mehnen. An overview of artificial intelligence in product design for smart manufacturing. In *2022 27th International Conference on Automation and Computing (ICAC)*, pages 1–6. IEEE, 2022.

Johan Arekrans. *Circling the Squares: Radical Innovation and Management Control Systems in the Circular Economy*. PhD thesis, KTH Royal Institute of Technology, 2023.

Sehrish Atif. Analysing the alignment between circular economy and industry 4.0 nexus with industry 5.0 era: An integrative systematic literature review. *Sustainable development (Bradford, West Yorkshire, England)*, 31(4):2155–2175, 2023.

Usama Awan et al. Industry 4.0 and circular economy in an era of global value chains: What have we learned and what is still to be explored? *Journal of Cleaner Production*, 371:133621, 2022.

Federico Barnabè and Sarfraz Nazir. Conceptualizing and enabling circular economy through integrated thinking. *Corporate social-responsibility and environmental management*, 29(2):448–468, 2022.

Christoph Jan Bartodziej. *The Concept Industry 4.0: An Empirical Analysis of Technologies and Applications in Production Logistics*. Springer Fachmedien Wiesbaden GmbH, Wiesbaden, 2017.

Mirjam Beltrami et al. Industry 4.0 and sustainability: Towards conceptualization and theory. *Journal of cleaner production*, 312:127733, 2021.

Holger Berg et al. Unlocking the potential of industry 4.0 to reduce the environmental impact of production. Technical report, European Environment Agency, European Topic Centre on Waste and Materials in a Green Economy: Mol, Belgium, 2021.

Erskin Blunck and Hedwig Werthmann. Industry 4.0: An opportunity to realize sustainable manufacturing and its potential for a circular economy. In *DIEM: Dubrovnik International Economic Meeting*, page 5650. Sveučilište u Dubrovniku, 2017.

Thomas Brekke et al. Overcoming barriers to transformation in manufacturing firms. a path-dependence perspective of digital servitization. *Review of managerial science*, 18(2):385–412, 2024.

Maija Breque, Lars De Nul, and Athanasios Petridis. Industry 5.0: Towards a sustainable. Technical report, European Commission, Directorate-General for Research and Innovation, 2021.

Malte Brettel et al. How virtualization, decentralization and network building change the manufacturing landscape: An industry 4.0 perspective. *International journal of information and communication engineering*, 8(1):37–44, 2014.

Giacomo Büchi, Monica Cugno, and Rebecca Castagnoli. Smart factory performance and industry 4.0. *Technological forecasting and social change*, 150:119790, 2020.

Mark Anthony Camilleri. The circular economy's closed loop and product service systems for sustainable development: A review and appraisal. *Sustainable Development*, 27(3):530–536, 2019.

Chen Chen, Tiong Lee Kong, and Wu Kan. Identifying the promising production planning and scheduling method for manufacturing in industry 4.0: A literature review. *Production & manufacturing research*, 11(1), 2023.

Marianna Ciccarelli et al. Advancing human-robot collaboration in handcrafted manufacturing: cobot-assisted polishing design boosted by virtual reality and human-in-the-loop. *The International Journal of Advanced Manufacturing Technology*, 2024.

Antonio Cicchetti, Federico Ciccozzi, and Alfonso Pierantonio. Multi-view approaches for software and system modelling: A systematic literature review. *Software and systems modeling*, 18(6):3207–3233, 2019.

Raffaele Cioffi et al. Artificial intelligence and machine learning applications in smart production: Progress, trends, and directions. *Sustainability*, 12(2):492, 2020.

Tiago Hennemann Hilario da Silva and Simone Sehnem. The circular economy and industry 4.0: Synergies and challenges. *Revista de Gestão*, 29(3):300–313, 2022.

TET Dantas et al. How the combination of circular economy and industry 4.0 can contribute towards achieving the sustainable development goals. *Sustainable production and consumption: transactions of the Institution of Chemical Engineers, Part E*, 26:213–227, 2021.

I David, M Latifaj, J Pietron, W Zhang, F Ciccozzi, I Malavolta, A Raschke, J Steghofer, and R Hebig. Blended modeling in commercial and open-source model-driven software engineering tools: A systematic study. *Software and Systems Modeling*, 22(1):415–447, 2023.

Jan-Philipp Disselkamp et al. Integrated product and production development-a systematic literature review. *Procedia CIRP*, 119:716–721, 2023.

Teresa Domenech et al. Mapping industrial symbiosis development in europe: Typologies of networks, characteristics, performance and contribution to the circular economy. *Resources, Conservation and Recycling*, 141:76–98, 2019.

Krzysztof Ejsmont, Bartlomiej Gladysz, and Aldona Kluczek. Impact of industry 4.0 on sustainability—bibliometric literature review. *Sustainability*, 12(14):5650, 2020.

Etieno Enang, Mahdi Bashiri, and David Jarvis. Exploring the transition from techno centric industry 4.0 towards value centric industry 5.0: A systematic literature review. *International Journal of Production Research*, 61(22):7866–7902, 2023.

Camila Favoretto et al. From servitization to digital servitization: How digitalization transforms companies' transition towards services. *Industrial Marketing Management*, 102:104–121, 2022.

Maximilian Gebhardt et al. Industry 4.0 technologies as enablers of collaboration in circular supply chains: A systematic literature review. *International Journal of Production Research*, 60(23):6967–6995, 2022.

Martin Geissdoerfer et al. Circular business models: A review. *Journal of Cleaner Production*, 277:123741, 2020.
Morteza Ghobakhloo. Industry 4.0, digitization, and opportunities for sustainability. *Journal of Cleaner Production*, 252:119869, 2020.
Morteza Ghobakhloo et al. Industry 5.0 implications for inclusive sustainable manufacturing: An evidence-knowledge-based strategic roadmap. *Journal of Cleaner Production*, 417:138023, 2023a.
Morteza Ghobakhloo et al. Behind the definition of industry 5.0: A systematic review of technologies, principles, components, and values. *Journal of Industrial and Production Engineering*, 40(6):432–447, 2023b.
Seyedehmalahat Ghoreishi. Assessing the role of artificial intelligence in product design towards circularity. *Journal of Cleaner Production*, 2019.
Omid Givehchi et al. Interoperability for industrial cyber-physical systems: An approach for legacy systems. *IEEE Transactions on Industrial Informatics*, 13(6): 3370–3378, 2017.
Lise Lillebrygfjeld Halse and Bjørn Jæger. Operationalizing industry 4.0: Understanding barriers of industry 4.0 and circular economy. In *Advances in Production Management Systems. Towards Smart Production Management Systems: IFIP WG 5.7 International Conference, APMS 2019*, page Springer International Publishing. Springer, 2019.
Peter Hehenberger et al. Design, modelling, simulation and integration of cyber physical systems: Methods and applications. *Computers in Industry*, 82:273–289, 2016.
M. Heithoff, A. Hellwig, J. Michael, and B. Rumpe. Digital twins for sustainable software systems. In *2023 IEEE/ACM 7th International Workshop on Green And Sustainable Software (GREENS)*, pages 19–23. IEEE, 2023. https://doi.org/10.1109/GREENS59328.2023.00010.
Mohd Javaid et al. Understanding the adoption of industry 4.0 technologies in improving environmental sustainability. *Sustainable Operations and Computers*, 3:203–217, 2022.
Henning Kagermann. *Change Through Digitization—Value Creation in the Age of Industry 4.0*. Springer Fachmedien Wiesbaden, Wiesbaden, 2015.
Henning Kagermann, Wolfgang Wahlster, and Johannes Helbig. Recommendations for implementing the strategic initiative industrie 4.0. In *Final Report of the Industrie 4.0*, 2013.
Sami Kara et al. Closed-loop systems to circular economy: A pathway to environmental sustainability? *CIRP Annals*, 71(2):505–528, 2022.
Iqra Sadaf Khan, Muhammad Ovais Ahmad, and Jukka Majava. Industry 4.0 and sustainable development: A systematic mapping of triple bottom line,

circular economy and sustainable business models perspectives. *Journal of Cleaner Production*, 297, 2021.

Daniel Kiel et al. Sustainable industrial value creation: Benefits and challenges of industry 4.0. *International Journal of Innovation Management*, 21(8):1740015, 2017.

Julian Kirchherr et al. Conceptualizing the circular economy (revisited): An analysis of 221 definitions. *Resources, Conservation and Recycling*, 194:107001, 2023.

Cristina Orsolin Klingenberg et al. Industry 4.0 as a data-driven paradigm: A systematic literature review on technologies. *Journal of Manufacturing Technology Management*, 32(3):570–592, 2021.

Marko Kohtamäki et al. Managing digital servitization toward smart solutions: Framing the connections between technologies, business models, and ecosystems. *Industrial Marketing Management*, 105:253–267, 2022.

Saydulu Kolasani. Revolutionizing manufacturing, making it more efficient, flexible, and intelligent with industry 4.0 innovations. *International Journal of Sustainable Development Through AI, ML and IoT*, 3(1):1–17, 2024.

Iker Laskurain-Iturbe et al. Exploring the influence of industry 4.0 technologies on the circular economy. *Journal of Cleaner Production*, 321:128944, 2021.

Jiewu Leng et al. Industry 5.0: Prospect and retrospect. *Journal of Manufacturing Systems*, 65:279–295, 2022.

Hongda Liu and Haifeng Zhao. Upgrading models, evolutionary mechanisms and vertical cases of service-oriented manufacturing in svc leading enterprises: Product-development and service-innovation for industry 4.0. *Humanities & Social Sciences Communications*, 9(1):1–24, 2022.

Ana Beatriz Lopes de Sousa Jabbour et al. When titans meet–Can industry 4.0 revolutionise the environmentally-ustainable manufacturing wave? The role of critical success factors. *Technological Forecasting and Social Change*, 132:18–25, 2018.

Yuqian Lu et al. Outlook on human-centric manufacturing towards industry 5.0. *Journal of Manufacturing Systems*, 62:612–627, 2022.

Mats Peter Winroth Machado Carla Gonçalves and Elias Hans Dener Ribeiro da Silva. Sustainable manufacturing in industry 4.0: An emerging research agenda. *International Journal of Production Research*, 58(5):1462–1484, 2020.

Praveen Kumar Reddy Maddikunta et al. Industry 5.0: A survey on enabling technologies and potential applications. *Journal of Industrial Information Integration*, 26:100257, 2022.

Marcello M Mariani, Isa Machado, and Satish Nambisan. Types of innovation and artificial intelligence: A systematic quantitative literature review and research agenda. *Journal of Business Research*, 155:113364, 2023.

Mohsen Moghaddam et al. Reference architectures for smart manufacturing: A critical review. *Journal of Manufacturing Systems*, 49:215–225, 2018.

S Venkata Mohan and Ranaprathap Katakojwala. The circular chemistry conceptual framework: A way forward to sustainability in industry 4.0. *Current Opinion in Green and Sustainable Chemistry*, 28:100427, 2021.

László Monostori et al. Cyber-physical systems in manufacturing. *CIRP Annals*, 65 (2):621–641, 2016.

Oksana Mont. Clarifying the concept of product–service system. *Journal of Cleaner Production*, 10(3):237–245, 2002.

Pieter J Mosterman and Justyna Zander. Industry 4.0 as a cyber-physical system study. *Software and Systems Modeling*, 15(1):17–29, 2016.

Julian Marius Müller, Daniel Kiel, and Kai-Ingo Voigt. What drives the implementation of industry 4.0? the role of opportunities and challenges in the context of sustainability. *Sustainability*, 10(1):247, 2018.

Rimsha Naeem, Marko Kohtamäki, and Vinit Parida. Artificial intelligence enabled product–service innovation: Past achievements and future directions. *Review of Managerial Science*, 2024.

Daniel Luiz Mattos Nascimento et al. Exploring industry 4.0 technologies to enable circular economy practices in a manufacturing context. *Journal of Manufacturing Technology Management*, 30(3):607–627, 2019.

Sónia Almeida Neves and António Cardoso Marques. Drivers and barriers in the transition from a linear economy to a circular economy. *Journal of Cleaner Production*, 341:130865, 2022.

Phu H. Nguyen, Shaukat Ali, and Tao Yue. Model-based security engineering for cyber-physical systems: A systematic mapping study. *Information and Software Technology*, 83:116–135, 2017.

Bernardo Nicoletti and Andrea Appolloni. Artificial intelligence for the management of servitization 5.0. *Sustainability*, 15(14):11113, 2023.

Olumide Emmanuel Oluyisola et al. Designing and developing smart production planning and control systems in the industry 4.0 era: A methodology and case study. *Journal of Intelligent Manufacturing*, 33(1):311–332, 2022.

Diana Penciuc et al. Product lifecycle management approach for integration of engineering design and lifecycle engineering. *AI EDAM*, 30(4):379–389, 2016.

Magdiel Pérez-Lara et al. Vertical and horizontal integration systems in industry 4.0. *Wireless Networks*, 26(7):4767–4775, 2020.

Shubhangini Rajput and Surya Prakash Singh. Connecting circular economy and industry 4.0. *International Journal of Information Management*, 49:98–113, 2019.

Tuija Rantala et al. Digital technologies for circular manufacturing. White paper, VTT Technical Research Centre of Finland, 2023.

Denise Reike, Walter J.V Vermeulen, and Sjors Witjes. The circular economy: New or refurbished as ce 3.0?—exploring controversies in the conceptualization of the circular economy through a focus on history and resource value retention options. *Resources, Conservation and Recycling*, 135:246–264, 2018.

Mengyang Ren and Pai Zheng. Towards smart product-service systems 2.0: A retrospect and prospect. *Advanced Engineering Informatics*, 61:101024, 2024.

Andreja Rojko. Industry 4.0 concept: Background and overview. *International Journal of Interactive Mobile Technologies*, 11(5):77–90, 2017.

Paolo Rosa et al. Assessing relations between circular economy and industry 4.0: A systematic literature review. *International Journal of Production Research*, 58 (6):1662–1687, 2020.

Jože M Rožanec et al. Human-centric artificial intelligence architecture for industry 5.0 applications. *International Journal of Production Research*, 61(20):6847–6872, 2023.

Manuel Sanchez, Ernesto Exposito, and Jose Aguilar. Industry 4.0: Survey from a system integration perspective. *International Journal of Computer Integrated Manufacturing*, 33(10–11):1017–1041, 2020.

Sebastian Saniuk, Sandra Grabowska, and Martin Straka. Identification of social and economic expectations: Contextual reasons for the transformation process of industry 4.0 into the industry 5.0 concept. *Sustainability*, 14(3):1391, 2022.

Josef-Peter Schöggl et al. Implementation of digital technologies for a circular economy and sustainability management in the manufacturing sector. *Sustainable Production and Consumption*, 35:401–420, 2023.

Gaurav Srivastava et al. *Artificial Intelligence and IoT-Assisted Sustainable Manufacturing for Industry 4.0*. Springer, 2023.

Walter R Stahel. The circular economy. *Nature*, 531(7595):435–438, 2016.

Sönnich Sönnichsen et al. The circular economy: A transformative service perspective. *Journal of Service Research*, 2024.

Saurabh Tiwari. Supply chain integration and industry 4.0: A systematic literature review. *Benchmarking: An International Journal*, 28(3):990–1030, 2021.

Ming-Lang Tseng et al. Circular economy meets industry 4.0: Can big data drive industrial symbiosis? *Resources, Conservation and Recycling*, 131:146–147, 2018.

Chris Turner et al. Industry 5.0 and the circular economy: Utilizing lca with intelligent products. *Sustainability*, 14(22):14847, 2022.

Etienne Valette, Hind Bril El-Haouzi, and Guillaume Demesure. Industry 5.0 and its technologies: A systematic literature review upon the human place into iotand cps-based industrial systems. *Computers & Industrial Engineering*, 184:109426, 2023.

Hans Vangheluwe, Juan De Lara, and Pieter J. Mosterman. An introduction to multiparadigm modelling and simulation. In *Proceedings of the AIS'2002 Conference (AI, Simulation and Planning in High Autonomy Systems), Lisboa, Portugal*, 2002.

Johannes W Veile et al. Lessons learned from industry 4.0 implementation in the german manufacturing industry. *Journal of Manufacturing Technology Management*, 31(5):977–997, 2020.

Timothy Gordon Walmsley et al. Circular integration of processes, industries, and economies. *Renewable & Sustainable Energy Reviews*, 107:507–515, 2019.

Junliang Wang et al. Big data analytics for intelligent manufacturing systems: A review. *Journal of Manufacturing Systems*, 62:738–752, 2022.

H. Winkler. Closed-loop production systems—a sustainable supply chain approach. *CIRP Journal of Manufacturing Science and Technology*, 4(3):243–246, 2011.

Erika Winquist et al. R-strategies in circular economy: Textile, battery, and agrifood value chains. Technical report, Natural Resources Institute Finland, Helsinki, 2023.

D. Wolfgang. Implementation strategy industrie 4.0 report on the results of the industrie 4.0 platform. Technical report, Bitkom eV, Alemania, 2016.

František Zezulka et al. Industry 4.0–an introduction in the phenomenon. *IFAC-PapersOnLine*, 49(25):8–12, 2016.

Ting Zheng et al. The applications of industry 4.0 technologies in manufacturing context: A systematic literature review. *International Journal of Production Research*, 59(6):1922–1954, 2021.

Ji Zhou et al. Human–cyber–physical systems (hcpss) in the context of new-generation intelligent manufacturing. *Engineering*, 5(4):624–636, 2019.

Zhijuan Zong and Yu Guan. Ai-driven intelligent data analytics and predictive analysis in industry 4.0: Transforming knowledge, innovation, and efficiency. *Journal of the Knowledge Economy*, pages 1–40, 2024.

13

Exploiting Machine Learning to Test Service Supply Scenarios: A Rescue Department Case

Mika Immonen, Heidi Huuskonen, Jouni Koivuniemi, and Jukka Hallikas

13.1 Introduction

Organizations' ability to monitor and test supply chains and processes supports adaptation to dynamic environments that enable agile strategies and optimized operations (Akter et al. 2016; Wamba et al. 2017; Yang et al. 2019). The achieved benefits of adopting novel analytics methods in decision-making are also related to increased awareness of operations risks and resiliency (Singh and Singh 2019). In practice, data-driven decision-making aims to address assessment operations and experimentation of alternative process structures where machine learning ("ML") and artificial intelligence ("AI") provide approaches for forecasting and

M. Immonen (✉) · J. Hallikas
LUT Business School, LUT University, Lappeenranta, Finland
e-mail: mika.immonen@lut.fi

H. Huuskonen
The Rescue Department of South Karelia, Lappeenranta, Finland

J. Koivuniemi
School of Engineering Sciences, LUT University, Lappeenranta, Finland

P. Aaltonen and E. Kurvinen (eds.), *Contemporary Issues in Industry 5.0*, Technology, Work and Globalization, https://doi.org/10.1007/978-3-031-74779-3_13

predicting the performance of solutions (Côrte-Real et al. 2017 2019). These analyses can focus on, for instance, supply chain planning, supplier selection and relationship prediction, supplier performance, and demand forecasting (Lima-Junior and Carpinetti 2019; Rezaei et al. 2019).

In Europe, population aging and public finance drive changes in public healthcare services, which increase the responsibility of individuals and bias independent home living as an essential environment for elderly people (Kumar et al. 2023). Changes in public health care lead to decentralized risks in residential areas from a safety management perspective and new approaches are needed to maintain awareness of urban regions, areas surrounding urban regions, and sparsely populated areas (Helminen et al. 2013; Helminen and Ristimäki 2008). In the Finnish context, 80% of people are living in or near urban regions, and the fastest-growing areas are those surrounding the urban regions of major cities. According to forecasts by the Ministry of the Interior (2016), approximately 25% of the population will be aged over 65 in 2030, and family structures are changing as well, with the number of single dwellers increasing in all age groups. To address these challenges, the harmonizing service management of rescue services and elderly service provision plays a remarkable role in guaranteeing a reasonable level of safety at home. Suburban growth also raises ethical questions about accessibility because public services are perceived as a subjective right regardless of economic, social, or geographic factors (Cordella and Willcocks 2010). As a result, novel approaches for assessing the risks and performance of safety management are needed to address challenges in changing operational environments.

The empirical context of this chapter connects predictive analytics to population changes and societal challenges, which are observed via an empirical performance assessment of a rescue department. In particular, focusing on the role of ML and AI as solutions to better understand the challenges of demographic shifts and operational complexities highlights Industry 5.0's human-centric, technology-enabled approach. The discussion on AI's role in advancing proactive risk management also connects the topic to data analytics premises indicating the potential of rescue services and healthcare data. Finally, the effectiveness of public services enabled via ML and AI represents an interaction that merges technological advancements with a focus on human well-being, hence embodying the principles of Industry 5.0.

This chapter demonstrates an ML-based approach to improve preparedness management in critical public services (Ghasemaghaei 2019) that relies on an artificial neural network regression model ("ANN") for enabling experiments of service system performance. This approach connects supply chain design with data analytics and employs empirical research to demonstrate the use of evidence-based approaches in public service performance management. The empirical context of the discussion wraps around the critical services of societies, where long-term changes or sudden societal shocks can cause disruptions to the public service supply and demand. Managing the effects of shocks requires systemic resiliency, which involves flexibility, redundancy, durability, collaboration, and financial stability to manage risks, mitigate immediate impacts, and restore operations (Pettit et al. 2013).

The present empirical study describes the datasets and outlines the modeling process for the experimentation of a service system. The empirical case focuses on building an estimator of accessibility for a rescue service network in residential areas in which societal changes and healthcare reforms drive fire station network reconfiguration. The data include emergency register data that are enriched with geospatial variables (demographic descriptors, geocoding building data, and route data). An empirical study utilized integrated data for training ANNs. The trained model enables scenario modeling for response time estimates of rescue services for commercial and residential buildings in a specific region. ANNs are selected as the regression method in this study because of their efficiency and adaptability in predictive modeling and their decision support for a variety of complex multivariate questions related to risk assessment (Lima-Junior and Carpinetti 2019; Rezaei et al. 2019; Tsai and Hung 2016). From a methodological perspective, this approach provides a protocol for testing the supply networks of other time-critical services and includes a baseline comparison of the ANN model with a linear regression model to justify the trained model.

13.2 Background of Supply Chain Resiliency

13.2.1 Risk and Information Management

Currently, risk management is progressively addressing vulnerabilities originating from supply chains and networks. This change signifies a deeper understanding of how organizations function as interlinked delivery systems or chains, appreciating the mix of external and internal resources necessary for an entity's operational tasks. These resources, which include suppliers of materials and services, subcontractors, and partners, are vital for upholding and boosting operational efficiency and competitive advantage (Choi and Wu 2009).

In the supply network context, information processing theory provides a background for modern risk management approaches because there is an increasing need to align information systems with risk management processes (Fan et al. 2017). In practice, collecting, processing, and sharing risk-related supply chain information are key tasks in risk management and should lead to improved capabilities or routines for organizations to detect, prevent, respond to, and recover from sudden changes in an operational environment (Fan et al. 2017; Vedel and Ellegaard 2013). Improved risk information-sharing also enhances proactive risk management capabilities in operations (Christopher and Lee 2004; Harju et al. 2023), which has proven to positively influence organizational performance (Fan et al. 2017)(Fan et al. 2017).

13.2.2 Demand Risk Management in Service Supply Chains

Supply chain disruption management is based on knowing how vulnerable the supply chain is (Wagner and Neshat 2012) and what kinds of disruptions can upset it (Wagner and Bode 2006). Indeed, managing risks in supply chains focuses on processes that include actors from multiple organizations that also link structural configurations as a unit of analysis, including both physical and information flow (Munir et al. 2020; Saha and Rathore 2024). Recognizing how different supply chain design options affect vulnerability is important because, depending on those design choices, different disruptions can occur; that is, the exposure to disruptions depends on the design choices of the supply chain (Chopra and Sodhi 2014; Wagner and Bode 2006). In particular, amid increasing digitalization and operational complexity, effectively managing structural complexity in supply chains is critical for mitigating inherent vulnerabilities and minimizing their impact on operational continuity and stability (Guo et al. 2024). Supply risks are the probability of an incident associated with an inbound supply from an individual supplier failure or the occurrence of a supply market (Zsidisin 2003). This definition encapsulates both the likelihood and impact dimensions of risk (Colicchia and Strozzi 2012), underscoring the goal of risk management to minimize both the possibility and impact of adverse events. The traditional approach to supply risk management, which offers numerous benefits for adequately executing the risk management process, spans risk identification, risk assessment, risk mitigation, risk performance, and continuous improvement (Kern et al. 2012). Building on this foundation, risk factors can generally include demand-side, supply-side, internal, and external factors, the latter of which are identified as the primary drivers (Guo et al. 2024). This is because a supply chain transmits demand information downstream to support management decisions.

Nonetheless, as demand information passes through a supply chain, it often becomes distorted (Sharma et al. 2023). The extent of this distortion significantly influences supply chain vulnerability, particularly in scenarios where chains are heavily reliant on market demands, further complicating the management and mitigation of supply risk. In addition, demand risk is an important dimension of supply chain risk. The reasons for demand risks include, for example, demand volatility and the consequent difficulty in predicting demand (Sodhi 2005). The literature shows that the low versus high unpredictability of demand has a moderating effect on supply chain volatility. When demand is relatively unpredictable, cross-functional integration should be able to manage variability in supply chain processes, thereby contributing to better performance (Germain et al. 2007). Improving supply chain visibility is regarded as an important mitigation strategy to help minimize the severity of supply chain disruptions caused by demand risks (Sodhi 2005). By improving forecasting models, it is possible to better anticipate changes in demand and reduce the uncertainty and risks related to demand (De Treville et al. 2014).

13.2.3 Supply Chain Resiliency

Resilience reflects the system's ability to recognize, anticipate, cope with, and recover from disruptions (Francis and Bekera 2014; Sheffi and Rice 2005). Managing resiliency requires competent organizations that can effectively adopt resources and strategies to anticipate the outcomes of disruptions in their operational environments, which are those capabilities that can positively affect firm performance (Lee and Rha 2016). The literature also shows that, in the realm of data analytics, firms need competencies in leveraging both internal and external data, enhancing analytics skills, and responding to early warnings, suggesting that viewing digitalization and supply chain resilience as strategic investments can foster strategic positioning and potentially improve expected performance (El Baz and Ruel 2024).

The ability to respond and recover quickly from disruptions is a key feature of a resilient organization's performance (Jüttner and Maklan 2011). Both proactive and reactive capabilities are important for improving supply chain system resilience under pre- and post-disaster conditions (Chowdhury and Quaddus 2017). Here, reactive resilience is the ability of an organization to respond and recover from disruptions (Sheffi and Rice 2005), while proactive resilience refers to the ability of a system to build capabilities, such as flexibility, redundancy, durability, collaboration, and financial stability (Pettit et al. 2013). Because certain features of supply chain design improve resilience, they need to be considered in the design process (Christopher and Lee 2004). Finally, there can also be predictive resilience, which predicts future exposure based on past performance data. In this case, the user can predict a problem before it occurs and offer mitigation strategies (Blackhurst et al. 2008).

Studies have highlighted the requirements and influencing factors for building resilience. Resilience development requires organizations to be disruption-oriented and have the resources to define and implement a risk management infrastructure (Chowdhury and Quaddus 2017). Resilience can be enhanced by supply chain planning strategies, collaboration, agility, and the creation of a risk management culture (Christopher and Lee 2004). Resiliency is also rooted in information-sharing capability throughout the supply chain and in the structure of the supply chain. Information-sharing and integration capabilities should cover both suppliers and customers, and network structures should be aligned to decrease risks that could negatively affect the overall performance of the supply chain (Ledwoch et al. 2018; Munir et al. 2020). Therefore, organizations need processes to support information processing so that big data analytics can be used to effectively anticipate and monitor supply chain disruptions (Gunasekaran et al. 2017). Information capability has been found to have a positive effect on supply chain resilience through supply chain visibility (Brandon-Jones et al. 2014), the creation of which depends significantly on the development of a company's analytical skills (Srinivasan and Swink 2018).

13.3 Methods

13.3.1 Process For Estimating Scenarios of Rescue Service Performance

In the current study, the assessment of service network responsiveness was based on an ANN regression model that produces estimates of operational response times for the rescue service system. The aim was to produce a "normal state"—estimates that do not take into account spatiotemporal variations in environmental conditions (traffic, weather, etc.). The final model excludes the spatiotemporal variables because of the limited cases in the training data, making it infeasible to add these contextual variables. Adding contextual variables results in an overly narrow sample for each condition, compromising the model's applicability and robustness.

The model utilized derived spatial data for commercial and residential buildings in the area, including the shortest distance to fire stations and agglomerations, an estimate of the shortest route length and duration to fire stations and the population density of an area, and the density of its built environment (1/km^2). Operational modeling was carried out in four main phases: (1) enriching the dataset from the statistics system of Finnish rescue services (PRONTO, a system for monitoring and developing rescue operations and resolving accidents), (2) training and validating a neural network estimator, (3) cross-validating the candidate ANN and (4) producing responsiveness scenarios for the modified fire station networks.

In the first phase of the analysis, source data were augmented by geocoding the addresses via the OpenStreetMap (REST/API) service and generating path lengths between the accident and the nearest fire station in the OpenStreetMap RouteMachine (REST/API) local service. The events in the source data were also accompanied by descriptive variables of the environment from the following: (i) open information by postal code area (PAAVO) and (ii) addresses of buildings (avoindata.fi). The second phase focused on (1) finding significant variables and (2) constructing an estimator. The selected features were distance variables and population density indicators. The selected variables encompassed distance metrics, capturing spatial relationships between addresses and nearby amenities, such as fire stations, while population density indicators were incorporated to account for variations in human settlement patterns, providing insights into potential risk factors. Here, the aim was to offer a comprehensive understanding of the spatial dynamics that influence addresses. Furthermore, recognizing the importance of contextual information for accurate predictions, indications were provided to the neural network regarding the regional context of distant locations, ensuring a more nuanced analysis of spatial patterns in addresses.

The second phase focused on creating an estimator. The neural network was chosen as a regression estimator (Fig. 13.1) because (1) the dependencies were nonlinear and (2) the environmental variables were categorical (Zhang 2004). Before the final estimation of the service scenarios, the neural network model was validated for estimation error and explanation power by comparing outputs to observations and linear

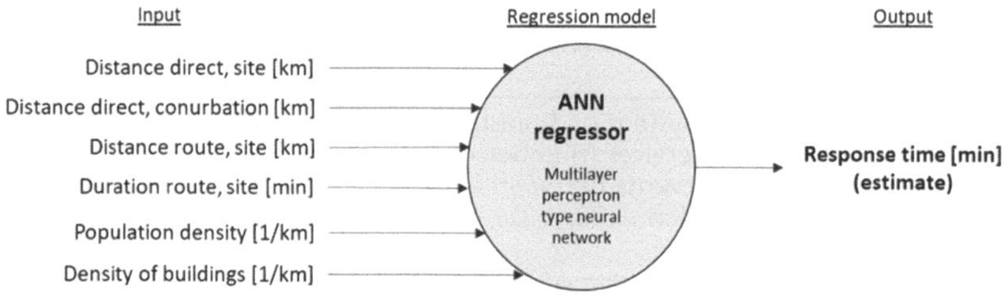

Fig. 13.1 Regression model to explain response times

estimates. In the third step, the ANN regressor was used to investigate three fire station network scenarios: (a) only permanent fire stations (no contract firefighters), (b) the existing service network (permanent and contract fire brigades), and (c) the existing service network with decentralized mobile complements.

13.3.2 Description of the Data

The research data can be divided into two groups at the general level: controlled data and open data sources. The data sources are summarized by title, description, format, and comments on availability in Table 13.1. The controlled data are from PRONTO and are used as the core data for model training. Access to PRONTO data is controlled by research permits. Open data can be divided into two groups according to the technical interface: (1) internet distributions of tabular formats (spreadsheets, CSV files, etc.) and (2) distributions via application programming interfaces (APIs). Tabular data typically include regional-level descriptions that contain aggregated summaries of the base data. APIs provide detailed information regarding a specific unit or time point. Because the information received from APIs is in machine-readable form (typically JSON or XML responses), the analysis requires further processing of the data. In the present study, regional statistics were gathered from open datasets across different interfaces, ranging from zip code-linked data to location coordinates.

Table 13.1 Applied data sources of the study

Data source	Description	Format	Data access
PRONTO	Statistics system of finnish rescue services (number of service events between 2007 and 2016 *n* = 22,153) *Key content: type of mission, timestamp, location*	Tabular data (SQL query)	Emergency services college/ research permit *a*
Building locations	Location data of buildings in Finland (*n* = 60,000 building IDs) *Key content: province, municipality, street address, postal area code coordinates (WGS84)*	Tabular data (download)	Population register centre/ open data
PAAVO	Open data by postal code area *Key content: population structure, buildings and dwellings, workplaces, main activities of the inhabitants*	Tabular data (download)	Statistics finland/ open data
OSM nominatim	OpenStreetMap (OSM) is a collaborative project designed to create a free editable map of the world *Key content: geocoding, reverse geocoding, route machine*	Interface (REST/API)	Nominatim API*b*, Open data
OSM routing	OpenStreetMap (OSM) is a collaborative project designed to create a free editable map of the world *Key content: geocoding, reverse geocoding, route machine*	Interface (REST/API)	OSRM virtual server *b, c, d*, Open data

13.3.3 ML Model Selection, Training, and Validation

The data content and objective of the research model defined the guidelines for ML algorithm selection. The data collected from a variety of sources included numeric inputs for the model, which could be interpreted categorically in certain cases, and the model should, in this case, include system features for predictions (Tsai and Hung 2016). The model building included two steps: (1) hyperparameter optimization and (2) model validation and cross-validation (Lima-Junior and Carpinetti 2019). To develop the most appropriate regression model, we tested ANN configurations (i.e., topology) defined by the number of hidden layers and neurons and employed training iterations to adjust the level of accuracy. The goal of these phases was to estimate the gradient descent of the training to avoid any remarkable overfitting or underfitting of the solution (Hastie et al. 2017). The KNIME Analytics Platform v3.7 was used for data preparation, model training, validation, and deployment of the model.

Valid cases of service response times from PRONTO provided reference data for ANN construction and training. The network type selected was a fully connected neural network. The training and validation data began from a random split of the data into training (80%) and validation (20%) sets. The model validation process also included the repetition of the random splits to check the robustness of the solutions. The performance of each construct was measured by cost functions, explanatory power (R^2), and the root-mean-square error of estimation (RMSE) (Metsämuuronen 2017).

The optimal structure of the ANN was determined in a two-step process: (1) the number of hidden layers was determined using a fixed number of neurons for each layer, and (2) the number of neurons in each layer was later iterated. Each iteration included a comparison of the given results with the observed response times, from which the performance was evaluated by cost functions. The structural configuration was defined with a fixed rate of iterations ($n = 200$), leading to six hidden layers and 50 neurons. The training rate was optimized by repeating the process from 50 to 800 iterations; the optimal level was found to be 100 iterations. The modeling errors were interpreted, and no clear trends were found (Fig. 13.2). A slight bias in the ANN may still occur because training and validation data have significantly higher counts of events at short distances, which follows the distribution of the population (Fig. 13.2c, d).

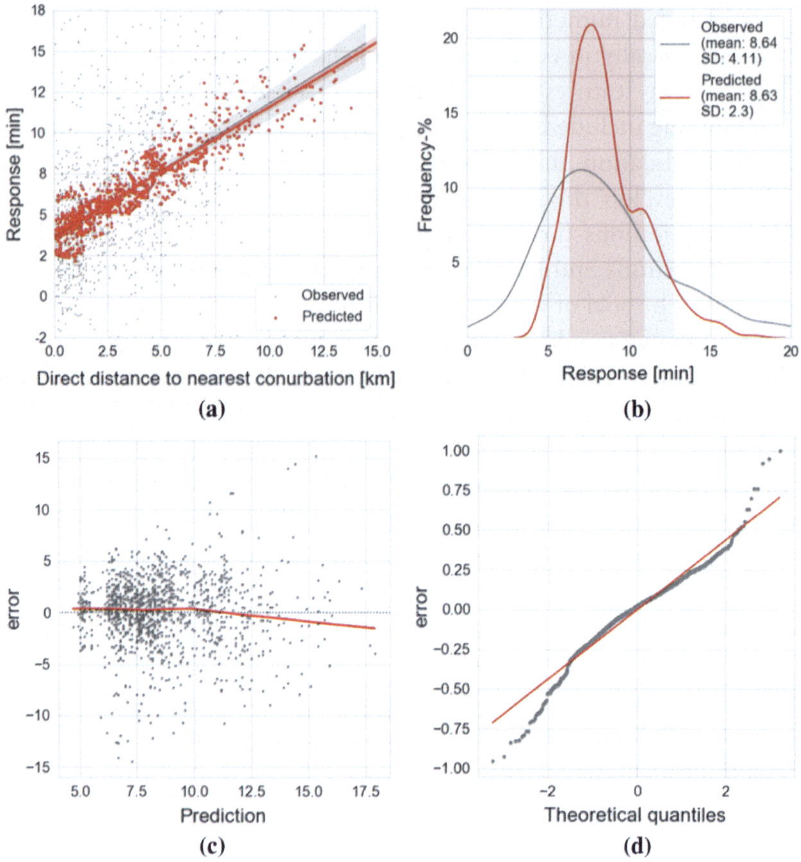

Fig. 13.2 Model validation

Finally, the optimized ANN was compared with an ordinary linear regression model to validate the ANN modeling approach against the baseline model (Table 13.2). The significant difference between the estimates, and the observed values was also tested. The developed ANN model was found to provide more accurate estimates than the linear regression model in terms of both estimation error and degree of explanation. No statistically significant differences were observed between the estimates and observations.

Table 13.2 Comparison of the ANN and linear regression models

	ANN[a] regression	Linear regression
Fit		
R-sqr	0.5	0.33
RMSE	362.7	386.05
Difference of means	Observation to prediction (paired sample *t*-test)	
	T; *df*; *p* (2-tailed)	*T*; *df*; *p* (2-tailed)
	− 0.42; 1166; 0.67	0.05; 1166; 0.96

In the final phase of testing, we aimed to assess the sensitivity of model training to sampling bias by using a random sampling cross-validation method (Lima-Junior and Carpinetti 2019). The cross-validation process was based on repeating the model training 400 times with resampled data, in which the sampling parameters were equal to those used in the model development phase. During model validation, the random decision forest algorithm ("RDF") was also tested as a competing solution. Experience shows that the RDF was not a suitable estimator for this case because cross-validation revealed remarkably high sensitivity to the training dataset. In other words, estimates from the RDF depend heavily on the biases of the sample, limiting its potential for generalizations.

A comparison of the cross-validation results between the ANN and linear regression models was accomplished using the explanatory power of the models as an indicator (see Fig. 13.3). The mean values of the R^2 model were 0.43 (SD 0.03) for the ANN model and 0.31 (SD 0.02) for the linear regression model. From the model comparison, we can conclude that neural networks provide greater accuracy and explanatory power over phenomena when dealing with the problems of a geospatial-related dataset. However, ANNs appear to be sensitive to training set bias, which can be seen in the seemingly wider variation in the explanatory power. To conclude, the neural network appears to produce an estimate of the response that is reasonably clear of random contextual variations.

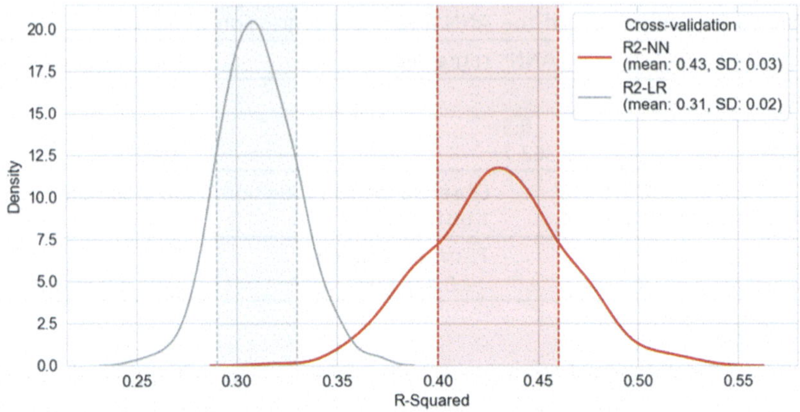

Fig. 13.3 Cross-validation of the ANN (red) and linear regression (grey) models using R^2 as an indicator

13.4 Findings

The regression model developed in the third and final steps of the analysis was used to examine three fire station network scenarios: (a) permanent fire stations only (no contract fire departments) (4 units), (b) existing service networks (permanent and contract fire departments) (22 units) and (c) existing service networks reinforced with decentralized units (29 units). The latter scenario is particularly interesting from the perspective of living at home as the relative share of first-response tasks increases. In scenario modeling, the first step was to generate input variables for all real estate in the region, which was grounded in the specifications described in the research model. A trained neural network (6 hidden layers, 50 neurons per layer, 100 iterations) was used to produce response time estimates for 60,366 property IDs in the given service network scenarios, the distributions of which were subsequently compared (Fig. 13.4).

The significant difference in the means of the response time estimates was assessed by a nonparametric Kruskal–Wallis test to detect variations in the service network performance. At the system-wide level, statistically significant differences ($p < 0.001$) were found in the means as follows: (a) Scenario 1 → Scenario 2: – 0.31 min, (b) Scenario 2 → Scenario 3: – 0.25 min, and (c) Scenario 1 → Scenario 3: – 0.57 min (Table 13.3).

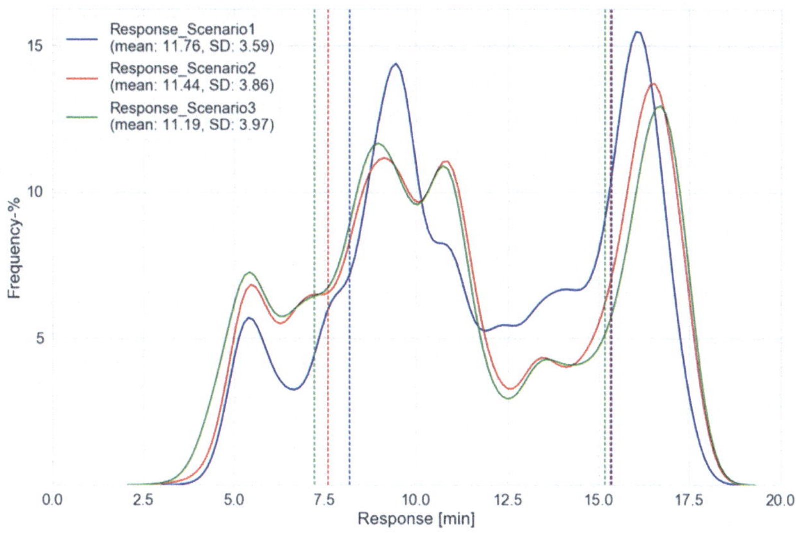

Fig. 13.4 Scenario results and distribution of estimates

In the analyzed region, city centers did not vary between the scenarios, but their areas were small, covering only several blocks. The magnitude of the effects of changes in the service network seems to dissolve further away from the borders of the suburbs about distance, which is reflected in a decreasing change between scenarios in distant rural residential areas. Based on the neural network, the greatest impact of service network change on the estimate of property-specific response times appears to be in detached areas dominated by urban suburbs, where the response change could be several minutes. The impact of service network change, based on the neural network, on response times appears to be in the residential sectors of urban fringe areas. The illustrations in Figs. 13.5, 13.6, and 13.7 (scenarios 1, 2, and 3, respectively) show the shifts in response times in the analyzed region.

Table 13.3 Data summary for different scenarios

	Response, predicted (std. deviation)		
	Scenario 1	Scenario 2	Scenario 3
General descriptors			
Mean	11.76 (3.59)	11.44 (3.86)	11.19 (3.97)
Median	11.28	10.86	10.65
Minimum	4.26	3.44	3.44
Maximum	17.80	17.90	17.90
Results for specific types of area			
Dense city centres	6 (1.9)	6 (1.9)	6 (1.8)
Dense suburban	8.4 (2)	8 (1.9)	7.6 (1.9)
Urban fringe	10.6 (2.8)	10.1 (3)	9.7 (3)
Rural areas	13.5 (2.9)	13.2 (3.4)	12.9 (3.5)

13.5 Discussion

Driven by global megatrends, the role of home living as an essential environment for elderly people is growing, and new, flexible ways to manage safety-related risks are needed. To optimize the safety of aging residents, specific information about organizations related to risk management and dedicated service supply chains for safety networks and well-being actors is needed. In aging societies, decentralized services are believed to be one answer to the challenges they present, but there have been no systematic approaches to comparing the effectiveness of different implementation approaches at the system level. A combination of the current service chain structure and new kinds of decentralized service units seems to be the most optimized alternative for the production of rescue services. This result is due to the changes in the operational environment, in which the rescue services provided by public authorities need to offset the increasing demands of safety services through a more information-based, dynamically formed, and precisely targeted combination of performances. In this context, modern ML-based solutions offer great potential for producing the novel information needed for the reformulation of public services and for future increases in their productivity and quality.

In the development of knowledge-based management and the required technology, the scalability and transferability of procedures outside the

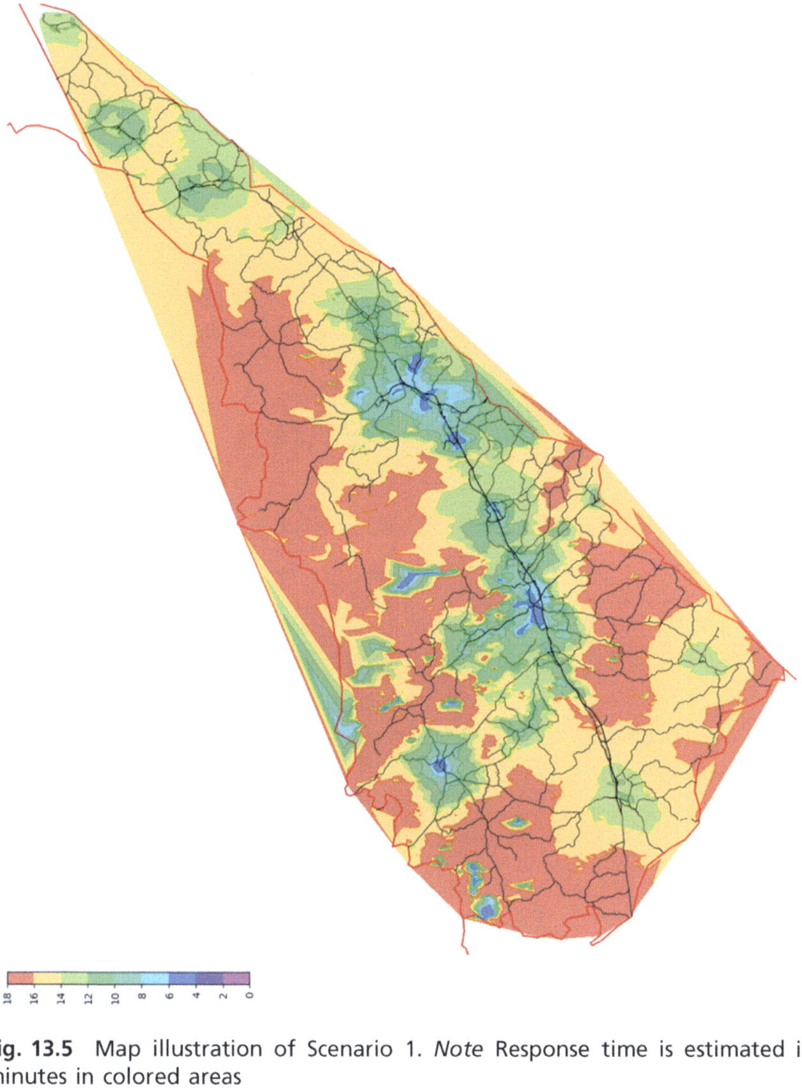

Fig. 13.5 Map illustration of Scenario 1. *Note* Response time is estimated in minutes in colored areas

development environment must also be considered. In the context of the present study, the national scalability of predictive data models is especially critical. The complexity of the required data, the sensitivity of the contents, the degree of modification of the data, permission, and the

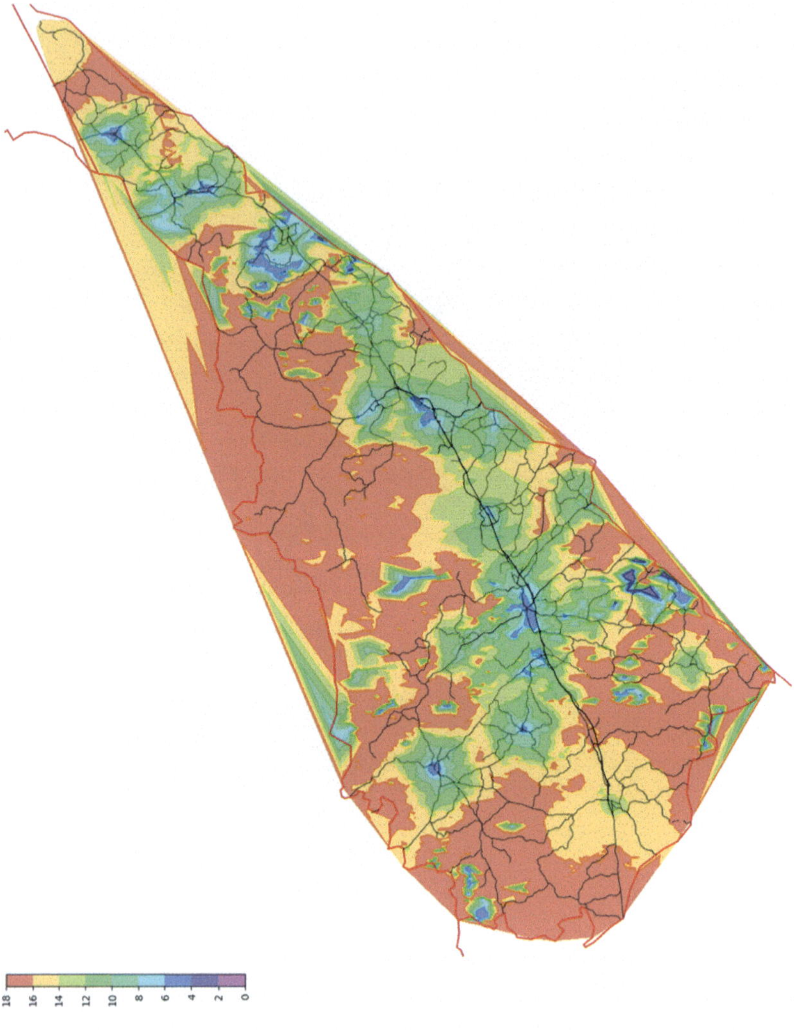

Fig. 13.6 Map illustration of Scenario 2. *Note* Response time is estimated in minutes in colored areas

availability of programming interfaces define the potential of the models for wide-scale utilization. Indeed, data enrichment processes influence the overall quality of the data if some critical data points are missing from the registry datasets. For instance, the geocoding phase was a major cause

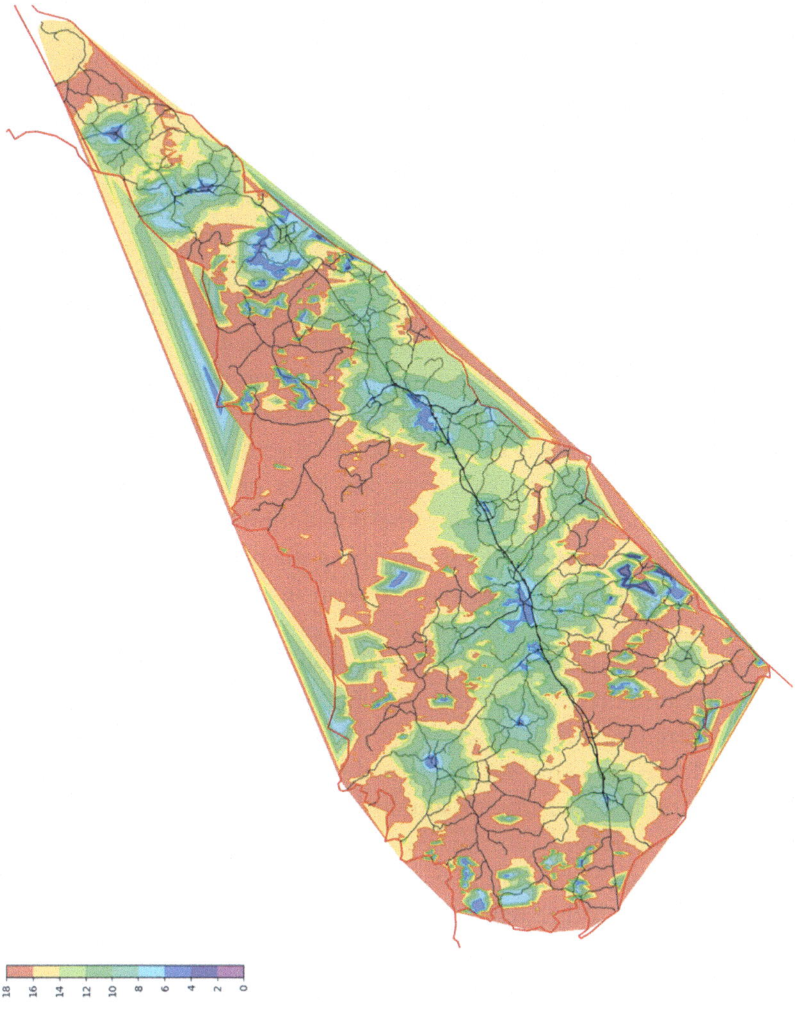

Fig. 13.7 Illustration of the Map of Scenario 3

of wasting data to be included in the training dataset because the correctness of the address fields in the registers and the technical characteristics of the interface affected the result. The structure of the data is also relatively heavy and complex, hence affecting the ease and replenishment of changes. In future phases, the data needs of spatial datasets and other models based on register data should be critically examined so that the models contain as few variables as possible. By minimizing the number of variables, the size of the model can be reduced. By optimizing the size of the models, the number of relevant features can also be increased, which has an impact on usability. In the future, the accuracy requirements of the presented data must be clarified. This will enable informed decision-making regarding the appropriate use of map tiles, statistical regions, or other region types for reporting data accuracy. In the current situation, a model at the national level could, for example, be based on statistical regions for which population data are openly available.

In the future, incorporating national information systems into process definitions will facilitate easier implementation of modeling across different counties. On the other hand, all other data are at the national level, from which the relevant sections have been selected for analysis. Further studies should utilize the population grid level of Statistics Finland as the basic geometry for describing the population and building an environment that increases the variation in input data and the resolution of the model. From the perspective of the usability of the spatial data model, it is essential to identify the confidentiality and location of the data because these factors affect the use of the data from the perspectives of different actors. The sensitivity of information must be assessed, and confidentiality issues must be resolved throughout the network of actors. Solutions to sensitivity should be sought through access rights and the aggregation of information to certain regions, where the data must be aggregated into spatial data so that data concerning individuals disappear. On the other hand, sensitivity and security concerns can be reduced by data-sharing platforms, which control access to data at user-level credentials and where properly developed interfaces also enable the monitoring of use.

13.6 Conclusions

Prior studies have highlighted the potential of applying big data analytics in supply chain risk management (Wang et al. 2016) to effectively anticipate and monitor supply chain disruptions (Gunasekaran et al.

2017). The presented case study provides a novel approach for integrating information processing into the risk management of supply chain systems. Based on the case study, the applications of data analytics in risk management were shown to be especially useful in accident prevention, responsiveness, and the development of proactive supply chain risk management. The current study has further developed the earlier findings of (Fan et al. 2017), who align risk management practices such as preventing, detecting, responding, and recovering with effective information processing systems in supply chains.

Furthermore, the present study contributes to supply chain resiliency research by illustrating the potential of data analytics in developing such resiliency. The study findings provide direct evidence for the development of proactive resiliency and risk management through advanced data analytics. Here, resilience refers to the capabilities built into the system, such as flexibility, redundancy, durability, collaboration, and financial stability against disruptions (Pettit et al. 2013). Moreover, based on the presented case study, there appears to be a high potential for building operational resiliency in supply chains through the utilization of real-time information from big data sources. Therefore, this utilization in risk management can be suggested as an important future research area.

This chapter aims to assess ML as a research approach for service provision performance in alternative service supply network scenarios. The present study contributes to the literature by providing an approach for utilizing complex data while framing a technique to test supply chain structures that support the management of resiliency in service provision networks as well as anticipate dynamics in environments (Akter et al. 2016; Ledwoch et al. 2018; Munir et al. 2020; Wamba et al. 2017; Yang et al. 2019). The present study has demonstrated a method for utilizing a trained ANN for scenario modeling within a bounded geographical area. The case consisted of an operational area (address space) of a single rescue facility for which response estimates were provided. The research data included two types of sources: controlled data and open data. The controlled data comprised rescue events from PRONTO, which included $n = 22{,}153$ service events covering the years 2007–2016. Core data were also acquired from PRONTO for model training, providing response time references for locations. The open datasets included data from internet distributions in tabular formats and distributions via APIs, which were applied to enrich the core dataset. The method found statistically significant differences between scenarios in the average response times, both in the whole dataset and locally, based on visual inspection.

The developed method has the potential for further development in testing the resilience of critical public services and assessing the impact of competing service systems. In addition, the optimization of performance provided by multiple actors in network-based structures for risk prevention and management needs to be specifically assessed in the future. Concerning a particular purpose, further development should consider temporal variations that can significantly affect occasional performance. We also need more research and a comparison of ML modeling approaches in general and with geospatial data. The adaptability of ML models needs to be further studied. The presented model is relatively reliable in densely populated areas for two reasons. Sufficient training data are available from the regions such that the model can vary the estimates according to the situation. In addition, the homogeneity of the area's structure and traffic conditions enhances the model's generalizability. In sparsely populated areas, the challenges are particularly related to obtaining sufficiently large amounts of teaching and validation data from only one administrative area. Based on the observed biases, further research should focus on developing sufficient validation procedures for deep learning models because the importance, significance, and reliability of predictors are difficult to validate. Thus, the lack of validation procedures remarkably limits the generalizability of deep learning for scientific research purposes. Further research should also provide more comparative studies between classic statistical methods (e.g., linear models), ML (e.g., decision trees), and deep learning (e.g., ANNs) to create standard rules for model selection by research problems, data features, and the volume of available research data.

The servitization of ANN models is a key prerequisite for their wider deployment and utilization in practical means. First, the models should be produced into programming interfaces that enable their integration into the management systems of rescue departments to support the creation of an up-to-date risk situational picture. Second, the planning and specification of platform requirements are essential steps in the productization process from the provider side. These are followed by the technical implementation of interfaces that enable access to the trained models. These procedures require further research to connect data management, AI development, and service design into a consistent framework. One important direction for further research is a discussion of the data quality and volume for modeling algorithm selection. From a supply chain management perspective, more research is needed to study approaches for effectively utilizing the signals derived from predictive modeling. Finally, additional studies that focus on the requisite organizational capabilities are needed to use complex datasets.

References

S. Akter et al. How can firm performance be improved through the use of big data analytics capability and business strategy alignment? *International Journal of Production Economics*, 182:113–131, 2016.

J. V. Blackhurst, K. P. Scheibe, and D. J. Johnson. Supplier risk assessment and monitoring for the automotive industry. *International Journal of Physical Distribution & Logistics Management*, 38(2):143–165, 2008.

E. Brandon-Jones, B. Squire, C. W. Autry, and K. J. Petersen. A contingent resource-based perspective of supply chain resilience and robustness. *Journal of Supply Chain Management*, 50(3):55–73, 2014.

T. Y. Choi and Z. Wu. Taking the leap from dyads to triads: Buyer–supplier relationships in supply networks. *Journal of Purchasing and Supply Management*, 15:263–266, 2009.

S. Chopra and M. S. Sodhi. Reducing the risk of supply chain disruptions. *MIT Sloan Management Review*, 55:73–80, 2014.

M. M. H. Chowdhury and M. Quaddus. Supply chain resilience: Conceptualisation and scale development using dynamic capability theory. *International Journal of Production Economics*, 188:185–204, 2017.

M. Christopher and H. L. Lee. Mitigating supply chain risk through improved confidence. *International Journal of Physical Distribution & Logistics Management*, 35:388–396, 2004.

C. Colicchia and F. Strozzi. Supply chain risk management: A new methodology for a systematic literature review. *Supply Chain Management: An International Journal*, 17(5):403–418, 2012.

A. Cordella and L. Willcocks. Outsourcing, bureaucracy and public value: Reappraising the notion of the "contract state". *Government Information Quarterly*, 27:82–88, 2010.

N. Côrte-Real, T. Oliveira, and P. Ruivo. Assessing business value of big data analytics in european firms. *Journal of Business Research*, 70:379–390, 2017.

N. Côrte-Real, P. Ruivo, T. Oliveria, and A. Popovic. Unlocking the drivers of big data analytics value in firms. *Journal of Business Research*, 97:160–173, 2019.

S. De Treville, N. Schürhoff, L. Trigeorgis, and B. Avanzi. Optimal sourcing and lead-time reduction under evolutionary demand risk. *Production and Operations Management*, 23(12):2103–2117, 2014.

J. El Baz and S. Ruel. Achieving social performance through digitalisation and supply chain resilience in the covid-19 disruption era: An empirical examination based on a stakeholder dynamic capabilities view. *Technological Forecasting and Social Change*, 201, 2024.

H. Fan, G. Li, H. Sun, and T. Cheng. An information processing perspective on supply chain risk management: Antecedents, mechanism, and consequences. *International Journal of Production Economics*, 185:63–75, 2017.

R. Francis and B. Bekera. A metric and frameworks for resilience analysis of engineered and infrastructure systems. *Reliability Engineering & System Safety*, 121:90–103, 2014.

R. Germain, C. Claycomb, and C. Dröge. Supply chain variability, organisational structure, and performance: The moderating effect of demand unpredictability. *Journal of Operations Management*, 26(5):557–570, 2007.

M. Ghasemaghaei. Does data analytics use improve firm decision making quality? the role of knowledge sharing and data analytics competency. *Decision Support Systems*, 120:14–24, 2019. https://doi.org/10.1016/j.dss.2019.03.004.

A. Gunasekaran, T. Papadopoulos, R. Dubey, S. Fosso Wamba, S. J. Childe, B. Hazen, and S. Akter. Big data and predictive analytics for supply chain and organisational performance. *Journal of Business Research*, 70:308–317, 2017.

X. Guo, Z. Yang, J. Sun, and Y. Zhang. Impact pathways of emerging its to mitigate supply chain vulnerability: A novel dematel-ism approach based on grounded theory. *Expert Systems with Applications*, 239, 2024.

A. Harju, J. Hallikas, M. Immonen, and K. Lintukangas. The impact of procurement digitalisation on supply chain resilience: Empirical evidence from finland. *Supply Chain Management*, 28(7):62–76, 2023.

T. Hastie, R. Tibshirani, and J. Friedman. *The elements of statistical learning: Data mining inference and prediction.* Springer, 2nd edition, 2017.

V. Helminen and M. Ristimäki. Village settlement in finnish peri-urban and rural areas. Technical Report The Finnish Environment 24/2008, Ministry of Agriculture and Forestry, Helsinki, Finland, 2008.

V. Helminen, S. Vienonen, M. Ristimäki, and M. Maunula. Settlement structure and water service in sparsely populated areas until 2030. Technical Report The Finnish Environment 4/2013, Ministry of Agriculture and Forestry, Helsinki, Finland, 2013.

U. Jüttner and S. Maklan. Supply chain resilience in the global financial crisis: An empirical study. *Supply Chain Management*, 16(4):246–259, 2011.

D. Kern, R. Moser, E. Hartmann, and M. Moder. Supply risk management: Model development and empirical analysis. *International Journal of Physical Distribution & Logistics Management*, 42:60–82, 2012.

S. Kumar, S. H. Underwood, J. L. Masters, N. A. Manley, I. Konstantzos, J. Lau, R. Haller, and L. M. Wang. Ten questions concerning smart and healthy built environments for older adults. *Building and Environment*, 244, 2023.

A. Ledwoch, H. Yasarcan, and A. Brintrup. The moderating impact of supply network topology on the effectiveness of risk management. *International Journal of Production Economics*, 197:13–26, 2018.

S. M. Lee and J. S. Rha. Ambidextrous supply chain as a dynamic capability: Building a resilient supply chain. *Management Decision*, 54(1):2–23, 2016.

F. R. Lima-Junior and L. C. R. Carpinetti. Predicting supply chain performance based on scor® metrics and multilayer perceptron neural networks. *International Journal of Production Economics*, 212:19–38, 2019.

J. Metsämuuronen. *Essentials of research methods in human sciences.* SAGE Publications India Pvt Ltd, finnish ed. edition, 2017.

M. Munir et al. Supply chain risk management and operational performance: The enabling role of supply chain integration. *International Journal of Production Economics*, 227:107667, 2020.

Ministry of the Interior. A safe and resilient finland rescue services strategy 2025. Technical Report Ministry of the Interior Publication 20/2016, Ministry of the Interior, Helsinki, Finland, 2016.

T. J. Pettit, K. L. Croxton, and J. Fiksel. Ensuring supply chain resilience: Development and implementation of an assessment tool. *Journal of Business Logistics*, 34:46–76, 2013.

S. Rezaei, S. Shokouhyar, and M. Zandieh. A neural network approach for retailer risk assessment in the aftermarket industry. *Benchmarking*, 26(5):1631–1647, 2019.

E. Saha and P. Rathore. The impact of healthcare 4.0 technologies on healthcare supply chain performance: Extending the organisational information processing theory. *Technological Forecasting and Social Change*, 201, 2024.

S. K. Sharma, P. R. Srivastava, A. Kumar, A. Jindal, and S. Gupta. Supply chain vulnerability assessment for manufacturing industry. *Annals of Operations Research*, 326(2):653–683, 2023.

Y. Sheffi and J. B. Rice. A supply chain view of the resilient enterprise. *MIT Sloan Management Review*, 47:41–48, 2005.

N. P. Singh and S. Singh. Building supply chain risk resilience: Role of big data analytics in supply chain disruption mitigation. *Benchmarking*, 26(7):2318–2342, 2019.

M. S. Sodhi. Managing demand risk in tactical supply chain planning for a global consumer electronics company. *Production and Operations Management*, 14(1): 69–79, 2005.

R. Srinivasan and M. Swink. An investigation of visibility and flexibility as complements to supply chain analytics: An organisational information processing theory perspective. *Production and Operations Management*, 27(10):1849–1867, 2018.

J. M. Tsai and S. W. Hung. Supply chain relationship quality and performance in technological turbulence: An artificial neural network approach. *International Journal of Production Research*, 54(9):2757–2770, 2016.

M. Vedel and C. Ellegaard. Supply risk management functions of sourcing intermediaries. *Supply Chain Management: An International Journal*, 18:509–522, 2013.

S. M. Wagner and C. Bode. An empirical investigation into supply chain vulnerability. *Journal of Purchasing and Supply Management*, 12:301–312, 2006.

S. M. Wagner and N. Neshat. A comparison of supply chain vulnerability indices for different categories of firms. *International Journal of Production Economics*, 50:2877–2891, 2012.

S. F. Wamba et al. Big data analytics and firm performance: Effects of dynamic capabilities. *Journal of Business Research*, 70:356–365, 2017.

G. Wang, A. Gunasekaran, E. W. Ngai, and T. Papadopoulos. Big data analytics in logistics and supply chain management: Certain investigations for research and applications. *International Journal of Production Economics*, 176:98–110, 2016.

Y. Yang, E. W. K. See-To, and S. Papagiannidis. You have not been archiving emails for no reason! using big data analytics to cluster b2b interest in products and services and link clusters to financial performance. *Industrial Marketing Management*, 86:1–14, 2019.

G. P. Zhang. *Neural networks in business forecasting*. IGI Global, 2004. https://doi.org/10.4018/978-1-59140-176-6.

G. A. Zsidisin. A grounded definition of supply risk. *Journal of Purchasing and Supply Management*, 9:217–224, 2003.

14

Boosting the Learning Process for IoT Data Utilization in Business Value

Sini-Kaisu Kinnunen, Lasse Metso, and Timo Kärri

14.1 Introduction

Companies are facing challenges in upgrading an increased amount of data into value in their business. The increased amount of data is collected with sensors and IoT-related advanced technologies, but not all data and technologies available are utilized or benefitted from as the support of decision-making, varying from operative level to managerial decisions and strategic management. Value from data can be achieved for example, by creating new business, e.g., developing data-driven services, digital services, and solutions to support decision-making. The key is understanding the process from data to decision-making, finding the technologies to support the process, and realizing the IoT solutions. (see, e.g., (Côrte-Real et al. 2020; Kinnunen, 2020, Kinnunen et al. 2018, Momeni and Martinsuo, 2018, Räikkönen et al. 2020)) IoT solutions

S.-K. Kinnunen (✉) · L. Metso · T. Kärri
LUT Industrial Engineering and Management, LUT University, Lappeenranta, Finland
e-mail: sini-kaisu.kinnunen@lut.fi

P. Aaltonen and E. Kurvinen (eds.), *Contemporary Issues in Industry 5.0*, Technology, Work and Globalization, https://doi.org/10.1007/978-3-031-74779-3_14

and artificial intelligence (AI) are essential parts of developing Industry 5.0. AI can be seen as a part of the IoT process, and it can be used to enhance the intelligence of IoT solutions, for example by automating decisions (Nolle, 2023; Vinugayathri, 2024). It has been emphasized that by combining IoT and AI, companies can enhance the power of both IoT and AI, develop more sophisticated and smart solutions, automate decision-making, increase efficiency, and achieve more value in their business (Gerlée, 2024; Nolle, 2023; Vinugayathri, 2024). However, data-driven decision-making and technology adoption are uneven in companies because companies are on a different economic scale, they lack education both in the IT department and the worker side, and they are on different levels in organizational learning (Brynjolfsson and McElheran, 2016).

Companies need new types of professionals, and this shortage of skilled workforce hinders the exploitation of advanced technologies and data utilization (see, e.g., (Brynjolfsson and McElheran, 2016; Gürdür Broo et al. 2022; Pomp et al. 2022). The actual need of companies has been the reason to develop education in this area. As a part of the Master's Programme in Industrial Engineering and Management at a Finnish university (University X), digital service processes and data analytics are taught to meet the needs of companies to get skilled professionals, who can develop new business from data and support business development with the aid of data. As a result of company collaboration, e.g., visiting lecturers and master's theses, it has been noticed that there is an increasing need for industry and the public sector to employ professionals who have skills to exploit data in business. The role of universities in transferring knowledge and skills for industrial needs, by considering the trends in scientific research and emerging technologies on artificial intelligence and IoT, has previously been studied by academics (see e.g., Gurdur Broo et al. 2022; Boltsi et al. 2024). It can be concluded that there is a need for professionals with IoT skills especially in the time of Industry 5.0, when companies should be able to take advantage of data utilization.

It is well known that to develop into a skilled expert, a person needs to apply theoretical models and frameworks, identify the need for a solution, and realize the solution with advanced technologies, such as with an IoT platform. As a part of the course "Industrial Applications of Internet of Things," a low-code/no-code solution or platform is utilized to enable students with varying computing skills to learn and develop solutions, including data models and dashboards, to support the real needs of companies. The solutions aim to meet the needs of different decision-makers, at different decision-making levels and to create value for business. Students develop solutions for various business and decision-making needs, from healthcare to maintenance management. The aim is to educate professionals on the practical needs of industry and the public sector and advance the development toward Industry 5.0 (see, e.g., Xu et al. 2021; Gürdür Broo et al. 2022).

This paper aims to develop a systematic process description that improves the student's knowledge and skills to utilize analytical IoT solutions for real decision-making needs related to business processes. The research questions are as follows:

RQ1: What kind of decision-making needs related to business processes can be solved with analytical IoT solutions?
RQ2: What kind of systematic process can support fulfilling these decision-making needs?
RQ3: How can the utilization of low-code/no-code IoT platforms support or improve the skills of students to create value for business?

As a result, the systematic process description is presented. By following the learning process, students achieve the knowledge and skills to utilize IoT solutions for the decision-making needs of companies. These learned improved skills lead to a stronger link between IoT solutions and business value, and make it possible to benefit from technology advances in creating value for business.

In this study, the research method is conceptual research where previous literature and concepts are analyzed and a systematic process description is developed. The systematic process description is based on observations from previous research and empirical observations from the first-course implementation (in 2020). The systematic process description is then tested with 19 cases, i.e., the group works that the students have done in the following course implementations. In the course, students have completed 19 group work projects during 2 years (2021–2022). The group works deal with the theoretical framework and practical IoT solution for a certain decision-making need to solve a problem. As an IoT platform, a commercial IoT tool is utilized, but the platform could be any other platform as well. The case can concern any industry, but according to the 19 cases, it can be said that maintenance management, the energy market, and healthcare are emphasized as the targets of solutions. The presented systematic learning process description responds to the need for companies to employ professionals with new skills to reap the benefits of advanced technologies and data utilization.

14.2 Literature Review

14.2.1 IoT Solution Development and Utilization

Recent literature is mainly focused on the technical development of IoT solutions, and the links to the business decision-making needs and the creation of business value are in a minor role. Although the technologies and technical solutions already exist, the actual revenues of IoT solutions have not yet met the expectations (Baltuttis et al. 2022). Several researchers have discussed the importance of defining the value creation potential of IoT solutions but stated that the value of IoT solutions is hard to define (Baltuttis et al. 2022; Kaiser et al. 2021; Kinnunen, 2020; Momeni and Martinsuo, 2018; Räikkönen et al. 2020). The focus has been on the technical perspective and how to, e.g., connect devices to the platform, do data preparation, warehousing, processing, and (advanced) analytics (Nast and Sandkuhl, 2021). IoT solutions often struggle to create business value, because the link to decision-makers is vague (Nast and Sandkuhl, 2021). The key is understanding the process from data to decision-making, finding the technologies to support the process, and realizing the IoT solutions (see, e.g., (Côrte-Real et al. 2020; Kinnunen, 2020; Kinnunen et al. 2018). When creating the solutions, the decision-making need and the decision-maker must be clear. The decision-making need defines what kind of decision-making situation it is, and what kind of data and analysis are needed to support the decision-making (Kinnunen et al. 2016).

Business value perspective is recently studied in IoT solutions (see, e.g., (Baltuttis et al. 2022; Kaiser et al. 2021), but the importance of the decision-maker is better acknowledged in business intelligence and analytics (BI&A), big data and decision support systems (DSS) literature (Phillips-Wren et al. 2021). BI&A and DSS studies discuss visualizations and user interfaces (UI), where business users and decision-makers are also emphasized. Whereas, IoT literature is highly technically oriented and not focused on the decision-maker. Only recently have some scholars acknowledged the need to also focus on business value evaluations of IoT solutions, yet the link to the decision-maker has remained vague. Thus, there needs to be collaboration with IoT solution developers and IoT solution users. The utilization of IoT solutions in creating business value requires analytical skills and business understanding from the decision-maker, including knowledge about value creation and business models. These aspects need to be emphasized more in IoT solution utilization literature as well (Baltuttis et al. 2022; Horváth and Szabó, 2019).

14.2.2 Decision-Making Level and Different Needs for Decision Support

If we consider the business value of an IoT solution, both the connections to the decision-maker and the decision-making need must be clear. This also means that the type and level of decision-making situation are defined. In general, decision-making situations can be categorized into operational-, tactical- and strategic-level decisions. These decision levels differ in type of decision, how often they occur, and how long-term the effects are. However, IoT and an increasing amount of real-time data have created a need for other types of categorizations for decision-making situations (Kinnunen et al. 2016; Sun et al. 2008). Decision-making situations can also be categorized into reactive, real-time, proactive, and strategic decisions (Kinnunen et al. 2016).

Figure 14.1 illustrates how different types of decisions are positioned with each other, when regarding the time scale, before or after an event where the decisions are made. Reactive decisions are made after an event has already occurred. The aim is to minimize the damages that are realized before corrective actions can be made (Räikkönen et al. 2020). In industry, especially in the asset management and maintenance contexts, the damages can be, for example, needed maintenance service, spare parts, and loss of production. Real-time decisions are aimed to be made just in time when something happens. Real-time decisions are often based on real-time monitoring, and the aim is to avoid damage. Proactive decisions are made before an event occurs. The aim is to predict an event or outcome, usually based on predictive models. Reactive, real-time, and proactive decisions can be seen as short-term decisions. Strategic decisions are long-term decisions and influence over the years. Strategic decisions are made long before an event or outcome occurs, and usually, extensive analyses and models can be utilized as support for decision-making. IoT solutions are not usually suitable in responding to the needs of strategic decisions, where decision-making situations and required data are often unstructured and not, e.g., routine decisions by nature. However, IoT technologies and sensors have improved the availability of real-time data that can be utilized later as support for strategic decision-making and models as well.

Thus, IoT solutions are mainly developed for the needs of operational- and tactical-level decisions. For decisions that occur relatively often and are routine decisions by nature, real-time data can bring benefits for decision-makers who work as managers, in middle management, or as experts or workers in operational tasks. Usually, top management focuses on strategic decisions, where real-time IoT data is not optimum to support long-term complex decisions. Thus, organizational hierarchy affects who the decision-maker is and the nature of the decisions they

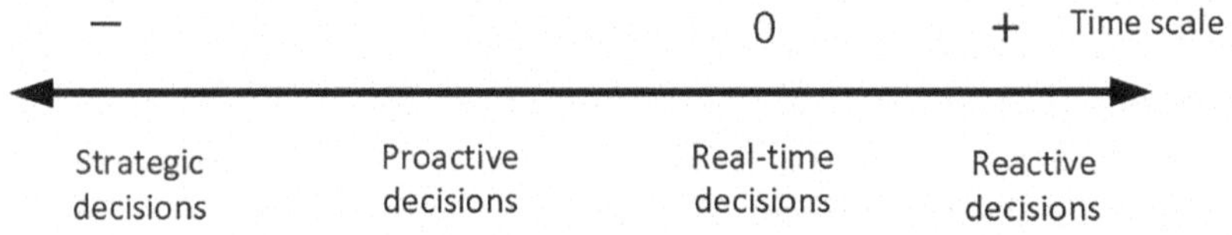

Fig. 14.1 Categorization of decision-making situations, based on time scale, before/after an event occurs (Kinnunen et al. 2016)

make. This also affects which analytics the decision-makers need or if there is a need for monitoring, analysis (reports), predictive models, or what kind of visualizations and dashboards can support the decision-making (see, e.g., Tokola et al. 2016). These are important issues to be acknowledged when developing analytical IoT solutions that can help decision-makers make the right decisions at the right times, and thus achieve the potential benefits. This link between decision-makers, decision-making types, and needs for decision support (e.g., need for monitoring, analysis, predictive models, etc.), and value in business, is not clear (Kinnunen 2020). By combining these different levels of decisions (operational, tactical, and strategic) and categorizations (reactive, real-time, and proactive decisions), we can understand better the nature of decision-making situations and the needs of decision-makers for decision support to which the IoT solutions are aiming to respond and create business value from IoT data utilization.

14.2.3 Industry 5.0 and IoT Skills

Industry 4.0 has brought on the technologies, so the technical solutions already exist, but the question is how we can intelligently benefit from them in business. Industry 5.0 has been introduced, and the emphasis is on "softer issues" and value-driven approach. The aim of Industry 5.0 is to create a sustainable, resilient, and human-centric industry. Industry 5.0 attempts to capture the value of new technologies while respecting planetary boundaries, and emphasizing the well-being of the industry worker. (Xu et al. 2021; European Commission et al. 2021). Industry 5.0 is also related to Society 5.0 which aims to solve social problems with the help of the integration of physical and virtual spaces. Industry 5.0 is expected to bridge this gap and create services and solutions that focus on social and environmental aspects by utilizing data and technological advancements. (Xu et al. 2021; Gürdür Broo et al. 2022).

Despite the introduction of the Industry 5.0 era, companies are at different levels of adaptation to Industry 4.0 and 5.0 (see, e.g., (Brynjolfsson and McElheran, 2016, Pomp et al. 2022)). Companies need skills to take advantage of technologies in creating value and acknowledging sustainability and well-being issues. Thus, new types of IoT skills are needed, but at the same time, the technology and data utilization skills are still in a key role (Cetrulo and Nuvolari, 2019; Gürdür Broo et al. 2022). Companies need to create an understanding of the changes needed and focus on training to develop employee knowledge in technologies (Horváth and Szabó, 2019). Companies need professionals with skills who understand the business value but also social, sustainability, and environmental values. It is essential to have analytical skills but also an understanding of business and the business environment. Thus, more research is needed in business models related to technologies but also both in social and economic aspects of Industry 5.0 (Gürdür Broo et al. 2022; Horváth and Szabó, 2019).

14.3 Methods and Data

This study applies a conceptual research approach, where a conceptual framework, a systematic process description, is developed based on analyzing theoretical and empirical information on IoT data utilization in creating business value (Kincheloe, 2001; Klag and Langley, 2013; Järvensivu and Törnroos, 2010). This approach combines the features of moderate constructionism and the benefits of abduction, which enables the assessment of previous theories and generates new knowledge through dialogue between theoretical conceptualization and empirical investigation (Järvensivu and Törnroos, 2010). The developed systematic process description aims to present how to utilize IoT data in business processes by creating an IoT solution for a certain decision-making need. The process description is presented in Sect. 14.4.2. The process is tested with 19 cases. The cases are 19 group work projects in the course "Industrial Applications of Internet of Things," in which students have developed IoT solutions for certain decision-making needs. Students can decide the topic of the IoT solution, and their previous work experience and background might have influenced the topic of the IoT solution. However, these cases reflect the practical needs and potential IoT data-utilization opportunities in companies. Some of the topics are related to the previous work experience of students, some topics are existing examples from companies that students have applied and some of the topics are descriptive solutions innovated by students.

The course was established in 2020, and there have been three implementations (2020–2022). The learning process was first developed for the purpose of the course 2020, based on a combination of previously presented theoretical frameworks and the experiences of the researchers. The systematic process description was further developed for the following course implementations based on empirical observations and experiences from the first implementation. The course has been developed in a way that the IoT platform was utilized in the years 2021 and 2022. The 19 cases used in this study took place in 2021 and 2022. Students create a report where they describe the IoT solution, including the decision-making need, theoretical framework, model architecture or data-to-decision process, description of IoT solution in the IoT tool and how the solution creates value for business, and for example, state the reasons the company should invest in the solution. The group work also includes a part where the students realize the solution with the IoT platform.

14.4 Process for IoT Data Utilization in Business

14.4.1 The Need for IoT Professionals

The knowledge gap is also recognized in practices in companies where the need for IoT professionals is increasing. For example, this phenomenon can be noticed in LinkedIn, which is the world's largest professional network on the internet, with more than 930 million members (LinkedIn, 2023). On LinkedIn, there were a total of 202 results, when conducting a job search 5.5.2023 with search terms "IoT" and "Finland." In Table 14.1, the results are divided by job function, in which LinkedIn filters can be used. The same job advertisement can belong to several job descriptions. Most job advertisements are in the IT sector or related to that. There is a shortage of professionals, especially in software

Table 14.1 LinkedIn job search (5.5.2023) with search terms "IoT" and "Finland" (total 202 results)

Filter	Results	Job description
Information technology	161	Software developer
Engineering	120	Software developer****IT**
Sales	17	Sales manager, product manager
Business development	13	Data-analysis, sales manager
Marketing	10	Marketing manager, sales manager
Quality assurance	5	Test automation
Consulting	4	Cloud architect
Administrative	3	AI data solutions
Human resources	3	HR
Product management	3	Product manager
Accounting/auditing	2	Accountant (electric vehicle)
Finance	2	Accountant
Other	12	

development. There are only a few jobs open for other than developing IoT software or analytics based on IoT.

The need for IoT professionals in companies is reflected in universities, where the topics of Master's theses originate from companies and their development needs. For example, the search for Master theses in a Finnish university (University X) with the keywords "IoT," "IIoT," "Internet of Things," and "Industrial Internet of Things" resulted in a total of 82 master theses from 2015 to 2022. Figure 14.2 demonstrates the number of Master's theses yearly (cumulative), and Fig. 14.3 demonstrates the number by department. It can be noticed that the numbers increased most rapidly in 2018–2019, and then the growth has been stabilized. As shown in Fig. 14.3, most of the Master's theses are done in computer science, electrical engineering industrial engineering, and management. This reflects that the IoT solution development has been rapid in software engineering and electrical engineering, but the high number of theses done by industrial engineering and management indicates that there has also been the need to apply IoT solutions in business processes. Also, several Master's theses have been related to business administration and supply management.

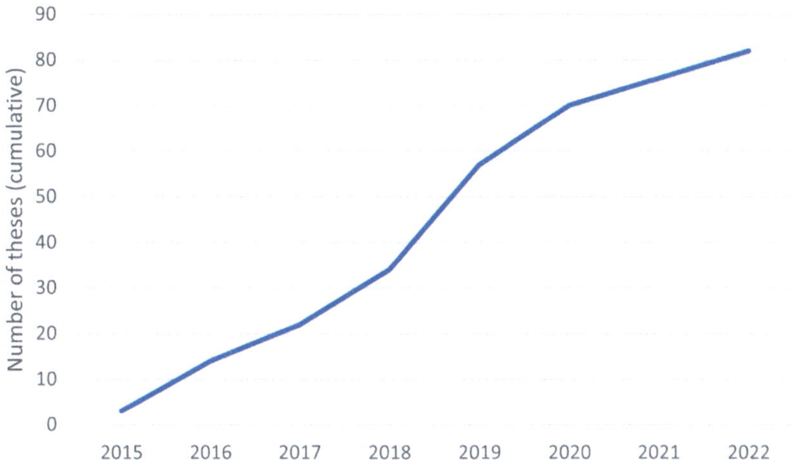

Fig. 14.2 The number of IoT-related Master's theses yearly (cumulative) in University X (2015–2022)

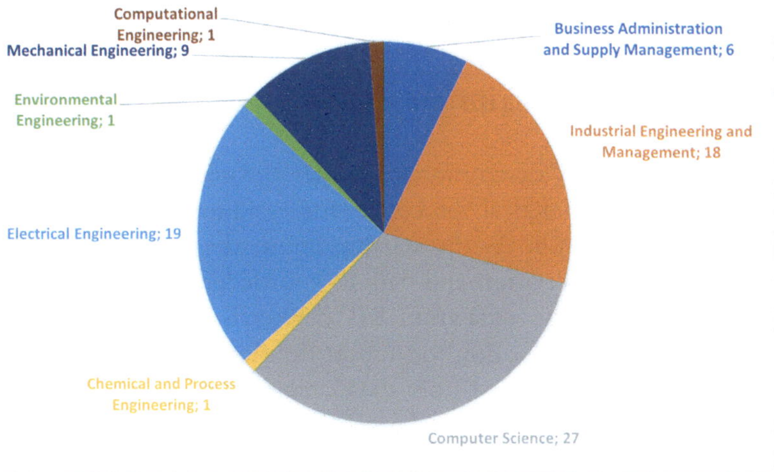

Fig. 14.3 The number of IoT-related Master's theses by department in University X (2015–2022)

To meet the need of companies to acquire skilled professionals, who can develop new businesses from data and support business development with the aid of data, teaching in the area of digital service processes and data analytics has been developed at University X. Especially, when recognizing the increasing interest around IoT technologies, a course, "Industrial Applications of Internet of Things," has been developed to increase the knowledge of students about business opportunities related to IoT technologies. As a part of the course, "Industrial Applications of Internet of Things," a low-code/no-code solution or platform is utilized to enable students with no computing skills to learn and develop solutions, including data models and dashboards, to support the real needs of companies. The solutions aim to meet the needs of different decision-makers, at different decision-making levels, and to create value for business. Students develop solutions to various business and decision-maker needs, from healthcare to maintenance management. The aim is to educate professionals on the practical needs of industry and the public sector and to advance the development toward Industry 5.0.

14.4.2 Process Description

A systematic process description combines theoretical knowledge and frameworks with practical processes and solutions. The process is presented in Fig. 14.4. As the starting point, the process description is based on data-to-decision and data-to-knowledge processes or frameworks. In other words, data from IoT devices is refined into analyses and models with visualization to support decision-making. Information or knowledge that is refined from data enables making better decisions than without that information or knowledge, which then can create value for business.

The process begins with defining the need for IoT solutions. This requires that the potential value is defined and the decision-making need is identified. After that, the process continues by defining the data sources, including, e.g., IoT devices and other data sources. In the third phase, the data model or architecture is defined, or the process from

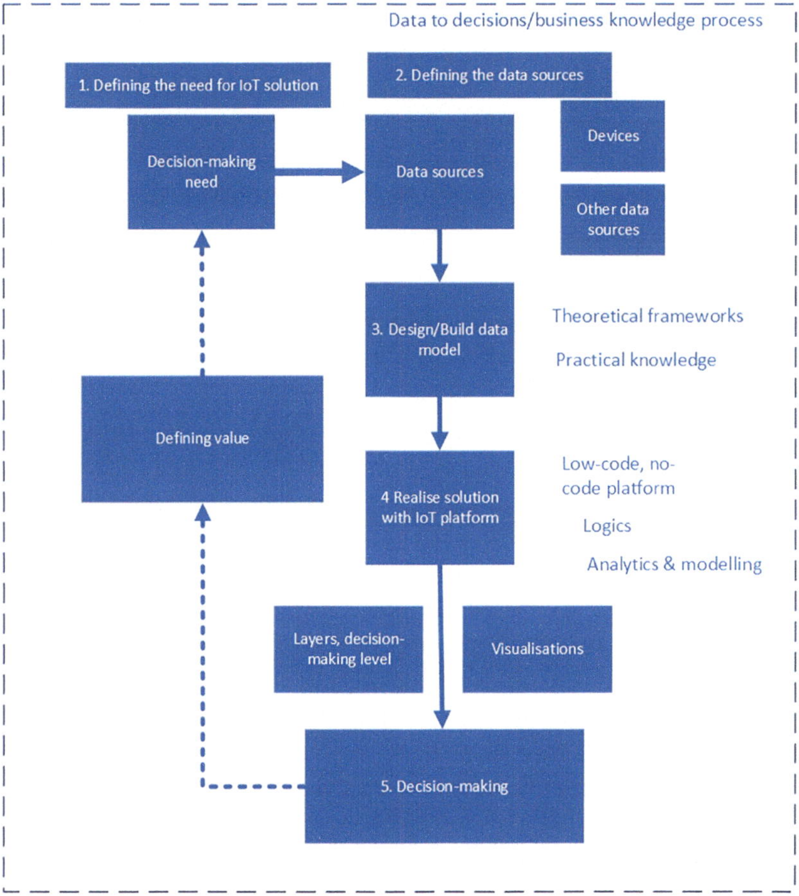

Fig. 14.4 A systematic process description for IoT data utilization in business

data to decisions is described based on theoretical frameworks and practical knowledge. This phase aims to understand the process of how data is utilized as a support of decision-making. In the fourth phase, the solution is realized with an IoT platform. Logics and the level of analysis, including analytics and modeling, (i.e., report, alarms, predictive elements) and visualizations for decision-makers, are built with low-code/no-code platforms. There can also be different layers for different decision-makers or different decision-making situations. For example, there can be an overview layer for upper-level decisions and opportunities to drill down for asset or component level. The fifth phase is decision-making, and in this phase, the IoT data is utilized in decision-making, and value is created for business. By following the systematic process for IoT data utilization, it becomes possible to improve and strengthen the abilities of students to develop their skills as professionals, and to reap the benefits of IoT technologies and data utilization.

14.4.3 Testing the Systematic Process Description: A Case Study

The developed systematic process description is tested with 19 group work projects done in the course "Industrial Applications of Internet of Things" in 2021–2022. The topics, business area, decision-making level and categorization, decision-maker, and business value, are analyzed and presented in Table 14.2.

All of the cases are based on real-time data, either on real-time data imported to the platform or simulated real-time data. Real-time data have affected the decision-making in a way that most of the decision-making situations in the cases are real-time decisions, or reactive decisions as near real-time as possible. However, some cases are reactive decisions, but real-time data bring improvements to previous decision-making when real-time monitoring has not been possible. Real-time data have also made it possible to make proactive decisions. Proactive decisions are emphasized in many cases. Figure 14.5 illustrates the distribution of different types of decision-making situations in the 19 cases. It needs to be acknowledged that some of the IoT solutions can include more than one type of decision-making situation and the solution may support all types of decisions: reactive, real-time, and proactive decisions, or just one or two of these. In some cases, it was also mentioned that the real-time data can later be utilized as history data to make a root cause analysis, or the data can be utilized in predictive models to identify behavior patterns. This can lead to improved predictive models and proactive decisions. Real-time data and history data can also be

Table 14.2 Case descriptions

	Topic/title	Business area	Decision making level and categorisation	Decision maker	Business value
G1	IoT solution for healthcare: supported living for elderly	Healthcare	Operational level, real-time data, reactive decisions	Healthcare profes-sional (or relative)	Working time savings for healthcare professional, improved quality of life for elderly
G2	IoT solution for packaging machine: production interrup-tions due to paper blocks/jam	Maintenance, industry	Operational and tactical levels, real-time data, reactive decisions	Production worker and produc-tion manager	Allocate resources to value-adding tasks, improved production processes and product quality, less production loss
G3	Increasing industry waste manage-ment	Industry waste manage-ment	Operational and tactical levels, real-time waste inventory and sales and supply data	Material manager	Cost savings in waste management, improve circular economy
G4	Protecting from the volatility of Bitcoin value in interna-tional business: monitoring the exchange risk	Blockchain or crypto-mining, exchange risk	Operational level, real-time data, reactive decisions	Finance director or manager	Avoid exchange rate losses, allocate resources to business development

(continued)

Table 14.2 (continued)

	Topic/title	Business area	Decision making level and categorisation	Decision maker	Business value
G5	IoT solution for monitoring wind power production: optimise energy production in changing conditions	Energy production and maintenance	Operational level, monitoring, real-time data, real-time and reactive decisions	Expert, operations and maintenance	Cost savings in maintenance costs, longer lifetime of components, increased production
G6	IoT hype—case hype train: condition monitoring and proactive maintenance of passenger train fleet	Maintenance, train fleet	Operational and tactical levels, real-time data, from reactive to proactive decisions	Fleet manager, different layers	Increased customer satisfaction and service quality, cost savings in claims, improved safety, cost savings in maintenance costs, cost savings in spare parts costs, less capital tied up in the fleet
G7	Smart home and smart construction: IoT-based building management system	Building management system, smart building	Operational level, real-time data, reactive decisions	Owner of a building	Increased lifetime of the building, cost savings in energy costs, safety, sustainable consumption habit

(continued)

Table 14.2 (continued)

	Topic/title	Business area	Decision making level and categorisation	Decision maker	Business value
G8	Sensor-enabled floor: preventing falls with activity monitoring	Healthcare, smart building	Operational level, real-time data, reactive and proactive decisions	Healthcare profes-sional	Fewer severe injuries, improved quality of life, working time savings of healthcare personnel, allocation of resources
G9	Smart office: IoT solution for improving working conditions	Smart building, facility services	Operational level, real-time data, real-time decisions	Maintenance manager or worker (facility)	Improved well-being of employees, improved productivity of employees, cost savings in facility maintenance
G10	IoT solution for remote monitoring of wind farm	Maintenance, windmill fleet	Operational and tactical levels, real-time data, reactive and proactive decisions (option for strategic decisions)	Operations and mainte-nance managers, different layers	Increased production, cost savings in maintenance costs

(continued)

Table 14.2 (continued)

	Topic/title	Business area	Decision making level and categorisation	Decision maker	Business value
G11	Real-time maintenance system for sewage pumping station	Maintenance, industry	Operational and tactical levels, real-time data, real-time and proactive decisions	Maintenance manager, different layers	Cost savings in maintenance and operating costs, increased utilization rate, cost savings in energy consumption, less capital tied up in spareparts inventory
G12	IoT solution for proactive industrial maintenance: case belt drive components	Maintenance, industry	Operational level, real-time data, real-time and proactive decisions	Operations and maintenance engineer	Cost savings in maintenance costs, increased production
G13	IoT solution for improving situational awareness of electricity market and grid	Energy market	Operational and tactical levels (strategic option) real-time data, reactive, real-time and proactive decisions	Power grid manager, operating engineer	Savings in electricity production and consumption, electricity sufficiency

(continued)

Table 14.2 (continued)

	Topic/title	Business area	Decision making level and categorisation	Decision maker	Business value
G14	Preventing slip injuries with IoT	Facility maintenance and services	Operational level, real-time data and forecasts, proactive decisions	Facility maintenance manager	Cost savings in maintenance services, savings in insurance compensations and healthcare costs, reduced health-related absences
G15	IoT solution for care and follow-up of diabetes	Healthcare	Operational and tactical levels, real-time data, reactive, real-time and proactive decisions	End-user (patient) and healthcare professional	Improved quality of life, decreased visits to the doctor and fewer severe attacks (due to low sugar levels), working time savings for healthcare professional, easier to make a treatment plan
G16	Data analysis of Lokotrack crusher IoT solution	Maintenance, mining industry	Operational and tactical levels, real-time data, proactive decisions	Maintenance manager	Cost savings in maintenance costs and spare parts, increased production

(continued)

Table 14.2 (continued)

	Topic/title	Business area	Decision making level and categorisation	Decision maker	Business value
G17	Smart home and IoT-based solutions: air humidity, temperature, electricity consumption	Smart building, consumer	Operational level, real-time data, reactive and real-time decisions	Owner of the building	Cost savings in energy consumption, well-being of residents
G18	Intelligent extraction ecosystem: cryptocurrency mining	Blockchain, crypto mining	Operational level, real-time data, real-time optimisation decisions	Business owner	Cost savings in energy costs, optimised profit
G19	IoT solution for improving grain logistics (grain drying)	Logistics	Operational and tactical levels, real-time data, optimization decisions (proactive decisions)	transport manager, truck fleet manager	Increased quality of product, cost savings in logistics costs, less capital tied up in the fleet

utilized as the support of strategic decisions, such as investment decisions, according to some cases. In strategic decisions, the long-term perspective is emphasized, but many of the cases were more focused on short-term operational or tactical decisions (see Fig. 14.6).

Figure 14.7 illustrates the distribution of IoT solutions for different business areas. It needs to be acknowledged that some of the IoT solutions can belong to, for example, two business areas, such as healthcare and smart building (see, e.g., G8). With these 19 cases, the business areas, such as maintenance, healthcare, smart building, and energy market, were emphasized. Even though the industry is emphasized in the form of multiple maintenance solutions, the business areas, such as

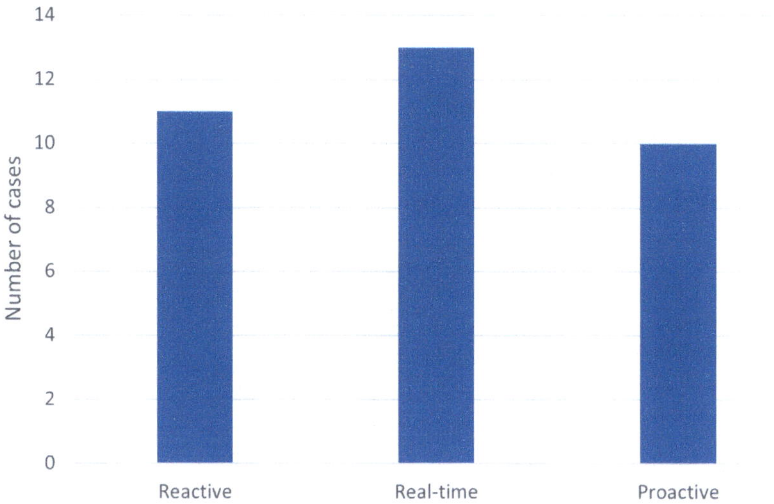

Fig. 14.5 Categorization of decision-making situations of cases

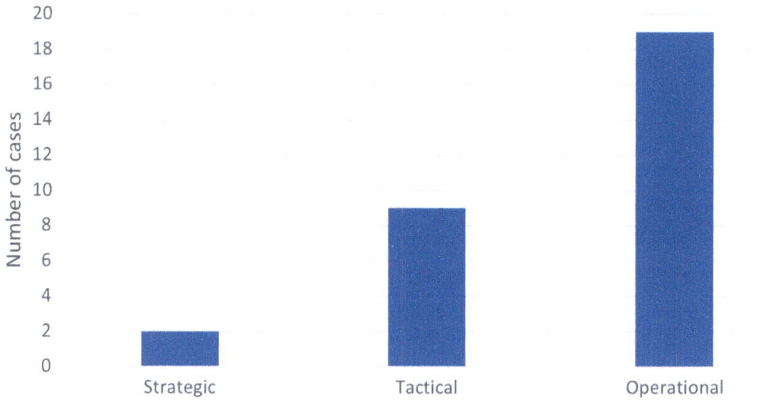

Fig. 14.6 Categorization of decision-making level of cases

healthcare, energy markets, and smart buildings were also emphasized. This same phenomenon can be seen as a trend in Industry 5.0 or Society 5.0, where the emphasis on technology applications is going to be more on well-being, environmental, and sustainability issues in the future (Xu et al. 2021; European Commission et al. 2021).

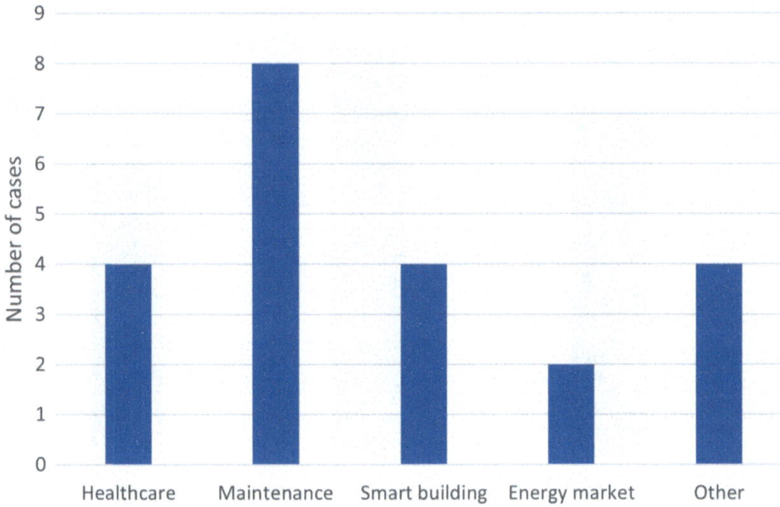

Fig. 14.7 IoT solutions in different business areas

Business value in the cases was recognized as cost savings, such as preventing production losses due to breakdowns or unplanned downtime, cost savings in spare parts costs, and cost savings in maintenance work. Many of these cases are trying to prevent disadvantageous and costly events from occurring or trying to plan the operations more cost-efficiently than previously. The emphasis here is on economic benefits and value, but in many cases, softer non-monetary values were emphasized as well. In the cases related to healthcare, in addition to the savings in the working time of healthcare personnel, the main value is considered as the well-being of patients, increased quality of life, identifying diseases, minimizing symptoms, and preventing accidents, attacks, falls, etc. Measuring the value of this kind of benefits is challenging or even immeasurable. Even though, in the industrial context, the monetary value is emphasized, e.g., cost savings and increased revenues from production, the softer values, such as well-being and the environment, are also discussed. Safety issues, such as preventing accidents (G14) and savings in energy consumption, can also be regarded as softer values, although they can also create monetary value. Examples of the increased interest in environmental consciousness as a business value were considered in smart building cases (G7, G9, and G17) and waste management and the circular economy case (G3).

In conclusion, in the 19 cases, the business value and the need for decision-making have been the main drivers in developing the IoT solutions described in the cases. It can be assumed that when value and decision-making needs are the focus and are well-defined, the potential benefits from these solutions can most likely be achieved. In some cases, hard values, i.e. monetary values, were at the center; and in other cases, soft values were more emphasized. Some of the cases considered both hard and soft values as key values of the IoT solution. In light of these 19 cases, it can be said that the interest in IoT solutions is in benefitting technology advances in the industrial, societal (healthcare), environmental, and sustainability contexts.

14.4.4 Benefits of the Systematic Process in Developing IoT Skills

The aim of creating the exercise to create IoT solutions was to develop the student's skills in IoT data utilization to create business value with IoT solutions. A systematic process description that forces students to define the need for IoT solutions was created. Defining the need for solutions includes defining the decision-making situation and the value that the solution produces. Students are required to plan the data-to-decision process in theory and then realize it in practice with an IoT tool. How the skills of students have developed can be observed from the statistics on how many students completed the course. In 2021–2022, 64 students started the course, and 62/64 completed the course. Some conclusions can be made from the student feedback. According to student feedback, the following comments were given:

> There was a good balance between studying theories and combining them with my own experiences." "It was useful to learn to utilize the IoT platform, even though it felt diflcult at first. In the course, there were plenty of examples of IoT solutions and utilization opportunities in different industries.

If we think that, by completing the group exercise and the whole course, students improve their IoT skills, this eventually leads to business value when they utilize these skills when they start work. It was shown that there is a demand for IoT professionals, and companies are highly interested in professionals who can benefit from IoT technologies and IoT data utilization (see, e.g., (Brynjolfsson and McElheran, 2016, Gürdür Broo et al. 2022, Pomp et al. 2022). In order for companies to reap the benefits of technological advances, they need professionals who understand the business value and how to utilize technologies and data to create business value.

14.5 Conclusions

As the result of this study, a systematic process description was created to improve the IoT skills of students to benefit from IoT data utilization in creating business value. Theoretical contribution and managerial implications are related to the investigation into which practical needs are needed for IoT solutions, in which business areas, and what kind of decision-making needs the IoT solutions can bring benefits and business value.

As a result of the first research question *(What kind of decision-making needs related to business processes can be solved with analytical IoT solutions?),* it was observed that the decision-making situations, where we can benefit from IoT data utilization, are increasingly real-time and proactive decisions. However, there is still a need for supporting reactive decisions with real-time data as well. It is also important to take into account the needs of the decision-maker and to create a practical view (layers) and dashboards for different decision-makers and their needs. Decision-making needs were most emphasized in the maintenance, or more broadly industrial asset management, context as well as in healthcare, smart building, and the energy market. As a conclusion, it was noticed that IoT data utilization enables shortening the time-scale of operational decision-making, i.e., decisions are aimed to be made faster than ever, as close to real-time as possible, or even proactively.

IoT solutions can also be used to automatize certain decision-making situations.

As an answer to the second research question *(What kind of systematic process can support fulfilling these decision-making needs?)*, the systematic process description is based on the data-to-decision process, where the decision-making need and potential value are the basis for IoT solutions. It is essential to identify the decision-making need and create value that is scalable to create adequate business value. Thus, if the decision-making need or situation is repeated enough, the generated value is easier to achieve and to justify the need for IoT solution development.

The third research question (How can the utilization of the low-code/no-code IoT platform support or improve the skills of students to create value for the business?) was taken on through group work projects in the course, where students with varying computing skills planned and realized an IoT solution with an IoT platform. Combining business skills with IoT skills can be advantageous for students in the job market. There is a need for IoT professionals who have business understanding and can attend to the IoT solutions development process and strengthen the link between the solutions and business value. By educating students in IoT skills, it is possible to benefit from technological advances and create business value in different business areas.

Future research is needed to understand the value of IoT data utilization and how the business value created with IoT solutions can be measured. The softer values are especially hard to measure, and these elements should be taken into account when evaluating the business value of technologies. It is also important to acknowledge the opportunities of artificial intelligence (AI) and how we could benefit if we combine real-time IoT data and AI.

References

D. Baltuttis, B. Häckel, C. M. Jonas, A. M. Oberländer, M. Röglinger, and J. Seyfried. Conceptualizing and assessing the value of internet of things solutions. *Journal of Business Research*, 140:245–263, February 2022.

A. Boltsi, K. Kalovrektis, A. Xenakis, P. Chatzimisios, and C. Chaikalis. Digital tools, technologies, and learning methodologies for education 4.0 frameworks: A stem oriented survey. *IEEE Access*, 12:12883–12901, 2024.

Erik Brynjolfsson and Kristina McElheran. The rapid adoption of data-driven decision-making. *American Economic Review*, 106(5):133–139, 2016.

Armanda Cetrulo and Alessandro Nuvolari. Industry 4.0: Revolution or hype? Re-assessing recent technological trends and their impact on labour. *Journal of Industrial and Business Economics*, 46:391–402, 2019.

N. Côrte-Real, P. Ruivo, and T. Oliveira. Leveraging internet of things and big data analytics initiatives in european and american firms: Is data quality a way to extract business value? *Information & Management*, 57(1):103141, 2020.

Directorate-General for Research European Commission, Innovation, M. Breque, L. De Nul, and A. Petridis. Industry 5.0: Towards a sustainable, human-centric and resilient european industry. Technical report, Publications Office of the European Union, 2021. URL https://data.europa.eu/doi/https://doi.org/10.2777/308407.

Dec G., Stadnicka D., Pasko L., Madziel M., Figliè R., Mazzei D., Tyrovolas M., Stylios C., Navarro J., and Solé-Beteta X. Role of academics in transferring knowledge and skills on artificial intelligence, internet of things and edge computing. *Sensors*, 22(7):2496, 2022.

K. Gerlée. AI in IoT: Enhancing the power of smart devices. Freeeway (Web page), 2024. URL https://freeeway.com/ai-in-iot-enhancing-the-power-of-smart-devices/. Referred 25.3.2024.

D. Gürdür Broo, O. Kaynak, and S. M. Sait. Rethinking engineering education at the age of Industry 5.0. *Journal of Industrial Information Integration*, 25:100311, January 2022.

D. Horváth and R.Z. Szabó. Driving forces and barriers of industry 4.0: Do multinational and small and medium-sized companies have equal opportunities? *Technological Forecasting and Social Change*, 146:119–132, 2019.

T. Järvensivu and J.-Å. Törnroos. Case study research with moderate constructionism: Conceptualization and practical illustration. *Industrial Marketing Management*, 39:100–108, 2010.

C. Kaiser, A. Stocker, G. Viscusi, M. Fellmann, and A. Richter. Conceptualising value creation in data-driven services: The case of vehicle data. *International Journal of Information Management*, 59:102335, August 2021.

J.L. Kincheloe. Describing the bricolage: Conceptualizing a new rigor in qualitative research. *Qualitative Inquiry*, 7:679–692, 2001.

S-K. Kinnunen, S. Marttonen-Arola, A. Ylä-Kujala, T. Kärri, T. Ahonen, P. Valkokari, and D. Baglee. Decision making situations define data requirements in fleet asset management. In K. T. Koskinen, H. Kortelainen, J. Aaltonen, T. Uusitalo, K. Komonen, J. Mathew, and J. Laitinen, editors, *Proceedings of the 10th World Congress on Engineering Asset Management (WCEAM 2015)*, Lecture Notes in Mechanical Engineering, pages 357–364. Springer, 2016.

S-K. Kinnunen, A. Ylä-Kujala, S. Marttonen-Arola, T. Kärri, and D. Baglee. Internet of Things in asset management: Insights from industrial professionals and academia. *International Journal of Service Science, Management, Engineering, and Technology*, 9(2):104–119, 2018.

Sini-Kaisu Kinnunen. *Modelling the value of fleet data in the ecosystems of asset management*. PhD thesis, Acta Universitatis Lappeenrantaensis, Lappeenranta, Finland, 2020.

M. Klag and A. Langley. Approaching the conceptual leap in qualitative research. *International Journal of Management Reviews*, 15(2):149–166, 2013.

LinkedIn. About linkedin, 2023. URL https://about.linkedin.com/. (Accessed: 12 June 2023).

K. Momeni and M. Martinsuo. Remote monitoring in industrial services: Need-to-have instead of nice-to-have. *Journal of Business and Industrial Marketing*, 33(6):792–803, 2018.

S. Nast and K. Sandkuhl. Meta-model and tool support for the organizational aspects of Internet-of-Things development methods: Organizational aspects of IoT development methods. In *International Conference on Advanced Information Science and System*, 2021.

T. Nolle. Ai and iot: How do the internet of things and AI work together? TechTarget (Web page), 2023. URL https://www.techtarget.com/iotagenda/tip/AI-and-IoT-How-do-the-internet-of-things-and-AI-work-together. Referred 25.3.2024.

G. Phillips-Wren, M. Daly, and F. Burstein. Reconciling business intelligence, analytics and decision support systems: More data, deeper insight. *Decision Support Systems*, 146:113560, July 2021.

A. Pomp, A. Burgdorf, A. Paulus, and T. Meisen. Towards unlocking the potential of the Internet of Things for the skilled crafts. In *Proceedings of the 24th International Conference on Enterprise Information Systems (ICEIS 2022)*, volume 1, pages 203–210, 2022.

M. Räikkönen, J. Keski-Rahkonen, H. Kortelainen, M. Tikkanen, P. Valkokari, A. Vehanen, and S. Pirttikangas. Towards a framework for assessing the customer value of digital solutions. In *Proceedings of the 30th European Safety and Reliability Conference and the 15th Probabilistic Safety Assessment and Management Conference*, pages 2358–2365, Venice, November 2020.

Y. Sun, C. Fidge, and L. Ma. A generic split process model for asset management decision-making. In *Proceedings of the 3rd World Congress on Engineering Asset Management and Intelligent Maintenance Systems*, Beijing, China, 2008.

H. Tokola, C. Gröger, E. Järvenpää, and E. Niemi. Designing manufacturing dashboards on the basis of a key performance indicator survey. In *Procedia CIRP*, volume 57, pages 619–624, 2016.

Vinugayathri. AI and IoT blended-What it is and why it matters? ClarionTechnologies, Technology Review, Data Analytics & BI (Web page), 2024. URL https://www.clariontech.com/blog/ai-and-iot-blended-what-it-is-and-why-it-matters. Referred 25.3.2024.

X. Xu, Y. Lu, B. Vogel-Heuser, and L. Wang. Industry 4.0 and Industry 5.0—inception, conception and perception. *Journal of Manufacturing Systems*, 61:530–535, 2021.

Index

P. Aaltonen and E. Kurvinen (eds.), *Contemporary Issues in Industry 5.0*, Technology, Work and Globalization, https://doi.org/10.1007/978-3-031-74779-3

S

T

U

V

The manufacturer's authorised representative in the EU is Springer Nature Customer Service Centre GmbH, Europaplatz 3, 69115 Heidelberg, Germany. If you have any concerns regarding our products, please contact ProductSafety@springernature.com

Printed and bound by CPI Group (UK) Ltd, Croydon, CR0 4YY
01/10/2026
02225852-0009